Mastering Object-Oriented Programming with C++

Revised Edition

R.S. Salaria

Alumnus of IIT, Delhi.
Certified Software Quality Professional, Govt. of India.
Sun Certified Programmer, SUN Microsystems, USA.
Sun Certified Trainer, SUN Microsystems, USA.

Former Head

Department of Computer Science & Engineering
Thapar University, PATIALA-147004.

Assisted by

Anita Salaria

KHANNA BOOK PUBLISHING CO. (P) LTD.

Publisher of Science, Technology and Engineering Books

4C/4344, Ansari Road, Darya Ganj, New Delhi-110002
Phone: 011-23244447-48 **Mobile:** +91-99109 09320
E-mail: contact@khannabooks.com
Website: www.khannabooks.com

Price: ₹ 450.00

ISBN: 978-93-82609-39-1

Mastering Object Oriented Programming Using C++
by R.S. Salaria

Edition: 2024

To view complete list of books, Please scan the QR Code:

Published by:
Khanna Book Publishing Co. (P) Ltd.
CIN: U22110DL1998PTC095547

Visit us at: **www.khannabooks.com**
Write us at: **contact@khannabooks.com**

Printed in India by: City Press, Delhi.

Preface to Revised & Enlarged Edition

Continuing with the tradition of providing the rich content on the subject of *"Object Oriented Programming With C++"*, which can make Computer Science and Information Technology students' competent professionals, the present edition lays more emphasis on the overall layout of the subject matter so as to make it more appealing and attractive. I am certain that the present edition will help the students in inculcating the habit of reading and self-learning.

Most of the topics are thoroughly revised, presented in a kind of manner with visuals where ever possible so that the students can grasp them with quite each.

Appendix A containing Frequently Asked Questions (FAQs) on Object Oriented Programming Concepts is added to help the students to prepare for short questions that are mostly asked in viva voce examinations and placement interviews.

I am hopeful that this edition will be going beyond your expectations. Do keep on writing, as your valuable feedback and suggestions will help me in tuning the book to your expectations.

. . . R. S. Salaria

Preface to First Edition

The C++ programming language is one of the popular programming languages that support object-oriented programming in addition to procedural programming. The course on object-oriented programming with C++ is usually offered after the foundation course on programming in C.

Since C++ language is build on the top of C language, therefore, to give the readers the jump start to object-oriented programming, this text book focuses only on object-oriented features of C++. However, an additional chapter is added (*Migrating from C to C++*) that explains enhancements and new features incorporated in C++ to improve few not so handy aspects of C, such as *stream based I/O*, *inline functions*, *default arguments*, etc.

This book will serve as a textbook for the students BCA, BSc (Computer Science), BSc (IT), PGDCA, MSc (Computer Science), MSc (IT), BTech and MCA.

The areas of strength of this book are in terms of that

- It provides a comprehensive coverage of the subject in a very lucid manner.
- It demonstrates the development of programs in a good programming style, as inline with the industry standards.
- It provides large number of ready to run example programs, for reference.
- It provides large number of multiple choice questions.
- It provides challenging review exercises to test your knowledge about the subject learned.
- It also provides large number of challenging programming exercises to test your programming skills acquired.

I am certain that you will enjoy reading this book. I do need a little favour from your side in the form of your response about the book. Your free and frank comments, suggestions, and positive criticism will help me to improve the book further to meet your expectations.

. . . R. S. Salaria

Acknowledgments

It is my pleasure to take this opportunity to sincerely thank all the teachers who have adopted my book and introducing it to their students. I am also thankful for their appreciations that I have been receiving from them in the form of emails and letters.

I would be failing in my duty if go without appreciating the response and interest shown by the students in my books. They are always a source of inspiration for me and I feel honoured because of their faith in me.

Finally, I must thank my publisher, Mr. Mukul Seth & Mr. Puneet Khanna for their aggressive marketing and thus establishing the book as one of the best text books on the subject of *"Mastering Object-Oriented Programming With C++"*.

. . . R. S. Salaria

Word of Advice for Students

My beloved students, I would like to remind you that we can categorize people as

People who watch the things happening,
People who look into how things are happening, and
People who make the things happen.

Now you are to find out where you fit-in and where you want to be.

I firmly believe that youth of our country is second to none, and this fact is recognized world wide.

Our honourable former president Dr. APJ Kalam (first and may be the last president known as *people's president*) has been saying at all the platform that in India there is no dearth of resources and talent, only thing we need to change is *the mindset* (we have to shed *chalta hai* attitude). He has set a vision for us to see India a developed country by 2020, and the basis for his vision is the talent of our youth.

Take some time to discover yourself and try to assess how much talent you possess. Utilize your period of study to harness that talent. I can assure you that you will have a great future.

I want to share a popular game with you which all of us used to play in our childhood. The game is of burning a peace of paper using a lens under the sun. When the lens and the paper are held stationery, it starts burning in a few seconds. However, if you keep moving either the paper or the lens, the paper will never burn. *Why it happens so*? The answer is simple – the light energy emitted by the sun is not focused. The same is with us. We have enough energy in ourselves, but we don't focus it, rather we waste it in meaningless acts. The next question arises is – *where to focus our energy*? The natural answer of this question should be – what you want to become in your life (that basically defines your goal). So you need to focus your entire energy on your goal, and surely you will achieve your goal.

I would also like to share with you a scene from the popular epic – *Mahabharta*. When Dronacharya, Guru of Pandvas, asked his disciples to aim at the eye of a fish hanged on a tree. All his disciples, except Arjuna, replied in a same manner – *Guru ji*, we see a fish. However, when the turn of Arjuna came, his reply was – *Guru ji, I see only the eye*. That is the kind of the focus you also need to develop in your life.

The next point is that when you have identified your goal, you need to identify the steps that you need to follow in order to accomplish your goal. Once the goal and the steps to accomplish your goal are identified, write them nicely on a piece of a paper and paste that paper at a place which you visit regularly. Whenever you will visit that place, the writing on the paper will remind you about your goal and what you have to do to achieve your goal.

The final word, you may set any goal for yourself and that may be of becoming a successful doctor, an engineer, an administrator or a businessman, but you must also try to be a *nice human being*. You know a nice human being is like a fruit of all seasons, and is welcome every where, anytime.

Contents at a Glance

Detailed Table of Contents

Chapter 1

Introduction to Object-Oriented Programming

Learning Objectives

After reading this chapter, students will be able to

- explain the object-oriented programming paradigm
- compare procedural programming paradigm with object-oriented programming paradigm
- understand the limitations of procedural programming paradigm
- understand how object-oriented programming paradigm is able to overcome the limitations of procedural programming paradigm
- explain the basic elements of object-oriented programming
- explain the benefits of object-oriented programming

1.1 INTRODUCTION

When Thermos Flask was invented, it was labeled as one of the greatest inventions in the sense that how it remembers to keep hot things hot and cold things cold. The same analogy holds true for object-oriented programming (OOP). OOP is the most dramatic innovation in software development and some of its features draw parallels to that of Thermos Flask.

The primary objective of OOP is to provide clearer, reliable, and easily maintainable approach to program design. OOP involves concepts that are new to programmers of traditional programming languages, also known as *procedural languages, imperative languages* or *problem oriented languages*, such as Pascal, C, FORTRAN, etc. These concepts, such as *data abstraction*, *encapsulation, data hiding*, *inheritance*, *overloading* and *polymorphism*, lie at the heart of object-oriented programming. It is very important to understand that object-oriented programming is not primarily concerned with the details of the program operation; instead it deals with the overall organization of the program.

Object-oriented programming is not just another way of programming; it is a new way of organizing programs.

In this chapter, before covering the concepts of object-oriented programming, let us have a look at procedural programming and object-oriented programming and their relative merits and demerits.

1.2 A LOOK AT PROCEDURAL PROGRAMMING

In *procedural programming*, also known by other names as *structured programming, functional programming* or *traditional programming*, the problem in hand is viewed as a sequence of things to be done such as reading, calculating and printing. Separate functions are written to accomplish these tasks. Thus, the primary focus is on functions.

In other words, we can say that a given problem is divided into small sized sub problems; each sub problem represents a specific task that can be handled efficiently and effectively. Then to solve each sub problem, a function/procedure is written.

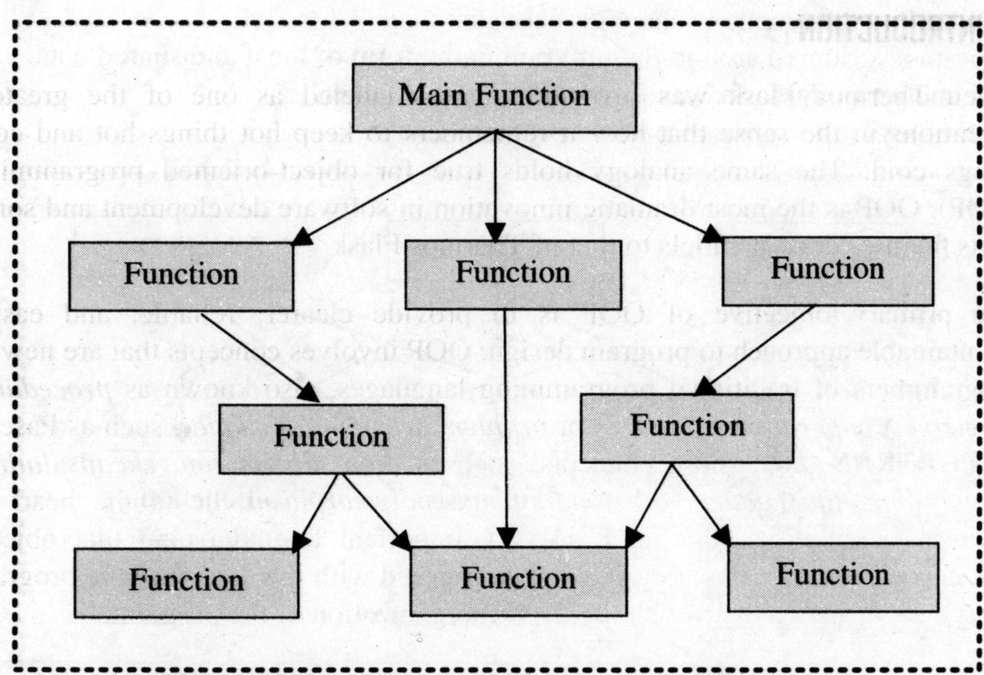

Figure 1.1: Typical structure of a procedural program

The technique of hierarchical decomposition has been used to specify the tasks to be completed to find the solution of a problem.

Note here that there is no mention of data. These functions are written to manipulate the data to accomplish a specific task. Thus, the data that is key to the existence of functions and hence a program gets a raw treatment.

Further, the data in a procedural program is spread across entire software in the form of local and global data structures. The global data is more vulnerable to an inadvertent change by a function. Functions communicate with each other either by passing arguments or by accessing and modifying data structures. In a very large program it is very difficult to identify what data is used by which function.

Key characteristics of procedural programming are:

- Emphasis is on doing things (algorithms).
- Large programs are divided into smaller independent subprograms known as functions or procedures (algorithmic decomposition).

- Majority the functions share global data.
- Data is scattered around the program in the form of local and shared data.
- Functions transform data from one form to another.
- Employs *top-down* approach to program design.

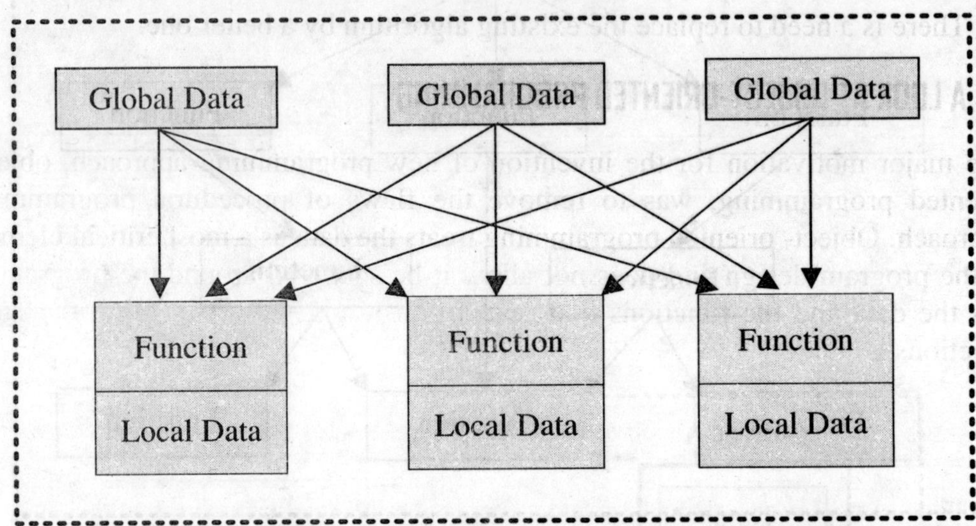

Figure 1.2: Relationship of data and functions in a procedural program

The organisation of programs using procedural programming approach suffers from following problems:

- The procedural programming approach does not model the real world problems very well.
- The program logic is dependent on the organisation of the data and the vice a versa. You cannot change one without change to another.
- The parts of the program are heavily dependent on each other, *i.e.*, tightly coupled to each other. Therefore, it is very difficult to make a change in one part of the program without affecting the other part.

These problems magnify further as the size and the complexity of the problem under consideration increases, and almost become unmanageable for very large and complex systems.

As change is inevitable, we want that our program design should be capable of handling a change without or with minimal effort and without introducing any anomalies.

The need of change can be because of the following reasons:

- There is problem in some part of the program and it needs to be fixed.
- There is need to extend the functionality of the program by including new features.
- There is a need to replace the existing algorithm by a better one.

1.3 A LOOK AT OBJECT-ORIENTED PROGRAMMING

The major motivation for the invention of new programming approach, object-oriented programming, was to remove the flaws of procedural programming approach. Object- oriented programming treats the data as a most critical element in the program design and does not allow it be scattered around the program. It ties the data and the functions that operate on it and protects it from the other functions.

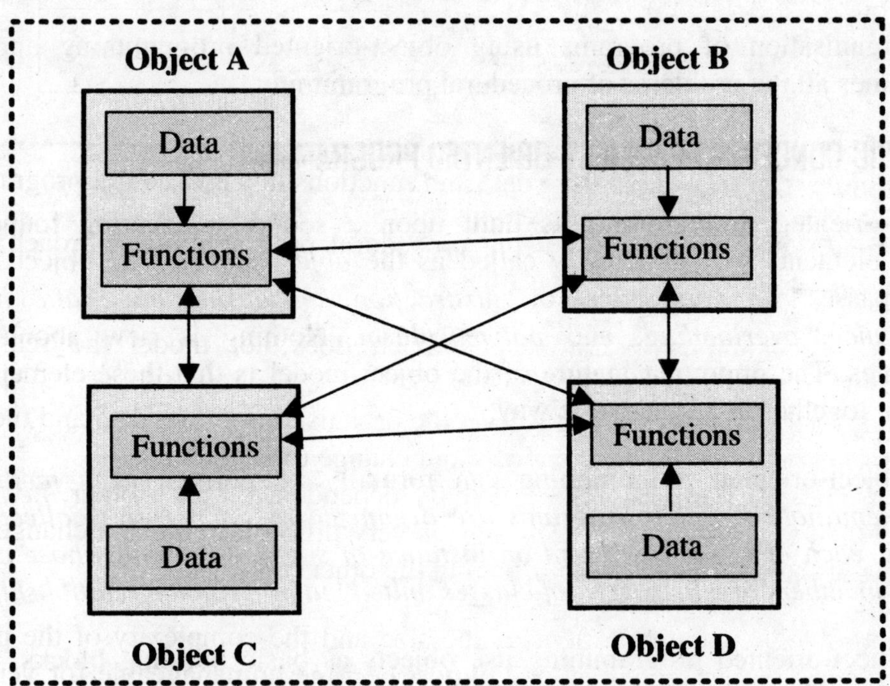

Figure 1.3: Typical Structure of an object-oriented program

Object-oriented programming allows decomposition of a problem into a number of entities called *objects* and then builds data and functions around these objects.

The typical structure of an object-oriented program and the relationship between the data and functions is shown in Figure 1.3.

The data of an object can only be accessed by functions associated with it. However, function of one object can access the function of another object. The communications among functions of different objects is called *messaging*.

Key characteristics of object-oriented programming are:

- Emphasis is on data rather than functions.
- Programs are divided into set of related objects.
- Data structures are designed in such way so as to characterize the objects.
- Functions that operate on the data of an object are tied together with the data structure.
- Data of an object is hidden and cannot be accessed by external functions.
- Objects communicate with each other through functions.
- Employs *bottom-up* approach to program design.

The organisation of programs using object-oriented programming approach overcomes all the problems of procedural programming.

1.4 BASIC CONCEPTS OF OBJECT-ORIENTED PROGRAMMING

Object-oriented programming is built upon a sound engineering foundation whose elements we collectively called as the *object model*. The object model encompasses the principles of *abstraction*, *encapsulation*, *data hiding*, *inheritance*, *overloading*, and *polymorphism*. Nothing is new about these principles. The important feature of the object model is that these elements are brought together in a synergistic way.

The object-oriented programming can formally be defined as *a method of implementation in which programs are organized as cooperative collection of objects, each of which represent an instance of some class, and whose classes are all members of a hierarchy of classes united via inheritance relationship.*

The object-oriented programming use objects as basic building blocks, where each object is an instance of some class, and classes are related to each other through inheritance.

Before we move on, it is necessary to understand some concepts that are used extensively in object-oriented programming.

These concepts include:

- Objects
- Classes
- Abstraction
- Encapsulation
- Data Hiding
- Inheritance
- Overloading
- Polymorphism
- Dynamic binding
- Message passing

1.4.1 Concept of an Object

An *object* is an entity that has *state*, *behavior* and *identity*. The structure and behavior of similar objects are defined in their common class. The term *instance* and *object* are interchangeable.

Each object has following characteristics:

- **State** – The *state* of an object encompasses all of the (usually static) property of the object plus the current (usually dynamic) values of each of these properties.
- **Behavior** – The *behavior* of an object tells how it acts and reacts to the outside world in terms of its state changes and message passing.

  With this, the state of the object can now be defined as - *the state of an object represents the cumulative results of its behaviour*.
- **Identity** – The *identity* of an object is that property which distinguishes it from all other objects.

1.4.1.1 Operations on Objects

The kind of operations that are performed on objects comprises:

- **Modifier** - An operation that alters the state of an object.
- **Selector** - An operation that access the state of the object but does not alter it.
- **Iterator** - An operation that permits all parts of an object to be accessed in some well-defined order.

- **Constructor** - An operation that creates an object and/or initializes its state.
- **Destructor** - An operation that frees the state of an object and/or destroys the object itself.

1.4.1.2 Relationship among Objects

Objects contribute to the behaviour of a system by collaborating with one another. The relationship between any two objects encompasses the assumptions that each make about the other, including what operations can be performed and what behaviour results.

Objects communicate with each other through links, where a link defined as a physical or a conceptual connection between objects.

As a participant in a link, an object may play one of the following roles:

- **Client/Actor** – that operate on other objects, but is never operated upon by other objects.
- **Server** – that never operates upon other objects, it is only operated upon by other objects.
- **Agent** – that can operate on other objects and be operated upon by other objects; an agent is usually created to do some work on behalf of an actor or another agent.

1.4.2 Concept of a Class

The concepts of class and object are tightly interwoven, for example, we cannot talk about an object without regard for its class. However, there are important differences between these two terms. An object is a concrete entity that exists in time and space. A class represents only an abstraction, the *essence* of an object, as it were. Thus, we may speak of the class mammal, which represents characteristics common to all mammals. To identify a particular mammal in this class, we must speak of *this mammal* or *that mammal*. In the context of object-oriented programming, we define class as a set of objects that share a common structure and a common behaviour. A single object is simply an instance of a class.

1.4.2.1 Interface of a Class

The interface of a class provides outside view of a class and encompasses the abstraction while hiding its structure and the secrets of its behaviour. This interface primarily consists of the declarations of all the operations applicable to instances of this class, but it may include the declarations of other classes, constants, variables, and exceptions that are needed to complete the abstraction.

1.4.2.2 Implementation of a Class

Implementation of a class is its inside view that encompasses the secrets of its behaviour. It primarily consists of implementation of all the operations defined in the interface of the class. Interface of a class is divided into following parts:

- **Public** – A part that is accessible to all clients.
- **Protected** – A part that is accessible to the class and its subclasses.
- **Private** – A part that is accessible to the class only.

Different object-oriented programming languages provide different mixtures of *public*, *protected*, and *private* parts, which developers can choose among to establish specific access rights for each part of the class's interface, and thereby exercise control over what clients can see and what they cannot see.

1.4.3 Abstraction and Encapsulation

The notion of abstraction and encapsulation are commonly used in human-machine interaction and are widely prevalent in the technology-oriented world in which we are living. Consider, far example, the videocassette recorder (VCR), which is an integral part of every household today.

We make two observations about how VCRs are packaged and used.

- All our interactions with a VCR are made through buttons on the control panel such as PLAY, FF (forward), REW (rewind), REC (record), STOP, EJECT, etc.
- The VCR is packaged in such a way that we cannot interact directly with the internal circuitry. So, the *internal representation* of the VCR is *hidden* from the user. This is the principle of *encapsulation*.
- The instruction manual that accompanies the VCR tells us what the VCR is supposed to do if we press a particular button. It does not tell us how it is implemented inside the VCR. For example, it does not explain the sequence

of electronic and mechanical events that result when the REW button is pressed. So, the instruction manual makes a clear distinction between what the VCR does and how it does. This distinction is the principle of *abstraction.*

1.4.3.1 Abstraction

Dictionary meaning of word *abstraction* refers to the act of emphasizing and representing essential features and ignoring the irrelevant features. In the context of object-oriented programming, word *abstraction* refers to the separation between the specification of data and its implementation. It results in better quality programs and more efficient programming techniques. These, in turn, reduce the number of man-hours required to develop a software system, and hence reduce the total cost of the final software product.

Since classes use the concept of data abstraction, they are also known as *abstract data types* (ADTs).

1.4.3.2 Encapsulation

Encapsulation is the concealing of the implementation details of a data object from the outside world. The data and functions are wrapped into a single unit, called class. Encapsulation is the most striking feature of a class.

1.4.4 Data Hiding

Data hiding deals with visibility of the members. The level of visibility determines which parts of the code can access the member. All most all the object-oriented programming languages provide three levels of visibility – *private*, *protected*, and *public*. Private members are accessible to members of the class only. Protected members are accessible to members of the class and members of the derived class. Public members are accessible from everywhere.

1.4.5 Inheritance

It means exactly what it says - *getting something from something that already exists*. For example, we inherit property, skills, features etc., from our parents.

Inheritance is a relationship among classes wherein one class inherits the structure and/or behavior defined in one (single inheritance) or more (multiple inheritance) classes. We call the class from which another class inherits its *super class, parent class* or *father class* and a class that inherits from one or more classes is a *subclass, derived class* or *child class*.

The concept of inheritance provides reusability. This means that we can add new features to an existing class without modifying it. The new class will have the combined features of both the classes.

1.4.6 Overloading

Overloading is the way of giving several meanings to an operator or a function. The meaning selected depends on the types of the arguments used by an operator or a function. The concept of overloading provides extensibility. This means that we can extend the existing features to meet new requirements. For example, by overloading operators, we make a new data type to behave like a built-in data type.

1.4.7 Polymorphism

Polymorphism is another important feature of object-oriented programming. Polymorphism is a combination of two words *poly* and *morphism*. The word *poly* means *many* and the word *morphism* means *forms*.

Thus, *polymorphism* means *many forms*. More formally, polymorphism can be defined as a technique that allow to define various forms of a single function or operator that can be shared by various objects to perform the operations.

The polymorphism is achieved using the following:

- ❑ Overloading
- ❑ Dynamic binding

1.4.8 Dynamic Binding

Binding is the linking of a function call to the function definition that will be executed on the call during program execution. Normally the function call is tied to the function definition during the linking process. This process is known as *early binding*.

However, the OOP permits dynamic binding, also called *late binding*, where the tie-up of function call to the address code is delayed until the run-time.

1.4.9 Message Passing

An object-oriented program consists of set of objects that communicate with each other in order to solve a particular problem. Objects communicate with one another by sending and receiving information much the same way as people pass messages to one another. A message for an object is a request for execution of a function, and therefore will invoke a function in the receiving object that generates the desired results. Message passing involves specifying the name of the object, the name of the function and the information to be sent.

Every object has a life cycle – they are created and destroyed. Communication with an object is feasible as long as it is alive.

1.5 ADVANTAGES OF OOP

The structured approach in developing software systems is able to handle the problem complexity to certain extent. But as soon as the complexity and the size of the problem increases, the strains of structured approach starts showing. In contrast, the object-oriented approach is aimed at developing large and complex software system. Even for moderate size problems, the object-oriented approach has many advantages over structured approach. Some of the advantages are enumerated below:

- We, the human being, perceive the world around us as being made of objects and the brain arranges these objects into groups. The object-oriented design uses these objects in a programming language that aids in imitating the existing pattern of human thought into programming.
- Object-oriented design involves the identification and implementation of objects of the problem in hand and their behavior. Since these objects map one-to-one to the objects in the real world, it becomes very easy to design and implement the system consisting of objects as observed and understood by the human brain.
- The core concept of OOP is data encapsulation and data abstraction that increases the reliability of the software systems by separating the procedural and representational specifications from its implementation.
- Since the objects are autonomous entities and communicate only through messages, thus each object lends itself to greater modularity. This independence of objects makes development and maintenance of programs very easy.

- Inheritance enhances the reusability of the code, thus increasing the productivity.
- Polymorphism increases the flexibility by permitting the addition of new classes without having to modify the existing ones.
- Object-orientations provide other benefits such as shorter development times, high degree of code sharing, etc. These benefits of OOP make it an important technology for building complex software systems.

QUICK RECAP

In this chapter, we have learnt that

- Object-oriented programming is a way of organizing programs.
- The key tenants of object-oriented programming are *encapsulation*, *inheritance* and *polymorphism*.
- Procedural programming views the task as a sequence subtasks such as reading, calculating and printing.
- Procedural programming employs *top-down* approach.
- Major problem with procedural programming is that it does not model the real world very well.
- Another problem with procedural programming is that parts of the program are tightly coupled to each other; therefore, corrections, changes and enhancements are very difficult to incorporate.
- Object-oriented programming overcomes all the problems of procedural programming approach.
- Object-oriented programming views the task as a collection of objects where objects communicate with each other to arrive at the solution.
- Object-oriented programming employs *bottom-up* approach.
- The building blocks of object-oriented programming are classes and objects.
- The real applications of object-oriented programming are in the areas where problems are large and complex.

MULTIPLE CHOICE QUESTIONS

1. Which of the following is not a key characteristic of structured programming?
   (*a*) Employs *bottom-up* approach to program design
   (*b*) Large programs are divided into smaller independent subprograms known as functions or procedures (algorithmic decomposition)
   (*c*) Data is scattered around the program in the form of local and shared data
   (*d*) None of above

2. Which of the following is not a key characteristic of object-oriented programming?
   (*a*) Employs *bottom-up* approach to program design
   (*b*) Emphasis is on data rather than functions
   (*c*) Makes extensive use of global data
   (*d*) Data of an object, in general, is hidden and cannot be accessed by non-member functions.

3. Which of the following is an attribute of an object?
   (*a*) State (*b*) Identity
   (*c*) Behaviour (*d*) All of above

4. Which of the following in not a valid access specifier?
   (*a*) protect (*b*) private
   (*c*) public (*d*) None of above

5. Process of giving several meanings to an operator or a function is known as
   (*a*) Abstraction (*b*) Overloading
   (*c*) Encapsulation (*d*) Binding

6. An operation that creates an object and/or initializes its state is known as
   (*a*) Modifier (*b*) Destructor
   (*c*) Constructor (*d*) Iterator

7. A class that inherits from one or more classes is known as
   (*a*) Sub class (*b*) Derived class
   (*c*) Child class (*d*) All of above

8. The process where tie-up of function calls to the function definition is delayed until the run-time is known as
   (*a*) Concurrent binding (*b*) Late binding
   (*c*) Early binding (*d*) Heuristics binding

9. A technique that allows to send identical messages to dissimilar but related objects and achieve identical actions while letting the software system determine how to achieve the required action for the given object is known as

   (*a*) Virtual mechanism (*b*) Data binding
   (*c*) Encapsulation (*d*) Polymorphism

10. Which of the following keyword is used to achieve runtime polymorphism?

   (*a*) mutable (*b*) const
   (*c*) explicit (*d*) virtual

11. Which of the following statement is not valid about operator overloading?

   (*a*) Only existing operators can be overloaded. New operators cannot be created.
   (*b*) Overloaded operator must have at least one operand of its class type.
   (*c*) Overloaded operators follow the syntax rules of the original operators.
   (*d*) None of above

12. Which of the following is not a valid type of relationship in the context of object-oriented programming?

   (*a*) The *is-a* relationship (*b*) The *has-a* relationship
   (*c*) The *was-a* relationship (*d*) None of above.

13. The use of inheritance facilitates . . . . . .

   (*a*) Extensibility (*b*) Reusability
   (*c*) Scalability (*d*) Interoperability

14. Which of the following statement is not true about polymorphism?

   (*a*) Polymorphism can be implemented at run time only.
   (*b*) To implement run time polymorphism, you need a pointer to the base class and virtual functions in the base class.
   (*c*) When a function is declared as virtual in base class, it is automatically becomes virtual in the derived classes.
   (*d*) Polymorphism provides uniform interface to access a method in a class hierarchy.

15. When a class contains at least one pure virtual function, it is known as

   (*a*) concrete class (*b*) container class
   (*c*) base class (*d*) abstract class

16. Which of the following is not included into signatures of a function/method?

   (*a*) Type of arguments (*b*) Number of arguments
   (*c*) Sequence of arguments (*d*) Return type

17. The size of a *class* is always equal to the sum of ....
    (*a*) Data members only
    (*b*) Data members as well as function members
    (*c*) Only non-static data members
    (*d*) None of above

REVIEW EXERCISES

1. What is procedural programming? What are its key characteristics?
2. What are the disadvantages of procedural programming?
3. What is object-oriented programming? What are its key characteristics?
4. What are the advantages of object-oriented programming?
5. Distinguish between the following:
    (*a*) Objects and classes
    (*b*) Abstraction and encapsulation
6. Explain the following terms:
    (*a*) Inheritance
    (*b*) Polymorphism
    (*c*) Dynamic binding
    (*d*) Message passing
    (*e*) Overloading
7. What is meant by the interface of a class?
8. What is meant by the implementation of a class?
9. What are the types of operations that can be performed on objects?
10. What are the relationships among objects?

❑ ❑ ❑

Chapter 2

Migrating from C to C++

Learning Objectives

After reading this chapter, students will be able to explain the

- new style of commenting, new data types
- enhanced approach of handling of structures and unions
- relaxation in the place of declaration of variables
- concept of reference variables
- new style of typecasting, new cast operators, new operator keywords, and new headers
- concept of namespaces
- parameter passing by reference
- concept of stream based I/O
- concept of inline functions and its comparison with macros
- enhancements of structures and unions to include functions as its members
- concept of default arguments
- concept of function overloading
- concept of function templates
- memory management operators

2.1 INTRODUCTION

The C++ language is a very powerful general-purpose programming language that supports procedural programming as well as object-oriented programming. It was developed by **Bjarne Stroustrup** at AT&T Bell Laboratories, New Jersey, USA, in the early 1980's. He found that as the magnitude of problem size and its complexity grows, it becomes extremely difficult to manage it, using most of procedural languages, including C language. He was a strong admirer of Simula67 and C languages, and wanted to have a language that combines the best of both of the languages, *i.e.*, a language that supports object oriented programming, and at the same time have the power and elegance of C language. The outcome of his efforts ultimately leads to the development of C++ language. Since classes were a major addition to the original C language, he initially called the new language **'C with Classes'**. Later on, the name was changed to C++ in the year 1983. The idea of suffixing C with ++ came from the increment operator as the new features were added to the C language which were in use since long.

During the early 1990's, the language underwent a number of changes and improvements. In the year 1997, the ANSI standards committee standardized these changes, and added several new features to the language specifications.

The C++ language is treated as super set of C language because the developer of C++ language have retained all features of C, enhanced some of the existing features, and incorporated new features to support for object-oriented programming.

In this chapter, we will discuss about the enhanced features of C++ language over C language. Every C programmer can very easily grasp these features without bothering about object-oriented features of C++ language.

2.2 NEW STYLE OF COMMENTING

The C++ language supports new style of commenting. It starts with two consecutive forward slashes '//'. This style of comments can appear on a separate line or following any instructions. The following are the examples of valid C++ comments:

```
// This is a C++ style comment.

int rno;  // variable for roll number
```

The only limitation of this style of commenting is that comments are limited to single line. There if you want to add multiple lines of comments, then every line of comment must be preceded by //.

As a guideline, whenever we want to add multiple line comments, we prefer C style commenting and for single line comments we prefer C++ style commenting. In the book we will be following these guidelines.

Listing 2.1

```
/*
 * Program to convert temperature from Centigrade scale to
 * Fahrenheit scale. This program also illustrates the use
 * of comments in a C++ program
*/
#include <iostream.h>
#include <iomanip.h>
void main()
{
    float fahrenheit, centigrade;          // declaration of variables

    cout << "Enter temperature in Celsius scale : ";
    cin >> centigrade;                     // keyboard input

    fahrenheit = 1.8 * centigrade + 32;
    cout << "Equivalent Temperature in Fahrenheit = ";
    cout << fahrenheit << endl;            // output computed temperature
}
```

2.3 NEW DATA TYPES

New standard of C++ language supports following new data types:

- The *bool* data type
- The *wchar_t* Data Type

Note that the old C++ compilers don't support these data types.

2.3.1 The *bool* Data Type

The *bool* data type has been added to hold a boolean value — *true* or *false*. The boolean values *true* or *false* have been declared as keywords. A *bool* value occupies 1 bytes of memory. Boolean value *false* is internally represented as integer value 0 whereas boolean value *true* is internally represented as integer value 1. Following statements show declarations and use of *bool* type variables.

```
bool b1, b2;        // declares variable of type bool

b1 = true;          // assigns boolean value true
b2 = 0;             // assign value 0, i.e. false
bool b3 = false;    // declares and initialize with Boolean
                    // value false
```

You can assign any non-zero value to a *bool* variable to represent boolean value true, however, it is always converted to value 1 before assignment.

When the display the values of bool variables, value 0 will be printed for boolean value false and 1 for boolean value true.

```
bool b1 = false, b2 = true;
cout << "\nb1 = " << b1;
cout << "\nb2 = " << b2;
```

The output will be as follows:

```
b1 = 0
b2 = 1
```

However, if you want the value of *bool* variable to be printed as boolean value, i.e., as *false* and *true*, then the *boolalpha* manipulator can be used to accomplish this task.

This is illustrated below:

```
bool test = true;
cout << boolalpha;
cout << "test = " << test;
```

The output will be as follows:

```
test = true
```

A *bool* variable and boolean value can be used in an arithmetic expression. For example, the following statements

```
int x, y = 10;
bool f = false;
x = true + 2 * y - f;
```

are valid.

2.3.2 The *wchar_t* Data Type

The new character data type named *wchar_t* is added to hold 16-bit wide characters called *unicode characters*. The 16-bit characters are used to represent the character sets of other languages such as Spanish, Japanese, French, etc. The use of *wchar_t* is particularly useful if we are writing programs for international distribution.

A new character literal known as *wide_character* is also added and it uses 2-bytes of memory. Wide_character literals begin with the letter L, as shown below:

```
L'xy' // wide_character literal
```

2.4 PROMOTION OF USER-DEFINED DATA TYPES

In C++ language, when you create a user-defined data type, the tag of the user-defined data type acts as a data type like basic data type and you can use tag to declare a variable.

Consider the following example:

```
struct EMPLOYEE
{
   int   code;
   char  name[20];
   int   deptCode;
   float salary;
};
```

The statement

```
EMPLOYEE aEmployee;
```

declaring the structure variable *aEmployee*. Here tag *EMPLOYEE* acts as a data type. To accomplish the same thing in C, we have to use the statement

```
struct EMPLOYEE aEmployee;
```

In C language, if variables of same user-defined data type are required at many parts of the program, then we have to repeatedly use the keyword for appropriate user-defined data type before the tag, which may be cumbersome and many a times becomes the source of errors.

Therefore, to overcome this difficulty in C language, when we create a new user-defined data type, and assign a symbolic name to it using *typedef* statement as illustrated below:

```
typedef struct
{
   int   code;
```

```
   char  name[20];
   int   deptCode;
   float salary;
} EMPLOYEE;
```

Now the statements of type

```
EMPLOYEE aEmployee;
```

will work in C language.

Similar treatment is with *union* and *enum* user-defined data types.

Though the keyword *typedef* is retained in C++ language, but it is not used much.

2.5 VARIABLE DECLARATION

In C language, local variables can only be declared at the top of the function or at the beginning of the nested block. While coding the program, it may not be known in advance the number and type variables to be used. As and when a new variable is required, we have to move to the top of the function definition and declare the variable. Many a times we use the variable and forget to declare it that leads to syntax error.

However, in C++ language, this restriction is relaxed. A variable in C++ language can be declared anywhere in the function, but in such a case the scope of the variable will be limited to part of the function following its declaration. Hence, most of the C++ programmers follow the practice of declaring the variables at its first use.

Listing 2.2

```
/* Program to demonstrate the declaration of variables
 * at the point of its first use
*/
#include <iostream.h>
#include <iomanip.h>
void main()
{
   // variable 'i' cannot be accessed before 'for' statement
   for ( int i = 0; i < 10; i++ )
   {
      cout << i << endl;
   }
   // variable 'i' can be accessed after 'for' statement
   cout << i << endl;
}
```

On other side, the declaration of variables at any position in the program reduces the readability of the program. Therefore, to enhance the readability of the program, it is better to declare the variables at the beginning of the function.

2.6 REFERENCE VARIABLES – VARIABLE ALIASES

In C language, we have used *value variables* and *pointer variables*. The value variables hold some value whereas the pointer variables are used to hold the address of some value variable. The C++ language supports one more type of variable called *reference variable*. A reference variable acts as an alias (alternative name) for other variable. Reference variables enjoy the simplicity of value variables and power of pointer variables.

A reference variable is bound to a value/pointer variable only at the point of its declarations using following syntax

```
DataType &ReferenceVariable = Variable;
```

The following examples illustrate the binding of reference variables.

```
char &ch1 = ch;          // ch1 is an alias of ch

int &x = y[100];         // x is an alias of y[100]

int n = 20;
int *p = &n;
int &m = *p;             // m an alias of *p and refers to n
```

Reference variables play important role while passing arguments to a function.

2.7 SCOPE RESOLUTION

The variables declared outside the functions are known as global variables. These variables are visible to all function following its declaration. But if there is a local variable with the same name in a function, there is no way to access the global variable in C language. In C++ LANGUAGE, a global variable can be accessed using *scope resolution operator* '::' (two consecutive colons).

The syntax of using the scope resolution operator is

```
::GlobalVariable
```

The next program illustrates the accessing of local and global variables with same name.

Listing 2.3

```
/*
 *  Program to demonstrate the accessing local and
 *  global variables with same name
*/

#include <iostream.h>
#include <iomanip.h>

int i = 10;    // declaration & definition of global variable

void main()
{
    int i=20;
    cout << "Local variable i = " << i << endl;
    cout << "Global variable i = " << ::i << endl;
}
```

2.8 NEW STYLE OF TYPECASTING

We know that basic data types are automatically converted to an appropriate type when used in assignments and expressions due to implicit type conversion facility provided by the language whereas this does not happen when the variable is passed as an argument during a function call. Similarly, this implicit type conversion facility does not work with user-defined data types. Through the use of explicit type conversion, (*the cast operator*), we can achieve the data type conversion for any sort of data type, *i.e.*, basic as well as user-defined.

In C language, the syntax for explicit type conversion is

```
(DataType) Variable/Expression
```

The data type is enclosed in parenthesis.

In C++ language, the syntax for explicit type conversion is

```
DataType(Variable/Expression)
```

The variable or expression is enclosed in parenthesis. This looks very similar to a function call.

2.9 NEW CAST OPERATORS

We have used *cast operator*, also known as *cast* or *typecast*, where the data type is used to convert a value from one type to another type as shown below:

```
float a = 12.45;            // variable of type float
```

```
int x;                    // variable of type int
x = int(a);               // conversion from float to int
```

This type of conversion is necessary where automatic conversions are not possible.

Following new type of cast operators have been added:

- static_cast
- const_cast
- dynamic_cast
- reinterpret_cast

2.9.1 The *static_cast* Operator

Like the conventional cast operator, the *static_cast* operator is used for any standard conversion of data types. It can also be used to cast a base class pointer into a derived class pointer. Its syntax is

```
static_cast<type>(variable/expression)
```

where *type* is one of standard data types, and specifies data type of target variable.

```
float a = 12.45;               // variable of type float
int x;                         // variable of type int
x = static_cast<int>(a);       // conversion from float to int
```

A trivial question arises in mind – *why to use this new cast operator when the old style cast operators still works*? Note that the old style, which looks like a normal function call, got mixed up with rest of the code and therefore it is difficult to spot it. This new cast operator is easy to spot and to search specially using automated tools.

2.9.2 The *const_cast* Operator

The *const_cast* operator is used for casting away *const* or *volatile*. Since the purpose of *const_cast* operator is to change its *const* or *volatile* attributes to normal attributes, the target variable should be of same type as that of source. Its syntax is

```
const_cast<type>(variable)
```

where *type* is one of the standard data types.

2.9.3 The *dynamic_cast* Operator

Run-time type identification (RTTI) provides a means of determining an object's type at run time. Two operators are added for this purpose - *dynamic_cast* and *typeid*. We will discuss these operators one-by-one.

The *dynamic_cast* operator is used to cast the type of an object at run-time. Its main application is to perform casts on polymorphic objects. Basically it is used for downcasting from a base class pointer to a derived class pointer.

Its syntax is

```
dynamic_cast<type>(baseClassPtr)
```

where *type* is pointer to the derived class and *baseClassPtr* is a pointer of the base class. If the object held by the base class pointer is of derived class, then it will return the address of the derived class object otherwise returns NULL value, *i.e.*, value 0.

The *typeid* operator is used to obtain the type of the unknown objects such as their class names at run-time. Its syntax is

```
typeid(object).name()
```

For example, in the following statement

```
const char *objectType = typeid(object).name();
```

It will assign the type of object (class name) to pointer variable *objectType*. To do this, it uses member function *name()* of *type_info* class. Remember that to use *typeid* operator, you have to include header file *typeinfo.h* in your program.

2.9.4 The *reinterpret_cast* Operator

The *reinterpret_cast* operator is used for non-standard casts, *i.e.*, to change one type to fundamentally different type. It is oftenly used to cast one type of pointer to a different pointer type. It cannot be used for standard cast such as *float*, *int*, *double*, etc. Its syntax is

```
reinterpret_cast<type>(sourcePtr)
```

where *type* is pointer to the target type and *sourcePtr* is a pointer of the source object.

Consider the following example

```
float a = 12.45, *floatPtr;
int *intPtr;
floatPtr = &a;
intPtr = reinterpret_cast<int *>(floatPtr);
```

Here it will convert a pointer of type *float* to a pointer of type *int*.

2.10 OPERATOR KEYWORDS

New operator keywords have been added that can be used in place of several operators.

Table 2.1: Operator keywords

Operator	Operator Keyword	Description
&&	and	Logical AND
||	or	Logical OR
!	not	Logical NOT
!=	not_eq	Inequality
&	bitand	Bitwise AND
|	bitor	Bitwise inclusive OR
^	xor	Bitwise exclusive OR
~	compl	One's complement
&=	and_eq	Bitwise AND assignment
|=	or_eq	Bitwise inclusive OR assignment
^=	xor_eq	Bitwise exclusive OR assignment

Following statement

```
x< y && z != k
```

using operator keywords can be written as

```
x < y and z not_eq k
```

2.11 NEW HEADERS

A new way of specifying header files is incorporated. Here you don't have to suffix the header file name with *.h* extension. This style of header files works in conjunction with namespaces, which are described in next section.

```
#include <iostream>
#include <fstream>
```

The traditional style *<iostream.h>*, *<fstream.h>*, etc., is still fully supported.

2.12 NAMESPACES

A program may include many identifiers defined in different scopes. Sometimes a variable of one scope may overlap (i.e. collide) with a variable of same name in a different scope, and thus creating a problem. Such overlapping can occur at many levels. This situation frequently occurs in third party libraries where same names are used for global identifiers such as functions.

To handle this problem, a new feature in the form of *namespace* is added. Each *namespace* defines a scope where all related identifiers are placed.

To use a *namespace member*, the member's name must be qualified with the *namespace* name and the scope resolution operator as shown below:

```
namespaceName::member
```

or a *using* statement must occur before the member is used. The *using* statements are generally placed in the beginning of the program. For example, the statement

```
using namespace namespaceName;
```

at the beginning of a program specifies that members of namespace *namespaceName* can be used in the program without preceding each member with the *namespaceName* and the scope resolution operator.

2.12.1 Defining a Namespace

We can define our own namespaces. The syntax for defining a namespace is

```
namespace namespaceName
{
   // declarations of variables, functions, and
   // classes
}
```

Note that there is no semicolon after the terminating brace.

2.12.2 Nesting of Namespaces

A namespace can be nested within another namespace as shown below:

```
namespace outerNamespaceName
{
   // . . .
   // . . .
```

```
    namespace innerNamespaceName
    {
        // . . .
        // . . .
        int m = 10;
    }
}
```

Variable *m* can be accessed using following ways:

```
cout << outerNamespaceName::innerNamespaceName::m;
```

OR

```
using outerNamespaceName;
cout << innerNamespaceName::m;
```

2.13 PARAMETER PASSING BY REFERENCE

In addition to *pass-by-value* and *pass-by-address*, parameters can also be *passed by reference* in C++ language. The parameter passed by reference has the functionality of pass-by-address and the syntax of pass-by-value. Any modification made through the formal reference parameter is also reflected in the actual parameter.

Consider the following implementation of a function to interchange values of two integer variables when the formal arguments are value variables.

Listing 2.4

```
/*
 * Program to demonstrate the argument passing using call by value
*/
#include <iostream.h>
#include <iomanip.h>
void main()
{
    int x = 10, y = 20;
    void swap ( int, int );  // function prototype
    cout << "Before call to swap function" << endl;
    cout << "Value of x = " << x << endl;
    cout << "Value of y = " << y << endl;
    swap (x, y);             // function call
    cout << "After call to swap function" << endl;
    cout << "Value of x = " << x << endl;
    cout << "Value of y = " << y << endl;
```

```
}
void swap ( int a, int b )
{
   int temp = a;
   a = b;
   b = temp;
}
```

In this case, the values of variables *x* and *y* are copied into formal parameters *a* and *b* respectively, which are value variables and acts as local variables to the function. The local copies of the variables are interchanged through another local value variable *temp*. The values of variables *x* and *y* are left unchanged.

Listing 2.5

```
/*
 * Program to demonstrate the argument passing using call by address (pointer)
*/
#include <iostream.h>
#include <iomanip.h>
void main()
{
    int x = 10, y = 20;
    void swap ( int *, int * );      // function prototype
    cout << "Before call to swap function" << endl;
    cout << "Value of x = " << x << endl;
    cout << "Value of y = " << y << endl;
    swap (&x, &y);                   // function call
    cout << "After call to swap function" << endl;
    cout << "Value of x = " << x << endl;
    cout << "Value of y = " << y << endl;
}
void swap ( int *a, int *b )
{
    int temp = *a;
    *a = *b;
    *b = temp;
}
```

Now consider the implementation of *swap()* function to interchange values of two integer variables when the formal arguments are pointer variables.

```
void swap ( int *a, int *b )
{
    int temp = *a;
    *a = *b;
    *b = temp;
}
```

The corresponding call to above function with *x* and *y* as actual parameters is

```
swap (&x, &y);
```

In this case, the addresses of variables *x* and *y* are copied into formal parameters *a* and *b* respectively, which are pointer variables and acts as local variables to the function. Here, values of the variables whose addresses are held in *a* and *b* are interchanged through local value variable *temp*. Here the values of variables *x* and *y* will be interchanged.

Listing 2.6

```
/*
 * Program to demonstrate the argument passing using call by reference (alias)
*/

#include <iostream.h>
#include <iomanip.h>

void main()
{
    int x = 10, y = 20;
    void swap ( int &, int & );  // function prototype
    cout << "Before call to swap function" << endl;
    cout << "Value of x = " << x << endl;
    cout << "Value of y = " << y << endl;
    swap (x, y);                  // function call
    cout << "After call to swap function" << endl;
    cout << "Value of x = " << x << endl;
    cout << "Value of y = " << y << endl;
}

void swap ( int &a, int &b )
{
    int temp = a;
    a = b;
    b = temp;
}
```

Now consider the implementation of *swap()* function to interchange values of two integer variables when the formal arguments are reference variables.

```
void swap ( int &a, int &b )
{
    int temp = a;
    a = b;
    b = temp;
}
```

In the function prototype

```
void swap ( int &a, int &b );
```

the operator & indicates that formal parameters are of reference type, and they must be bound to the memory locations of actual arguments. Thus access made to these formal reference variable in the *swap()* function refers to the actual parameters. Here the values of variables *x* and *y* will be interchanged.

The call statement

```
swap ( x, y );
```

is translated into

```
swap ( &x, &y );
```

during the compilation process.

By comparing above versions of *swap()* functions, you will find that reference variables enjoy the simplicity of value variables and power of pointer variables.

The only limitation of reference variables is that they don't provide the flexibility of pointer variables. Once they are bound to a variable that binding cannot be changed. All accesses made to the reference variables are the same as the access to the variable. On the other side you can assign the address of any value variable of same type to a pointer variable of that type and change the binding of pointer variables at your will.

2.14 STREAM BASED I/O

The C++ I/O subsystem is designed to work with a wide variety of devices that includes keyboard, monitor, disks, tape drives, etc. The working principle (characteristics) of each of these devices is quite different. The C++ I/O subsystem is designed in such a way that it provides a uniform interface that is independent of the actual device being used.

Thus, the programmer can write a C++ program that can receive input from, and send output to any device without bothering about the characteristics of device being used. This interface is called a *stream*. Figure 2.1 shows this uniform interface.

Streams in C++ language are classified as

- Input streams
- Output streams
- File streams

A stream basically is a sequence of bytes. It can either act as a *source* from which the program can take (extract) input data or as a *destination* to which the program can send (insert) output data. The source stream that supplies data to the program is called *input stream* and the destination stream that receives data from the program is called *output stream*. These streams collectively are called *data streams*.

Figure 2.3 shows the interaction of data streams with program. We will learn more about data streams and their use in *Chapter 3* (for handling keyboard input and screen output) and *Chapter 12* (for managing data files).

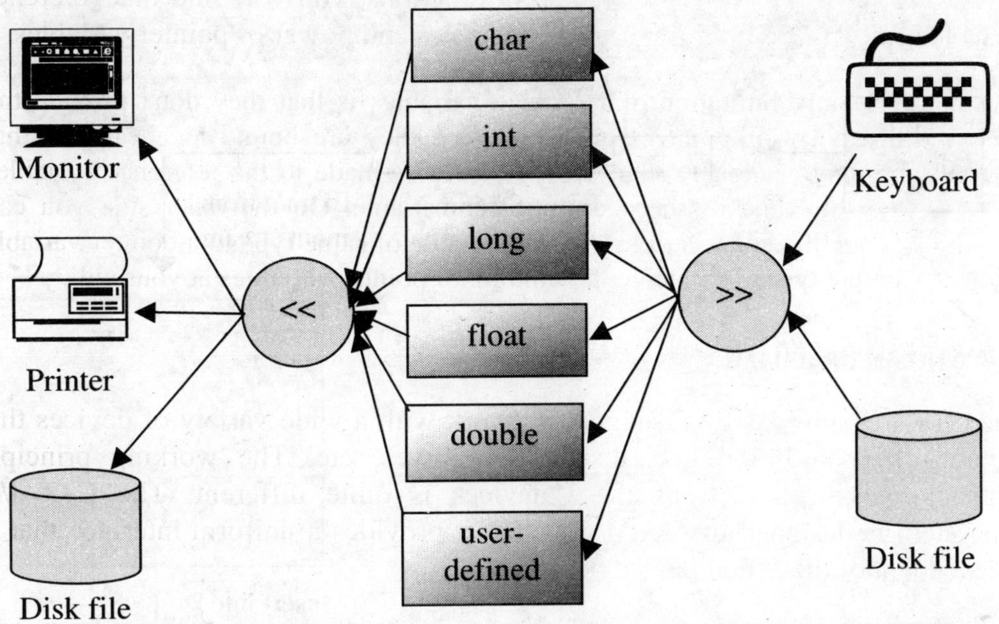

Figure 2.1: Consistent stream interface with I/O devices

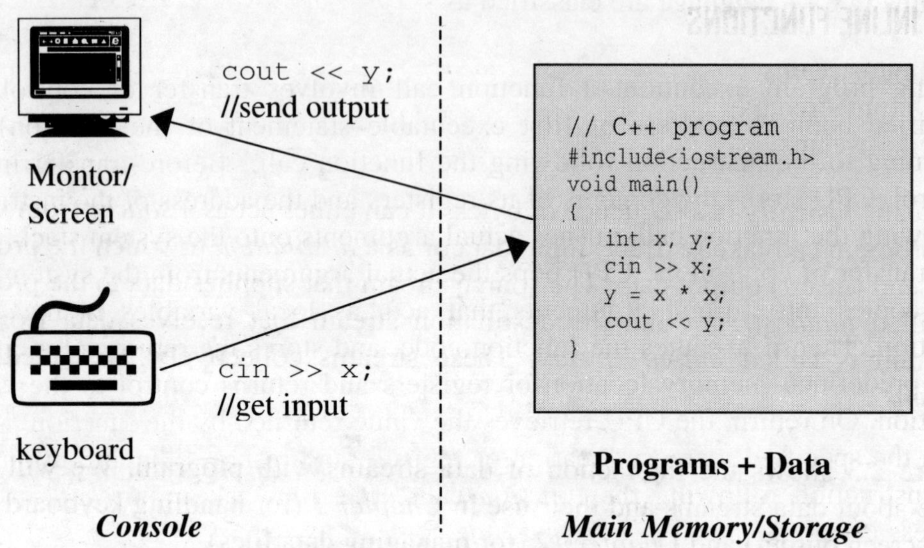

Figure 2.2: Console-program interaction

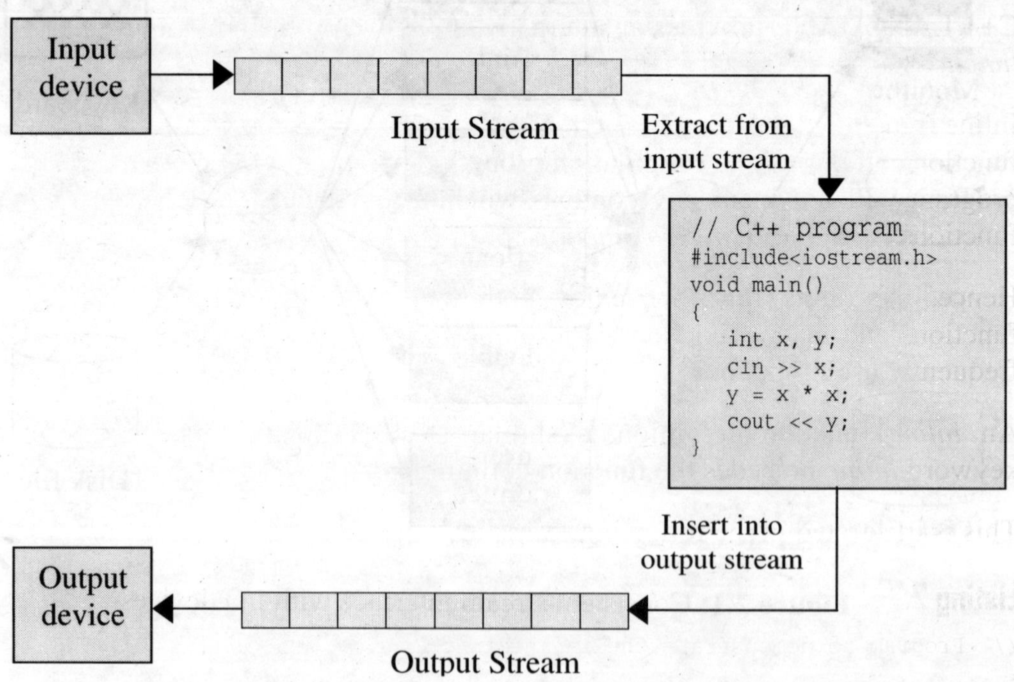

Figure 2.3: Data streams and program interaction

2.15 INLINE FUNCTIONS

During program execution, a function call involves transfer of control to a specified address (address of first executable statement of the function), and returning to the instruction following the function call. Before transferring the control, CPU stores the contents of its registers and the address of the instruction following the function call, pushes actual arguments onto the system stack. After the transfer of control, the CPU pops the actual arguments from the system stack and copies into formal arguments that acts as local variables in the called function. Then it executes the function code, and stores the return value, if any, in a predefined memory location or registers and returns control to the calling function. On return, the CPU retrieves the value returned by the function, if any, from the specified memory location or register, and resumes the execution from the instruction following the function calls. The time taken during this whole process is called *context switch time*, and constitutes an overhead in the execution of the program.

This overhead is relatively large if the time required to execute a function is small than the context switch time. In that case, we would like to repeat the code in multiple places in a function rather than creating a separate function for it. The C++ LANGUAGE provides an alternative to above problem in the form of *inline functions*.

Inline functions are those functions whose body is inserted in place of the function call during the compilation process. Therefore, with inline functions, the program will not incur any context-switching overhead. The concept of inline functions is similar to *macro functions* of C.

Hence, the inline functions enjoy both the flexibility and power of normal functions and macro functions. The inline functions are best used for small and frequently used functions.

An *inline* function definition is similar to an ordinary function except the keyword *inline* precedes the function definition.

This is illustrated in the following example:

Listing 2.7

```
//  Program to demonstrate the inline functions

inline float square( float x )
{
    return x*x;
}
```

```
void main()
{
    float a, b, r, z;
    // some statements
    a = square ( z );
    b = square ( r );
    // some more statements
}
```

After preprocessing, the above code will be treated as

Listing 2.8

```
//  Program to demonstrate the inline functions
void main()
{
    float a, b, r, z;
    // some statements
    a = z * z;
    b = r * r;
    // some more statements
}
```

2.15.1 Inline Functions Versus Macros (#define)

Given a choice, prefer *inline* over *#define*. Let us see why?

Like anything else in the world, there are advantages and disadvantages to everything and macros are not an exception to that. However, the list of advantages is over shadowed by list of disadvantages.

Consider the following macro:

```
#define MAX( a, b )  a < b ? b : a// 1
```

The problem here is that since variables *a* and *b* are not properly parenthesized, an expression in their place could produce side effects.

For example, macro call

```
MAX( x += 2, y )
```

expands to

```
x += 2 < y ? y : x += 2
```

which, by C++'s precedence rules, evaluates to

```
x += (( 2 < y ) ? y : x += 2 )
```

where as the required was

```
if ( x+ = 2 < y ) then result is y else result is x += 2
```

This pitfall can be taken care of in the following manner

```
#define MAX(a,b)   (a) < (b) ? (b) : (a)      // 2
```

Though the fix may look bug-free now, there is another similar subtler pitfall to it. The problem here is that though the single variables are parenthesised now, the whole expression is not properly parenthesised. Remember that a macro can be a part of larger expression and since it expands into plan stupid text, there is no evidence of a macro having been there once the expansion has taken place. If we do not want the parts of a macro to mix-and-match with others, we have to parenthesize the macro as a whole and not only its variables. For example the expression

```
z = MAX( a, b ) + 23
```

will expand to

```
z = ( a )< ( b ) ? ( b ):( a ) + 23
```

which, by C++'s precedence rules, evaluates to

```
z = (( a ) < ( b )) ? ( b ):(( a ) + 23 )
```

which is not the intended functionality.

The above problem can now be fixed by putting parentheses around the whole macro as

```
#define MAX( a, b )  (( a ) < ( b ) ? ( b ) : ( a ))    // 3
```

This is not the end of problems that macro can create. Consider the use macro for the expression

```
MAX( ++x, y )
```

This would expand to

```
(( ++x ) < ( y ) ? ( y ):( ++x ))
```

which will twice increment the value of *x* in case ++*x* is greater than *y*. This is generally not the accepted result.

Another problem with the macros is that about their scope. Macros always have global scope.

Some more disadvantages of macros are

Macros do no have address – Macros are not code. They do not have existence of their own in the object code. They have been replaced by the pre-processor in the resulting code.

Macros are debugger-unfriendly – Till date, I think, there is no compiler that is macro friendly and provides similar functionality for stepping in/out, watching, etc. as it does for functions.

Macros are not type-safe – Static type checking of arguments and return value is carried out by the compiler for functions, but not for macros.

Macros are not recursive – Macros are not code. They do not have existence of their own in the object code. They have been replaced by the pre-processor.

The *inline* functions overcome all these disadvantages.

2.16 FUNCTION AS MEMBERS OF STRUCTURES

Structures in C language provide a mechanism to group elements (usually) of different data types in one unit that belong to the same family. For example, if we want to create a user-defined data type to represent an employee in an organization, the structure definition in C may look like

```
struct EMPLOYEE
{
    int empCode;
    char empName[20];
    float empSalary;
};
```

Here, for simplicity, we have considered only three elements viz. employee's code (*empCode*), employee's name (*empName*) and employee's salary (*empSalary*) while leaving out other elements such as date of birth, date of joining, educational and professional qualification, etc.

In order to process a variable (that represents an employee, an instance of family *employees*), either it must declared as global variable so that it is accessible to all functions or must be passed as an argument to an appropriate set of functions in order to process it.

However, a structure in C++ LANGUAGE permits the inclusion of functions in addition to data members, and thus provides a true mechanism of handling data abstraction. The general syntax of structure in C++ LANGUAGE is

```
struct structureName
{
   public:
      // data and functions
   protected:
      // data and functions
   private:
      // data and functions
};
```

The structure has two types of members: *data member* and *function members*. Function defined in a structure can access any data member. The keywords *public*, *protected* and *private* are called *access specifiers*. If none of the above specifier appears in the structure definition, all the members have default access.

The private and protected members of a structure can only be accessed by the member function where as public members are accessible by members functions as well its instances (structure variables). Therefore, with appropriate use of these access specifiers, we can control the access to data members as desired in the application.

When we define a structure, member functions can be defined within the structure definition or outside the structure definition. When they are defined outside the structure definition, they are just declared (prototyped) in the structure definition and are bound to an appropriate structure definition by using scope resolution operator. Both of the ways are illustrated below:

When the member functions are defined inside the structure definition:

```
struct EMPLOYEE
{
   private:
      int empCode;           // private data members
      char empName[20];
      float empSalary;
   public:
      // public member function defined inside the class
      void readData()
      {
```

```
        cout << "Enter code : ";
        cin >> empCode;
        cout << "Enter name : ";
        cin >> empName;
        cout << "Enter salary : ";
        cin >> empSalary;
    }
    void showData()
    {
        cout << endl << "Employee information" << endl;
        cout << "Code   : " << empCode << endl;
        cout << "Name   : " << empName << endl;
        cout << "Salary : " << setprecision(2);
        cout << empSalary << endl;
    }
};
```

When the member functions are defined outside the structure definition:

```
struct EMPLOYEE
{
  private:
    int empCode;          // private data members
    char empName[20];
    float empSalary;
  public:
    // public member function declared inside the
    // class and defined outside the class
    void readData ();
    void showData ();
};
void employee :: readData()
{
  cout << "Enter code : ";
  cin >> empCode;
  cout << "Enter name : ";
  cin >> empName;
  cout << "Enter salary : ";
  cin >> empSalary;
}
void employee :: showData()
{
  cout << endl << "Employee information" << endl;
  cout << "Code   : " << empCode << endl;
  cout << "Name   : " << empName << endl;
  cout << "Salary : " << setprecision(2);
  cout << empSalary << endl;
}
```

The use of both of these definitions is illustrated in following programs.

Listing 2.9

```
/* Program to illustrate the mechanism of defining
   member functions inside the structure definition
*/
#include <iostream.h>
#include <iomanip.h>
struct EMPLOYEE {
   private:
      int empCode;           // private data members
      char empName[20];
      float empSalary;
   public:
      // public member function defined inside the class
      void readData ()
      {
         cout << "Enter code : ";
         cin >> empCode;
         cout << "Enter name : ";
         cin >> empName;
         cout << "Enter salary : ";
         cin >> empSalary;
      }
      void showData ()
      {
         cout << endl << "Employee information" << endl;
         cout << "Code   : " << empCode << endl;
         cout << "Name   : " << empName << endl;
         cout << "Salary : " << setprecision(2);
         cout << empSalary << endl;
      }
};
void main()
{
   EMPLOYEE aEmployee;
   aEmployee.readData();    //member function invoked on instance
   aEmployee.showData();    //member function invoked on instance
}
```

Listing 2.10

```
/* Program to illustrate the mechanism of defining
   member functions outside the structure definition
*/
#include <iostream.h>
#include <iomanip.h>
#include <conio.h>
struct EMPLOYEE {
```

```
    private:
        int empCode;            // private data members
        char empName[20];
        float empSalary;

    public:
        // public member function declared inside the
        // class and defined outside the class
        void readData ();
        void showData ();
};
void employee :: readData() {
    cout << "Enter code : ";
    cin >> empCode;
    cout << "Enter name : ";
    cin >> empName;
    cout << "Enter salary : ";
    cin >> empSalary;
}
void employee :: showData() {
    cout << endl << "Employee information" << endl;
    cout << "Code   : " << empCode << endl;
    cout << "Name   : " << empName << endl;
    cout << "Salary : " << setprecision(2);
    cout << empSalary << endl;
}
void main()
{
    EMPLOYEE aEmployee;
    aEmployee.readData(); //member function invoked on instance
    aEmployee.showData(); //member function invoked on instance
}
```

The following points about structures in C++ laguage are important to remember:

1. When we compute the size of a structure, the member functions are not included in its size. This fact you can verify using *sizeof* operator. For example, for employee structure defines above, the *sizeof* operator will return value 26, *i.e.*, size of structure employee is 26 bytes (2 bytes for *empCode*, 20 bytes for *empName* and 4 bytes for *empSalary*).
2. The data member can be *private*, *protected* or *public*, but the member functions must be *public* otherwise it will not be possible to call member functions on a structure variable and thus serves no purpose.
3. If the access specifier for the data members is *private*, then a structure variable initialization cannot be combined with declaration. Therefore, we have to write a member functions to initialize a structure variable.

Consider the following structure definition

```
struct DATE
{
    int day;     //data members with default access public.
    int month;
    int year;
    // member functions
};
```

or

```
struct DATE
{
    public:
        int day;  //public data members
        int month;
        int year;
      // member functions
};
```

Then compiler permits the following

```
DATE dd = { 10, 12, 2003 };
```

However, if the structure definition is

```
struct DATE
{
    private:
        int day;  //private data members
        int month;
        int year;
        // member functions
};
```

Then compiler will not permits the following

```
DATE dd = { 10, 5, 2003 };
```

Therefore, in this case the only way is to use a member function as illustrated below:

```
struct DATE
{
    private:
        int day;  //private data members
        int month;
```

```
        int year;
        void initialize(int dd, int mm, int yy)
        {
            day = dd;
            month = mm;
            year = yy;
        }
        // more member functions
};
```

Now, we can declare a structure variable and then call member function *initialize()* to form the initialization.

```
DATE d;
d.initialize(10,5, 2003);
```

You may think that these two statements can be combined as we do in normal case, but it is not permitted. You first have to create a variable (instance), and only then you can call member function. Therefore, following statement is not permitted:

```
DATE d.initialize(10,5, 2003);
```

Like structures, unions in C++ language also can have member functions.

2.17 DEFAULT ARGUMENTS

In C language, a function call must specify all the arguments used in the function definition. In a C++ function call, one or more arguments can be omitted with the condition that function is defined to take default values for the arguments that can be omitted by providing the default values in the function prototype or declarator.

In the function prototype or declarator, parameters without default arguments are placed first and those with default values are placed later. The arguments specified in the function call explicitly override the default values.

This following example illustrates the definition of a function with default arguments and how it can be used.

Listing 2.11

```
/*
 *  Program to illustrate the mechanism of defining
```

```
 *  function with default arguments
*/
#include <iostream.h>
void printline ( char ch = '-', int count = 80)
{
   cout << endl;
   for ( int i = 0; i < count; i++ )
      cout << ch;
   cout << endl;
}
void main()
{
   printline();              // use both default arguments
   printline('*');           // use second argument as default
   printline('+', 45);       // use explicit arguments
}
```

The above program can also be written with function prototype as

Listing 2.12

```
/*
 *  Program to illustrate the mechanism of defining
 *  function with default arguments
*/
#include <iostream.h>
void printline ( char ch = '-', int count = 80); // prototype
void main()
{
   printline();              // use both default arguments
   printline('*');           // use second argument as default
   printline('+', 45);       // use explicit arguments
}
void printline ( char ch, int count )
{
   cout << endl;
   for ( int i = 0; i < count; i++ )
      cout << ch;
   cout << endl;
}
```

The following prototype statement is also acceptable

```
void printline ( char = '-', int = 80 );
```

If you are using prototype for a function with default arguments, then the default values need to be specified only in the prototype. Specifying default values in the declarator too will lead to error indicating the default argument(s) is re-declared.

2.18 FUNCTION OVERLOADING

Suppose in our program we require the functionality to swap two values of *int* type, *float* type, *double* type, *char* type. Normally, this situation is dealt with by writing four different functions with different names as shown below:

```
// function to swap two int values
void swapInt ( int &first, int &second )
{
   int temp;
   temp = first;
   first = second;
   second = temp;
}
// function to swap two float values
void swapFloat ( float &first, float &second )
{
   float temp;
   temp = first;
   first = second;
   second = temp;
}
// function to swap two double values
void swapDouble ( double &first, double &second )
{
   double temp;
   temp = first;
   first = second;
   second = temp;
}
// function to swap two char values
void swapChar ( char &first, char &second )
{
   char temp;
   temp = first;
   first = second;
   second = temp;
}
```

Thus we have four different functions with different names for identical functionality. It would have been nice if we can use single name instead of four different names.

In C++ language, it is possible to use the same function name to perform identical operation. Such functions are called *overloaded functions* and the process of defining such functions is called *function overloading*.

Overloaded functions must differ in argument list in either of the following ways:

- They may differ in number of arguments.
- They may differ in data types of arguments.
- They may differ both in number and type of arguments.

Therefore, in the above example case, we can use one name, say *swap*, for all four versions of the swap function to swap different values and depending on the type of actual arguments in the function call; the compiler will resolve the function call.

Listing 2.13

```
/* Program to calculate the square of an int and float number
 * using overloaded function sqr()
*/
#include <iostream.h>
#include <iomanip.h>
int sqr ( int intArg );              // prototype for int version
float sqr ( float floatArg );    // prototype for float version
void main()
{
    int intNumber;
    float floatNumber;
    cout << "Enter integer number : ";
    cin >> intNumber;
    cout << "Enter float number : ";
    cin >> floatNumber;
    cout << endl << "square of " << intNumber << " = "
         << srq ( intNumber ) << endl;
    cout << "square of " << floatNumber << " = "
         << srq ( floatNumber ) << endl;
}
// function that returns square of a integer number
int sqr ( int intArg )
{
    return ( intArg * intArg );
}
// function that returns square of a float number
float sqr ( float intArg )
{
    return ( floatArg * floatArg );
}
```

Note that the return type does not play any role in function overloading. The reason is that it is not necessary to collect the returned value even if the called function returns a value.

This is demonstrated below:

Listing 2.14

```
/*
 * Program to demonstrate that return type does play any
 * role in overloading
*/
#include <iostream.h>
void f(void);          // prototype
int f(void);           // prototype
void main()
{
   f();                // function call
}
void f(void)           // function definition
{
   cout << "\nNo args., No return type\n";
}
int f(void)            // function definition
{
   cout << "\nNo args., int return type\n";
   return 10;
}
```

In function call, there will be ambiguity because just by seeing the call the system will not be able to figure out which version of function *f()* to call. Even, if we are not collecting the value, we cannot assume that function that does not return a value would be called.

2.18.1 Name Mangling – *Mechanism For Handling Function Overloading*

If there have been no overloading, then functions are always called by their name as given by the programmer. But, in case the compiler permits overloading, then to handle overloading, the compiler changes the names of all functions during compilations. This is known as *name mangling*.

Name mangling, also known as *name decoration*, is the process where the compiler changes the names of the functions to facilitate overloading.

2.19 FUNCTION TEMPLATES

The C++ language allows defining a single function capable of processing elements of different data types. Such a function is known as *function template* or *generic function*.

The syntax of function template is

```
template <class T1, class T2, . . .>
DataType FunctionName (arguments of type T1, T2, . . . )
{
   // local variables of type T1, T2, or any other type
   // function body, operating on variable of type T1, T2
   // any other variables
}
```

where *template* is the keyword for declaring function template

Following is the function template for swapping the values of two variables that are passed by reference.

```
Template <class T1>
void swap ( T1 &a, T1 &b )
{
    T1 temp;          // temporary variable
    temp = a;
    a = b;
    b = temp;
}
```

Following program illustrates the definition and use of function template.

Listing 2.15

```
/*
 * Program to illustrate the mechanism of defining and using function templates
*/
#include <iostream.h>
template <class T1>
void swap ( T1 &a, T1 &b)
{
    T1 temp;
    temp = a;
    a = b;
    b = temp;
}
void main()
{
    char ch1 = '*', ch2 = '+';
    int a1 = 10, a2 = 20;
    float b1 = 10.25, b2 = 22.75;
    double d1 = 12.67, d2 = 67.8;
    swap ( ch1, ch2 );
    cout << "\n" << ch1 << "," << ch2 << "\n";
```

```
    swap ( a1, a2 );
    cout << "\n" << a1 << "," << a2 << "\n";
    swap ( b1, b2 );
    cout << "\n" << b1 << "," << b2 << "\n";
    swap ( d1, d2 );
    cout << "\n" << d1 << "," << d2 << "\n";
}
```

2.20 DYNAMIC MEMORY MANAGEMENT OPERATORS

The C++ language provides the following operators to perform dynamic memory management:

- ***new* operator** – for dynamic memory allocation.
- ***delete* operator** – for dynamic memory deallocation.

2.20.1 The *new* Operator

The new operator allocates the memory in a manner similar to *malloc()* function in C language. The only difference is that it always return a pointer to an appropriate type, and there is no need for typecasting whereas the *malloc()* function returns a generic pointer (pointer to *void* data type) that must be typecasted to appropriate data type prior to its use otherwise system may behave inconsistently.

The *new* operator is defined as

```
type * new type [ size in integer ];
```

The following example illustrates its use.

```
int *intPtr;
intPtr = new int[100];
```

Allocate a memory block of 200 bytes, 2 bytes for one integer value, total of 100 integers.

Similar statements will be used for other primitive data types.

```
struct DATE {
    int day;
    int month;
    int year;
};
DATE *datePtr;
datePtr = new date;
```

Allocate memory for one structure item of type *DATE, i.e.*, 6 bytes.

The *new* operator also permits the initialization of memory locations during allocation. The syntax for doing so is

```
type *ptrVar = new type ( InitialValue );
```

This is illustrated in following example:

```
int *intPtr = new int(100);
```

This statement allocates memory for an integer number and initializes it with value 100. The address of the memory allocated memory is assigned to pointer variable *intPtr*.

```
float *floatPtr = new float(125.75);
```

This statement allocates memory for a float number (single precision real number) and initializes it with value 125.75. The address of the memory allocated memory is assigned to pointer variable *floatPtr*.

2.20.2 The *delete* Operator

The *delete* operator is a counterpart of new operator and it deallocates (releases) memory allocated by the new operator back to the free poll of memory in a manner similar to *free()* function in C language.

The syntax of *delete* operator is defined as

```
delete pointerVariable;
```

The *free()* function in C language is defined as

```
void free ( void * pointerVariable );
```

The following statement in C++ language

```
delete ( ptrVar );
```

is equivalent to following statement in C language

```
free ( ptrVar );
```

where *ptrVar* is pointer variable that holds the address of the dynamically allocated memory using *new* operator and *malloc()* function, respectively. The memory allocated using *new* operator or *malloc()* function must be released by the *delete* operator and *free()* function, respectively.

Following program demonstrates the use of *new* and *delete* operators. The program reads two vectors of same size from keyboard, add these vectors and outputs the resultant vector.

Listing 2.16

```
/*  Program to add two vectors. This program illustrates the use
 *  of new and delete operators
 */
#include <iostream.h>
#include <iomanip.h>
// function to input elements of a vector
void readVector ( float *vector, int size )
{
    for ( int i=0; i < size; i++ )
       cin >> vector[i];
}
// function to output elements of a vector
void writeVector ( float *vector, int size )
{
    for ( int i=0; i < size; i++ )
       cout << vector[i] << "  ";
    cout << endl;
}
// function to add to vectors
void addVectors ( float *x, float *y, float *z, int size )
{
    for ( int i=0; i < size; i++ )
       z[i] = x[i] + y[i];
}
void main()
{
    int vec_size;
    float *a, *b, *c;
    cout << "Enter size of vectors : ";
    cin >> vec_size;
    a = new float[vec_size];          // allocate memory for all vectors
    b = new float[vec_size];
    c = new float[vec_size];
    cout << "Enter elements of vector a : ";
    readVector(a, vec_size);
    cout << "Enter elements of vector b : ";
    readVector(b, vec_size);
    addVectors(a, b, c, vec_size);   // c = a + b
    cout << "Elements of resultant vector are : ";
    writeVector(c, vec_size);
```

```
    delete a;   // free memory allocated for all vectors
    delete b;
    delete c;
    // above three statements can also be combined as "delete a, b, c;"
}
```

A QUICK RECAP

In this chapter, we have learnt that

- C++ language is a superset of C.
- C++ language supports object-oriented programming in addition to procedural programming.
- C++ language supports new style of comments. Every comment line begins with two slash characters (//).
- C++ language supports two new data types – *bool* and *wchar_t*.
- For a structure, union and enumerated user-defined data types, you don't need to prefix keyword *struct*, *union* and *enum* before the *tag*.
- A variable in C++ language can be declared anywhere in the code.
- C++ language supports reference variables. A reference variable acts as alias for other variable.
- Reference variables enjoy the simplicity of value variables and power of pointer variables.
- A reference variable can only be bound to a value/pointer variable at the point of its declaration.
- A global variable can be accessed using *scope resolution operator* '::' (two consecutive colons).
- C++ language supports new style of typecasting that looks similar to function call.
- C++ language provides specialized cast operators – *static_cast*, *const_cast*, *dynamic_cast*, *reinterpret_cast*.
- C++ language provides operator keywords for *relational*, *bitwise* and some *short-hand* operators.
- New standard of C++ language also supports new style of header files, where you don't need to include the extension.
- New standard of C++ language also introduces the concept of namespaces that allows managing the large and complex software in an efficient manner.
- In addition to *call by value*, *call by address* (pointer), the arguments can also be passed using *call by reference* mechanism.

- C++ language introduces the concept of streams that streamlines the handling of input/output. Streams provide a uniform interface of doing the I/O irrespective of the I/O devices being used.
- C++ language also introduces the concept of *inline* functions. The inline functions are substitutes of *macros* that suffer from many inherit problems.
- In C++ language, structures can have function members in addition to data members.
- In C++ language, a function can have default arguments.
- C++ language supports the feature of function overloading, where you can give same function name for the functions that provide the same functionality but on different type of operands.
- C++ language also supports concept of *function templates* (*generic functions*), where you can define a single function capable of processing elements of different data types.
- C++ language provides two memory management operators – *new* and *delete*. These operators have added to support the requirements of object-oriented programming.

REVIEW EXERCISES

1. Trace the history of C++ language.
2. What are the types comments supported by C++ language?
3. Name the new basic data types added in C++ language over C language.
4. What is a reference variable?
5. Is it possible to access a global variable in a block when the local variable shares the name as that of a global variable? If yes, how?
6. Name the new cast operators in C++ language.
7. Name the operator keywords added in C++ language.
8. What is a namespace? How namespaces are useful?
9. By taking an example, demonstrate how the arguments can be passed using call by reference mechanism.
10. What is a stream? Name the predefined streams in C++ language.
11. What are inline functions? How they compare with normal functions?
12. What is function overloading? How is it useful?
13. What is function template? How is it useful?
14. Explain the usage of memory management operators incorporated in C++ language.

❑ ❑ ❑

Chapter 3

Standard Input/Output

Learning Objectives

After reading this chapter, students will be able to

- understand the standard I/O facility provided by C++ I/O subsystem
- understand the concept of streams
- understand the hierarchy of console stream classes
- understand the predefined console streams
- perform I/O using overloaded >> and << operators
- perform I/O using members function of istream class
- format the output using member functions of ostream class
- format the output using predefined manipulators
- format the output using user-defined manipulators

3.1 INTRODUCTION

In almost every computer program, the users have to input some data that will be stored in computer's memory, and then subsequently processed. This input data may be from a keyboard, a disk file, or from another computer via a communication channel. The intermediate and final results of the computations are also stored in computer's memory. And finally, there is need to output the results of the computations so that user can use them in their day-to-day work. The output can be displayed on the computer screen, stored on a disk, or transmitted via a communication channel to other computer.

The most common input device is the keyboard and the output device is a computer screen, sometimes called the *monitor*. This subsystem comprising keyboard and monitor is referred to as a *console*.

The C++ language provides uniform way for reading and writing of data without the knowledge of underlying data types through the use of streams.

In this chapter, we discuss in detail about streams, stream classes, and the way input/output can be performed.

3.2 CONCEPT OF STREAMS

The C++ I/O subsystem is designed to work with a wide variety of devices that includes keyboard, monitor, disks, tape drives, etc. The working principle (characteristics) of each of these devices is quite different. The C++ I/O subsystem is designed in such a way that it provides a uniform interface that is independent of the actual device being used. Thus, the programmer can write a C++ program that can receive input from, and send output to any device without bothering about the characteristics of device being used. This interface is called a *stream*.

Figure 3.1shows this uniform interface.

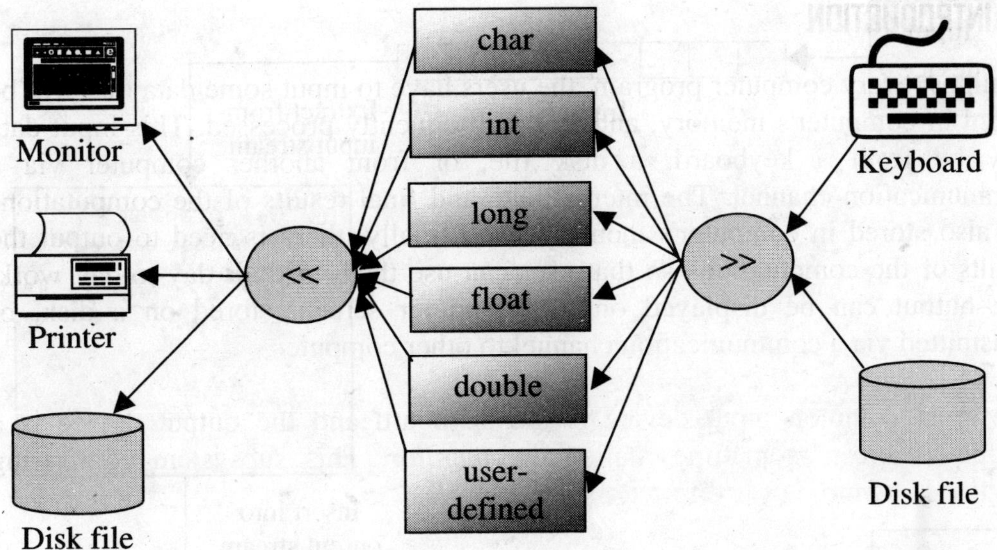

Figure 3.1: Consistent stream interface with I/O devices

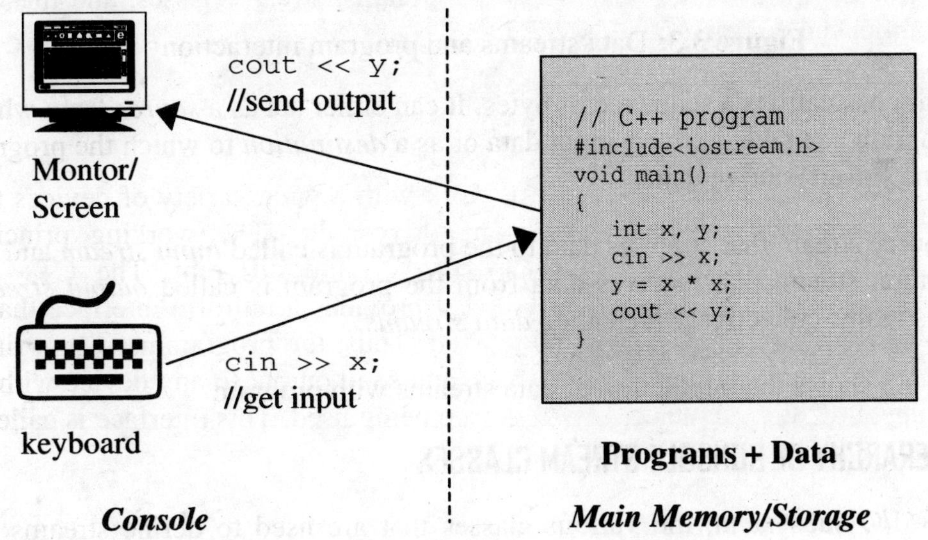

Figure 3.2: Console-program interaction

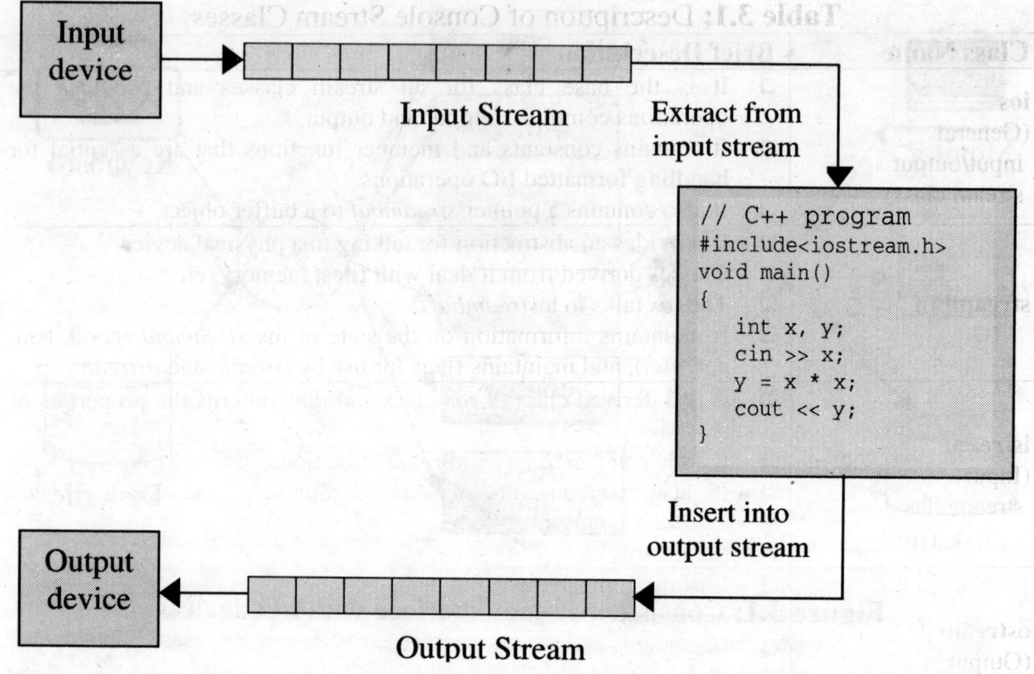

Figure 3.3: Data streams and program interaction

A stream basically is a sequence of bytes. It can either act as a *source* from which the program can take (extract) input data or as a *destination* to which the program can send (insert) output data.

The source stream that supplies data to the program is called *input stream* and the destination stream that receives data from the program is called *output stream.* These streams collectively are called *data streams*.

Figure 3.3 shows the interaction of data streams with program.

3.3 HIERARCHY OF CONSOLE STREAM CLASSES

In C++ I/O subsystem, the various classes that are used to define streams for dealing with both the console and disk files, called *stream classes*, are organized into a hierarchy of classes. Figure 3.4 shows the partial hierarchy of stream class dealing with the console.

A brief description of each class is given in Table 3.1.

Table 3.1: Description of Console Stream Classes

Class Name	Brief Description
ios (General input/output stream class)	❑ It is the base class for all stream classes and provides the operations common to input and output. ❑ It contains constants and member functions that are essential for handling formatted I/O operations. ❑ It also contains a pointer *streambuf* to a buffer object.
streambuf	❑ It provides an abstraction for talking to a physical device. ❑ Classes derived from it deal with files, memory, etc. ❑ The *ios* talks to a *streambuf*. ❑ It maintains information on the state of the *streambuf* (good, bad, eof, etc.), and maintains flags for use by *istream* and *ostream*.
istream (Input stream class)	❑ It is a derived class of *ios* class and thus inherits the properties of *ios* class. ❑ It adds *get()*, *getline()* and *read()* functions. ❑ It also contains an overloaded operator >>, called *stream extraction operator*, to read data from a standard input device (keyboard) and assign to memory variables.
ostream (Output stream class)	❑ It is also a derived class of *ios* class and thus inherits the properties of *ios* class. ❑ It adds *put()* and *write()* functions. ❑ It also contains an overloaded operator <<, called *stream insertion operator*, to write data from memory variables to a standard output device (screen/monitor).
iostream (Input/output stream class)	It is a derived class of *istream* and *ostream* classes and thus inherits the properties of *istream* and *ostream* classes. Hence, it provides the facility for handling both input and output streams.

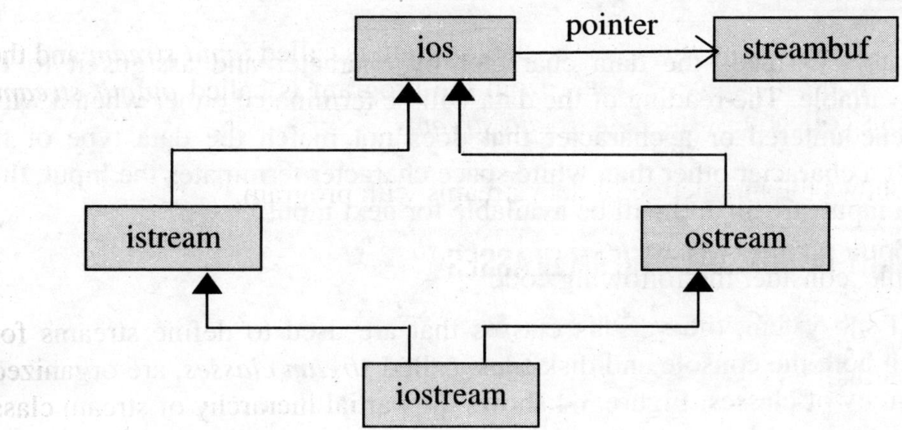

Figure 3.4: Partial hierarchy of console stream classes

3.4 PREDEFINED CONSOLE STREAMS

When a C++ program begins execution, the following streams are automatically opened and are closed when the program finished execution:

- The first one, known as the *standard input stream*, represented by an object *cin* of *istream* class, is the stream from which input is received. This stream usually receives input from keyboard, but using redirection, the stream can obtain input from a disk file or another input device.
- The second one, known as *standard output stream*, represented by an object *cout* of *ostream* class, is the stream to which output is sent. The stream usually sends output to computer screen, but using redirection, the stream can send output to a disk file or to another output device.
- The third one, known as *standard error stream*, represented by an object *cerr* of *ostream* class, is the stream to which error messages are sent. This stream always sends error messages to computer screen. The redirection does not work for this stream. Therefore, even if you use redirection, the output of the program will be send to the specified disk file or device, the error messages, if any, continue to appear on computer screen.

3.5 INPUT/OUTPUT USING OVERLOADED OPERATORS >> AND <<

The syntax for reading the data from the input device using operator >> is

```
cin >> VariableName;
```

The operator >> reads the data character by character and assigns it to the specified variable. The reading of the data will be terminated either when a white space is encountered or a character that does not match the data type of the variable. If a character other than white space character terminates the input, then it is left in input stream and will be available for next input.

For example, consider the following code

```
int radius;
cin >> radius;
```

If the input is given as

```
1234e
```

The operator >> will read the character upto 4 because character 'e' does not match with the integer values which can have digits only, and the value 1234 is assigned to variable *radius*. The character 'e' will be left in the input stream.

If the input is given as

```
1234.75
```

The operator >> will again read characters upto 4, and the value 1234 is assigned to variable *radius*. The characters '.', '7' and '5' will be left in the input stream.

If you want to input data for two or more variable, then either we can use separate statements or we can cascade operator >> as shown below:

```
cin >> VarName1 >> VarName2 >> VarName3 >> ... >> VarNameN;
```

The variables can be of different data type. The input data must match the data type of the variables and must be separated by white space character.

For example, consider the following code

```
int var1, var2, var3;
cin >> var1 >> var2 >> var3;
```

Suppose we want to input data as: 100 for *var1*, 105 for *var2*, and 200 for *var3*. The input data can be entered in any of the following ways:

1.	100	105	200↵	(input values separated by space)
2.	100	105	200↵	(input values separated by tabs)
3.	100↵			(input values separated by newline character)
	105↵			
	200↵			

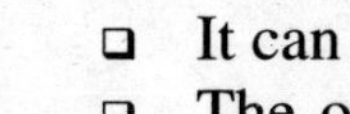

- The use of comma as a separator is not permitted.
- It can read only non-white space characters.
- The operator >> cannot read multiword strings as these strings use embedded space character which operator >> will interpret as value terminating character.

The syntax for writing data to the output device using operator << is

```
cout << item;
```

The overloaded operator << sends the item to the output device. This item may be a constant of any basic data type, a string constant, a variable, and arithmetic or a relational expression.

For example, consider the following code

```
int radius = 5;
cout << radius;
```

The operator << will send the value 5 to the output stream.

If you want to send two or more items to the output stream, then either we can use separate statements or we can cascade operator << as shown below:

```
cout << item1 << item2 << item3 << ... << itemN;
```

For example, consider the following code

```
int lengh = 5, width = 6;
cout << "Length of room = " << length << "Mts" << endl;
cout << "Width of room = " << width < "Mts" << endl;
cout << "Area of room = " << length * width;
cout << "Sq. Mts" << endl;
```

This code segment will produce the output

```
Length of room = 5 Mts.
Width of room = 6 Mts.
Area of room = 30 Sq. Mts.
```

Listing 3.1

```
//  Program to convert time given in seconds to time
//  in hours, minutes and seconds
#include<iostream.h>
void main()
{
    int seconds, minutes, hours, total_seconds, temp;
    cout << "Enter time in seconds : ";   // user prompt
    cin >> total_seconds;   // read time in seconds
```

```
    temp = total_seconds;  // create a copy of input
    hours = temp / 3600;   // calculate hours
    temp %= 3600;          // calculate remaining seconds
    minutes = temp / 60;   // calculate minutes
    seconds = temp % 60;   // calculate remaining seconds
    cout << endl;
    cout << "Time in " << total_seconds << " seconds = ";
    cout << hours << " hour(s), " << minutes
         << " minute(s) and " << seconds << " seconds" << endl;
}
```

Test Run

```
Enter time in seconds : 3678

Time in 3678 seconds = 1 hour(s), 1 minute(s) and 18 seconds
```

3.6 CHARACTER INPUT USING *get()* FUNCTION

The *get()* function reads one character, including white space characters, at a time from the input stream.

It is overloaded in *istream* and its prototypes are as follows:

```
int get(void);              // it returns character
void get(char &);     // it reads character into variable
```

It can be used with standard input stream object or with user defined object of *istream* class.

For example, consider the following code

```
char ch;
ch = cin.get();
```

It reads a single character and returns the same, which is subsequently assigned to character variable *ch*.

Now consider the following code

```
char ch;
cin.get(ch);
```

It reads a single character into variable *ch*.

3.7 CHARACTER OUTPUT USING *put()* FUNCTION

The *put()* function sends one character at a time to the output stream. Its prototype is:

```
void put(char);
```

It can be used with standard output stream object or with user defined object of the *ostream* class.

For example

```
cout.put('X');
```

displays the character X, and

```
char ch = 'A';
cout.put(ch);
```

displays the value of the character variable *ch*, *i.e.*, character A.

Listing 3.2

```
// Program to demonstrate the use of get() and put() functions.
// Program accepts a text terminated by newline character

#include <iostream.h>
void main()
{
    int count = 0;
    char ch;
    cout << "Enter Any Text" << "\n\n";
    ch = cin.get();          // input character
    while ( ch != '\n' )
    {
       cout.put(ch);         // output character
       count++;              // increment character count
       ch = cin.get();       // input character
    }
   // output character count
   cout << "\nNumber of characters = " << count << "\n";
}
```

Following program is another version of above program and both are functionally equivalent.

Listing 3.3

```
// Program to demonstrate the use of get() and put() functions.
// Program accepts a text terminated by newline character
#include <iostream.h>
void main()
{
    int count = 0;
    char ch;
    cout << "Enter Any Text" << "\n\n";
    cin.get(ch);             // input character
    while ( ch != '\n' )
    {
       cout.put(ch); // output character
       count++;              // increment character count
       cin.get(ch);     // input character
    }
    // output character count
    cout << "\nNumber of characters = " << count << "\n";
}
```

Test Run

```
C++ supports Object Oriented Programming. ↵

C++ supports Object Oriented Programming.
Number of characters = 41
```

3.8 STRING INPUT USING *getline()* FUNCTION

Using *getline()* function, we can read a line of text at a time. Every line of text is automatically terminated by null character ('\0').

The prototype for *getline()* function is

```
void getline(char *, int, char = '\n');
```

Input of line of text is terminated either by character specified by third argument, which is a newline character (Enter key ↵) by default, or by maximum limit.

If the number of character in the input line of text is less than the maximum limit, *i.e.*, input is terminated by a specified character, then all the characters are read.

However, if the number of characters in the input line of text is equal to maximum limit or more, then number of character read will be maximum limit minus one, because the last character position will be used for null character to terminate the string. The remaining characters will be left in the input stream.

After reading the line of text, it removes the input terminating string from the input stream.

For example, consider the following code

```
char name[20];
cin.getline(name,20);
```

Valid input line of text can be maximum of 19 characters.

If we enter the following input line of text

```
Lucky Ali↵
```

It will accept is correctly and assign this string to variable `name`.

However, if we enter the following input line of text

```
Inder Mohan Jit Singh Sidhu↵
```

It will accept only

```
Inder Mohan Jit Sin
```

and the remaining characters

```
gh Sidhu
```

will be left in the input stream.

Now consider the following code

```
char name[20];
cin.getline(name,20, ',');
```

Here the input will be terminated either by the presence of comma character ',' in the input lines of text or by the maximum limit.

If we enter the following input line of text

```
Programming is fun, enjoy it.↵
```

It will accept only

```
Programming is fun
```

and the remaining characters

```
enjoy it.
```

will be left in the input stream.

3.9 STRING OUTPUT USING *write()* FUNCTION

Using *write()* function, we can write a line of text at a time. The prototype for *write()* function is

```
void write ( const char *, int);
```

If the maximum limit is less than the number of characters in the stored line of text, then the *write()* function sends number of characters equal to the maximum limit from the beginning of the line of text

However, if the maximum limit is more than the number of characters in the stored line of text, then the *write()* function continues to send the character beyond the line of text i.e. it does not stop automatically when the null character is encountered. In this case, you may see some spaces or some other characters printed after the actual line of text.

Consider the following declaration

```
char *title = "C++ support object-oriented programming";
```

If we use the following statement

```
cout.write(title,25);
```

it will display

```
C++ support object-orient
```

However, if we use the following statement

```
cout.write(title,45);
```

the it will display

```
C++ support object-oriented programming++++++
```

where six occurrences of character '+' represents the characters that will be printed as a result of the maximum limit that is more that the actual number of characters in the variable *title* by a factor of 6.

Listing 3.4

```
// Program to demonstrate the use of getline() and write()
// functions. Program accepts a line of text terminated
// by newline character

#include <iostream.h>
#include <string.h>
void main()
{
    char text[80];
    int length;
    cout << "Enter Line of Text" << endl;
    cin.getline(text, 80);          // input line of text
    length = strlen(text);          // find length of input text
    cout << endl << "Line of text entered by you" << endl;
    cout.write(text, length);       // write line of text
    cout << "\n";
}
```

Test Run

```
Enter Line of Text
Programming is fun, enjoy it.↵

Line of text entered by you
Programming is fun, enjoy it.
```

3.10 FORMATTING OUTPUT

We know that data processing system involves input, process and output. We usually have control over the input, but may not have control over the form of output. We would be interested to control the output as per our procedures and requirements.

The default settings for the output are as follows:

- Values are always displays from left to right character by character.
- The columns used to print a value are always equal to the number of characters of that particular item.
- The trailing zeros in the fractional part of a real number are not displayed. If the fractional part is zero, then the decimal point is also not displayed.

Therefore, if you want to control the output in your own way, we have to use formatted output operations. C++ provides a number of features that can be used to format the output as desired.

These features include:

- *ios* class functions and flags.
- Predefined Manipulators.
- User-defined manipulators.

3.10.1 Formatting *ios* Class Functions and Flags

The *ios* class contains a large number of functions and flags that can be used to format the output in variety of ways. The most common and important of these functions are listed in Table 3.2.

The use and effect of each of these functions is described below and is supported by illustrative examples.

3.10.1.1 Defining Field Width with *width()* Function

The *width()* function is a member function of the *ios* class and is used to specify the minimum number of columns to be used to display a particular item. It can only be invoked on an object of output stream. Its prototype is:

```
int width(int);
```

where the integer argument specifies the number of columns for displaying output.

Table 3.2: The *ios* Class Functions and Flags

Function	Action Performed
`width()`	Specifies the minimum number of columns used to display a value. If the number of characters in an output item are less that the specified number of columns, then some columns will be left unused and will be filled by fill character, which space by default. These unused columns can be leading or trailing depending on the justification of the value in the field. By default, all value are displayed right justified.
`precision()`	Specifies the number of digits to be displayed after the decimal point. The fractional part is rounded to specified number of digits. For example, if the value is 25.7689, it will be display as 25.77, and if the value is 50.7326, it will be displayed as 50.73.
`fill()`	Specifies a character to be used to fill the unused area of a display field if the number of columns specified is more than the character in an output value. The default fill character is space.
`setf()`	Sets the format flags that control the output such as left-justification and right justification.
`unsetf()`	Clears the specified flag.

It can specify field width for only one item (item that follows immediately). It sets the width to the specified integer value, and returns the previous width. After displaying one item it reverts back to previous width. This previous width is usually a default width i.e. number of columns equal to the number characters in the output item. Therefore, you have to set the width for every item on the display list.

Consider the statement

```
int x = 2345, y = 1785;
```

It declares two integer variables *x* and *y* and initializes them to value 2345 and 1785, respectively.

If we use the statement

```
cout << x << y;        // both are displayed using default width
```

Output will appear as

2	3	4	5	1	7	8	5

If we use the statements

```
cout << x;          // display x using default width
cout.width(6);      // set width to 6 columns
cout << y;          // display y and return to default width
```

Output will appear as

2	3	4	5			1	7	8	5

If we use the statements

```
cout.width(6);      // sets width to 6 columns
cout << x;          // display x and return to default width
cout << y;          // displays y
```

Output will appear as

		2	3	4	5	1	7	8	5

If we use the statements

```
cout.width(3);      // set width to 3 columns
cout << x;          // display x and return to default width
cout.width(5);      // set width to 5 columns
cout << y;          // displays y and return to default width
```

Output will appear as

2	3	4	5		1	7	8	5

While displaying item *x*, it uses 4 columns rather than 3 columns as set by *width()* function because the items contains four character value.

3.10.1.2 Setting Precision with *precision()* Function

By default, floating-point numbers are displayed with a maximum of six decimal digits. However, we can specify the number of digits to be displayed after the decimal point using *precision()* function, which is a member function of the *ios* class. It can only be invoked on an object of output stream. Its prototype is:

```
int precision(int);
```

where the integer argument specifies the number of digits to be displayed after decimal point.

The precision once set remains effective for subsequent items till it is changed. To reset the precision to default, we call *precision()* function with 0 value as its argument.

Consider the statement

```
float a = 23.478, b = 178.532;
```

It declares two float variables *a* and *b* and initializes them to value 23.478 and 178.532, respectively.

If we use the statement

```
cout << x << y;        // both are displayed using default width
                       // and default precision
```

Output will appear as

If we use the statements

```
cout.width(7);         //set width to 7 columns
cout.precision(2);     //set precision 2 decimal digits
cout << a;             //display a in 7 columns with 2 decimal digits
cout.width(8);         //set width to 8 columns
cout.precision(1);     //set precision 2 decimal digits
cout << b;             //display x in 8 columns with 1 decimal digit
cout.precision(0);     //reset the precision to default
```

Output will appear as

3.10.1.3 Filling and Padding with *fill()* Function

If the field width is larger than the required by the value, the unused position of the field are filled with space, by default. However, using *fill()* function, we can fill the unused position of the field with any character. The *fill()* function is a member function of the *ios* class, and can be invoked only on an object of output stream. Its prototype is:

```
char fill(char);
```

where the character argument specifies the fill character. It set the new fill character to the specified character and returns the previous character.

The fill character once specified remains effective for subsequent items till it is changed. To reset the fill character to default character (space), we call *fill()* function with 0 value as its argument.

Consider the statement

```
int a = 2300, b = 532;
```

It declares two integer variables *a* and *b* and initializes them to value 2300 and 532, respectively.

If we use the statements

```
cout.fill('*');        // set character '*' as fill character
cout.width(10);        // set field width to 10
cout << a << "\n";     // output value of a
cout.width(10);        // set field width to 10
cout << b << "\n";     // output value of a
cout.fill(0);          // reset fill character to default
```

Output will appear as

*	*	*	*	*	*	2	3	0	0
*	*	*	*	*	*	*	5	3	2

Financial institutions use this kind of filling and padding so that the amount printed at different places in their financial documents cannot be tampered (changed). You must have observed this feature on bank drafts and cheques issued by a fully computerized bank.

3.10.1.4 Setting Flags and Bit-fields with *setf()* Function

We have seen that when the field width is larger than the required by the value, the values are printed right justified. But there is standard practice of printing text left justified and numeric data right justified. Similarly, we may like to print the float values in scientific notation. Also when the float value is printed the trailing zeroes in the decimal part are not printed, and even if the decimal part is zero, the decimal point is also not printed. We may like to print the decimal point and trailing zeros, even if the decimal part is zero. All this is possible using *setf()*

function, which is a member function of the *ios* class, and can be invoked only on an object of output stream. It is overload function with prototypes:

```
long setf(long _setbits, long _field);
long setf(long _setbits);
```

where the first argument *_setbits* is one of the flags defined in *ios* class and it specifies action required for the output. The second argument _field that is also defined in *ios* class, specifies the group to which formatting flag belongs.

The first form is used with those flags that have associated bit fields whereas the second form is used with those flags that don't have associated bit fields.

Different flags defined in *ios* class along with their associated bit fields, if any, along with their action on output are listed in Table 3.3 and Table 3.4.

Table 3.3 : Flags that don not have bit fields for *setf()* function

Flag	Action on Output
showbase	Show base indicator on output.
showpoint	Include decimal point and trailing zeros in the output.
showpos	Output '+' before positive numbers. By default, if the number is positive then the sign character is not printed.
uppercase	Use uppercase letters when integer number is output using hex base.
skipws	Skip white space on input.
unitbuf	Flush all streams after insertion.
stdio	Flush *stdin* and *sterr* after insertion.

Table 3.4: Flags that have bit fields for *setf()* function

Flag	Field	Action on Output
left	adjustfield	Left-justified output. Padding occurs before the sign or the base indicator.
right		Right-justified output. Padding occurs after the number.
internal		Padding occurs between the sign or the base indicator and the number when the field width is more that the required by the value.

Table 3.4: Flags that have bit fields for *setf()* function *contd.*

scientific	floatfield	Float values are output using exponential normalized floating-point notation.
fixed		Float values are output using ordinary floating-point notation (without exponent).
doc	basefield	Integer value is output in the decimal base.
oct		Integer value is output in the octal base.
hex		Integer value is output in the hexadecimal base.

3.10.1.4.1 Justifying the Output

Consider the statement

```
int a = 2300, b = -532;
```

It declares two integer variables *a* and *b* and initializes them to value 2300 and 532, respectively.

If we use the statements

```
cout.setf(ios::left, ios::adjustfield);
cout.fill('*');
cout.width(10);
cout << a << "\n";

cout.setf(ios::right, ios::adjustfield);
cout.width(10);
cout << b << "\n";
cout.fill(0);
```

Output will appear as

2	3	0	0	*	*	*	*	*	*
*	*	*	*	*	*	–	5	3	2

Financial institutions use this kind of filling and padding so that the amount printed at different places in their financial documents cannot be tampered (changed). You must have observed this feature on bank drafts and cheques issued by a fully computerized bank.

If we use the statements

```
cout.fill('*');
cout.setf(ios::internal, ios::adjustfield);
cout.width(10);
cout << b << "\n";
```

Output will appear as

–	*	*	*	*	*	*	5	3	2

3.10.1.4.2 Display Trailing Zeros

When float numbers are output, the trailing zeros are not printed. And if the fractional part of a float number is zero, then decimal point is also not printed. Consider the following code segment

```
float a = 1023.75, b = 29.00, c = 175.50;
cout.precision(2);
cout.width(8);
cout << a << "\n";
cout.width(8);
cout << b << "\n";
cout.width(8);
cout << c << "\n";
```

The output would appear as

	1	0	2	3	.	7	5
						2	9
			1	7	5	.	5

Where would like the above output to be in the following form

	1	0	2	3	.	7	5
			2	9	.	0	0
		1	7	5	.	5	0

This is possible using *setf()* functions with *showpoint* flag as its argument.

The above output can be achieved using the following code segment:

```
float a = 1023.75, b = 29.00, c = 175.50;
cout.setf(ios::showpoint);
```

```
cout.precision(2);
cout.width(8);
cout << a << "\n";
cout.width(8);
cout << b << "\n";
cout.width(8);
cout << c << "\n";
```

3.10.1.4.3 Display Plus Sign

When numbers are output, the sign is printed only if the number is negative. If the number is positive, the positive sign is not printed. However, there may be situations where we want to print the sign irrespective of whether the number is positive or negative. This is possible using *setf()* functions with *showpos* flag as its argument. When *showpos* flag is set, the positive sign will be printed if the number is positive and negative sign will be printed if the number is negative.

Consider the following example code segment

```
float a = -1023.75, b = 29.25;
cout.setf(ios::showpos);
cout.precision(2);
cout.fill('*');
cout.width(10);
cout << a << "\n";
cout.width(10);
cout << b << "\n";
```

The output would appear as

*	*	–	1	0	2	3	.	7	5
*	*	*	*	+	2	9	.	2	5

For the following example code segment

```
float a = -1023.75, b = 29.25;
cout.setf(ios::internal, ios::adjustfield);
cout.setf(ios::showpos);
cout.precision(2);
cout.fill('*');
cout.width(10);
cout << a << "\n";
cout.width(10);
cout << b << "\n";
```

The output would appear as

–	*	*	1	0	2	3	.	7	5
+	*	*	*	*	2	9	.	2	5

3.10.1.5 Resetting Flags with *unsetf()* Function

A flag once set remains in effect till either it reset or the flag of the same group is set because flag belonging to a group are mutually exclusive. Whenever we set a flag of a given group, the precious flag is automatically reset. However, any flag can be reset any time using *unsetf()* function. Its prototype is:

```
long unsetf(long);
```

It resets specified flag as specified by the argument, and returns the previous flag.

3.10.2 Formatting with Predefined Manipulators

Manipulators are special functions that are designed to modify the working of streams. These are defined in *iomanip.h* header file. They provide the same features as that of the member functions of *ios* class, but are more convenient to use. They don't need an object to invoke them as in the case of *ios* member function that can only be invoked on an object of output stream.

Further, two or more manipulators can be chained in one statement as shown below:

```
cout << manip1 << manip2 << manip3 << item1;
cout << manip1 << item1 << manip2 << item2;
```

The manipulators are categorized into following two types:

- Non-parameterized Manipulators – manipulators that take an argument.
- Parameterized Manipulators – manipulators that take no argument.

Table 3.5: Predefined non-parameterized manipulators

Manipulator	Action Performed
dec	Sets the conversion base to 10.
hex	Sets the conversion base to 16.
oct	Sets the conversion base to 8.
ws	Extracts white space characters from an input stream until a non-white space character is found.
endl	Outputs a newline character ('\n') to the output stream and flushes it.
ends	Outputs a NULL character ('\0') to the output stream.
flush	Flushes the output stream.

Table 3.6: Predefined parameterized manipulators

Manipulator	Action Performed	Equivalent member function in *ios* Class
`setw(int)`	Sets the field width.	`width(int)`
`setprecision(int)`	Sets the floating-point precision.	`precision(int)`
`setfill(int)`	Sets the fill character.	`fill(char)`
`setbase(int)`	Sets the conversion base: 0: Use decimal for output. 8: Use octal for input and output. 10: Use decimal for input and output. 16: Use hexadecimal for input and output.	No equivalent
`setiosflags(long)`	Sets the format flag.	`setf(long)`
`resetiosflags(long)`	Resets (clears) the format flags.	`unsetf(long)`

The following code segment using the `ios` member functions and flags

```
float a = 1023.75, b = 29.00, c = 175.50;
cout.setf(ios::showpoint);
cout.precision(2);
cout.width(8);
cout << a << endl;
cout.width(8);
cout << b << endl;
cout.width(8);
cout << c << endl;
```

produce the output

	1	0	2	3	.	7	5
			2	9	.	0	0
		1	7	5	.	5	0

The same out can be realized using manipulators as shown in following code segment:

```
float a = 1023.75, b = 29.00, c = 175.50;
cout.setf(ios::showpoint);
cout << setprecision(2) << setw(7) << a << endl;
cout << setw(7) << b << endl;
cout << setw(7) << c << endl;
```

By comparing these two code segments, you can find that the use of manipulators is more convenient.

Listing 3.5

```
//  Program to demonstrate the use of pre-defined manipulators

#include <iostream.h>
#include <iomanip.h>
#include <math.h>
void main()
{
   float x;
   cout.setf(ios::right, ios::adjustfield);
   cout << "---------------------------------------------\n";
   cout << setw(5)  << "x";
   cout << setw(10) << "x^2";
   cout << setw(15) << "log(x)";
   cout << setw(15) << "exp(x)" << endl;
   cout << "---------------------------------------------\n";
   cout << setiosflags(ios::showpoint);
   cout << setprecision(2);
   for ( x = 0.5; x <= 5; x += 0.5 )
   {
      cout.setf(ios::fixed, ios::floatfield);
      cout << setw(5)  << x;
      cout << setw(10) << x * x;
      cout << setw(15) << log(double(x));
      cout.setf(ios::scientific, ios::floatfield);
      cout << setw(15) << exp(double(x));
      cout << endl;
   }
   cout << "---------------------------------------------\n";
}
```

Test Run

```
---------------------------------------------
    x       x^2         log(x)         exp(x)
---------------------------------------------
 0.50      0.25          -0.69       1.65e+00
 1.00      1.00           0.00       2.72e+00
 1.50      2.25           0.41       4.48e+00
 2.00      4.00           0.69       5.39e+00
 2.50      6.25           0.92       1.21e+01
 3.00      9.00           1.10       2.01e+01
 3.50     12.25           1.25       3.31e+01
 4.00     16.00           1.39       5.46e+01
 4.50     20.25           1.50       9.00e+01
 5.00     25.00           1.61       1.48e+02
---------------------------------------------
```

3.10.3 Formatting with User-defined Manipulators

We can design our own manipulators, called user-defined manipulators, to control the output in a certain manner.

The syntax for creating user-defined output manipulators is

```
ostream & manipulator(ostream & output)
{
      . . . .
      . . . .    // manipulator code
      . . . .
      return output;  //return reference to the output stream
}
```

The following segment defines an output manipulator named *currency* that display "Rs.":

```
ostream & indian_currency (ostream & output)
{
      output << "Rs.";
      return output;
}
```

Then the following statements

```
float amount = 125.50;
cout << indian_currency;
cout << setw(10) << setfill('*') << setprecision(2);
cout.setf(ios:showpoint);
cout << amount << endl;
```

will produce the output

R	s	.	*	*	*	*	1	2	5	.	5	0

The following segment defines a manipulator named *float_format* that sets the filed width to 10 columns, set the *showpoint* flag, specifies '*' as fill character, sets precision to two decimal digits, and sets the fixed flag for a float value:

```
ostream & float_format (ostream & output)
{
   output << setw(10);                          //set field width
   output << setiosflags(ios::showpoint); // set showpoint flag
   output << setfill('*');                     // set fill character
```

```
   output << setprecision(2);          // set precision
   output << setiosflags(ios::fixed);  //without exponent format
   return output;    // return reference to output stream
}
```

Listing 3.6

```
//  Program to demonstrate the creation and use
//  of user-defined output manipulators

#include <iostream.h>
#include <iomanip.h>
ostream & currency (ostream & output)
{
   output << "Rs.";
   return output;
}
ostream & float_format (ostream & output)
{
   output << setw(10);                          //set field width
   output << setiosflags(ios::showpoint); //set showpoint flag
   output << setfill('*');             // set fill character
   output << setprecision(2);          // set precision
   output << setiosflags(ios::fixed); //fixed format
   return output;    // return reference to output stream
}
void main()
{
   float amount = 125.50;
   cout << endl << currency;
   cout << float_format;
   cout << amount << endl;
}
```

Test Run

```
Rs.****125.50
```

The syntax for creating user-defined input manipulators is

```
istream & manipulator(istream & input)
{
      . . . .
      . . . .// manipulator code
      . . . .
      return intput;  //return reference to the input stream
}
```

The following segment defines an input manipulator named *get_password* that display generates one audio tone and display user prompt "Enter password":

```
istream & get_password (istream & input)
{
      cout << '\a'; // beep (sound bell)
      cout << "Enter password : ";
      return intput;
}
```

Listing 3.7

```
//   Program to demonstrate the creation and use
//   of user-defined input manipulators

#include <iostream.h>
#include <iomanip.h>
istream & get_password (istream & input)
{
    cout << '\a';    // beep (sound bell)
    cout << "Enter password : ";
    return input;
}
void main()
{
    char pass[12];
    cin >> get_password;
    cin >> pass;
    cout << "Password entered by you : ";
    cout << pass << endl;
}
```

Test Run

```
Enter password : harry

Password entered by you : harry
```

3.11 SUPPLEMENTARY PROGRAMMING PROBLEMS

Let us write a few C++ programs to use the features that we have learned so far.

Problem 3.1:

Program to find the sum of digits of a given four-digit positive integer number.

Listing 3.8

```
// Program to find sum of digits of a four digit
// positive integer number

#include<iostream.h>
#include <iomanip.h>

void main()
{
    int number,sum,digit1,digit2,digit3,digit4,temporary;
    cout << "Enter four digit positive number : ";
    cin >> number;
    temporary = number;
    digit1 = temporary % 10;
    temporary /= 10;
    digit2 = temporary % 10;
    temporary /= 10;
    digit3 = temporary % 10;
    temporary /= 10;
    digit4 = temporary % 10;
    sum = digit1 + digit2 + digit3 + digit4;
    cout << "Sum of digits of " << number << " = ";
    cout << sum << endl;
}
```

Test Run

```
Enter four digit positive number : 2375
Sum of digits of 2375 = 17
```

Problem 3.2:

Program to reverses the digits of a given four-digit positive integer number.

Listing 3.9

```
//  Program to print four digit positive integer number
//  in reverse order

#include<iostream.h>
#include<iomanip.h>

void main()
{
    int number,sum,digit1,digit2,digit3,digit4,temporary;
    cout << "Enter four digit positive number : ";
    cin >> number;
    temporary = number;
    digit1 = temporary % 10;
```

```
    temporary /= 10;
    digit2 = temporary % 10;
    temporary /= 10;
    digit3 = temporary % 10;
    temporary /= 10;
    digit4 = temporary % 10;
    sum = digit1 * 1000 + digit2 * 100 + digit3 * 10 + digit4;
    cout << "Number after reversing digits of " << number;
    cout << " is " << sum << endl;
}
```

Test Run

```
Enter four digit positive number : 2375
Number after reversing the digits of 237
```

Problem 3.3:

Given the temperature in Fahrenheit scale. Find the equivalent temperature in Celsius scale.

We know the relation between temperature in Celsius and Fahrenheit is:

$$\frac{C}{100} = \frac{F-32}{180} \qquad \text{simplifying, we get} \qquad F = \frac{5}{9}(F-32)$$

Listing 3.10

```
//  Program to convert temperature from Fahrenheit scale to
//  Centigrade scale
#include<iostream.h>
#include<iomanip.h>
void main()
{
    float fahrenheit, centigrade;
    cout << "\nEnter temperature in fahrenheit scale : ";
    cin >> fahrenheit;
    centigrade = ( 5.0/9.0 ) * (fahrenheit - 32 );
    cout << "Equivalent Temperature in Fahrenheit ";
    cout << " = " << centigrade << endl;
}
```

Test Run

```
Enter temperature in Fahrenheit scale : 86
Equivalent Temperature in Celsius = 30
```

Problem 3.4:

Program to find the largest of three integer numbers.

Listing 3.11

```
//  Program to find the largest of three integers
#include<iostream.h>
#include<iomanip.h>
void main()
{
    int a, b, c, larger;
    cout << "Enter three integer number : " << endl;
    cin >> a >> b >> c;
    larger = a > b ? ( a > c ? a : c ) : ( b > c ? b : c);
    cout << "\nLargest number is " << larger << endl;
}
```

Test Run

```
Enter three integer number : 86 125 75
Largest number is 125
```

Problem 3.5:

Program to compute the area of a triangle whose sides are given.

Suppose that length of sides is *a*, *b* and *c*, then area of triangle is given by formula

$$\text{Area of triangle} = \sqrt{s(s-a)(s-b)(s-c)}\,, \quad \text{where} \quad s = \frac{a+b+c}{2}$$

Listing 3.12

```
//  Program to find the area of triangle whose sides are given
#include<iostream.h>
#include<iomanip.h>
#include<math.h>

void main (void)
{
    float sideA, sideB, sideC, s, area;
    cout << "Enter side A: ";
    cin >> sideA;
    cout << "Enter side B: ";
    cin >> sideB;
    cout << "Enter side C: ";
```

```
    cin >> sideC;
    s = ( sideA + sideB + sideC ) / 2;
    area = sqrt(double((s*(s-sideA)*(s-sideB)*(s-sideC))));
    cout << setprecision(3) << endl
         << "Area of triangle: " << area
         << endl;
}
```

Test Run

```
Enter side A: 3
Enter side B: 3
Enter side C: 3

Area of triangle: 3.897
```

The program is run for an equilateral triangle with each side equal to 3 units.

Problem 3.6:

On an amount of rupees, say *P*, program to compute simple interest and compound interest if the interest rate is *R%* annually and the time is *N* years.

We know that formulae to compute simple interest and compound interest are

$$\text{simple interest } (si) = \frac{P \times R \times N}{100}, \text{ compound interest } (ci) = P\left(1+\frac{R}{100}\right)^{N} - P$$

Listing 3.13

```
// Program to compute simple interest and compound interest
#include<iostream.h>
#include<iomanip.h>
#include<math.h>
void main (void)
{
    float p, r, n, si, ci;
    cout << "Enter amount: ";
    cin >> p;
    cout << "Enter rate of interest: ";
    cin >> r;
    cout << "Enter time: ";
    cin >> n;
    si = ( p * r * n ) / 100;
    ci = p * pow(double(1.0+r/100), double(n) ) - p;
    cout.setf(ios::showpoint);
    cout << setprecision(2) << endl
```

```
        << "Simple Interest   : " << si << endl
        << "Compound Interest : " << ci << endl;
}
```

Test Run

```
Enter amount: 100
Enter rate of interest: 5
Enter time: 5

Simple Interest   : 25.00
Compound Interest: 27.63
```

Problem 3.7:

Program that reads lowercase alphabet and prints it in uppercase.

Note that characters are internally represented using ASCII code. The ASCII for lowercase alphabet letters (*a-z*) is 97 decimal to122 and for uppercase alphabet letters (*A-Z*) it is 65 to 90. It means that the ASCII code of lowercase alphabet letters is more by a factor of 32 than corresponding uppercase alphabet letters. Therefore, given a lowercase alphabet letter, by subtracting a value of 32, we get corresponding uppercase alphabet letter. The following program does this.

Listing 3.14

```
//  Program to reads a lowercase character and
//  outputs it as uppercase character
#include<iostream.h>
void main (void)
{
    char ch;
    cout << "Enter lowercase alphabet letter: ";
    cin >> ch;
    ch = ch - 32;
    cout << "\nUppercase alphabet letter: " << ch << endl;
}
```

Test Run

```
Enter lowercase alphabet letter: a

Uppercase alphabet letter: A
```

Problem 3.8:

Program that reads a decimal integer number and prints it equivalent octal number without doing any explicit conversion.

Note that integer numbers (in general all kind of data) are internally represented as binary numbers whether you input as decimal number, octal number or hexadecimal number. The stored binary integer number can be printed either as decimal number, octal number or hexadecimal number using *dec*, *oct* and *hex* pre-defined non-parameterized manipulators. The following program does this.

Listing 3.15

```
//  Program that reads decimal integer number and
//  prints it as octal integer number
#include<iostream.h>
#include<iomanip.h>
void main (void)
{
    int number;
    cout << "Enter decimal integer number: ";
    cin >> number;
    cout << "\nEquivalent octal number: " << oct << number;
}
```

Test Run

```
Enter decimal integer number: 250

Equivalent octal number: 372
```

QUICK RECAP

In this chapter, we have learnt that

- Input/output is a vital part of every program.
- By default, every C++ program has access to *cin*, *cout*, *cerr* and *clog* streams.
- Input can be performed either by using extraction operator (>>) or by using member functions *get()* and *getline()* of the input stream.
- Output can be performed either by using insertion operator (<<) or by using member functions *put()* and *write()* of the output stream.
- Output of a C++ program can be formatted or unformatted.
- You can use member functions of *ios* class or manipulators to format output.
- You can also create your manipulators.
- Using escape sequences, we can format the output as per our requirements.

MULTIPLE CHOICE QUESTIONS

1. In order to use *cin* and *cout* stream objects, you need to include ______ header file.
   (*a*) stdio.h (*b*) iostream.h
   (*c*) iomanip.h (*d*) cincout.h
2. The member function *precision()* of *cout* object is used to specify the ______.
   (*a*) number of decimal position (*b*) field width
   (*c*) desired accuracy in the output (*d*) none of above
3. Which of the following statement is true about the default setting for the output stream?
   (*a*) Values are left aligned
   (*b*) Field width used for the value equals number of character positions in the value
   (*c*) If the fractional part of a real value is zero, then even decimal point is not displayed
   (*d*) All of above
4. The manipulator *endl* performs the task equivalent to
   (*a*) tab character '\t' (*b*) formfeed character '\f'
   (*c*) carriage return character '\r' (*d*) newline character '\n'
5. Which of the following statement is not true about streams?
   (*a*) A stream is a sequence of bits
   (*b*) A stream is a sequence of bytes
   (*c*) A stream can act as either source stream or destination stream
   (*d*) The *ios* class is base class for all stream classes
6. Which of the following is not a predefined stream?
   (*a*) cin (*b*) cout
   (*c*) cerr (*d*) None of above
7. Which of the following can be used to input multiword strings?
   (*a*) Operator '>>'
   (*b*) The *get()* member function of input stream
   (*c*) The *getline()* member function of input stream
   (*d*) All of above
8. To fill the unused section of the field with a specified character, the ____ function can be used?
   (*a*) fil() (*b*) fill_field()
   (*c*) fill_char() (*d*) None of above

9. Which of the following member function of input stream class is overloaded?
   (*a*) get() (*b*) getline()
   (*c*) put() (*d*) All of above
10. Which of the following flag is used to output the sign irrespective whether the number is positive or negative?
    (*a*) showsign (*b*) showbase
    (*c*) showpos (*d*) printsign
11. If we want that padding should occurs between the sign the number when the field width is more that the required by the value, which of the following flag we have to use?
    (*a*) left (*b*) internal
    (*c*) between (*d*) right
12. Which of the following statement is not true about manipulators?
    (*a*) More handy as compared to member functions of the *ios* class.
    (*b*) To use manipulators in your program you have to include header file *iomanip.h*.
    (*c*) You can create customized input as well as output manipulators.
    (*d*) All of above.
13. Which of the following function can be used to reset the previous set flags?
    (*a*) resetflags() (*b*) clearflags()
    (*c*) unsetf() (*d*) unsetflags()
14. Which of the following manipulator don't have its equivalent member function of *ios* class?
    (*a*) setw() (*b*) setbase()
    (*c*) resetiosflags() (*d*) setfill()
15. Name the stream whose input/output cannot be directed?
    (*a*) cin (*b*) cout
    (*c*) cerr (*d*) None of above

REVIEW EXCERCISES

1. What is a stream?
2. Describe the I/O subsystem supported by C++.
3. Describe the hierarchy of stream classes that deals with the console.
4. By default, every C++ program has access to certain stream class. Describe those stream classes.
5. Describe the I/O using overloaded insertion '<<' and extraction '>>' operators.
6. Describe the I/O using *get()* and *put()* functions.

7. Describe the I/O using *getline()* and *write()* functions.
8. What do you understand by formatting the output? What are the default settings for the output?
9. Describe the features provided by C++ that can be used to format the output.
10. Describe various flags defined in *ios* class that can be used to format output.
11. Describe the features provided by C++ that can be used to format the output.
12. What are manipulators?
13. Given a choice, will you prefer using member functions of an *ios* class or manipulators? Justify your answer with suitable examples.
14. Is it possible to design customized manipulators? If yes, describe the syntax for doing so.

PROGRAMMING EXERCISES

1. Write a program that accepts a decimal integer and prints it in the hexadecimal form.
2. Write a program that accepts a character in uppercase and prints it as lowercase.
3. Write a program that accepts a temperature in Fahrenheit scale and prints its equivalent temperature in Centigrade scale.
4. An amount of rupees, say *P*, is deposited in a commercial bank for *N* years, which pays simple interest at the rate of *R*% annually. Write a C++ program that prints the amount after *N* years.
5. Write a C++ program to find the real roots of a quadratic equation of type $ax^2+bx+c = 0$, where $a \neq 0$
6. Basic salary (BS) of an employee is input through the keyboard. The dearness allowance (DA) is 25% of the basic salary while the house rent allowance (HRA) is 15% of the basic salary. Provident fund (PF) is deducted at the rate of 10% of the gross salary (BS+DA+HRA). Write a C++ program to calculate the net salary (NS).

❑ ❑ ❑

Chapter 4

Classes and Objects

Learning Objectives

After reading this chapter, students will be able to explain the

- syntax for creating a class
- effect of access specifier on class members
- syntax for creating objects
- syntax for accessing class members
- syntax for defining the member functions inside the class
- syntax for defining the member functions outside the class
- syntax for making the member functions defined outside the class as inline
- syntax for passing objects as function arguments
- syntax for functions that can return an object
- mechanism of friendship of a class and how it can help in program design
- meaning and purpose of nested, empty, abstract, local and container classes

4.1 INTRODUCTION

A class and an object are tightly interwoven, for example, we cannot talk about an object without regard for its class. However, there are important differences between these two terms. An object is a concrete entity that exists in time and space and has an identity, whereas a class represents only an abstraction, the *essence* of an object. Thus, we may speak of the class *student*, which represents characteristics common to all students. To identify a particular student in this class, we must speak of *this student* or *that student*.

In the context of OOP, we define class as a set of objects that share a common structure and a common behaviour. An object is simply an instance of a class.

4.2 SPECIFYING A CLASS

Syntax for specifying a class is much like specifying a structure as shown below:

```
class ClassName
{
    AccessSpecifier:
        // data members
        // function members
};
```

Figure 4.1: Syntax for class declaration

The *AccessSpecifier* (*private*, *protected* or *public*) determines which parts of a software system can access these members of a class. By default, access specifier for a class is *private*, and an access specifier remain in effect till overridden by another access specifier.

The data members describe the structure of the objects and at particular instant the values of these data members represents the state of an object. The function members describe the behavior of the objects, *i.e.,* how object responds to external events.

Each of these members can be declared as *private*, *protected* or *public*. The private members can only be accessed from within the class. Members of the class and members of its subclass can access a protected member. The public members can also be accessed by non-members of the class, *i.e.*, from outside the class.

Declaring all members (data and function) as *private* will not serve any purpose because the entire class will be hidden from the external world.

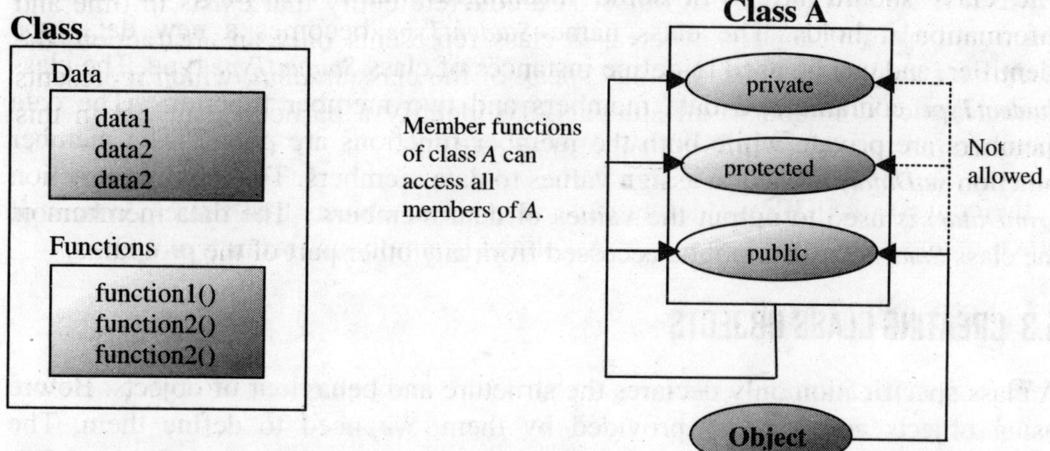

Figure 4.2: Class contains data and functions

Figure 4.3: Access limits within a class

The following declaration illustrates the specification of a class called *StudentType* having *studentRollNo* and *studentName* as its data members; *setData()* and *printData()* as its member functions.

```
class StudentType
{
   private:                    // data members
      int  studentRollNo;
      char studentName[20];
  public:                   // function members
      void setData( int rollNo, char *name ) {
        studentRollNo = rollNo;
        strcpy ( studentName, name );
      }
      void printData() {
        cout << "\nRoll No of Student : ";
        cout << studentRollNo << endl;
        cout << "Name of Student    : ";
        cout << studentName << endl;
      }
};
```

In the above class definition, even if we omit the use of keyword private, the data members will be declared as private since private is the default access, and remain in effect till new access specifier is encountered in the class definition.

The class should be given some meaningful name reflecting the kind of information it holds. The class name *StudentType* becomes a new data type identifier, and can be used to define instances of class *StudentType* type. The class *StudentType* contains two data members and two member functions. The data members are private while both the member functions are public. The member function *setData()* is used to assign values to data members. The member function *printData()* is used to output the values of data members. The data members of the class *StudentType* cannot be accessed from any other part of the program.

4.3 CREATING CLASS OBJECTS

A class specification only declares the structure and behaviour of objects. Before using objects and services provided by them, we need to define them. The process of defining the objects is known as *instantiation*. It is the definition of an object that creates object in a program and sets aside memory for its storage *i.e.*, necessary resources are allocated only when a class is instantiated.

Syntax for defining objects of a class as shown below:

```
ClassName objectName;
```

Declaration of an object is similar to that of a value variable of any basic data type.

```
StudentType student;
```

Class specification and object definition can also be combined by placing the name of objects after the closing brace of the class specification as shown below:

```
class StudentType
{
      private:                        // data members
         int  studentRollNo;
         char studentName[20];
     public:                     // function members
          void setData( int rollNo, char *name ) {
            studentRollNo = rollNo;
            strcpy ( studentName, name );
          }
          void printData() {
            cout << "\nRoll No of Student : ";
```

```
        cout << studentRollNo << endl;
        cout << "Name of Student    : ";
        cout << studentName << endl;
    }
} student;
```

But this practice is seldom used because the developer would always prefer to declare the objects close to the place where they will be used and not at the time of the class definition.

4.4 ACCESSING CLASS MEMBERS

Syntax for accessing a class member is similar to that of accessing a member of a structure, *i.e.*, using dot operator as shown below:

```
ObjectName.publicDataMemberName;
ObjectName.publicFunctionMemberName(actualArguments);
```

Note that only public members can be accessed outside the class specification. The private and protected class members can only be accessed by member functions that can be private or public. Similarly, the function members that are declared as public are accessible from outside the class specification. These public functions can access private data members as well as private functions of the class.

For example, the statement

```
student.setData( 100, "Ravi Kiran" );
```

will invoke member function *setData()* which assign value 100 to data member *studentRollNo* and string "Ravi Kiran" to data member *studentName.*

Similarly, the statement

```
student.printData();
```

will output the values of the data members.

A member function can only be called (invoked) by using an object. Thus, the statement

```
setData();
```

is illegal.

The following statements are also illegal:

```
student.studentRollNo = 10;
strcpy( student.studentName, "Ravi Kiran" );
```

These data members being private can only be accessed from within the class. Thus, to assign values to them, to process them or to output their values, a class specification must incorporate a set of appropriate member functions.

4.5 MORE ABOUT ACCESS SPECIFIERS

As mentioned earlier, the *AccessSpecifier* (*private*, *protected* or *public*) determines which parts of a software system can access these members of a class. By default, access specifier for a class is *private*, and an access specifier remain in effect till overridden by another access specifier.

4.5.1 The *public* Access Specifier

The *public* access specifier allows the object to access the members of a class directly like structure. In addition, a non-member function that takes object of a class as an argument can also access the public members. The following program illustrates the use of public access specifier.

Listing 4.1

```
//  Program to demonstrate use of public members. Members are
//  accessed using object as well as non-member function
#include <iostream.h>
#include <iomanip.h>
class Example
{
   public:
       int a;
       char b;
       float c;
};    // end of class definition
void testFunction(Example arg)
{
   arg.a += 5;
   arg.b = 'b';
   arg.c +=2.5;
   cout << "\na = " << arg.a<<endl; //display data members
   cout << "\nb = " << arg.b<<endl;
   cout << "\nc = " << arg.c<<endl;
}
void main()
{
```

```
    Example obj;        // Create object
    obj.a = 10;         // initialize the data members
    obj.b = 'a';
    obj.c = 13.25;
    cout << "\na = " << obj.a<<endl; //display data members
    cout << "\nb = " << obj.b<<endl;
    cout << "\nc = " << obj.c<<endl;
    testFunction(obj);
}
```

As you can see in this program, the data members are declared as public, and the object, *obj*, of the *Example* class accesses the members directly. The members are initialized and displayed on the screen.

Further, a non-member function, *testFunction()*, that takes an object of class *Example* as its argument, can also access the public members.

Thus we can conclude that the members that are declared as public can be accessed from any section of the program.

4.5.2 The *private* Access Specifier

The *private* access specifier prevents the direct access to members. The default access specifier for a class is *private*. To see its effect, just change the public access specifier to private and compile the program, you will see the following list of error messages.

When the compiler processes the *testFunction()* function, it will displays following error messages:

```
'Example::a' is not accessible.
'Example::b' is not accessible.
'Example::c' is not accessible.
```

Similarly, when the compiler processes the *main()* function, it will displays following error messages:

```
'Example::a' is not accessible.
'Example::b' is not accessible.
'Example::c' is not accessible.
```

Thus we can conclude that the object cannot access the members directly those are declared as *private*. Likewise, a non-member function also cannot access the private members of a class.

4.5.3 The *protected* Access Specifier

The *protected* access specifier plays its role in the inheritance, i.e., when the new classes are derived from the existing classes. In the context class under consideration, the protected access specifier behaves as a *private* access specifier.

We will discuss more about *protected* access specifier in *Chapter 14*.

Table 4.1 gives the comparative view of various access specifiers indicating which part of the program can access the members, *i.e., what are the access limits of a class member*?

Table 4 1: Access Limits of Class Member

Access Specifier	Access Permission		
	Class	Subclass	Object
private	yes	no	no
protected	yes	yes	no
public	yes	yes	yes

It is general practice and a recommendation also, specify the data members as private and members functions as public.

Listing 4.2

```
//  Program to demonstrate the use of private data members
//  and public member functions
#include <iostream.h>
#include <string.h>
class StudentType
{
   private:                   // data members
      int  studentRollNo;
      char studentName[20];
   public:                    // function members
      void setData( int rollNo, char *name )
      {
         studentRollNo = rollNo;
         strcpy ( studentName, name );
      }
      void printData()
      {
         cout << "\nRoll No of Student : ";
         cout << studentRollNo << endl;
         cout << "Name of Student    : ";
```

```
        cout << studentName << endl;
    }
};    // end of class definition
void main()
{
    StudentType student;    // Create object
    student.setData( 100, "Ravi Kiran" );
    student.printData();
    student.setData( 101, "Kiran Jot" );
    student.printData();
}
```

4.6 CONSTRUCTORS AND DESTRUCTORS

These are special types of member functions. These are special in the sense that they are invoked automatically and have the same name as that of a class. The constructor is invoked when the object is created whereas the destructor is invoked when the object goes out of scope or deleted with the *delete* operator if the object is created dynamically using *new* operator. Like, other member functions, they can also be defined inside or outside the class template.

Consider the following class declaration

```
class Test
{
    private:
          // . . . data member declared here
    public:
          Test() {              // constructor
              // code for initializing data members
          }
          ~Test() {             // destructor
              // code for releasing the resources held by the object
          }
          // . . . other member functions
};
```

Here *Test()* is a constructor while *~Test()* is a destructor.

In general, every class must have these member functions. However, if no constructor is defined in the class, the compiler automatically inserts a constructor of following type

```
ClasName() { }  // default constructor, that does nothing
```

Therefore, when an object is created using following statement

```
ClasName objectName;
```

The default constructor is invoked. As default constructor does nothing, the initial values of the data members will be undefined, and thus the object will have undefined state.

In practice, we want the object should have a well-defined initial state whenever it is created. In order to achieve this, we have to write our own constructor that initializes the object to a specified state.

On the other side, we have to write destructor in the class, especially when an object claims resources dynamically. Remember that compiler does not provide any default destructor.

We will learn in more detail about constructors and destructors in *Chapter12*.

4.7 DEFINING MEMBER FUNCTIONS

The data members of a class can only de declared within the body of the class, whereas the member functions of the class can be defined in following ways:

- Inside class definition
- Outside class definition

The syntax for defining a member function depends on whether it is defined inside or outside the class definition. However, irrespective of the location of the definition, the member function must perform the same operation. Therefore, the code inside the function body will be identical in both the cases. The compiler treats these definitions in a different manner.

4.7.1 Member Functions Inside the Class Definition

The syntax for defining a member function is same as of a normal function except that it is enclosed within the body of a class. All the member functions defined inside the class definition are treated as inline by default except those members having looping statements. If the member functions are defined inside the class definition, then there is no need for function prototype (declaration).

Next example illustrates the definition of member function inside class definition.

```
class StockItem
{
  private:                    // data members
     int   itemCode;
     char  itemDescription[20];
     int   itemQuantity;
     float itemUnitPrice;
  public:                     // function members
    void readData()
    {
       cout << "\n\nEnter particulars of Stock item\n\n";
       cout << "Enter item code          : ";
       cin  >> itemCode;
       cout << "Enter item description : ";
       cin  >> itemDescription;
       cout << "Enter item quantity     : ";
       cin  >> itemQuantity;
       cout << "Enter item unit price   : ";
       cin  >> itemUnitPrice;
    }
    void displayData()
    {
       cout << "\n\nParticulars of Stock item are\n\n";
       cout << "Enter item code          : ";
       cout << itemCode << endl;
       cout << "Enter item description : ";
       cout << itemDescription << endl;
       cout << "Enter item quantity     : ";
       cout << itemQuantity << endl;
       cout << "Enter item unit price   : ";
       cout << itemUnitPrice << endl;
    }
};
```

4.7.2 Member Functions Outside the Class Definition

When the member functions are to be defined outside the class definition, then following tasks are need:

- Declare the prototypes of the member functions inside the class definition.
- Bind the member function definition to a class to whom it belongs. This is done using the *scope resolution operator* "::".

Syntax for defining a member function outside the class definition is

```
ReturnType ClassName :: memberFunctionName(formalArguments)
{
    // body of the function
}
```

Figure 4.4: Syntax for defining the member function outside the class

Class *StockItem* is rewritten here to demonstrate the writing of member functions outside the class definition.

```
class StockItem
{
   private:                  // data members
      int   itemCode;
      char  itemDescription[20];
      int   itemQuantity;
      float itemUnitPrice;
   public:
        void readData();     // prototypes of member functions
        void displayData();
};
void StockItem :: readData()
{
    cout << "\n\nEnter particulars of a Stock item\n\n";
    cout << "Enter item code         : ";
    cin  >> itemCode;
    cout << "Enter item description : ";
    cin  >> itemDescription;
    cout << "Enter item quantity    : ";
    cin  >> itemQuantity;
    cout << "Enter item unit price  : ";
    cin  >> itemUnitPrice;
}
void StockItem :: displayData()
{
    cout << "\n\nParticulars of a Stock item are\n\n";
    cout << "Enter item code         : ";
    cout << itemCode << endl;
    cout << "Enter item description : ";
    cout << itemDescription << endl;
    cout << "Enter item quantity    : ";
    cout << itemQuantity << endl;
    cout << "Enter item unit price  : ";
    cout << itemUnitPrice << endl;
}
```

A member function defined inside the class is by default inline function except those functions involving loops. However, when a member function is defined outside the class definition it is treated as a normal function. If the developer wants a member function to be inline, then one has to make it inline explicitly.

4.8 MAKING AN OUTSIDE FUNCTION INLINE

The C++ language provides features where member functions can be defined outside the class definition, and still they can be made inline. The syntax for doing so is

```
inline ReturnType ClassName::memberFunctionName(formalArguments)
{
   // body of the function
}
```

The class *StockItem* is rewritten once again here to demonstrate the writing of member functions outside the class definition.

```
class StockItem
{
   private:                    // data members
      int   itemCode;
      char  itemDescription[20];
      int   itemQuantity;
      float itemUnitPrice;
   public:
       void readData();      // prototypes of member functions
       void displayData();
};
inline void StockItem :: readData ()
{
    cout << "\n\nEnter particulars of a Stock item\n\n";
    cout << "Enter item code         : ";
    cin  >> itemCode;
    cout << "Enter item description : ";
    cin  >> itemDescription;
    cout << "Enter item quantity     : ";
    cin  >> itemQuantity;
    cout << "Enter item unit price   : ";
    cin  >> itemUnitPrice;
}
```

```
inline void StockItem :: displayData()
{
    cout << "\n\nParticulars of a Stock item are\n\n";
    cout << "Enter item code          : ";
    cout << itemCode << endl;
    cout << "Enter item description : ";
    cout << itemDescription << endl;
    cout << "Enter item quantity      : ";
    cout << itemQuantity << endl;
    cout << "Enter item unit price   : ";
    cout << itemUnitPrice << endl;
}
```

4.9 ACCESSING MEMBER FUNCTION FROM WITHIN THE CLASS

An object using dot operator can only access a member function of a class. However, a member function of a class can call other member functions irrespective of its privilege. Such a situation is called *nesting* of member functions. Method of calling a member functions from within a member function is same as of calling a normal function. This is illustrated in the following example.

Listing 4.3

```
//  Program to demonstrate the way member functions can be
//  called from within the class

#include <iostream.h>
#include <iomanip.h>

class PairOfNumbers
{
   private:                    // data members
      int firstNumber;
      int secondNumber;
   public:                     // function members
      void readNumbers()
      {
         cout << "\nEnter two integer numbers\n\n";
         cout << "Enter first number : ";
         cin >> firstNumber;
         cout << "Enter second number : ";
         cin >> secondNumber;
      }
      int pickLargest()
      {
         if ( firstNumber > secondNumber )
            return firstNumber;
         else
```

```
            return secondNumber;
        }
        void displayLargest()
        {
            cout << "\n\nThe largest number = ";
            cout << pickLargest() << endl;
        }
};      // end of class definition

void main()
{
    PairOfNumbers pairOfNumbers;   // Create object
    pairOfNumbers.readNumbers();
    pairOfNumbers.displayLargest();
}
```

Test Run

```
Enter two integer numbers

Enter first number  : 66
Enter second number : 75

The largest number = 75
```

4.10 CLASSES, OBJECTS AND MEMORY

You may be having this impression that each object created from a class contains separate copies of that class's data and member functions. This may seem to be a good approximation in the beginning as it emphasizes that objects are complete, self-contained entities, created using the class definition.

However, the things are not that simple. In fact, each object has its own copy of data and on contrary; all the objects use the same member functions. The member functions are placed in the memory only once and it happens when the class definition is loaded. This makes sense since there is no point in duplicating all the member functions in a class every time a new object is created, since functions for each object are identical. The data members, however, will hold different values, so there must be separate instance of each data member for each object.

Therefore, data is placed in memory when each object is created, so there is a separate set of data for each object.

Suppose we have created four objects of class *StudentType* using following statement

```
StudentType student1, studen2, student3, student4;
```

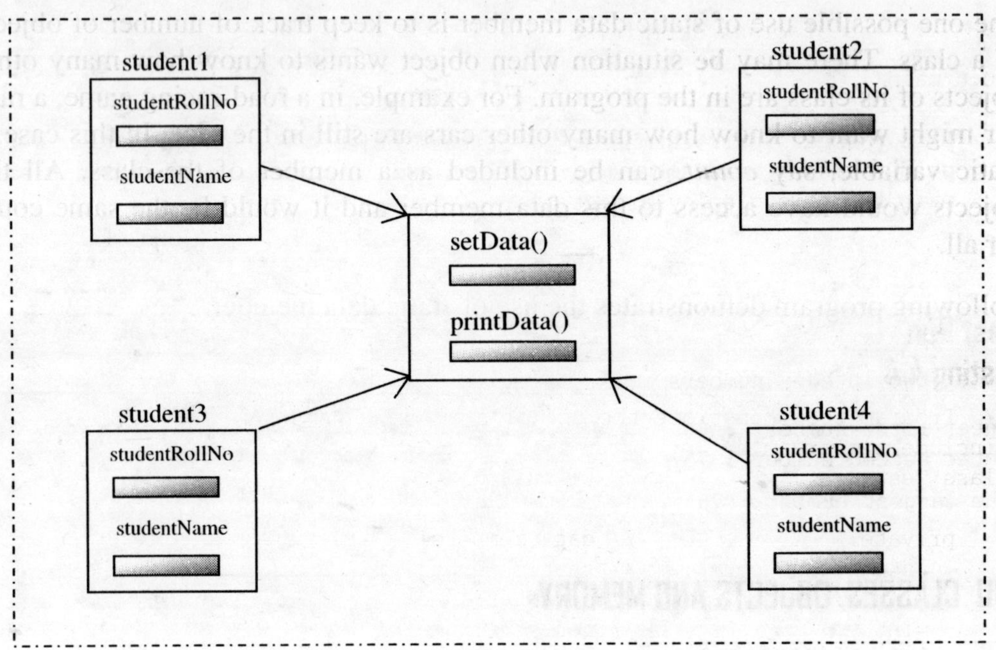

Figure 4.5: Representation of objects in memory

4.11 STATIC MEMBERS

4.11.1 Static Data Members

There can be data members that are common to all objects, whereas there can be data members that belong to an individual object. The data members common to all objects are known as *class variables* and are declared with *static* modifier. The static data member is useful when all the objects of the same class must share a common piece of information. A member variable defined as static has characteristics similar to a normal static variable. It is visible only within a class, but its lifetime is the entire program. It continues to exist even there are no objects of the class. However, while a normal static variable is used to retain information between function calls to a function; static data member is used to share information among the objects of a class.

Memory is allocated for class variables when the class is loaded and only one copy of the class variables is kept irrespective of number of objects of that class. Every object has access to class variables.

A static variable is initialized before the *main()* function.

The one possible use of static data member is to keep track of number of objects of a class. There may be situation when object wants to know how many other objects of its class are in the program. For example, in a road-racing game, a race car might want to know how many other cars are still in the race. In this case, a static variable, say *count*, can be included as a member of the class. All the objects would have access to this data member and it would be the same count for all.

Following program demonstrates the use of static data member.

Listing 4.4

```
//  Program to demonstrate the use of static data member
#include <iostream.h>
class Test
{
    private:                    // data members
       static int count;        // static member
       int x;                   // non-static member
       int y;                   // non-static member
    public:                     // function members
       Test()
       {
          count++;
       }
       int getCount()
       {
          return count;
       }
};
int Test::count = 0;         // initialize static data member
void main()
{
    Test obj1;
    cout << "\nCurrent count is " << obj1.getCount();
    Test obj2;
    cout << "\nCurrent count is " << obj2.getCount();
    Test obj3;
    cout << "\nCurrent count is " << obj3.getCount()<<"\n";
}
```

Test Run

```
Current count is 1
Current count is 2
Current count is 3
```

The class *Test*, in above program, has three data members, which are of type *static int*, *int*, and *int*, respectively. The data members *x* and *y* are non-static. The constructors for this class increments the count. The *getCount()* member functions returns the current value of the *count*.

Static data members are not used as often as ordinary data members (non-static), but they are important in many situations. Figure 4.6 shows how static data members compare with non-static data members.

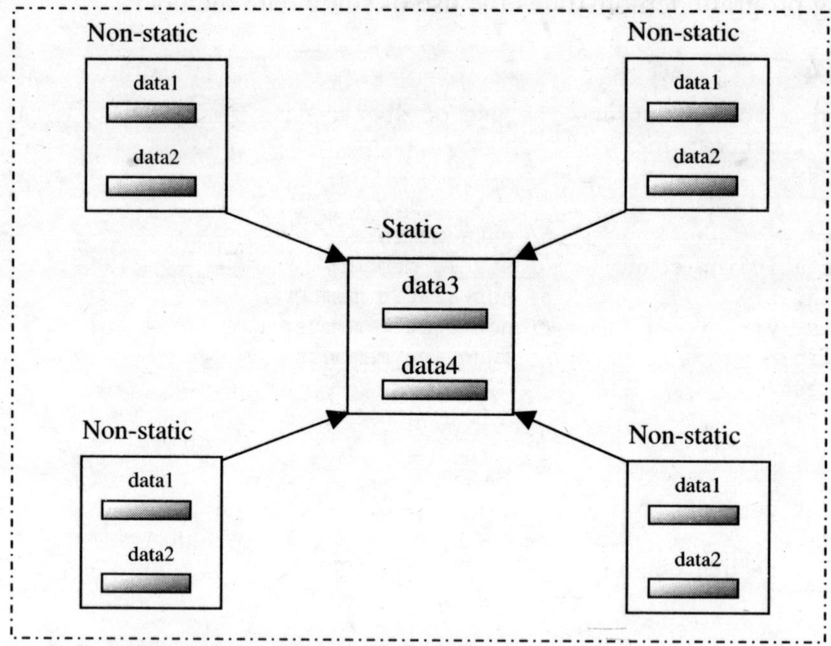

Figure 4.6: Static versus non-static data members

4.11.2 Static Member Functions

Like, data members that are common to all objects, the member function can also be declared as *static*. Since static members (data members as well as member functions) are associated with the class, static member functions can access static data members only. In contrast non-static member functions can access non-static data members as well as static data members. The static member functions can be invoked using class name or object name.

A static member function is declared and defined by prefixing keyword *static* before the return type of the function.

Listing 4.5

```
//  Program to demonstrate the use of static data member
#include <iostream.h>
#include <iomanip.h>
class Test
{
   private:
      static int count;
      int code;
   public:
      Test() {                     // constructor
         code = ++count;
      }
      static void showCount() { // static member function
         cout << "\nValue of count : " << count << endl;
      }
      void showCode() {
        cout << "\nObject code : " << code << endl;
      }
};
int Test::count = 0;
void main()
{
   Test t1, t2;      // Create two objects
   Test::showCount();
   Test t3;
   Test::showCount();
   t1.showCode();
   t2.showCode();
   t3.showCode();
   t3.showCount();
}
```

Test Run

```
Value of count : 2
Value of count : 3
Object code : 1
Object code : 2
Object code : 3
Value of count : 3
```

The class *Test*, in above program, has two data members, one is static (*count*) while the second is non-static (*code*). The class also has two member functions, one is static (*showCount()*) while the second is non-static (*showCode()*). The class also has a constructor that increment the static data member *count* and assigns the incremented value of *count* to non-static data member *code* when a new object is created. In the main function, it is shown that a static member function can be invoked with class name or with object, where as non-static member function can only be invoked with an object.

4.12 PRIVATE MEMBER FUNCTIONS

The normal practice in a class design is to place data members in private section and function members in public section. However, there may be some situations where you want to hide a particular member function from outside world.

As an example, consider an application that deals with the employees of an organization. The tasks such as deleting an employee record or providing increment to an employee are of serious consequences, and therefore the member functions handling such tasks should have restricted access. This can be achieved by placing the member functions in the private section.

A private member function can only be called by another member function of its class. Even an object of the class cannot invoke a private member function using the dot operator.

Following example demonstrates this:

```
class Employee
{
   private:
      int  code;
      char name[30];
      float basicPay;
       . . .
      void readData()       // private member function
      {
           . . .
      }
   public:
      void updateData()     // public member function
      {
           . . .
       readData();  // call to private member function
         . . .              // just as normal call
      }
```

```
    void writeData()      // public member function
    {
        . . .
        readData();      // call to private member function
        . . .
    }
};
```

4.13 OBJECTS AS FUNCTION ARGUMENTS

Like built-in data type, user-defined data types such as structures, unions, objects can also be passed as arguments. The following program demonstrates this, where two objects of class *ComplexNumber* are passed as arguments, the function adds these complex numbers.

Listing 4.6

```
// Program to demonstrate passing of objects
// as arguments to a function
#include <iostream.h>
#include <iomanip.h>
class ComplexNumber
{
   private:
       float realPart;
       float imaginaryPart;
   public:
         void  setComplexNumber(float real, float imaginary) {
         realPart = real;
         imaginaryPart = imaginary;
       }
       // member function to output complex number
       void displayComplexNumber() {
         cout << setiosflags ( ios::showpoint )
              << setprecision ( 2 )
              << endl
              << realPart << " + j" << imaginaryPart
              << endl;
       }
       void addComplexNumbers(ComplexNumber n1, ComplexNumber n2)
       {
         realPart = n1.realPart;
         imaginaryPart = n1.imaginaryPart;
         realPart += n2.realPart;
         imaginaryPart += n2.imaginaryPart;
       }
};
```

```
void main()  // main program
{
   ComplexNumber n1, n2, n3;      // create object
   n1.setComplexNumber( 1.2, 2.5 );
   n2.setComplexNumber( 2.0, 5.2 );
   n3.addComplexNumbers(n1,n2);
   n3.displayComplexNumber(); // display object
}
```

Test Run

```
3.20 + j7.70
```

Two complex numbers, *n1* and *n2*, are passed as arguments to member function *addComplexNumbers()*, and the result is stored in the object of which *addComplexNumbers()* is a member, namely *n3*.

Note that the syntax for arguments is same as that for simple data types like *int*: the object name is supplied as an argument. Since *addComplexNumbers()* is a member function of *ComplexNumber* class, it can access the private data in any object of class *ComplexNumber* supplied to it as an argument, using names like *n1.realPart* and *n1.imaginaryPart*.

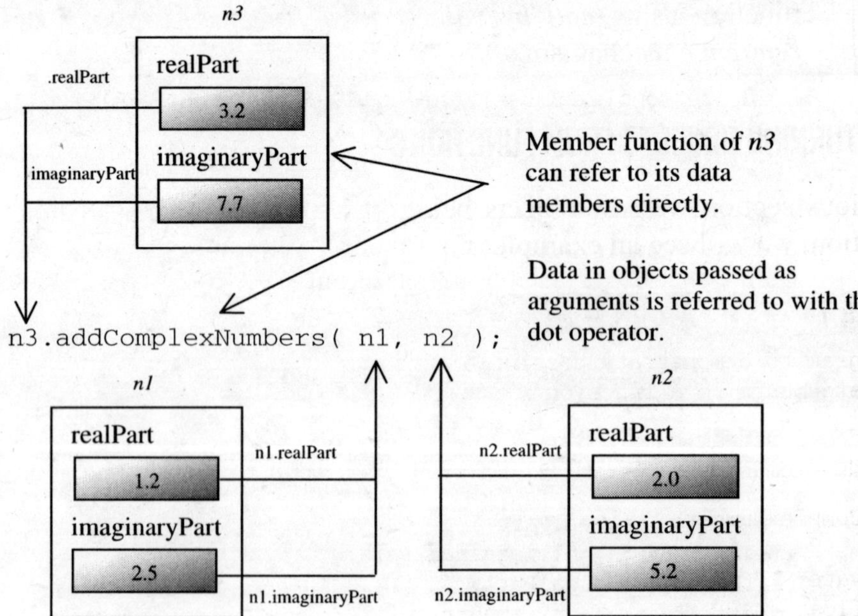

Figure 4.7: Illustration of passing objects as arguments to a function

Careful examination of *addComplexNumbers()* member function reveals few key points about members functions. When a member function is called, it is given access to only one object – *the object of which the function is a member*.

In the following example, what objects can *addComplexNumbers()* access?

```
n3.addComplexNumbers(n1,n2);
```

It can access *n1* and *n2*, because they are supplied as arguments. It can also access *n3*, because it is a member function of *n3*. When the variables (data members) *realPart* and *imaginaryPart* are referred to within this function, they refer to *n3.realPart* and *n3.imaginaryPart*. Later on we will see that a member function can refer to the entire object of which it is a member with the keyword *this*. The keyword *this* emphasizes the close relationship between a function and the object of which it is a member.

Note that the result is not returned by the function. The return type of *addComplexNumbers()* is *void*. The result is stored automatically in the *n3* object. Figure 4.7 shows the two complex numbers *n1* and *n2* being added together, with the result stored in *n3*.

Like normal variables, objects can be passed as an argument to a function using *call by value*, *call by address* (*pointer*) or *call by reference* mechanism.

4.14 RETURNING OBJECTS FROM FUNCTIONS

In previous section we saw objects being passed as arguments to functions. In this section, we will see an example of a function that returns an object.

Listing 4.7

```
// Program to demonstrate passing of objects
// as arguments to a function

#include <iostream.h>
#include <iomanip.h>

class ComplexNumber
{
   private:
      float realPart;
      float imaginaryPart;
```

```
public:
    void setComplexNumber( float real, float imaginary )
    {
        realPart = real;
        imaginaryPart = imaginary;
    }

    // member function to output complex number
    void displayComplexNumber()
    {
        cout << setiosflags ( ios::showpoint )
             << setprecision ( 2 )
             << endl
             << realPart << " + j" << imaginaryPart
             << endl;
    }

    ComplexNumber addComplexNumbers(ComplexNumber n1)
    {
        ComplexNumber temp;
        temp.realPart = realPart + n1.realPart;
        temp.imaginaryPart = imaginaryPart + n1.imaginaryPart;
        return temp;
    }
};

void main()   // main program
{
    ComplexNumber n1, n2, n3;        // create object
    n1.setComplexNumber( 1.2, 2.5 );
    n2.setComplexNumber( 2.0, 5.2 );
    n3 = n1.addComplexNumbers(n2);
    n3.displayComplexNumber(); // display object
}
```

Test Run

```
3.20 + j7.70
```

From the user's viewpoint of view, this program is very similar to the previous program, but the difference lies in how the function works with objects. One complex number, *n2*, is passed as an argument. It is added to the complex number, *n1*, of which *addComplexNumbers()* is a member function, and the result is held in a temporary object, *temp*, that is subsequently returned from the function and assigned to complex number *n3*. This is illustrated in Figure 4.8.

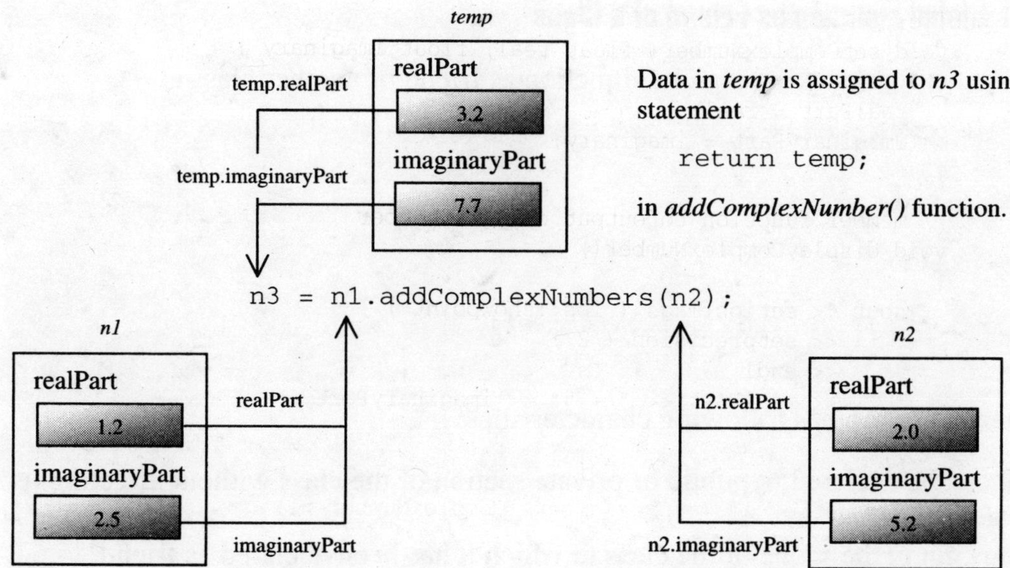

Figure 4.8: Illustration of a function returning an object

4.15 FRIENDS OF A CLASS

The concepts of encapsulation and data hiding demands that non-member function should not be allowed to access an object's private or protected data. The policy is simple — if you are not a member, you cannot get it. However, there may be some situations when such rigid discrimination leads to considerable inconvenience. Such inconvenience can be overcome to some extent by allowing non-members of a class to gain access to its data members. This is possible by making non-members as friends of a class.

Consider a situation, where you want a function to operate on objects of two or more classes in order to manipulate their private data. One possible solution is to make this function member function of every class. The other alternative, and better in design, is to define the function as global function and make it friend of the class so that it can gain access to class's private data.

For making friends, the following situation can arise:

- Global function (a function that is not member of any class) as friend of a class.
- Member function of a class as friend of another class
- Class as a friend of another class.

4.15.1 Global Function as Friend of a Class

The syntax for declaring a global function as friend of another class is

```
class TestClass1
{
      private:
            //. . .
      public:
            // . . .
      friend ReturnType functionName( argList );
};
```

A friend function has following characteristics:

- It can be declared in public or private section of the class without affecting its meaning.
- It is not in the scope of the class to which it has been declared as friend.
- It cannot access the members directly. To access members, it uses *object* and *dot* operator.
- It takes objects of classes as arguments.

The following program illustrates the use of a global function as friend function of two classes. Each of these classes has one data member of type *int*. The friend function returns the sum of these data members.

Listing 4.8

```
// Program to demonstrate the use of global function
// as a friend function of a class

#include <iostream.h>
#include <iomanip.h>

class Two;            // forward declaration

class One
{
    private:
       int a;
    public:
       void setData(int x)
       {
          a = x;
       }
       void ShowData()
       {
```

```
        cout << endl << "One::a = " << a << endl;
     }

     friend int addBoth( One, Two );
};
class Two
{
   private:
     int b;
   public:
     void setData(int y)
     {
         b = y;
     }
     void ShowData()
     {
       cout << endl << "Two::b = " << b << endl;
     }
     friend int addBoth( One, Two );
};
int addBoth( One r, Two s )
{
   return ( r.a + s.b );
}
void main()
{
   One aa;
   Two bb;
   int result;
   aa.setData(10);
   aa.showData();
   bb.setData(20);
   bb.showData();
   result = addBoth(aa, bb);
   cout << "\nOne::a + Two::b = " << result << endl;
}
```

Test Run

```
One::a = 10
Two::b = 20
One::a + Two::b = 30
```

The friend function *addBoth()* takes two arguments where first is of type class *One* and the second is of type class *Two*. The *addBoth()* function being a friend of both class is able to access the private data of both objects.

4.15.2 Member Function of a Class as Friend of another Class

Syntax for declaring member function of a class as a friend of another class is

```
class TestClass2
{
      private
            //. . .
      public:
            // . . .
      friend ReturnType className::funtionName(argList);
};
```

The following program illustrates the use of a member function of a class as friend function of another class. Each of these classes has one data member of type *int*. The friend function displays the data member of another class.

Listing 4.9

```
// Program to demonstrate the use of member function of one
// class a friend function of another class
#include <iostream.h>
#include <iomanip.h>
class Two;              // forward declaration
class One
{
   private:
      int a;
   public:
      void setOne(int x) {
         a = x;
      }
      void showBoth(Two); // cannot provide definition here
};
class Two
{
   private:
      int b;
   public:
      void setTwo(int y) {
         b = y;
      }
      void showTwo() {
         cout << endl << "Two::b = " << b << endl;
      }
      friend void One::showBoth(Two);
};
```

```
void One::showBoth(Two obj)
{
   cout << endl << "One::a = " << a << endl;
   cout << endl << "Two::b = " << obj.b << endl;
}
void main()
{
   One aa;
   Two bb;
   aa.setOne(10);
   aa.setTwo(20);
   aa.showBoth(bb);
}
```

Test Run

```
One::a = 10
Two::b = 20
```

The member function *showBoth()* of class *One* that is declared as friend of class *Two* takes an object of class *Two* as an arguments and displays the data members of both the classes. It can access it own data member directly and data member of class *Two* through its object.

The member function, which you want to make a friend of another class, can only be defined after the definitions of both the classes.

4.15.3 Class as Friend of another Class

The syntax for declaring a class as a friend of another class is

```
class TestClass3
{
      private:
            //. . .
      public:
            // . . .
      friend class className;
}
```

The following program illustrates the use of a class as friend function of another class. Class *One* has three member functions; each takes an object of class *Two* as an argument, and is declared as a friend of class *Two*.

Listing 4.10

```
// Program to demonstrate use of class as a friend of another class
#include <iostream.h>
#include <iomanip.h>
class Two;          // forward declaration
class One
{
   private:
     int a;
   public:
     void setOne(int x) {
        a = x;
     }
     void show1(Two);
     void show2(Two);
     void show2(Two);
};
class Two
{
   private:
     int b;
     int c;
     int d;
   public:
     void setData(int x, int y, int z) {
        b = x; c = y; d = z;
     }
     void showTwo() {
        cout << endl << "Two::b = " << b << endl;
     }
     friend One;
};
void One::show1(Two obj)
{
   cout << endl << "Two::b = " << obj.b << endl;
}
void One::show2(Two obj)
{
   cout << endl << "Two::c = " << obj.c << endl;
}
void One::show3(Two obj)
{
   cout << endl << "Two::d = " << obj.d << endl;
}
void main()
{
   One aa;
   Two bb;
```

```
    aa.setOne(10);
    bb.setData(20,30,40);
    aa.show1(bb);
    aa.show2(bb);
    aa.show3(bb);
}
```

Test Run

```
Two::b = 20
Two::c = 30
Two::d = 40
```

Class *One* is declared as a friend of class *Two*. Each of the three member functions of class *One* – *show1()*, *show2()*, and *show3()*, take an object of class *Two* as an argument and displays the data members *b*, *c*, and *d*, respectively, of class *Two*.

4.16 EMPTY CLASSES

Although the main reason for using a class is to encapsulate data and code, it is however, possible to have a class that has neither data nor code. In other words, it is possible to have empty classes. The declaration of an empty class is as follows:

```
class xyz { };
```

During the initial stages of development of a project, some of the classes are either not fully identified, or not fully implemented. In such cases, they are implemented as empty classes during the first few iteration of project development. Such empty classes are also called as *stubs*. The significant use of empty classes can be found with exception handling.

4.17 NESTED CLASSES

A class can be defined within another class. Such a class is called *nested class*. A nested class is a member of its enclosing class. The definition of a nested class can occur within a public, protected, or private section of its enclosing class. The name of a nested class is visible only in its enclosing class scope.

Following points must be taken into considerations while defining and using local classes:

- Nested classes can use member of its enclosing class.
- Nested classes cannot have static data members.

- Member functions can only be defined inside the local class.
- The enclosing class cannot access the private members of a nested class. However, by making the enclosing function as friend function makes it possible.

The following code segment gives an example of nested classes, where the *StudentType* class is enhanced to include date of birth of a student:

```
class StudentType
{
    private:
        int  studentRollNo;
        char studentName[20];
   public:
        class Date           // nested class
        {
            private:
                int day;
                int month;
                int year;
           public:
                  // . . . member functions of Date class
        } dateOfBirth;
        // . . . member functions of StudentType class
};
```

4.18 LOCAL CLASSES

Classes can be defined and used inside a function or a block, such classes are known as local classes.

Following points must be taken into considerations while defining and using local classes:

- Local classes can use global variables (variables declared before the function) and local static variables to the function but cannot use local automatic variables.
- If a data member have the same name as global variable, then global variable can be used with the scope resolution operator '::'.
- Local classes cannot have static data members.
- Member functions can only be defined inside the local class.
- The enclosing function cannot access the private members of a local class. However, by making the enclosing function as friend function makes it possible.

The following example shows a class defined inside a function

```
void testFunction()
{                      // function definition
   // . . .
   // . . .
   class LocalClass // local class definition
   {
       // . . .
       // . . .
   };
   // . . .
   LocalClass obj;  // create object of local class
   // . . .
   // . . .
}
```

4.19 ABSTRACT CLASSES

These are the classes, which are not complete and cannot be used to create objects. These classes contain at least one pure virtual function. Pure virtual functions are discussed in *Chapter 9.* These classes are used as framework upon which new classes can be built to provide new functionality.

4.20 CONTAINER CLASSES

These are the classes, also known as *container types*, which are used to hold objects of other classes. These classes are very helpful in managing resources required by the application. There is a rich collection of container classes supported by most of the modern C++ compilers in the form of Standard Template Library (STL). The STL not only contains container classes but also set of functions that can manipulate these container classes.

QUICK RECAP

In this chapter, we have learnt that

- Like a structure, a class can have data members as well as member functions.
- Though, class is similar to structure, it is incorporated in tune with the philosophy of object orientation, where we talk of class of objects or an object of a particular class.
- Default access for a structure is public whereas for a class it is private.
- Member functions of a class can be defined inside or outside the class. Member functions inside the class are inline by default. Member functions

defined outside class can be made inline by prefixing the keyword inline before the return type.

- Data member are non-static by default. However, members can be declared as static.
- For static data members, only one copy is created and it is shared among all objects of a class.
- Static data members are initialized before the main function.
- A class can be defined inside another class. Such a class is called nested class.
- A class can also be defined inside a function. Such a class is called local class.
- An abstract class is class from which no object can be created.
- A class that can hold objects of another class(es) is known as container class.

MULTIPLE CHOICE QUESTIONS

1. Which of the following statement is not true about a friend function?
   (*a*) It can be declared in public or private section of the class without affecting its meaning.
   (*b*) It is not in the scope of the class to which it has been declared as friend.
   (*c*) It can access the members directly.
   (*d*) None of above.
2. Which of the following statements is true about a static data member?
   (*a*) It is always initialized to zero whenever first object of its class is created.
   (*b*) It needs to be initialized before the main function.
   (*c*) Each object has its own copy of static data member.
   (*d*) All of above.
3. The members of a class, by default, are
   (*a*) Public (*b*) Protected
   (*c*) Private (*d*) Mandatory to specify.
4. Which of the following statement is not true about a class?
   (*a*) A class can have constant data members.
   (*b*) All members are non-static unless declared static explicitly.
   (*c*) Data members can be declared inside the class as well as outside the class.
   (*d*) Member functions can be defined inside the class as well as outside the class.
5. Which of the following statements is true about a static member function?
   (*a*) It can access only static data members of its class.
   (*b*) It can access all data members of its class.
   (*c*) Each object has its own copy of static member function.
   (*d*) None of above.

6. The members of a structure, by default, are
   (*a*) Public (*b*) Protected
   (*c*) Private (*d*) Access specifier is irrelevant to a structure.
7. When a class is declared inside the function, it is called . . .
   (*a*) Nested class (*b*) Empty calls
   (*c*) Local class (*d*) Abstract class
8. A bit-field can be of type
   (*a*) int (*b*) float (*c*) double (*d*) All of above
9. Fill in the blank: The size of a *class* is always equal to the sum of . . . .
   (*a*) All data members only (*b*) All data members as well as function members
   (*c*) Only non-static data members. (*d*) None of above
10. Which of the following statement(s) is/are true about bit fields?
    (*a*) The address of bit fields cannot be obtained
    (*b*) A pointer cannot be used to access bit fields
    (*c*) The *sizeof* operator cannot be applied on bit fields
    (*d*) All of above
11. Consider the following program

```
#include <iostream.h>
class Sample {};
void main()
{
    cout << sizeof(Sample);
}
```

    What will happen if we attempt to compile and execute the program?
    (*a*) Program will fail to compile because *Sample* class must have at least one member.
    (*b*) Program will compile but will not run because no object of *Sample* class is created.
    (*c*) Program will compile and execute and will output value 0.
    (*d*) Program will compile and execute and will output value 1.
12. A bit-field is a
    (*a*) Pointer variable in a class.
    (*b*) Data members of a class can be passed as arguments.
    (*c*) One or more adjacent bits within a word.
    (*d*) none of above.

13. If the client code is to be allowed to modify a particular data member, which of the following keyword can be used as modifier for that data member?

    (*a*) volatile (*b*) mutable (*c*) const (*d*) static

14. Which of the following is not a keyword?

    (*a*) mutable (*b*) protect (*c*) const (*d*) static
    (*e*) None of above

15. Which of the following statement is true about friend function?

    (*a*) A global function can be declared a friend of more that one class.
    (*b*) A member function of one class can be declared as a friend of another class.
    (*c*) All member functions of a one class can be declared as friends of another class by declaring the class as friend of another class.
    (*d*) All of above.

REVIEW EXERCISES

1. What is a class? Describe the syntax for declaring classes, creating objects, and accessing members of a class, with the help of examples.
2. What is the difference between a class and an object?
3. What are the differences between a class and a structure in C++?
4. Can we initialize a data member in class template? If not, why?
5. Explain the uses of *private*, *protected*, and *public* visibility specifiers with the help of suitable examples.
6. When a member of class be declared as static? Give example to illustrate your viewpoint.
7. How a member function can be defined outside the class template? Give example.
8. What are the different ways of passing objects as arguments to a function? Give example for each case.
9. How a function can return an object? Is it safe to return a reference to a local non- static object? If not, why?
10. How static data member is initialized? Give example to demonstrate the same.
11. What are empty classes? What purpose they serve?
12. What is an abstract class?
13. What is a container class?
14. What is a nested class?
15. What is a local class?

16. Can member functions be made private? If yes, what purpose they will serve?

17. What are constructors and destructors?

18. What is a friend function? How friend functions are useful?

19. What are the characteristics of a friend function?

20. What are the various ways in which friend functions can be used?

21. Is any thing wrong with the following?

```
class Test
{
  private;
    int x;
  public;
    void setX(int a)
    {
       x = a;
    }
    int getX()
    {
       return x;
    }
    void showX()
    {
       cout << "\nx = " << getX();
    }
};
```

22. Is any thing wrong with the following?

```
class Test
{
  private:
     int x = 20;
  public:
    void setX(int a)
    {
       x = a;
    }
    int getX()
    {
       return x;
    }
    void showX(
   ) {
       cout << "\nx = " << getX();
    }
};
```

23. Is any thing wrong with the following?

```
class Test
{
    private:
       int x;
    public:
       void setX(int a)
       {
           x = a;
       }
       int getX()
       {
           return x;
       }
       void showX()
       {
           cout << "\nx = " << getX();
       }
};
```

24. Is any thing wrong with the following?

```
#include <iostream.h>
#include <iomanip.h>
class Test
{
    int x;
    public:
    void showX()
    {
        cout << "\nx = " << x << endl;
    }
};
void main()
{
   Test obj;
   Obj.x = 10;
   Obj.showX();
}
```

25. Is any thing wrong with the following?

```
#include <iostream.h>
#include <iomanip.h>
class Test
{
   private:
     int x;
   public:
     void setX(int);
     int getX();
```

```
    void showX();
};
void setX(int a)
{
    x = a;
}
int getX()
{
    return x;
}
void showX()
{
    cout << "\nx = " << getX() << endl;
}
void main()
{
    Test obj;
    Obj.setX(10);
    Obj.showX();
}
```

26. Consider the following program

```
#include <iostream.h>
class Sample {};
void main()
{
    cout << sizeof(Sample);
}
```

What will be the output of the program?

PROGRAMMING EXERCISES

1. An employer plans to pay a bonus to all employees. A bonus of 10% is to be paid to employees with earning at least Rs. 2000/- and 20% of the earning to others. The input contains name and earnings of an employee and the desired output is name and bonus to be paid to the employee.

Create a class to represent an *employee*. It should include the following:

Data Members:

Name
Earning
Bonus

Member Functions:

To input data
To compute bonus

To output the desired information

Using this class, write a program to accomplish the intended task.

2. The monthly telephone bill is to be computed as follows:

   Minimum Rs. 200 for upto 100 calls
   plus Rs. 0.60 per call for next 50 calls
   plus Rs. 0.50 per call for next 50 calls
   plus Rs. 0.40 per call for any call beyond 200 calls.

   The input contains name of the customer and number of calls made and the desired output is the name and telephone bill to be paid by the customer.

   Create a class to represent an *employee*. It should include the following:

   Data Members:

   Name
   Number of calls
   Bill amount

   Member Functions:

   To input data
   To compute bill
   To output the desired information

   Using this class, write a program to accomplish the intended task.

3. Income tax for individuals is computed on slab rates as follows:

Income	Tax Payable
Upto Rs. 1,00,000/-	Nil
From Rs. 1,00,001/- to Rs. 1,50,000/-	10% of the excess over Rs. 1,00,000/-
From Rs. 1,51,001/- to Rs. 200,000/-	20% of the excess over Rs. 1,50,000/-
Above Rs. 2,00,000/-	30% of the excess over Rs. 2,00,000/-

   The input contains name of the individual and income and the desired output is the name of the individual and amount of tax to be paid by the individual.

   Create a class to represent an *employee*. It should include the following:

   Data Members:

   Name
   Income
   Tax due

   Member Functions:

   To input data

To compute tax
To output the desired information

Using this class, write a program to accomplish the intended task.

4. Create a class to represent a *bank account*. It should include the following:

   Data Members:

   Name of account holder
   Account number
   Type of account
   Balance amount

   Member Functions:

   To initialize the data members with appropriate data
   To deposit an amount
   To withdraw an amount after checking the balance
   To display details of account holder

   Write a program to use this class.

5. Create a class to represent a *vector*. It should include the following:

   Data Members:

   Elements of vector (in the form of an array)
   Size of vector

   Member Functions:

   To input the elements of the vector
   To compute the sum of elements of vector
   To find the largest element of the vector
   To display the vector in the form [10, 20, 30, . . .]

   Write a program to use this class.

6. Create a class named *Student* with the following specifications:

   Private Members:

admno	of type integer to represent admission number
name	of type character to represent name (max 20 characters)
marksEng	of type float to represent marks in the subject of English
marksMaths	of type float to represent marks in the subject of mathematics
marksSci	of type float to represent marks in the subject of Science
total	of type float to represent total marks
compute()	A function to compute sum of marks in English, Maths and Science

Public Members:

readData()	A function to accept the data for admNo, name, marksEng, marksMaths, marksSci. It also invokes *compute* function to calculate total marks.
showData()	A function that display all the data members on the computer screen.

7. Create a class named *Teacher* with the following specifications:

Private Members:

name	of type character (max 20 characters)
subject	of type character (max 10 characters)
basic, hra, da	of type float
netpay	of type float
calculate()	function to calculate netpay as basic + hra + da with return type float

Public Members:

readData()	A function to accept the data for *name*, *subject*, *basic*, *hra*, *da* and invoke function *calculate()* to compute *netpay*
displayData()	A function that display all the data members on the computer screen.

8. Create a class named *Student* with the following specifications:

Private Members:

rollno	of type integer
name	of type character (max 20 characters)
marks[4]	array of type float
grade	of type float
calculate()	function to calculate grade with return type void

Public Members:

readData()	A function to accept data for *rollno*, *name*, *marks*[4], and invokes the function *calculate()* to compute grade
displayData()	A function that display *rollno*, *name*, and *grade* on the computer screen.

9. Create a class named *Worker* with the following specifications:

   Private Members:

wno	of type integer
name	of type character (max 20 characters)
hrwrk, wgrate	of type float (hours worked and wage rate per hour)
totwage	of type float
calcwg()	function to calculate total wages (*hrwrk* * *wgrate*) with return type *float*

   Public Members:

inData()	A function to accept the data for *wno*, *name*, *hrwrk*, *wgrate*, and invokes the function *calcwg()* to compute total wages
outData()	A function that display wno, name, and total wages for a worker

10. Create a class named *Crickter* with the following specifications:

    Private Members:

bcode	of type integer (4 digit code)
name	of type character (max 20 characters)
innings, notout, runs,	of type integer
batavg	of type float, and is computed as "*runs/(innings-notout)*"
calcavg()	function to compute bating average

    Public Members:

readData()	A function to accept the data for *bcode*, *name*, *innings*, *notout*, *runs* and invokes the function *calcavg()* to compute bating average
displayData()	A function that display *bcode*, *name*, and *batavg* for a batsman

❑ ❑ ❑

Chapter 5

Pointers and Dynamic Memory Management

Learning Objectives

After reading this chapter, students will be able to

- comprehend the world of pointers, one of the richest feature of C++ language
- explain how main memory is organized and addresses are assigned to each memory location
- declare , initialize and access through pointer
- explain the usefulness of pointers in passing arguments to a function
- explain the permissible operations on pointers
- explain the concept of memory allocation
- distinguish between static allocation and dynamic allocation
- comprehend and use memory management operators for dynamic memory management
- explain what possible problems can occur while working with pointers
- write efficient programs using pointers to solve variety of problems

5.1 INTRODUCTION

Pointers are one of the most important features of C++ language. Pointers, by most people, are regarded as one of the most difficult topics in C. Let me tell you frankly, it is more a myth rather a fact. I would prefer to say that pointers are one of the most delicate aspects of C++ language, and you know delicate things need very careful handling. Therefore, pointers need very careful handling.

There are many reasons for using pointers; some of them are enumerated below:

- A pointer allows a function or a program to access a variable (better we say memory location) outside the preview of function or a program. In fact, using a pointer, your program can access any memory location in the computer's memory.
- Since using *return* statement, a function can only pass back a single value to the calling function, pointers allows a function to pass back more than one value by writing them into memory locations that are accessible to the calling function.
- Use of pointer increases makes the program execution faster.
- Using pointers, arrays and structures can be handled in more efficient way.
- Without pointers, it will be impossible to create complex data structures, such as *linked lists*, *trees* and *graphs*.
- To communicate with operating system about memory. For example, the operator *new* returns the location of free memory block by using a pointer and the operator *delete* returns the memory block pointed to by a pointer to the operating system.

In totality, we can say that the real power of C++ language lies in the judicious use of pointers. Therefore, every reader of C++ must learn and master the art of using pointers.

In this chapter our goal is to explain the pointers as clearly as possible. In an attempt to achieve our goal, we ensure that the groundwork is laid carefully before we move on to use pointers in more advanced situations.

5.2 UNDERSTANDING POINTERS

Computer's memory is organized as a linear collection of bytes or words. For Intel processors, memory is byte-organized whereas for most of the non-Intel processors, memory is word-organized. In byte-organized memory, each memory location is of one byte, whereas in word-organized, each memory location is of one word. Each memory location is assigned a unique number called *location number* or *address*. Figure 5.1 shows the schematic of memory organization.

Figure 5.1: Memory Organization

We know that one byte is equal to 8 bits, whereas one word may be made up of two or more bytes. A word is a measure of the capacity of processor in terms of the size of operands that it can process (*i.e.* add, subtract, multiply, divide, compare, etc.) in single operation. When we say that a processor is a 16-bit processor, it means that its word size is 16-bits (2 bytes) and it can process 16-bit operands in single operations. For large size operands, it needs more operations.

A *memory cell* is either of one byte/word or more contiguous bytes/words. Each cell can store one value at a given time. The address of a cell is always the address of the first byte/word.

When you give a command to run a program, the operating system first finds a free block of requisite size from computer (main) memory, and then loads the program into that block. Even in that block, usually, the program's code is loaded in one part and the program's data in another part of the block. Each of the data operand is stored in a cell and the system associates each of the variables with these addresses. This is illustrated in Figure 5.2.

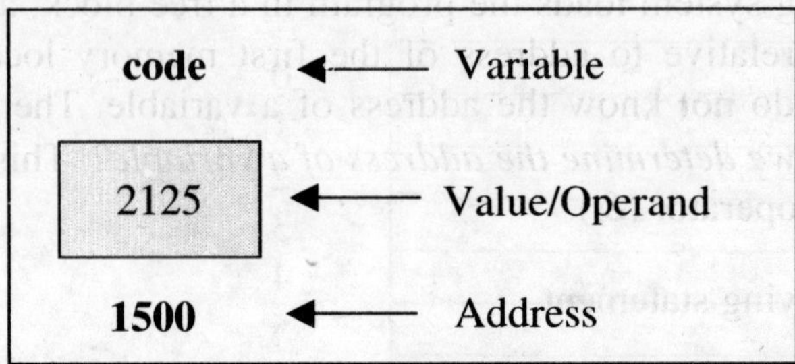

Figure 5.2: Representation of a Variable in Memory

In order to access the data operand either we use either variable name or we can use address of the memory cell. Since these addresses are simply positive integer numbers, they can also be assigned to some variables and stored in memory, like any other variable. Such variables that hold addresses are known as a *pointer*. A pointer is, therefore, nothing but a variable that contains address of another variable in memory.

Since pointer is a variable, its value is also stored in memory in another address. Suppose we assign the address of variable *code* to a variable *ptr*. The link between the variable *ptr* and *code* can be visualized as shown in Figure 5.3.

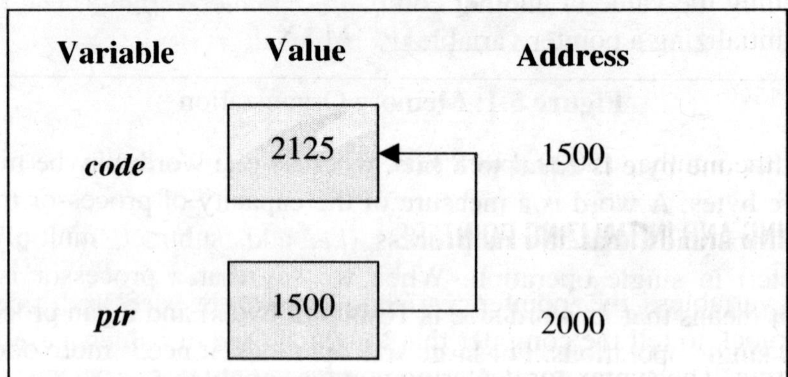

Figure 5.3: Pointer as a Variable

Since the value of the variable *ptr* is the address of the variable *code*, we can access the value of variable *code* by using the value of variable *ptr* and therefore, we say that the variable *ptr* points to the variable *code*, and hence *ptr* gets the name pointer.

5.3 ACCESSING ADDRESS OF A VARIABLE

The actual address of a variable is a system dependent. During compilation and linking, addresses are assumed to be relative to some base address, usually 0. When the operating system loads the program in a free block, all the address are transformed with relative to address of the first memory location of the free block. Hence, we do not know the address of a variable. Therefore, a question arises — *how can we determine the address of a variable*? This is done with the help of *address of* operator (&).

Consider the following statement

```
ptr = &code;
```

It will assign the number 1500 (address of variable *code*) to the variable *ptr*.

The following restrictions must be observed carefully:

1. The address of operator can only be used with variables or an array element. The following are illegal use of *address of* operator:

   (*a*) `&1200` (pointing at constant expression)
   (*b*) `&(a/b)` (pointing at expression)

2. Pointer variable can be initialized only with the use of *address of* operator or by assigning the value of another compatible pointer variable. The following way of initializing a pointer variable *ptr* is illegal:

   ```
   ptr  = 1500;
   ```

   Though, the number 1500 happen to be the address of variable code.

5.4 DECLARING AND INITIALIZING POINTERS

Like other variables, the pointer variables are to be declared first in the declaration block to tell the compiler that to which kind of values these variables will be pointing. The syntax for declaring pointer variable is

```
type *ptr_name;
```

where *type* is a *pre-defined* or *user-defined* data types and indicates that the pointer will point to the variables of that specific data type, and character '*' indicates that variable is a pointer variable.

For example, the statement

```
int *ptr1;
```

declares a pointer variable *ptr1* that can point to an integer type variable.

For example, the statement

```
float *ptr2;
```

declares a pointer variable *ptr2* that can point to a float type variable.

The pointer variable(s) declaration can also be combined with the declaration of other variables, provided they are of same type. For example, the statement

```
int x, *ptrX;
```

declares an integer variable *x* and a pointer variable *ptrX*.

Once a pointer has been declared, it must be initialized prior to its use. It is important to note here that like other variables, a pointer variable will take a garbage value, which can be an address of any storage location. Therefore, if not properly initialized, a pointer may point to any location in memory including those locations where operating system is running, and your system may hang-up i.e. stop responding. Such un-initialized pointers are sometimes referred to as *dangling/wild pointers*.

5.5 ACCESSING A VARIABLE THROUGH ITS POINTER

Once a pointer has been assigned the address of a variable, the question remains as how to access the value of the variable using the pointer. This is done using indirection operator (*). Consider the following statements

```
   :
int *ptrX, x = 10, y;
ptrX = &x;
y = *ptrX;
cout << "\nValue of variable x = " << x;
cout << "\nValue of variable pointed to by ptrX = " << *ptrX;
cout << "\nAddress of variable x = " << ptrX;
cout << "\nValue of variable y  = " << y << "\n";
   :
```

The declaration statement tells the compiler that *ptrX* is pointer variable that will point to an integer value, *x* is an integer variable and it also initializes the variable *x* with value 10, and *y* is another integer variable.

And suppose that during the execution of the above segment, a memory location with address 1098 is set aside for variable *x*. The output of the above segment will look like:

```
Value of variable x = 10
Value of variable pointed to by ptrX = 10
Address of variable x = 1098
Value of variable y = 10
```

Note that writing the statements

```
ptrX = &x;
y = *ptrX
```

is equivalent to writing

```
y = *&x;
```

or for more clarity as

```
y = *(&x);
```

which in turn is equivalent to writing

```
y = x;
```

It is important to note that assignment of pointers and addresses is always done symbolically, by means of symbolic names. You cannot access the value stored at address 1098 by writing *1098. It will not work.

Listing 5.1

```
//  Program to illustrate the use of address of
//  and indirection operators
#include <iostream.h>
void main()
{
     int *ptrX, x = 10, y;
     ptrX = &x;
     y = *ptrX
     cout << "\nValue of variable x = " << x;
     cout << "\nValue of variable pointed to by ptrX = "
          << *ptrX;
     cout << "\nAddress of variable x = " << ptrX;
     cout << "\nValue of variable y  = " << y << "\n";
}
```

5.6 POINTER ARITHMETIC

The C++ language is very consistent in its approach to pointer arithmetic. The integration of pointers, arrays, and pointer arithmetic is one of the strengths of the C++ language. In this section, we will briefly describe the various operations permissible on pointers.

The following operations are permitted on pointers.

1. **Addition of a number to a pointer variable.**

   Suppose *p* is a pointer variable pointing to an element of integer type, then the statement

   ```
   p++;      or    ++p;
   ```

   increments the value of *p* by a factor of 2, so that it points to the next location that holds another value of integer type. This increment factor will be 1 for *character*, 4 for *long integer* and *float*, and 8 for *long float*. The statement

   ```
   p += i;
   ```

   where *i* is either a positive integer constant or an integer variable having positive value, increments *p* such that it points to the *i*th location beyond the location to which it is currently pointing.

2. **Subtraction of a number from a pointer variable.**

   Suppose *p* is a pointer variable pointing to an element of integer type, then the statement

   ```
   p—;       or    —p;
   ```

   decrements the value of *p* by a factor of 2, so that it now points to the location preceding the current location. The statement

   ```
   p -= i;
   ```

   where *i* is either a positive integer constant or an integer variable having positive value, decrements *p* such that it points to the *i*th location before the location to which it is currently pointing.

3. **Subtraction of one pointer variable from another.**

   One pointer variable can be subtracted from another provided both point to the same data type. The difference of the two indicates the number of bytes separating the corresponding elements.

In addition to these arithmetic operations, the pointer variables can be compared with one another, provided they are compatible, *i.e.*, point to the variables of same data type.

The following arithmetic operations on pointers are not permitted.

- Addition of two pointer variables.
- Multiplication of a pointer variable by a number.
- Division of a pointer variable by a number.

5.7 GENERIC POINTERS

As the name suggests, *a generic pointer* is a kind of pointer that can be used to hold addresses of operands of different types at certain times. The syntax for declaring a generic pointer is

```
void *ptr;
```

The following program demonstrates the use of generic pointers.

Listing 5.2

```
// Program to illustrate the use of generic pointers
#include<iostream.h>
void main()
{
    void *ptr;
    int x = 5;
    float y = 20.5;
    ptr = &x;     // assign address of integer variable
    cout << "\nValue pointed to generic pointer now is "
         << ( * ( int* ) ptr );
    ptr = &y;    // assign address of float variable
    cout << "\nValue pointed to generic pointer now is "
         << ( * ( float* ) ptr );
}
```

Though, a generic pointer is very versatile pointer, it suffers from following serious problems:

1. Generic pointers cannot be directly de-referenced. They need to appropriately type casted.
2. Pointer arithmetic cannot be performed on generic pointers.

The reason for both of these problems is that the compiler cannot determine the size of the operand whose address is held in the generic pointers.

5.8 POINTER TO A POINTER

As mentioned, a pointer is variable that holds the address of another variable. This concept can be further extended. We can have a variable that hold an address of a variable that in turn holds an address of another variable. This type of variable will be known as *pointer to a pointer*. The underlying concept is known as *double indirection*. This concept can be further extended to triple level, fourth level, and so on.

A pointer to a pointer will be declared as

```
int **ptr;
```

The value pointed to by a pointer to another pointer will be accessed as

```
**ptr;
```

Listing 5.3

```
// Program to illustrate the use of double indirection
#include <iostream.h>
void main()
{
    int a = 5, *ptrA, **ptrPtrA;
    ptrA = &a;
    ptrPtrA = &ptrA;
    cout << "\nAddress of a = " << &a;
    cout << "\nValue of a = " << a;
    cout << "\nAddress of ptrA = " << &ptrA;
    cout << "\nValue of ptrA = " << ptrA;
    cout << "\nValue pointed to by ptrA = " << *ptrA;
    cout << "\nAddress of ptrPtrA = " << &ptrPtrA;
    cout << "\nValue of ptrPtrA = " << ptrPtrA;
    cout << "\nValue pointed to by ptrPtrA = " << **ptrPtrA;
    cout << "\n";
}
```

Test Run

```
Address of a = 65524
Value of a = 5
Address of ptrA = 65522
Value of ptrA = 65524
Value pointed to by ptrA = 5
Address of ptrPtrA = 65520
Value of ptrPtrA = 65522
Value pointed to by ptrPtrA = 5
```

A practical example of using pointers to pointers is when pointers are passed by address to a calling function.

The following skeleton of code demonstrates this:

```
void main()
{
    int *ptr1;
    // . . .
    func1( &ptr1, . . . );
    // . . .
}
void func1( int **ptr2, . . . )
{
    // . . .
    func2( &ptr2 );
    // . . .
}
void func2( int ***ptr3, . . .)
{
    // . . .
    // . . .
}
```

and so on.

In the rest of the sections, we will extensively demonstrate the of use pointers. This is the area that is given a secondary treatment in most of the textbooks on C++ language. It is important to remember that pointers are the backbone of C++ language. Therefore every reader of C++ language must master them.

5.9 MEMORY ALLOCATION

It is important to note that anything that needs to be executed (programs) or processed (data) must be loaded into memory before it can be executed or processed. Therefore, for every program to be executed or data to be processed, some memory must be allocated for them. The memory allocation can be done in two ways – *statically* and *dynamically*. Let us look at both the ways.

5.9.1 Static Memory Allocation

When you give a command to run your program, the operating system allocates a block of memory for your program, loads it from the secondary storage (Floppy disk, hard disk, CD or DVD, etc.) into that block and then initiates its execution.

When the program finishes its execution, the memory occupied by the program is automatically released. It means that the memory requirements are determined prior to execution of your program, and thereafter your program neither can acquire more memory nor can release the free memory, if not required.

The above situations depicts a situation where the amount of memory required is known before hand, and the compiler then can determine the memory requirements for the data as well as the instructions. In such a situation, memory allocation is known as *static memory allocation*.

5.9.2 Dynamic Memory Allocation

Further, it is important to note that the memory requirements for the instructions are always fixed. However, there may be situation when the exact memory requirements for the data may not be known in advance or the data requirements may vary from one program execution to another program execution, *i.e.*, memory requirements for the data are dynamic.

Therefore, when the amount of memory is not known before hand for a particular data item(s), then it is allocated at the execution time, *i.e.*, when the program is running. In such a situation, memory allocation is known as *dynamic memory allocation*.

5.9.3 Heap/Free Store

As mentioned earlier, every program is provided with a pool of unallocated memory that it can utilize during execution. This pool of unallocated memory is known as *heap* or *free store*. Therefore, whenever the memory of requisite size (amount) is required by the program, it is taken from the free store, and when the previously allocated memory is not required further, it is returned back to the free store.

The memory requirements for the instructions (program code) are always fixed.

5.10 DYNAMIC MEMORY MANAGEMENT

As mentioned earlier, when you give a command to run your program, the operating system allocates a block of memory for your program, loads it from the disk into that block and then initiates its execution. When the program finishes its execution, the memory occupied by the program is automatically released. It means that the memory requirements are determined prior to execution of your program, and thereafter your program can neither acquire more memory nor can release the free memory, if not required.

However, C++ language provides a set of operators, called *dynamic memory management operators*, to allocate and de-allocate memory at execution time, *i.e.*, dynamically. By allocation, we mean that your program can obtain as much memory as required by your program even during execution of your program. By de-allocation, we mean that the memory acquired dynamically can be released at any time during your program execution. It is important to note that memory allocated dynamically, must be de-allocated before your program finishes its execution. Otherwise, even if your program terminates, memory allocated dynamically is never released automatically, and from operating system point of view that memory is still in use. Therefore, if you run the same program many times, many users are using your program concurrently, the operating system may run out of memory.

In this section, we will discuss following memory management functions:

- *new* operator
- *delete* operator

5.10.1 The *new* Operator

The *new* operator allocates the memory and always returns a pointer to an appropriate type. The *new* operator is defined as

```
type * new type [ size in integer ];
```

The following example illustrates its use.

```
int *intPtr;
intPtr = new int[100];
```

Allocate a memory block of 200 bytes, 2 bytes for one integer value, total of 100 integers.

Similar statements will be used for other primitive data types.

```
struct DATE {
int day;
int month;
int year;
```

```
};
DATE *datePtr;
datePtr = new date;
```

Allocate memory for one structure item of type *DATE*, *i.e.*, 6 bytes.

The *new* operator also permits the initialization of memory locations during allocation. The syntax for doing so is

```
type *ptrVar = new type ( InitialValue );
```

This is illustrated in following example:

```
int *intPtr = new int(100);
```

This statement allocates memory for an integer number and initializes it with value 100. The address of the memory allocated memory is assigned to pointer variable *intPtr*.

```
float *floatPtr = new float(125.75);
```

This statement allocates memory for a float number (single precision real number) and initializes it with value 125.75. The address of the memory allocated memory is assigned to pointer variable *floatPtr*.

5.10.2 The *delete* Operator

The *delete* operator is a counterpart of *new* operator and it deallocates (releases) memory allocated by the new operator back to the free poll of memory.

The syntax of *delete* operator is defined as

```
delete ptrVar;
```

where *ptrVar* can be a simple pointer variable or the name of the array of pointer to all types excepts class type.

However, if *ptrVar* is an array of pointers to objects, then we have to use the delete operator as shown below:

```
delete ptrVar[];          or          delete [] ptrVar;
```

The second form is very handy if we want to deallocate more that one array with single use of *delete* operator.

It is important to note that in case of array of pointers to objects, writing

```
delete ptrVar;
```

is equivalent to writing

```
delete ptrVar[0];
```

and hence destructor will be invoked only for the first object. Since we want that destructor should be invoked on all objects, we have to use delete operator as

```
delete ptrVar[];
```

5.11 POINTERS AND ARRAYS

When we declare an array, the compiler allocates a block of memory of appropriate size so that all the elements of an array can be stored in contiguous memory locations. The address of the first memory location (also the address of the first element of the array) of allocated block is known as the *base address*, and is assigned to the array name. Thus, array name behaves as a pointer variable.

5.11.1 Pointers and One-dimensional Arrays

Consider the following declaration statement

```
float a[9] = { 0, 1, 2, 3, 4, 5, 6, 7, 8 };
```

This statement set aside a contiguous block of 9 memory locations for the array named *a*. Here the array named *a* holds the address of the first element of the array i.e. base address of the array. The memory map of the array *a* is shown in Figure 5.4. By adding offset (index of the element) to this base address, the other elements of the array can also be accessed. For example, using pointer notation, the elements of array *a* can be accessed as

```
*(a+0), *(a+1), *(a+2), ..., *(a+8)
```

999	1003	1007	1011	1015	1019	1023	1027	1031
0	1	2	3	4	5	6	7	8
a[0]	*a*[1]	*a*[2]	*a*[3]	*a*[4]	*a*[5]	*a*[6]	*a*[7]	*a*[8]

Figure 5.4: Memory map of one-dimensional array *a* with a base address 999

In comparison to subscript notation, accessing array elements using pointers is always faster.

Listing 5.4

```
// Program to demonstrate passing of an entire array
// using pointer notation
#include<iostream.h>
#include<iomanip.h>
void main()
{
    int arr[10] = { 12, 15, 20, 17, 25, 50, 11, 10, 8, 13 };
    int i, sum, count, *intPtr;
    float average;
    intPtr = arr;
    for ( sum = 0, i = 0; i < 10; i++ )
        sum += *(intPtr+i);
    average = float(sum)/10;
    for ( count = 0, i = 0; i < NUM; i++ )
    {
        if ( *(ptr + i ) > average )
            count++;
    }
    cout << "\nNumber of elements greater than average = "
         << count << endl;
}
```

5.11.2 Pointers and Two-dimensional Arrays

Consider the following declaration statement

```
float a[3][3] = { { 1, 2, 3 }, { 4, 6, 9 }, { 3, 2, 7 } };
```

This statement set aside a contiguous block of 9 memory locations for the array named *a*. Here the array named *a* holds the address of the first element of the array i.e. base address of the array. As we know that there is no concept of rows and columns in memory. The elements of the array, irrespective of that whether it is one-dimensional, two-dimensional or three-dimensional, are stored in a continuous chain, *i.e.*, one after the other.

	Col #0	Col #1	Col #2
Row #0	1	2	3
Row #1	4	6	9
Row #2	3	2	7

999	1003	1007	1011	1015	1019	1023	1027	1031
1	2	3	4	6	9	3	2	7
a[0][0]	*a*[0][1]	*a*[0][2]	*a*[1][0]	*a*[1][1]	*a*[1][2]	*a*[2][0]	*a*[2][1]	*a*[2][2]

Figure 5.5: Memory map of two-dimensional array *a* with base address 999

Now let us see how we can access individual elements of the above two-dimensional array using pointers. The procedure is slightly difficult. As mentioned earlier that two-dimensional array can be treated as an array of arrays, where each element of the array is one-dimensional array.

For example, the above array can be visualized as

a[0]	1	2	3
a[1]	4	6	9
a[2]	3	2	7

Figure 5.6: Two-dimensional array *a* as array of one-dimensional arrays

We can refer to individual elements as *a*[0], *a*[1], and *a*[2]. More specifically, *a*[0] gives address of first one-dimensional array, *a*[1] gives address of second one-dimensional array, *a*[2] gives the address of the third one-dimensional array.

Listing 5.5

```
// Program to illustrate 2D array as array of 1D arrays
#include<iostream.h>
#include<iomanip.h>
void main()
{
   float a[3][3] = {{ 1, 2, 3 },{ 4, 6, 9 },{ 3, 2, 7 } };
   int i;
   for ( i = 0; i < 3; i++ ) {
      cout << "Address of 1D array number " << i+1
         << " = ";
      cout << a[i] << endl;
   }
   cout << endl;
}
```

Now the question is — *How can we access the individual elements of these arrays*? Suppose we want to access the *j*th element of the *i*th row. We know that *a*[*i*] will give address of the *i*th one-dimensional array (i.e. *i*th row). And we also know from our knowledge of one-dimensional arrays that writing *a*[*i*] in subscript notation is equivalent to *(*a*+*i*). Further if *a*[*i*] is the address of the *i*th row, the address of the *j*th element of *i*th row will be (*a*[*i*]+*j*), and thus the element can be accessed as *(*a*[*i*]+*j*), which on replacing *a*[*i*] by *(*a*+*i*) becomes *(*(*a*+*i*)+*j*).

Thus, all of the following expressions refer to element a_{ij}.

```
a[i][j]
*(a[i]+j)
*(*(a+i)+j)
```

Listing 5.6

```
//  Program to print the elements of the 2D array using
//  pointer notation
#include<iostream.h>
#include<iomanip.h>
void main()
{
    int a[3][3] = { { 1, 2, 3 }, { 4, 6, 9 }, { 3, 2, 7 } };
    int i, j;
    cout << "\nElements of two-dimensional array are\n\n";
    for ( i = 0; i < 3; i++ ) {
        for ( j = 0; j < 3; j++ )
            cout << "\t" << *(*(a+i)+j);
        cout << endl;
    }
}
```

5.11.3 Dynamic Arrays

The declaration of arrays at the compilation time (i.e. using subscripted notation) has one major limitation. The memory is allocated during the compilation time. If the number of actual data elements is very less as compared to the declared size, then a lot of memory is wasted. On the other hand, if the number of actual data elements is more than the declared size then we have to modify the source code. However, this limitation can be overcome if the memory is allocated at the execution time. The following program illustrates this concept.

Listing 5.7

```
// Program to illustrate the allocation of memory for
// one-dimensional array at execution time
#include<iostream.h>
#include<iomanip.h>
void main()
{
    int *a, n, i, big;
    cout << "\nEnter size of one-dimensional array : ";
    cin >> n;
    a = new int[n]; // allocate memory for array
    if ( a == NULL ) {
       cout << "\nUnable to allocate memory\n";
       return;
    }
    cout << "Enter " << n << " elements of array\n";
    for ( i = 0 ; i < n ; i++)
        cin >> a[i];
    for ( big = *a, i = 1 ; i < n ; i++ ) {
       if ( *(a+i ) > big )
           big = *(a+i);
    }
    cout << "\nLargest element of the array = " << big << endl;
    delete a;           // release memory held by array
}
```

The following program illustrates the processing of two-dimensional arrays by allocating memory for them during execution time. This program is for matrix multiplication.

Listing 5.8

```
// Program to multiply matrix A of size mxn by matrix B of
// size pxq using pointer notation. Program also checks
// the feasibility of product.
#include<iostream.h>
#include<iomanip.h>
void main()
{
    int *a, *b, *c, n, m, p, q, i, j, k, temp;
    cout << "\nEnter size of matrix A as m, n : ";
    cin >> m >> n;
    cout << "\nEnter size of matrix B as p, q : ";
    cin >> p >> q;
    if ( n != p ) {
       cout << "\nMatrix Product AxB is not feasible\n";
       return;
    }
    a = new int[m*n];    // allocate memory
    b = new int[p*q];
    c = new int[m*q];
    cout << "\nEnter " << m*n;
```

```
    cout << " elements of matrix A row-wise\n";
    for ( i = 0 ; i < m * n; i++ )
        cin >> a[i];
    cout << "\nEnter " << p*q;
    cout << " elements of matrix B row-wise\n";
    for ( i = 0 ; i < p * q; i++ )
        cin >> b[i];
    for ( i = 0 ; i < m ; i++ ) {
        for ( j = 0 ; j < q ; j++ ) {
            for ( temp = 0, k = 0; k < n; k++ )
                temp += *( a + i * n + k )*(*( b + k * q + j ));
            *( c + i * q + j ) = temp;
        }
    }
    cout << "\nProduct AxB is \n";
    for ( i = 0 ; i < m * q; i++ ) {
       if ( i % m == 0 )
           cout << endl;
       cout << c[i] << "\t";
    }
    delete a, b, c;
}
```

5.12 POINTERS AND STRINGS

As we know that a string is an array of characters, terminated with a null character '\0'. Therefore, like one-dimensional arrays, we can use individual characters in a string. This is illustrated in program listing 5.7.

Listing 5.9

```
//  Program to illustrate the access of individual
//  characters in a string using a pointer
#include<iostream.h>
void main()
{
   char city[]= "Chandigarh is a beautiful city";
   char *ptr;
   ptr = city;
   cout << "\nIndividual characters of the strings are\n\n";
   while ( *ptr != '\0' ) {
      cout << "\n" << *ptr << " is stored at address " << ptr;
   }
   cout << "\n";
}
```

As mentioned in *Chapter 6,* that storing/representing a table of strings (list of strings) using a two-dimensional array is not an efficient way. We will take up that issue here.

Consider the following declaration

```
char names[4][12] = { "Ram",
                      "Inder Mohan",
                      "Amanpreet",
                      "Rajan"
                    };
```

Where we have considered that each string can be of 20 characters, at maximum excluding the null character. This list of strings will be represented in memory as shown below:

R	a	m	'\0'								
I	n	d	e	r		M	o	h	a	n	'\0'
A	m	a	n	p	r	e	e	t	'\0'		
R	a	j	a	n	'\0'						

Total memory requirements are 48 bytes. However, if we count, first string requires 4 bytes, second string requires 12 bytes, third string requires 10 bytes, and the fourth string requires 6 bytes. Thus total memory requirements come out to be 32, wastage of 16 bytes. In practice, it has been shown that, on average, half of the allocated space is mere wastage.

However, this kind of representation of list of strings can be practical only if all strings are of equal length, but this happens rarely in practice.

Therefore, more practical and efficient way of storing a list of strings is using array of pointers to strings. The following declaration illustrates this point

```
char *names[4] = { "Ram",
                   "Inder Mohan",
                   "Amanpreet",
                   "Rajan"
                 };
```

This will be represented in memory as

R	a	m	'\0'								
I	n	d	e	r		M	o	h	a	n	'\0'
A	m	a	n	p	r	e	e	t	'\0'		
R	a	j	a	n	'\0'						

This declaration allocates only 32 bytes of memory, *i.e.*, what is actually needed.

Following code shows I/O of list of strings represented using array of pointers.

Listing 5.10

```
//  Program to illustrate input/output of strings
//  represented using array of pointer
#include<iostream.h>
#include<string.h>
#define  MAX  30
void main()
{
    char *names[MAX];
    int i, n;
    cout << "\nEnter number of strings : ";
    cin >> n;
    for ( i = 0; i < n; i++ ) {
       cout << "\nEnter string #" << i+1 << " : ";
       cin.getline(names, 30, '\n');
    }
    cout << "\nYou have entered following strings\n\n";
    for ( i = 0; i < n; i++ )
       cout << names[i];
}
```

5.13 POINTERS AND STRUCTURES

As we can use pointers with other data types, we can also use pointers for structure variables. Consider the following declarations

```
struct EMPLOYEE
{
   int    code;
   char   name[20];
   int    deptCode;
   float  salary;
};

EMPLOYEE emp, *empPtr;
```

These declarations create user-defined data type and give it name *EMPLOYEE*. It also declares *emp* as variable of type employee and *empPtr* as pointer variable to type employee. Now the following statement

```
ptr = &emp1;
```

can be used to assign the address of variable *emp1* to pointer variable *ptr*. Now, we can access members of structure variable *emp1* using pointer variable *ptr*.

You may expect that the elements can be accessed as shown below:

```
*ptr.code        *ptr.name        *ptr.dept_code        *ptr.salary
```

But this approach will not work as the *dot operator* '.' has higher priority than the *indirection operator* '*'. The correct way is to write as

```
(*ptr).code     (*ptr).name     (*ptr).dept_code     (*ptr).salary
```

There is another approach that is more elegant and simple. In this approach, the elements of structure are accessed using *arrow operator* '–>' which is a combination of two characters, *i.e.*, hyphen '–' and greater-than '>'.

The syntax for accessing members of structure using arrow operator is:

```
ptr->vname
```

where *ptr is* pointer variable pointing to a structure, and *vname* is the name of element of the structure.

Using arrow operator, the elements of structure of type *employee* pointed to by pointer variable *ptr* can be accessed as

```
ptr->code      ptr->name      ptr->dept_code      ptr->salary
```

Listing 5.11

```
// Program to illustrate I/O of structure using pointers
#include <iostream.h>
struct employee
{
   int code;
   char name[20];
   int  dept_code;
   float  salary;
};

void main()
{
    employee emp1, *ptr;
    ptr = &emp1;

    cout << "Enter code of employee as integer number : ";
    cin >> ptr->code;

    cout << "Enter name of employee : ";
```

```
    cin >> ptr->name;

    cout << "Enter department code of as integer number : ";
    cin >> ptr->dept_code;

    cout << "Enter Salary : ";
    cin >> ptr->salary;

    cout << "Particulars of employee as entered by you are\n\n"
    cout << "Employee code   : " << ptr->code << endl;
    cout << "Employee name   : " << ptr->name << endl;
    cout << "Department code : " << ptr->dept_code << endl;
    cout << "Employee salary : " << ptr->salary << endl;
}
```

5.13.1 Self-referential Structures

The self-referential structures are structures that include an element that is a pointer to another structure of the same type. These structures find their application in building complex data structure such as *linked lists*, *trees* and *graphs*.

Following are some examples of self-referential structures.

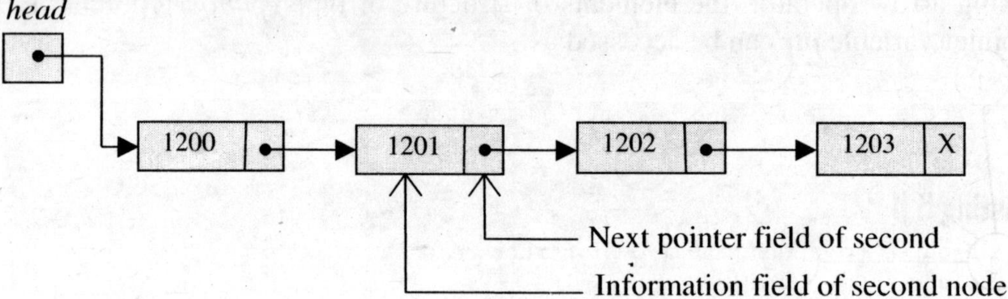

Figure 5.7: Linear linked list of integer values with nodes 4

To represent the above linear linked list in memory, we need following declarations

```
struct NODE
{
    int info;
    NODE *next;
};

NODE *start;
```

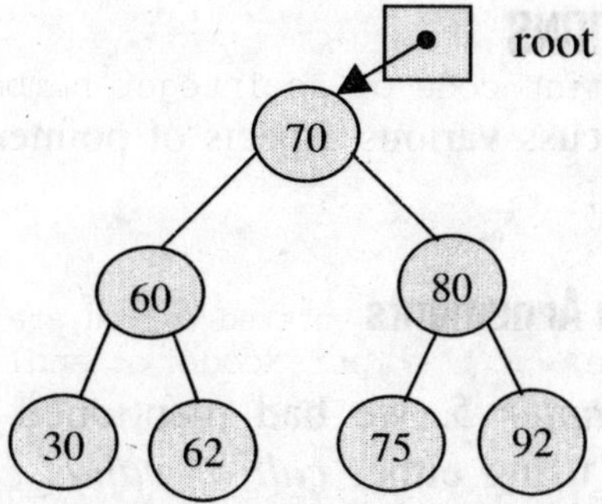

Figure 5.8: Binary tree

To represent a binary tree in memory, we need following declarations

```
struct NODE
{
   NODE *left;
   int info;
   NODE *right;
};

NODE *root;
```

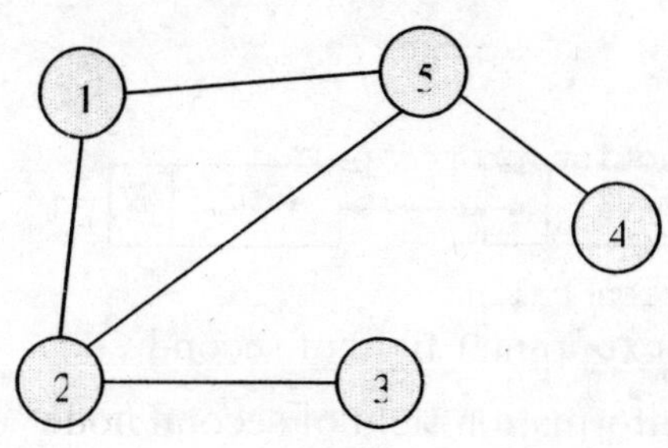

Figure 5.9: Undirected graph

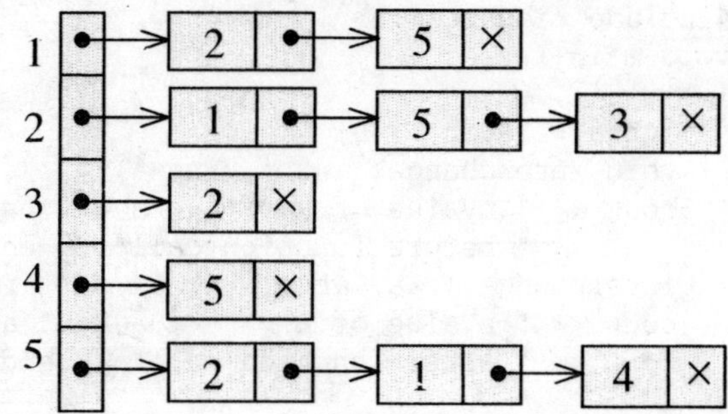

Figure 5.10: Adjacency list for graph

To represent a graph in memory, one of the best representation schemes is adjacency list as shown in Figure 5.10. Therefore, for a graph with maximum of 50 vertices/nodes, we need following declarations

```
#define MAX 50
struct NODE{
   int vertex;
   NODE *link;
};

NODE *adj[MAX];
```

5.14 POINTERS AND FUNCTIONS

In this section, we will discuss various aspects of pointers concerning user-defined functions.

5.14.1 Pointers as Function Arguments

If you remember, *in Chapter 5*, we had mentioned that the arguments to a function could be passed using either *call by value*, *call by address* or *call by reference* mechanism. When we use call by value mechanism, the formal arguments of the function are declared as simple variable, and at execution time the values of the actual arguments are copied into formal arguments (formal arguments are local to the function), and the execution of the function begins.

However, when we use call by address mechanism, the formal arguments are declared as pointers, and at execution time, the addresses of the actual arguments are copied into formal arguments and the execution of the function begins.

Listing 5.12

```
// Program to illustrate pointers as function arguments
#include <iostream.h>
void main()
{
   int a = 10, b = 20;
   void interchange( int *, int *);  //  function prototype
   cout << "\nValue of a = " << a << " and b = " << b
        << " before function call" << endl;
   interchange ( &a, &b );          // function call
   cout << "\nValue of a = " << a << " and b = " << b
        << " after function call" << endl;
}
void interchange( int *x, int *y ) // function definition
{
   int temp;
   temp = *x;
   *x = *y;
   *y = temp;
}
```

Test Run

```
Value of a = 10 and b = 20 before function call
Value of a = 20 and b = 10 after function call
```

Consider the following program listing.

Listing 5.113

```
// Program to illustrate the consequence of not using
// pointers as function arguments

#include <iostream.h>
void main()
{
    int a = 10; b = 20;
    void interchange(int, int);  // function prototype
    cout << "\n\nValue of a =  << a
         << " and b = " << b << " d before function call";
    interchange ( a, b);          //   function call
    cout << "\n\nValue of a =  << a
         << " and b = " << b << " d after function call";
}

// function definition
void interchange(int x, int y)
{
    int temp;
    temp = x;
    x = y;
    y = temp;
}
```

Test Run

```
Value of a = 10 and b = 20 before function call
Value of a = 10 and b = 20 after function call
```

Why this version of the program could not complete the task of interchanging the values of the arguments. In this version, values of *a* and *b* are copied into *x* and *y*, which act as local variables. Thus the values, in fact, of *x* and *y* are interchanged in the workspace of the *interchange()* function, but as soon as the function completes its execution, these variables are destroyed. Thus, the values of the variables remain un-effected. However, in the first version of the program, the addresses of variables *a* and *b* are copied into pointer variables *x* and *y*. These pointer variables, though local to the function *interchange()*, interchanges the values of *a* and *b* indirectly in the work space of the *main()* function, with the help of a local variable *temp*. When the function *interchange()* completes its execution, the variables *x*, and *y* along with temp are destroyed, but the task has been accomplished.

Listing 5.14

```
// Program to illustrate passing of array of
// strings to a function

#include <iostream.h>
#define    DAYS   7
void print_strings ( char **, int );  // function prototype
void main()
{
   char *week[DAYS] = { "Sunday", "Monday", "Tuesday",
                        "Wednesday", "Thursday",
                        "Friday",  "Saturday"
                      };
   print_strings ( str1, N );
}
void print_strings ( char **temp, int n )
{
   int i;
   cout << "\nStrings passed to this function are\n\n";
   for ( i = 0; i < n; i++ )
       puts(temp[i] );
}
```

5.14.2 Function Returning a Pointer

Like any type of value, a function can also return a pointer pointing to an appropriate type of values. Syntax for declaring a function that return a pointer is

```
type *funName( args  )
{
   // Local declarations
   // statements
}
```

The following program listing illustrates the various steps.

Listing 5.15

```
// Program to illustrate a function that returns a pointer
#include <iostream.h>
void main()
{
   int x = 20;
   int *address ( int );     /*  function prototype  */
   cout << "\nAddress of " << x << " in main function is "
        << &x;
   cout << "\nand in function it is copied at address\n"
        << address(x) << "\n";
}
```

```
int *address( int y )
{
   return &y;
}
```

5.15 POINTERS AND CLASSES

Pointer can be used in a variety of ways with classes – *pointer to object*, *pointer to member*, passing objects as arguments using *call-by-address* mechanism.

5.15.1 Pointer to an Object

Like pointers can be used to hold an address of a value of basic type, likewise pointers can also be used to hold address of object. Once a pointer is initialized with the address of an object, then its members can be accessed using arrow '->' operator. The following program illustrates the use of pointer to an object.

Listing 5.16

```
// Program to demonstrate the use of pointer to an object
#include <iostream.h>
#include <iomanip.h>
class Test
{
    private:
       int b;
       int c;
       int d;
    public:
       void setData(int x, int y, int z) {
          b = x;
          c = y;
          d = z;
       }
       void showData()
       {
          cout << "\nb = " << b;
          cout << "\nc = " << c;
          cout << "\nd = " << d << endl;
       }
};
void main()
{
   Test obj;         // create object
   Test *ptrToObj;   // declare pointer to type Test
   ptrToObj = &obj; // initialize pointer with address of object
   ptrToObj->setData(10,20,30);
   ptrToObj->showData();
}
```

Test Run

```
b = 10
c = 20
d = 30
```

5.15.2 Pointer to a Member

It is possible to obtain the addresses of members of a class and assign it to pointers of appropriate type. To obtain address of a member, the *address of* '&' operator is used along with fully qualified member name. A class member pointer is declared using the operator '::*', a combination of two characters '::' and '*' without any embedded space. The general syntax for declaring and using a pointer for data member is

```
// syntax for declaration of pointer to a data member
DataType ClassName::* dataPointer;

// syntax for initializing a pointer to a data member
ClassName::* dataPointer = &ClassName::dataMember;

// syntax for accessing value of data member through
// a pointer to a data member using object itself
Object.* dataPointer

// syntax for accessing value of data member through
// a pointer to a data member using a pointer to a object
objectPointer->* dataPointer
```

The general syntax for declaring a pointer to member function is

```
// syntax for declaration of pointer to a member function
ReturnType (ClassName::* FunctionPointer)(formalArgList);

// syntax for initializing a pointer to a member function
ClassName::* functionPointer = &ClassName::functionMember;

// syntax for accessing value of member function through
// a pointer to a member function
Object.*functionPointer(actualArgList);

// syntax for accessing value of member function through
// a pointer to a member functio  using a pointer to a object
pointerObject->*functionPointer(actualArgList);
```

Consider the following class

```
class Sample
{
  private:
```

```
      int m;
      // . . .
   public:
      void show() {
         // . . .
      }
};
```

Pointer to data member *m* will be declared and initialized as

```
int Sample::* intPtr = &Sample::m;
```

Note that the following statement will not work

```
int *intPtr = &m;
```

Listing 5.17

```
// Program to demonstrate the use of pointer to members
#include <iostream.h>
#include <iomanip.h>
class Test
{
   private:
      int b;
      int c;
      int d;
   public:
      void setData(int x, int y, int z)
      {
         b = x;
         c = y;
         d = z;
      }
      void showData() {
         cout << "\nb = " << b;
         cout << "\nc = " << c;
         cout << "\nd = " << d << endl;
      }
      friend int sum ( Test );
};
int sum ( Test ob )
{
   int temp;
   int Test:: *ptrB = &Test::b;  // pointers to data members
   int Test:: *ptrC++ = &Test::c;
   int Test:: *ptrD = &Test::d;
   temp = ob.*ptrB + ob.*ptrC++ + ob.*ptrD;
   return temp;
}
```

```
void main()
{
   Test obj;
   Test *objPtr;     // pointer to object
   // declare and initialize pointer to first member function
   void (Test::*functionPtr1)(int,int,int) = &Test::setData;
   // declare and initialize pointer to second member function
   void (Test::*functionPtr2)() = &Test::showData;
   objPtr = &obj;
   // call member functions through object and pointer
   // to member function
   (obj.*functionPtr1)(10,20,30);
   (obj.*functionPtr2)();
   // call to friend function that returns sum of data members
   cout << "\nSum of data member = " << sum(obj) << endl;
   // call member functions through object and pointer
   // to member function
   (objPtr->*functionPtr1)(40,50,60);
   (objPtr->*functionPtr2)();
   cout << "\nSum of data member = " << sum(obj) << endl;
}
```

Test Run

```
b = 10
c = 20
d = 30

Sum of data member = 60

b = 40
c = 50
d = 60

Sum of data member = 150
```

Following is the equivalent version of friend function *sum()*, where member elements are accessed using pointer to object.

```
int sum ( Test ob )
{
  int temp;
  Test *objPtr = &ob;
  int Test:: *ptrB = &Test::b;
  int Test:: *ptrC++ = &Test::c;
  int Test:: *ptrD = &Test::d;
  temp = objPtr->*ptrB + objPtr->*ptrC++ + objPtr->*ptrD;
  return temp;
}
```

5.15.3 The *this* Pointer

All non-static member functions of an object have access to a special pointer named *this*. The *this* pointer holds the address of the object whose member function is invoked. Therefore, any non-static member function can find out the address of the object of which it is a member. Basically, *this* pointer is not part of the object, i.e., *this* pointer is not reflected in the result of a *sizeof* operation on the object. Rather, *this* pointer is passed as an implicit first argument to every non-static member function.

Listing 5.18

```
// Program to demonstrate that this pointer is passed as
// implicit first argument to a member function
#include <iostream.h>
#include <iomanip.h>
class Sample
{
  private:
    int a;
    int b;
  public:
    void showAddress() {
       cout << endl << "My object's address is :"
              << this << endl;
    }
};
void main()
{
   Sample s1, s2, s3       // create objects
   s1.showAddress();     // call member function
   s2.showAddress();
   s3.showAddress();
}
```

Test Run

```
My object's address is : 0x8fa6fff2

My object's address is : 0x8fa6ffee

My object's address is : 0x8fa6ffea
```

In the class *Sample*, a member function *showAddress()* is defined that outputs the value of this pointer. In main function, three objects are created. Then on each object, the member function *showAddress()* is invoked, that in turn prints the address of each object through *this* pointer.

Since the data in each object consists of 4-bytes, the objects are spaced 4 bytes apart in memory. Further, since local automatic variable are stored in *stack*, that grow from higher addresses towards lower addresses, the first object gets higher address that second object that in turn gets higher address than third object.

The type of *this* pointer depends on the type of the object and whether the member function in which *this* pointer is used is declared as *const*. In a non-constant member function for *Sample*, *this* pointer has the data type *Sample * const* (a constant pointer to a *Sample* object). In a constant member function of the class *Sample*, *this* pointer has the data type *const Sample * const* (a constant pointer to a *Sample* object that is constant).

5.15.3.1 Accessing Data Members with *this* Pointer

When a call to a non-static member function is made, the *this* pointer is created and set to the address of the object, for which it is called, and then passed as first implicit argument. The *this* pointer can be treated like any other pointer to an object, and thus can be used to access the data in the object it points to.

As a specific case, if the name of arguments of a member function is same as that of data members, then the arguments takes precedence over data members being local to the member function. In this case, to refer to data members, you have to use *this* pointer. The following programs demonstrate these concepts.

Listing 5.19

```
// Program to demonstrate these use of this pointer

#include <iostream.h>
#include <iomanip.h>

class Sample
{
  private:
     int a;
     int b;
  public:
      void setData( int a, int b ) {
         a = a;
         b = b;
      }
      void showData() {
         cout << endl
              << " a = : " << a << endl
              << " b = : " << b << endl;
      }
};
```

```
void main()
{
    Sample s1;
    s1.showData();
    s1.setData(12,15);
    s1.showData();
}
```

In both the calls to *showData()*, the output will be same. The reason being, in *setData()* member function, the values of the arguments gets assigned to themselves, being local, and the data members left unchanged.
In order to accomplish the intended task, we should write the *setData()* member function as

```
void setData( int a, int b )
{
   this->a = a;
   this->b = b;
}
```

5.15.4 Self-referential Classes

Like structures, there are the classes where at least one of the data members is a pointer to itself, *i.e.*, pointer to its own type. These types of classes are useful for building complex data structures.

The following code shows an example of a self-referential class to implement a singly (linear) linked list:

```
class List
{
   private:
       int data;
     List *next;
   public:
     // . . . member functions
};
```

5.16 POSSIBLE PROBLEMS WITH THE USE OF POINTERS

Pointers can be the source of mysterious and catastrophic program bugs. Common bugs related to pointers and memory management is *dangling/wild pointers*, *memory leaks*, and *allocation failures*. Each of these problems is discussed below. Every student must understand these carefully.

5.16.1 Problem of Dangling/Wild Pointers

The most common problem with pointers is that the programmer fails to initialize a pointer with a valid address. Such an initialized pointer, referred to as *dangling/wild pointer*, can end up pointing anywhere in memory that may include the program code itself or to the code of the operating system. If the programmer assign a value to such pointer, the value will overwrite the program or operating system instructions, and the computer program may show undesirable behaviour or may even crash, *i.e.*, stop responding. When the system stop responding, we say the system has hanged up and the only option left is to reboot the system. Therefore, care must be taken to initialize pointers with valid address.

5.16.2 Problem of Null Pointer Assignment

One particular situation that happens is when the pointer points to address 0, which is called NULL. For example, this may happen that if the pointer variable is declared as global since global variables are initialized to 0. Likewise, this can also happen for a local un-initialized pointer variable, particularly for local static variables, they are also initialized to 0. When it happens, and no catastrophic situations had occurred, then the system will display a message "*Null pointer assignment*" on termination of the program.

Listing 5.20

```
// Program to illustrate the cause of NULL pointer
#include <iostream.h>
//  global pointer variable, initialized to 0
int *intPtr;
void main()
{
   *intPtr = 200;          // write value on 0 address
   cout << "\nValue stored at address 0 = " << *intPtr;
}
```

5.16.3 Problem of Memory Leak

Another very serious problem with pointers is that of *memory leak*. Memory leak is a situation where the programmer fails to release the memory allocated at run time in a module. Note that when memory is allocated, a pointer variable is used to hold the address of the allocated block, however, when the module completes its execution, the pointer variable goes out of scope and there will be no way to reach that memory block. Therefore, care must be taken to release the allocated memory block in a module where memory was allocated.

Listing 5.21

```
// Program to illustrate the cause of memory leak
#include <iostream.h>
void main()
{
    . . . . .
    fun();    //  invoke function named 'fun'
    . . . . .
}
void fun()
{
   int *intPtr;
   // allocate memory for 'n' integer numbers
   intPtr = new [n*sizeof(int)];
   //  work on the allocated block
}
```

5.16.4 Problem of Allocation Failures

Allocation failure is a situation when the program through *new* operator request for a block of memory, and the operating system could not fulfill the request of the program because the sufficient memory may not be available in the free pool of memory. In that case, *new* operator returns a NULL pointer indicating the allocation failure. Therefore, the programmer should take care of allocation failures and provide a safe exit in their programs on such failures.

Listing 5.22

```
// Program to illustrate the allocation failure, and
// the way it should be handled
#include <iostream.h>
void main()
{
   int *intPtr;
   //  allocate memory for 'n' integer numbers
   intPtr = new [n*sizeof(int)];
   if ( intPtr == NULL )
   {
      cout << "\nUnable to allocate memory . . .\n";
      return;
   }
   //   work on the allocated block
   delete intPtr;    // release the memory
}
```

QUICK RECAP

In this chapter, we have learnt that

- Pointer is a variable that holds an address of an operand.
- Pointers offers many advantages such as returning more than one value from a function, building complex data structures, communicating with hardware, etc.
- Pointers can be designated as integer pointers, character pointers, float pointers or double pointers depending on type of operand whose address it holds.
- An addition operation on pointers is permitted. A subtraction operation is permitted in the restricted sense that it must give positive difference. Multiplication and division operation is not permitted.
- Memory allocation can be done in two ways – *statically* and *dynamically*.
- Static memory allocation is that which is done at compilation time.
- Dynamic memory allocation is that which is done at execution time.
- Every program is provided with a pool of unallocated memory that it can utilize during execution. This pool of unallocated memory is known as *heap* or *free store*.
- The process of managing the memory at execution time is known as *dynamic memory management*.
- The *new* and *delete* operators are used for dynamic memory management.
- The *new* operator allocates the requisite amount of memory while the *delete* operator deallocates the memory previously allocated with *new* operator.
- Pointers are used to pass arguments by address.
- Arrays, strings and structures can be efficiently passed as arguments to a function.
- A function can return a pointer.
- A self-referential structure is a structure that includes at least one element that is a pointer to itself.
- An initialized pointer is referred to as *dangling/wild pointer*, as it can end up pointing anywhere in memory.
- Whenever there is attempt to write on zero address (also known as *Null pointer*) or the system will flag and a message "*Null pointer assignment*" on termination of the program.
- Memory leak is a kind of situation when memory is allocated in a called function but it is not deallocated in that function after it use. As a result, when

the called function completes its execution, the pointer variable is destroyed and there is no means to reach that allocated memory block.

- **Allocation failure is a situation when system is not able to find a requisite block of free memory. System indicates this situation by returning a *NULL* pointer.**

MULTIPLE CHOICE QUESTIONS

1. The address of a variable can be obtained using ___ operator.

   (*a*) * (*b*) & (*c*) ? (*d*) ->

2. Which of the following operator is known as *indirection* operator?

   (*a*) & (*b*) << (*c*) ^ (*d*) *

3. Which of the following operator is known as *address of* operator?

   (*a*) & (*b*) * (*c*) -> (*d*) **

4. Identify the correct declarations of pointer variables *ptr1*, *ptr2*.

   (*a*) int ptr1, *ptr2; (*b*) int *ptr1, ptr2;
   (*c*) int ptr1, ptr2; (*d*) int *ptr1, *ptr2;

5. The operators exclusively used with pointers are

   (*a*) * and / (*b*) & and * (*c*) & and ^ (*d*) * and +

6. The operand of *address of* operator can be

   (*a*) a constant (*b*) an array element
   (*c*) an expression (*d*) None of above

7. Pointer variables may be assigned

   (*a*) address value represented in hexadecimal notation
   (*b*) address value represented in octal notation
   (*c*) address of another variable
   (*d*) address value represented in binary notation

8. Operand of *indirection* operator is

   (*a*) pointer variable (*b*) ordinary variable
   (*c*) integer constant (*d*) none of above

9. Identify the operator that is not used with pointers

   (*a*) -> (*b*) & (*c*) * (*d*) >>

10. The operator used for dynamic memory allocation is

    (*a*) memalloc (*b*) alloc (*c*) new (*d*) mcalloc

11. Pointer can be used to achieve

    (*a*) call by function (*b*) call by name
    (*c*) call by address (*d*) call by procedure

12. Which of the following statements about functions is not correct?

    (*a*) function can return a pointer
    (*b*) function cannot return a pointer
    (*c*) function can have its formal arguments declared as pointer
    (*d*) function can be called using a pointer to a function

13. Which of the following operation is not permitted on pointers?

    (*a*) incrementing a pointer variable
    (*b*) adding a number to a pointer variable
    (*c*) division of a pointer variable by a number
    (*d*) difference of two pointer variables

14. When address of operator (&) is prefixed to a variable, it yields

    (*a*) variable's value (*b*) variables data type
    (*c*) variable's address (*d*) none of above

15. Consider the following statements

```
char *ptr;
ptr = "abba";
cout << *ptr;
```

    What will be printed?

    (*a*) first letter (*b*) entire string
    (*c*) it is a syntax error (*d*) last letter

16. Which of the following statement is not true about *this* pointer?

    (*a*) It is implicitly passed as a first argument to every member function.
    (*b*) It can be used to refer to data members as well as member functions.
    (*c*) It always acts as a constant pointer.
    (*d*) It can be used to return a reference to an object.

17. What can you say about the following declarations?

```
int *f(void);
int (*f)(void);
```

    (*a*) Both are identical.
    (*b*) The first is a correct declaration and the second is wrong.

(*c*) The first declaration is a function returning a pointer to an integer and the second is a pointer to function returning an integer.
(*d*) Both are different ways of declaring a pointer to a function.

18. What will be the output of the following program?

```
#include <iostream.h>
void main() {
    const int i = 5;
    int *p;
    i = 20;
    p = &i;
    cout << "\n" << *p << ", " << i;
}
```

(*a*) -5, 5 (*b*) 5, 20 (*c*) 20, 5 (*d*) Error

19. Consider the following code segment

```
int *p, a[10];
p = a;
```

Which of following is incorrect way to access the 5th element of array?

(*a*) *(*a*+4) (*b*) *a*[4] (*c*) *(**p*+4) (*d*) *p*[4]

20. Consider the following program

```
#include <iostream.h>
void main()
{
    int *p, a[] = { 1, 2, 3, 4, 5 };
    p = &a[2];
    cout << p[-1];
}
```

Which of the following is correct about above program?

(*a*) Compiler time error because *p* is not an array
(*b*) Output will be 2
(*c*) Compiler time error because subscript cannot be negative
(*d*) None of above

REVIEW EXERCISES

1. How can we get the address of a variable?
2. What is a pointer variable?
3. How is a pointer variable declared?
4. How can the values pointed to by a pointer variable be accessed?

5. **What are the various types of pointers?**
6. **Pointers are double-edged weapons. Comment.**
7. **What are the operations permissible on pointers?**
8. **What are the operations, which are not permissible on pointers?**
9. **What is the difference between *static* and *dynamic* memory allocation?**
10. **What do you mean by a *dangling/wild pointer*? What type of problems it may cause?**
11. **What is a NULL pointer assignment?**
12. **What is a memory leak? What can be the possible reason for it? How can memory leaks be avoided?**
13. **What is an allocation failure?**
14. **What is a self-referential structure? How are they useful?**
15. **Consider the following declarations**

```
struct Book
{
    int accessionNo;
    char title[31];
    char author[21];
    char publisher[41];
    float price;
};
int *intPtr;
float *floatPtr;
char *charPtr;
Book *bookPtr;
```

How much memory will be allocated for each of these pointer variables?

16. **Predict the output and explain the working of the following program, and identify the error, if any?**

```
#include <iostream.h>
void main()
{
    int i = 6, j = 4;
    void kudo( int, int * );   // function prototype
    kudo(j, &i);
    cout << "\ni = " << i << ", j = " << j << "\n";
}
void kudo( int x, int *y )  // function definition
{
    x = *y * x;
    *y = x * *y;
}
```

17. Predict the output and explain the working of the following program, and identify the error, if any?

```
#include <iostream.h>
void main()
{
    int i = 156;
    int *j, *k;
    j = &i;
    k = j;
    cout << "\ni = " << i << ", *(&i) = " << *(&i)
         << ", *j = " << *j << ", *k = " << *k << "\n";
}
```

18. Identify the error, if any, in the following program, and explain the reason.

```
#include <iostream.h>
void main()
{
    int x[6] = { 1, 2, 3, 4, 5, 6 };
    int *r, *s;
    r = x;
    s = x + 4;
    r *= 2;
    s /= 2
    cout << "\n*r = " << *r << ", *s = " << *s << "\n";
}
```

19. Identify error, if any, in following program, and explain the reason.

```
#include <iostream.h>
void main()
{
    int x[6] = { 1, 2, 3, 4, 5, 6 };
    int i = 0;
    while ( i < 6 )
    {
        cout << "\nx[" << i << "] = " << *x;
        ++i;
        x++;
    }
    cout << "\nThe End\n";
}
```

20. Predict and explain output of following program.

```
#include <iostream.h>
void func(int, int *);// prototype
void main()
{
    int x[] = { 2, 4, 6, 8 };
    int i = 0, b = 6;
    while ( i < 4 )
```

```
        {
            func(x[i],&b);
            cout << "x[" << i << "] = " << x[i]
                 << ", b = " << b << "\n";
            i++;
        }
    }
    void func(int a, int *p)
    {
        a = *p += 2;
        cout << "\na = " << a << ", ";
    }
```

21. What is the difference between following statements?

`int *fname(int a, int b);` **and** `int (*fname)(int a, int b);`

22. What is the difference between the following declarations?

`const int *intptr;` **and** `int *const intptr;`

23. Identify errors, if any, in following program, and also give appropriate reasons.

```
#include <iostream.h>
void main()
{
    int i = 5;
    const int j = 100;
     int * const ptr = &j;
    *ptr++;
    ptr = &i;
    cout << "\n" << *ptr << ", " << i
         << ", " << j << "\n";
}
```

PROGRAMMING EXERCISES

1. Write a function that takes three arguments *x*, *y*, *z* of type *float* through reference, and changes the values of *x*, *y*, and *z* so that *x* has *y*'s value, *y* has *z*'s value, and *z* has *x*'s value.
2. Write a function that takes an array as its argument and returns the largest, smallest and range of its elements.
3. Write a function to compute the roots of a quadratic equation by using call by reference mechanism to pass computed roots to calling function.
4. Write a program that dynamically allocates memory for an array of size *n*, reads elements of array and sorts them in ascending order.
5. Depending on which computing system you use, you will have to consider byte order in which multi-byte numbers are stored, particularly when you are

writing those numbers to a file. These two orders are called "Little Endian" and "Big Endian".

"Little Endian" means that the low-order byte of the number is stored in memory at the lowest address, and the high-order byte at the highest address. (The little end comes first.)

For example, a 4 byte *long int*

```
Byte3 Byte2 Byte1 Byte0
```

will be arranged in memory as follows:

```
Base Address+0  Byte0
Base Address+1  Byte1
Base Address+2  Byte2
Base Address+3  Byte3
```

Intel processors (those used in PC's) use "Little Endian" byte order.

"Big Endian" means that the high-order byte of the number is stored in memory at the lowest address, and the low-order byte at the highest address. (The big end comes first.)

Our *long int*, would then be stored as:

```
Base Address+0  Byte3
Base Address+1  Byte2
Base Address+2  Byte1
Base Address+3  Byte0
```

Motorola processors (those used in Mac's) use "Big Endian" byte order.

Write a program in C++ language to check that whether the computer on which you are working is *little endian* or *big endian*.

6. Consider the following structure definition:

```
struct Box
{
    char make[25];
    float length;
    float breadth;
    float height;
};
```

Write a function that takes the address of the *Box* structure and returns its volume.

7. Consider the following declaration:

```
struct employeeType
{
    int code;
    char name[31];
    float salary;
};
```

Given that there are *n* (≤50) employees in an organization. Write a program, using pointer notation to access the data of an employee that output the details of the employee having highest salary.

8. Consider the following declaration:

```
char *names[] = { "Vimal", "Amit", "Anuj", "Rohit", "Abhijit" };
```

Write a program to produce the following output:

```
char *names[] = { "tijihbA", "tihoR", "junA", "timA", "lamiV" };
```

9. Write a function *substr()* whose prototype is given as

```
char *substr(char *str1, char *str2);
```

that scan the first string for the occurrence of a second string, and returns a pointer to the element in the first string where the second string begins. However, if the second string does not occur in the first string, the function should return NULL.

Write a program to test the above function.

10. Write a function *replace()* whose prototype is given as

```
int replace(char *str, char c1, char c2);
```

that replace every occurrence of character *c1* with character *c2*, and returns the total replacements made.

Write a program to test the above function.

❑ ❑ ❑

Chapter 6

Constructors and Destructors

Learning Objectives

After reading this chapter, students will be able to

- explain the need of constructors and destructors
- explain the special features of constructors
- declare and define the constructor
- explain the various type of constructors
- explain the special features of destructors
- declare and define the destructor
- explain the role of initializer list

6.1 INTRODUCTION

In *Chapter 4*, we have seen that after an object is created, we use members functions like *getData()*, *setData()* to provide the initial values to the data members. This approach of initializing the data members does not conform to the philosophy of object-oriented languages such as C++, Java, etc. As we have discussed earlier that one of the objectives of C++ is to create user-defined data types, such as class that behave like built-in data types. This means that we should be able to initialize a class type variable (object) when it is declared, much the same way initialization of an ordinary variable. Likewise, when a class type variable (object) goes out of scope, it should be destroyed automatically.

Consider the following statements

```
int intVariable = 25;
float floatVariable = 12.25;
```

These statements are valid declarations and initialization statements for built-in data types. When these variables go out of scope, they are destroyed automatically.

But this is not the case with objects the way we have discussed so far. Therefore, it means that some more features are needed in the class so that objects can be initialized when they are created and destroyed when they go out of scope.

The C++ language provides following member functions to accomplish these tasks:

- ***Constructor*** - special member function that enables an object to initialize itself when it is created. This process is known as *automatic initialization*.
- ***Destructor*** - special member function that destroys the object when it goes out of scope.

This chapter describes the various aspects of these special member functions.

6.2 CONSTRUCTORS

A constructor is a special member function whose task is to initialize an object of a class when it is created. It is special in the sense that it has a name that is same as that of its class.

A constructor is automatically invoked when an object of its associated class is created. It is called constructor because it constructs object with its initial state by assigning initial values to it data members.

6.2.1 Special Characteristics of Constructors

The following are some special characteristics of a constructor:

- They are generally declared in the public section.
- Though it is not mandatory, they are usually declared before other member functions.
- They are invoked automatically when the objects of a given class are created.
- They do not have any return type.
- They cannot be inherited. However, the derived class can invoke the base class constructor.
- Like other member functions, they can be overloaded.
- They can have default arguments.
- Constructors cannot be declared as *virtual*.

6.2.2 Need of Constructors

If you remember that an array as well a structure can be initialized at the time of their declaration. Look at the following code fragments where an array and structure are initialized:

```
int abc[10] = { 0, 1, 2, 3, 4, 5, 6, 7, 8, 9 };

struct studentType
{
   int   rollno;
   char  name[25];
    int   age;
   float height;
};

studentType student = { 1000, "Surbhi Salaria", 18, 5.6 };
```

However, such initializations do not work for a class since the access for the data member is usually private or protected (if class is involved in derivation of new classes). In that case, the data members are not accessible from outside the class definition.

The following code fragment will not be acceptable:

```
class Student
{
  private:
     int   rollno;
     char  name[25];
     int   age;
     float height;
  public:
     // member functions
};
Student std = { 1000, "Surbhi Salaria", 18, 5.6 };
```

One possible alternative solution is to write a member function, say *init()*, to initialize the data members as shown below:

```
class Student
{
   private:
     int   rollno;
     char  name[25];
     int   age;
     float height;
   public:
     void init()
     {
        rollno = 1000;
        strcpy(name, "Surbhi Salaria");
        age = 18;
        height = 5.6;
     }
     // other member functions
};
Student std;  // create object
std.init();   // call to member function to initialize data members
              // immediately after the declaration of the object
```

As you can see that now we have an additional member function to give initial values to the data members. However, the programmer has to explicitly call/invoke it in order to initialize the object. In other words, responsibility of initializing the object lies with the programmer. Imagine the situation where the programmer forgets to do so. The object in that case might be full of garbage and might cause the program to behave in very unpredictable manner and even the program may cause the system to crash.

Is there any way to tackle this situation so that the object is initialized automatically as and when a new object is created?

The only answer to this situation is the use of constructor.

6.2.3 Declaration and Definition of Constructors

A constructor is a member function whose name is same as that of the class. A constructor is declared and defined in the same manner as other member functions. It is placed in the public section of the class. It can be defined in the class itself or outside the class. When the constructor is defined outside the class, its declaration is placed inside the class. These situations are illustrated in the following code fragments.

Constructor defined inside the class:

```
class Student
{
  private:
      int   rollno;
      char  name[25];
      int   age;
      float height;
  public:
      Student()      // definition of the constructor
      {
         rollno = 1000;
         strcpy(name, "Surbhi Salaria");
         age = 18;
         height = 5.6;
      }
      // other member functions
};
Student std;   // create object, constructor is invoked implicitly
```

Constructor defined outside the class:

```
class Student
{
  private:
      int   rollno;
      char  name[25];
      int   age;
      float height;
  public:
      Student();              // declaration of the constructor
```

```
    // other member functions
};
Student::Student()          // definition of the constructor
{
    rollno = 1000;
    strcpy(name, "Surbhi Salaria");
    age = 18;
    height = 5.6;
}
Student std; // create object, constructor is invoked implicitly
```

Note that constructors must be defined in the public section of the class otherwise so that objects can be created in all sections of the program. If you place the constructor in the private or protected sections of the class then object cannot be created and initialized using that constructor.

6.2.4 Default Constructor

In case no constructor is defined by the programmer for a class, then compiler automatically inserts one constructor in the class definition prior to compiling the class. This constructor has following structure

```
className() { }
```

Note that this constructor takes no arguments and does nothing as it carries no statements. You must be thinking that *what values will be assigned to the object when the object is created using the default constructor*? The garbage (unpredictable) values will be assigned to the object.

Just to confirm this, try the following program:

Listing 6.1

```
// Program to demonstrate the creation of object using
// default constructor
#include <iostream.h>
#include <iomanip.h>
class Sample
{
    private:
        int a;
        float b;
        double c;
    public:
        void  display()
```

```
    {
        cout << setiosflags ( ios::showpoint )
             << setprecision ( 2 );
        cout << "\na = " << a << endl;
        cout << "\nb = " << b << endl;
        cout << "\nc = " << c << endl;
    }
}; // end of class definition
void main()    // main program
{
   Sample obj;        // create object
   obj.display();  // display object
}
```

Test Run

```
a = 13081
b = 9.44e-41
c = 1.75e-130
```

When you run the above program, you may get different values printed.

Note that if the class contains at least one constructor, of any type, the compiler will not insert the default constructor in the class definition.

6.2.5 Zero Argument Constructor

Zero argument constructor is a kind of constructor that takes no arguments. It is used to initialize the every created object to a same specific state, *i.e.*, same initial values for all objects. This constructor has the following form

```
className()
{
   datamemeber1 = value1;
   datamemeber2 = value2;
   datamemeber3 = value3;
        :
}
```

Consider the following code fragment

```
class ComplexNumber
{
   private:
      float realPart;
```

```
        float imaginaryPart;
    public:
        ComplexNumber()                    // zero argument constructor
        {
            realPart = 0.0;
            imaginaryPart = 0.0;
        }
              // other member functions
};
void main()
{
    ComplexNumber n1, n2, n3;    // create the objects
    // more statements
}
```

The data members, *realPart* and *imaginaryPart* of all three objects – *n1*, *n2* and *n3*, are initialized to zero value.

6.2.6 Parameterized Constructors

The constructor in *ComplexNumber* class, in previous section, initializes the data members of every object of that class to zero value. However, in practice, it is required to initialize the data members of different members with different values when they are created. The C++ language permits to achieve this objective by allowing the programmer in defining a constructor that can take arguments. Such a constructor is called a *parameterized constructor*.

The following code shows the rewritten version of *ComplexNumner* class with a parameterized constructor:

```
class ComplexNumber
{
    private:
        float realPart;
        float imaginaryPart;
    public:
          // parameterized constructor that takes two real
        // number as its arguments
        ComplexNumber( float real, float imaginary )
        {
            realPart = real;
            imaginaryPart = imaginary;
        }
       // other member functions
};
```

Note that when a parameterized constructor is used, declaration statement of type

```
ComplexNumber number;
```

will not work. We have to pass initial values as arguments to the constructor when an object is declared.

This can be done in following ways:

- By calling the constructor explicitly as shown by the declarations statement

```
ComplexNumber number = ComplexNumber ( 2.0, 3.0 );
```

- By calling the constructor implicitly as shown by the declarations statement

```
ComplexNumber number ( 2.0, 3.0 );
```

The second approach, sometimes called shorthand method, is often used and we will also follow this approach.

Listing 6.2

```
// Program to demonstrate the creation of object using
// parameterized constructor with explicit call and implicit call
#include <iostream.h>
#include <iomanip.h>
class ComplexNumber
{
    private:
        float realPart;
        float imaginaryPart;
    public:
        //  parameterized constructor
        ComplexNumber( float real, float imaginary ) {
            realPart = real;
            imaginaryPart = imaginary;
        }
        // member function to output complex number
        void displayComplexNumber() {
            cout << setiosflags ( ios::showpoint )
                 << setprecision ( 2 )
                 << endl << realPart
                 << " + j" << imaginaryPart << endl;
        }
};
void main()  // main program
{
    // object created with explicit call to constructor
    ComplexNumber firstNumber = ComplexNumber(1.25,2.75);
```

```
    cout << "First Complex Number" << endl;
    firstNumber.displayComplexNumber(); // display object
    // object created with implicit call to constructor
    ComplexNumber secondNumber ( 7.5, 12.25);
    cout << endl << "First Complex Number" << endl;
    secondNumber.displayComplexNumber(); // display object
}
```

Test Run

```
First Complex Number
1.25 + j2.75
Second Complex Number
7.50 + j12.25
```

6.2.7 Copy Constructor

The parameters of a constructor can be of any type except an object of the class to which it belongs. For example, the following constructor is not acceptable.

```
class ComplexNumber
{
    private:
        float realPart;
        float imaginaryPart;
    public:
        // parameterized constructor that takes another
        // object of its own class as its argument
        ComplexNumber( ComplexNumber cn ) {
            realPart = cn.realPart;
            imaginaryPart = cn.imaginaryPart;
        }
       // other member functions
};
```

However, a constructor can accept a reference to its own class as a parameter. A constructor that accepts a reference to its own class is called a *copy constructor*. A copy constructor is used to initialize an object from another object of same class. For example, the following constructor is acceptable.

```
class ComplexNumber
{
     private:
         float realPart;
         float imaginaryPart;
```

```
public:
    //  parameterized constructor that takes reference
    //  to an object of its own class as its argument
    ComplexNumber( ComplexNumber &cn )
    {
        realPart = cn.realPart;
        imaginaryPart = cn.imaginaryPart;
    }
    // other member functions
};
```

A copy constructor is used to declare and initialize an object from another object of its class.

For example, the statement

```
ComplexNumber secondNumber ( firstNumber );
```

would declare the object *secondNumber* and initialize with the values of *firstNumber*.

The same task can also be performed in the following manner

```
ComplexNumber secondNumber = firstNumber;
```

The process of initialization with the help of a copy constructor is known as *copy initialization*.

What you can expect from the following statement when both are objects of *ComplexNumber* class?

```
secondNumber = firstNumber;
```

This statement will not invoke copy constructor, however, will assign the value of *firstNumber* to *secondNumber* member-by-member.

When no copy constructor is defined, the compiler supplies its own copy constructor.

6.2.8 Overloaded Constructors

In the previous example, we have used the default constructor, zero argument constructor, parameterized constructor or copy constructor. However, the C++ language permits to use all of these constructors in a same class. The constructor actually used in initializing an object depends on the way the object is declared.

Consider the following definition of *ComplexNumber* class that contains three types of constructors:

```
class ComplexNumber
{
   private:
      float realPart;
      float imaginaryPart;
   public:
     //  zero argument constructor
      ComplexNumber()
      {
         realPart = 0.0;
         imaginaryPart = 0.0;
      }
      // parameterized constructor that takes two real
      // number as its arguments
      ComplexNumber( float real, float imaginary )
      {
         realPart = real;
         imaginaryPart = imaginary;
      }
      //  parameterized constructor that takes reference
       //  to an object of its own class as its argument
      ComplexNumber( ComplexNumber & cn )
      {
         realPart = cn.realPart;
         imaginaryPart = cn.imaginaryPart;
      }
       // other member functions
};
```

The declaration statement of type

```
ComplexNumber thirdNumber;
```

will invoke the zero argument constructor that initializes both its data members *realPart* and *imaginaryPart* to zero..

The declaration statement of type

```
ComplexNumber thirdNumber ( 1.5, 10.5 );
```

will invoke the parameterized constructor that takes two real numbers as its arguments that initializes *realPart* data member to 1.5 and *imaginaryPart* data member to 10.5.

The declaration statement of type

```
ComplexNumber thirdNumber ( secondNumber );
```

will invoke the copy constructor that takes reference to an object as its arguments and copies the value of data members *realPart* and *imaginaryPart* of object *secondNumber* to data members *realPart* and *imaginaryPart* of object *thirdNumber*, respectively.

Listing 6.3

```
// Program to demonstrate overloading of multiple constructors
#include <iostream.h>
#include <iomanip.h>
class ComplexNumber
{
   private:
      float realPart;
      float imaginaryPart;
   public:
         //  zero argument constructor
       ComplexNumber() {
          realPart = 0.0;
          imaginaryPart = 0.0;
       }
       //  parameterized constructor
       ComplexNumber( float real, float imaginary ) {
         realPart = real;
         imaginaryPart = imaginary;
       }
       //  parameterized constructor that takes reference
       //  to an object of its own class as its argument
       ComplexNumber( ComplexNumber & cn ) {
         realPart = cn.realPart;
         imaginaryPart = cn.imaginaryPart;
       }
       // member function to output complex number
       void  displayComplexNumber() {
         cout << setiosflags ( ios::showpoint )
             << setprecision ( 2 ) << endl
             << realPart << " + j"
             << imaginaryPart << endl;
       }
};
void main()  // main program
{
    // create object with zero argument constructor
    ComplexNumber firstNumber;
```

```
        cout << "First Complex Number = ";
        firstNumber.displayComplexNumber(); // display object
        // create object with parameterized constructor that takes
        // two real number as its arguments
        ComplexNumber secondNumber ( 70.5, 120.25 );
        cout << endl << "Second Complex Number = ";
        secondNumber.displayComplexNumber(); // display object
        // create object with parameterized constructor that takes
        // reference to object as its argument (copy constructor)
        ComplexNumber thirdNumber ( secondNumber );
        cout << endl << "Third Complex Number = ";
        secondNumber.displayComplexNumber(); // display object
}
```

Test Run

```
First Complex Number
0.00 + j0.00
Second Complex Number
70.50 + j120.25
Third Complex Number
70.50 + j120.25
```

6.2.9 Constructors With Default Arguments

Like other functions, a constructor can also have default arguments. But remember that the default arguments must be trailing ones. For example, the parameterized constructor for *ComplexNumber* class that takes two real numbers as its argument can be written as

```
// parameterized constructor that takes two real
// number as its arguments, with second argument
// as default argument with default value 0.0
ComplexNumber( float real, float imaginary = 0.0 )
{
    realPart = real;
    imaginaryPart = imaginary;
}
```

Then the statement

```
CompexNumber fourthNumber ( 22.5 );
```

assigns value 22.5 to *realPart* and 0.0 to *imaginaryPart*.

However, the statement

```
CompexNumber fifthNumber ( 22.5, 33.5 );
```

assigns value 22.5 to *realPart* and 33.5 to *imaginaryPart*.

Thus, the actual parameter, when specified overrides the default value.

Listing 6.4

```
//  Program to demonstrate use of parameterized constructor
//  with default arguments
#include <iostream.h>
#include <iomanip.h>
class ComplexNumber
{
    private:
       float realPart;
       float imaginaryPart;
    public:
       // parameterized constructor that takes two real
       // number as its arguments, with second argument
       // as default argument with default value 0.0
       ComplexNumber( float real, float imaginary = 0.0 )
       {
          realPart = real;
          imaginaryPart = imaginary;
       }
       // member function to output complex number
       void  displayComplexNumber()
       {
         cout << setiosflags ( ios::showpoint )
               << setprecision ( 2 )
               << endl << realPart
               << " + j" << imaginaryPart << endl;
       }
};
void main()  // main program
{
    // create object using constructor with only one argument
    ComplexNumber firstNumber ( 22.5 );
    cout << "First Complex Number = ";
    firstNumber.displayComplexNumber(); // display object
    // create object using constructor with two arguments
    ComplexNumber secondNumber ( 22.5, 33.5 );
    cout << endl << "Second Complex Number = ";
    secondNumber.displayComplexNumber(); // display object
}
```

Test Run

```
First Complex Number
22.50 + j0.00
Second Complex Number
22.50 + j33.50
```

If we use two constructors in a class where one is a default constructor and the other is parameterized constructor that takes one argument that is declared as default. This situation can cause ambiguity. This situation is illustrated in following example.

Consider the following class

```
class OnlyNumber
{
    private:
        int number;
    public:
        //  zero argument constructor
        OnlyNumber()  {
            number = 0;
        }
        // parameterized constructor with default argument
        OnlyNumber( int num = 5 )
        {
            number = num;
        }
        // other member functions
};
```

Here, it is important to distinguish between the default constructor *OnlyNumber()* and the parameterized constructor *OnlyNumber(int)* with default argument. If we declare an object with statement

```
OnlyNumber firstNumber;
```

It causes confusion and ambiguity regarding whether to call *OnlyNumber()* or *OnlyNumber(int)*. This type of situations must be taken care of.

Listing 6.5

```
// Program to demonstrate ambiguity that arises when a class
// contains default constructor and parameterized constructor
// with one argument that is also declared as default argument
#include <iostream.h>
```

```
#include <iostream.h>
class OnlyNumber
{
    private:
       int number;
    public:
       //  zero argument constructor
       OnlyNumber() {
          number = 0;
       }
       // parameterized constructor with default argument
       OnlyNumber( int num = 5 ) {
          number = num;
       }
        //  show number
       void showNumber()
       {
          cout << "\nNumber = " << endl;
       }
};
void main()   // main program
{
    OnlyNumber firstNumber;         // create object
    firstNumber.showNumber();       // show the data member
}
```

When attempt is made to compile this program the compiler flags the following error message

```
Ambiguity between 'OnlyNumber::OnlyNumber()' and
'OnlyNumber::OnlyNumber(int)'
```

6.2.10 Dynamic Initialization of Objects

Till this section we have initialized the objects at declarations time. However, the objects can also be initialized at program execution time, called *dynamic initialization*. One of the advantages dynamic initialization formats using overloaded constructors. This provides flexibility of using different formats of data at run time depending upon the situation.

Listing 6.6

```
//  Program to demonstrate use of dynamic initialization
//  of objects at runtime
#include <iostream.h>
#include <iomanip.h>
```

```
class ComplexNumber
{
    private:
        float realPart;
        float imaginaryPart;
    public:
        // parameterized constructor that takes two real
        // number as its arguments
        ComplexNumber( float real, float imaginary )
        {
            realPart = real;
            imaginaryPart = imaginary;
        }
        // member function to output complex number
        void  displayComplexNumber()
        {
            cout << setiosflags ( ios::showpoint )
                 << setprecision ( 2 ) << endl
                 << realPart
                 << " + j" << imaginaryPart << endl;
        }
};
void main()  // main program
{
    float real, imag;
    cout << "Enter real part of Complex Number = ";
    cin >> real;
    cout << "Enter imaginary part of Complex Number = ";
    cin >> imag;
    // dynamic initialization of object
    ComplexNumber firstNumber ( real, imag );
    cout << endl
        << "Dynamically initialized Complex Number = ";
    firstNumber.displayComplexNumber(); // display object
}
```

Test Run

```
Enter real part of Complex Number = 15.75
Enter imaginary part of Complex Number = 25.5

Dynamically initialized Complex Number = 15.75 + j25.50
```

In this program user inputs the real and imaginary part of the number, and using these values an object named *firsNumber* of *ComplexNumber* class is created.

6.2.11 Dynamic Constructors

Constructors can also be used to allocate memory while creating objects. This will allow the system to allocate the desired amount of memory for each object when the objects are not of same size, thus resulting in the saving of the memory. Allocation of memory to objects at the time of their construction is known as dynamic construction of objects. The memory is allocated with *new* operator.

Listing 6.7

```
//  Program to demonstrate dynamic construction of objects
#include <iostream.h>
#include <iomanip.h>
#include <string.h>
class MyString
{
    private:
       char *stringName;
       int length;
    public:
       MyString () {// zero argument constructor
          length = 0;
          stringName = new char [ length + 1 ];
       }
       // parameterized constructor that takes string as argument
       MyString ( char *str ) {
          length = strlen ( str );
          stringName = new char [ length + 1 ];
          strcpy ( stringName, str );
       }
       // member function to display the string
       void  displayString() {
          cout << endl << stringName << endl;
       }
};
void main()  // main program
{
    char *temp = "C++ Programming";
    MyString myString ( temp );
    myString.displayString();
}
```

Test Run

```
C++ Programming
```

6.2.12 Explicit Constructors

Consider the following class definition

```
class Sample
{
    private:
          int a;
    public:
          Sample(int x)
          {
            a = x;
          }
          // . . .
};
```

The constructor for *Sample* class takes one parameter. In order to create an object of *Sample* class, we generally write either of the following statements

```
Sample obj(5);          OR       Sample obj = Sample(5);
```

This statement will create an object named *obj* of *Sample* class and initialize its dada member *a* with integer value 5.

However, the same object can also be created by using the following statement

```
Sample obj = 5;
```

This statement will automatically be converted in to a call to the *Sample* constructor with 5 being the argument, *i.e.*, the statement is handled by the compiler if it were written like

```
Sample obj(5);
```

Note that this type of implicit conversion happens only for a constructor with single argument. However, if you do not want this implicit conversion to happen, you can prevent it by prefixing the keyword *explicit* before the single argument constructor as shown below:

```
class Sample
{
    private:
        int a;
    public:
```

```
        explicit Sample(int x) {
            a = x;
        }
        // . . .
};
```

Now only statements like

```
Sample obj(5);        OR        Sample obj = Sample(5);
```

will work, and the statement like

```
Sample obj = 5;
```

will not be allowed. Doing so will cause a syntax error.

6.3 DESTRUCTORS

A destructor, as its name implies, is a special member function that is used to release the resource held by the object before the object is destroyed. Like a constructor, the destructor also has the same name as that of class but is preceded by character tilde ('~').

For example, the destructor for *ComplexNumber* class will be defined as

```
~ComplexNumber() { . . . }
```

6.3.1 Special Characteristics of Destructors

Like constructors, destructors also have some special characteristics that are listed below:

- They are declared in the public section.
- Though it is not mandatory, they are usually declared after other member functions.
- They are invoked automatically when the objects go out of scope.
- They do not have any return type.
- They cannot be inherited. However, the derived class can invoke the base class destructor.
- They don't have any argument.
- They cannot be overloaded.
- Destructors can be declared as *virtual*.
- A destructor can call other member functions.

6.3.2 Need of Destructors

During construction of an object by the constructor, resources may be allocated for use. Constructor may have opened files, may have created a connection to another computer on the network or internet, or may have allocated memory dynamically.

These allocated resources must be deallocated (released) before the object is destroyed.

One possible alternative solution is to write a member function, say *destroy()*, to deallocate the resources held by the object as shown below:

```
class Sample
{
    private:
        // data members
    public:
        void destroy()
        {
            // statement to release the resources
        }
        // other member functions
};
Sample obj;    // create object
// more statements
obj.destroy();    // call to member function to release the resources
```

As you can see that now we have an additional member function to release the resources held by the object. However, the programmer has to explicitly call/invoke it in order to release the resources before the object is destroyed (the control leaves the function in which the object was created). In other words, responsibility of deallocating the resources held by the object lies with the programmer. Imagine the situation where the programmer forgets to do so. The situation may arise when the system may run out of resources and may not be in a position provide them to other programs wanting for these resources.

Is there any way to tackle this situation so that the when the object is going to be destroyed the resources should be deallocated automatically as and when the object is destroyed?

The only answer to this situation is the use of destructor.

6.3.3 Declaration and Definition of Destructors

A destructor is a member function whose name is same as that of the class but is prefixed with character tilde '~'. Note that a destructor takes no arguments. It is declared and defined in the same manner as other member functions. It is placed in the public section of the class. It can be defined in the class itself or outside the class. When the constructor is defined outside the class, its declaration is placed inside the class. These situations are illustrated in the following code fragments.

Destructor defined inside the class:

```
class Sample
{
    private:
        // data members
    public:
        ~Sample() {           // definition of the destructor
            // statements for the destructor
        }
        // other member functions
};
```

Destructor defined outside the class:

```
class Sample
{
    private:
        // data members
    public:
        ~Sample();    // declaration of the destructor
        // other member functions
}; // end of class definition
Sample :: ~Sample() // definition of the destructor
{
    // statements for the destructor
}
```

The following program illustrates the dynamic construction of a two-dimensional array as data member of class to hold a matrix of size $m \times n$. The destructor is used to free the allocated memory with *new* operator.

Listing 6.8

```
// Program to demonstrate dynamic construction of objects
#include <iostream.h>
#include <iomanip.h>
#include <conio.h>
```

```
class Matrix
{
  private:
     int **ptrVariable;  // pointer to a pointer
     int m;                          // number of rows
     int n;                          // number of columns
  public:
     // declaration of parameterized constructor that takes
     // two integer number as its arguments that represents
     // size of matrix
     Matrix ( int rows, int cols );
     // member function to assign each element of matrix
     void  setElement( int i, int j, int value ) {
          ptrVariable[i][j] = value;
     }
     // member function to retrieve element of matrix
     int retrieveElement( int i, int j ) {
          return  ptrVariable[i][j];
     }
     // member function to display the matrix
     void  displayMatrix();
    // declaration of destructor that deallocate memory
    // allocated to matrix using new operator in constructor
    ~Matrix ();
};
// definition of constructor
Matrix :: Matrix ( int rows, int cols )
{
   m = rows;
   n = cols;
   // allocate memory for array of pointer
   ptrVariable = new int *[m];
   // allocate memory for each row
   for ( int i = 0; i < m; i++ )
       ptrVariable[i] = new int [n];
}
// definition of destructor
Matrix :: ~Matrix()
{
   for ( int i = 0; i < m; i++ ) {
       // deallocate memory for each row
       delete ptrVariable[i];
   }
   // deallocate memory array of pointers
   delete ptrVariable;
}
void Matrix :: displayMatrix()
{
   for ( int i = 0; i < m; i++ ) {
```

```
        for ( int j = 0; j < n; j++ ) {
            cout << setw ( 4 )
                 << ptrVariable[i][j];
        }
        cout << endl;
    }
}
void main()   // main program
{
    int i, j, value, rows, cols;
    clrscr();
    cout << "Enter size of matrix as m n : ";
    cin >> rows >> cols;
    Matrix firstMatrix ( rows, cols );
    cout << "Enter " << rows * cols
         << " elements of matrix row wise " << endl;
    for ( i = 0; i < rows; i++ ) {
        for ( int j = 0; j < cols; j++ ) {
            cin >> value;
            firstMatrix.setElement ( i, j, value );
        }
    }
    cout << "\nMatrix entered by you" << endl << endl;
    firstMatrix.displayMatrix();
    // changeelement at (1, 2)
    firstMatrix.setElement ( 1, 2, 12 );
    cout << endl
         << "Matrix after changing value at row 1 column 2"
         << endl << endl;
    firstMatrix.displayMatrix();
}
```

Test Run

```
Enter size of matrix as m n : 3 3
Enter 9 elements of matrix row wise
1 1 1 2 2 2 3 3 3

Matrix entered by you

   1   1   1
   2   2   2
   3   3   3

Matrix after changing value at row 1 column 2

   1   1   1
   2   2  12
   3   3   3
```

The constructor first creates a one-dimensional array of pointers to *int* of size *m* (3). Then it allocates one-dimensional array of type *int* of size *n* (3) for each value of *i*. The final memory for *firstMatrix* of size 3×3 is shown in Figure 6.1.

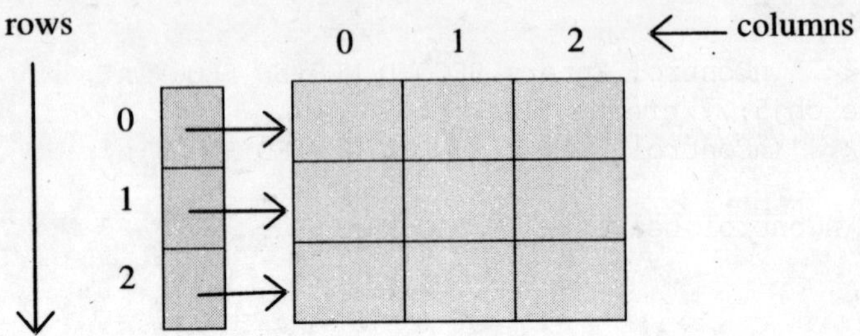

Figure 6.1: Dynamic allocation for object *firstMatrix* of size 3×3

A destructor is invoked implicitly (automatically) when an object goes out of scope. Therefore, as soon as the program finishes its execution the destructor is invoked. The *destructor* first deallocates the memory allocated for each one-dimensional array (row) and then deallocates the memory allocated for one-dimensional array of pointers. This way a *firstMatrix* object is destroyed. Following program further illustrates invoking of constructors and destructors.

Listing 6.9

```
//  Program to demonstrate the invoking of constructors
//  and destructors
#include <iostream.h>
#include <iomanip.h>
// global variable to track number of objects created
int count = 0;
class Sample {
    public:
        Sample() {    // zero argument constructor
           count++;          // increment object count
           cout << "\nConstructor invoked\n"
                << "Current object count = "<<count<<endl;
        }
        ~Sample()    {         // destructor
           count--;          // decrement object count
           cout << "\nDestructor invoked\n"
                << "Current object count = "<<count<<endl;
        }
};    // end of class definition
void main()  // main program
{
    cout << endl << "Control Enters MAIN BLOCK" << endl;
    Sample obj1, obj2, obj3;      // create three objects
```

```
    {
        cout << "\nControl Enters FIRST NESTED BLOCK\n";
        Sample obj4;// create fourths object
        cout << "\nControl Leaves FIRST NESTED BLOCK\n";
    }
    {
        cout << "\nControl Enters SECOND NESTED BLOCK\n";
        Sample obj5;// create fifth object
        cout << "\nControl Leaves SECOND NESTED BLOCK\n";
    }
    cout << "\nControl Leaves MAIN BLOCK\n";
}
```

Test Run

```
Control Enters MAIN BLOCK

Constructor invoked
Current object count = 1

Constructor invoked
Current object count = 2

Constructor invoked
Current object count = 3

Control Enters FIRST NESTED BLOCK

Constructor invoked
Current object count = 4

Control Leaves FIRST NESTED BLOCK

Destructor invoked
Current object count = 3

Control Enters SECOND NESTED BLOCK

Constructor invoked
Current object count = 4

Control Leaves SECOND NESTED BLOCK

Destructor invoked
Current object count = 3

Control Leaves MAIN BLOCK

Destructor invoked
Current object count = 2

Destructor invoked
Current object count = 1

Destructor invoked
Current object count = 0
```

6.4 CONSTRUCTORS & DESTRUCTORS WITH STATIC MEMBERS

The static data member is useful when all the objects of the same class must share a common piece of information. Memory is allocated for static variables when the class is loaded and only one copy of the class variables is kept irrespective of number of objects of that class. Every object has access to class variables. A static variable is initialized before the *main()* function.

The one possible use of static data member is to keep track of number of objects of a class. There may be situation when object wants to know how many other objects of its class are in the program. For example, in a road-racing game, a race car might want to know how many other cars are still in the race. In this case, a static variable, say *count*, can be included as a member of the class. All objects would have access to this data member and it would be the same count for all.

The constructors and destructors, being member functions, can access the static data members in the same way as other member functions. The following program demonstrates this.

Listing 6.10

```
// Program to demonstrate the use of constructors and destructors
// with static members
#include <iostream.h>
#include <iomanip.h>
class Sample
{
    private:
        static int count;
        int x, y;
    public:
        Sample() {      // zero argument constructor
            count++;    // increment object count
            cout << "\nIncluding newly created object,"
                 << " the object count = " << count << endl;
        }
        ~Sample() {     // destructor
        {
            count--;    // decrement object count
            cout << "\nExcluding object being destroyed,"
                 << " the object count = " << count << endl;
        }
};      // end of class definition
int Sample::count = 0;
void main()
{
    Sample s1, s2, s3;
}
```

Test Run

```
Including newly created object, the object count = 1
Including newly created object, the object count = 2
Including newly created object, the object count = 3
Excluding object being destroyed, the object count = 2
Excluding object being destroyed, the object count = 1
Excluding object being destroyed, the object count = 0
```

6.5 INITIALIZER LIST

The most common task of a constructor is to initialize the data members. This initialization takes place in the body of the constructor function. There is another approach of doing so, where the initialization takes place following the function declarator but before the function body. A colon precedes the initializer list. The value is placed in parentheses following the data member name. The following example illustrates this.

```
class Example
{
    private:
        int a;
        int b;
        int c;
  public:
        Example( int i, int j, int k ) : a(j), b(i), c(k) { }
        void show() {
            // . . .
        }
};
```

When we create an object as shown

```
Example obj(1,2,3);
```

The constructor is invoked and values 1, 2 and 3 are passed as arguments, which are collected in formal arguments *i*, *j* and *k*. These values are collected in data members *a*, *b* and *c*, respectively. This happens even before the constructor start executing.

This approach is important in some situations. One such situation is where a data member is *const*. A *const* data member cannot be initialized in the body of the constructor. An attempt of doing so will be treated as an attempt of modifying the value of a *const* and compiler will flag a syntax error.

Consider the following example:

```
class Example
{
    private:
        const float pie;
        int k;
    public:
        Example( float a, int b )
        {
            pie = a;
            k = b;
        }
        void show()
        {
            cout << "\nPie = " << pie << "\nk = " << k <<endl;
        }
};
```

When we create an object as shown

```
Example obj(3.142,12);
```

Compiler will generate the message "*Constant member 'pie' is not initialized*" followed by message "*Cannot modify const object*".

However, the problem will be solved if we write the code as

```
class Example
{
    private:
        const float pie;
        int k;
    public:
        Example( float a, int b ) : pie(a)
        {
            k = b;
        }
        void show() {
            cout << "\nPie = " << pie << "\nk = " << k <<endl;
        }
};
```

QUICK RECAP

In this chapter, we have learnt that

- Constructors and destructors are member functions that perform the automatic initialization and cleanup for the objects.
- Constructors can be overloaded whereas destructors cannot be overloaded.
- A constructor can have default argument.
- If a class has at least one parameterized constructors, it will be programmer's duty to provide the zero argument constructor in the class.
- Constructor and destructors have same name as that of class.
- A copy constructor is a special constructor that is used to create an object from an existing object. If there is no copy constructor in the class, compiler provides default copy constructor.
- *Const* data members can only be initialized through initializer list.

MULTIPLE CHOICE QUESTIONS

1. Given a class named *Book*, which of the following is not a valid constructor?

   (*a*) Book () { }
   (*b*) Book (Book b) { }
   (*c*) Book (Book &b) { }
   (*d*) Book (char *author, char *title) { }

2. Which of the following statement is not true about a constructor?

   (*a*) Constructors are not inherited.
   (*b*) Constructors can be overloaded.
   (*c*) Constructors can be made virtual.
   (*d*) Constructors can have default arguments.

3. Which of the following statements is not true about a destructor?

   (*a*) Destructors are not inherited.
   (*b*) Destructors cannot call other member functions.
   (*c*) Destructors can be made virtual.
   (*d*) Destructors cannot be overloaded.

4. Which of the following statement is true about *const* data member of a class?

   (*a*) A class cannot have *const* data members.
   (*b*) A *const* data member can be initialized inside the constructor.

(*c*) A *const* data member can be initialized before the main function.
(*d*) A *const* data member can only be initialized through initializer list.

5. Which of the following statements is not true about a copy constructor?

(*a*) It takes reference to an object of its own class as its argument.
(*b*) It is used to create an object from another object of its own class.
(*c*) It can be made virtual.
(*d*) If programmer has not provided copy constructor, compiler inserts copy constructor from its own.

6. In which case it is mandatory to provide a destructor in a class?

(*a*) Almost in every class.
(*b*) Class for which two or more than two objects will be created.
(*c*) Class for which copy constructor is defined.
(*d*) Class whose object will be created dynamically.

7. Consider the following skeleton of code.

```
class SampleClass
{
   private:
      int a;
      int b;
   public:
      SampleClass()
      {
            // . . .
      }
      SampleClass( int i = 5, int j = 6 )
      {
            // . . .
       }
      // . . .
};
void main()
{
   SampleClass obj1(3,12);
   // . . .
};
```

Which of the following statement is true?

(*a*) Program will compile successfully.
(*b*) There will be ambiguity.
(*c*) Problem in the class definition as constructors cannot be overloaded.
(*d*) None of above.

8. Consider the following skeleton of code.

```
class Example {
   private:
      static int count;
      int k;
   public:
     Example( int b ) {
        count++;
        k = b;
     }
     void show() {
        // . . .
     }
};
void main()
{
   Example obj(12);
   // . . .
}
```

Which of the following statement is true?

(*a*) Program will compile successfully.
(*b*) Static variable cannot be modified in constructor.
(*c*) Static variable *count* not initialized.
(*d*) None of above.

9. Consider the following skeleton of code.

```
class Example
{
   private:
      const float pie;
      int k;
   public:
      Example( float a, int b ) {
         pie = a;
         k = b;
      }
      void show() {
         // . . .
      }
};
void main()
{
   Example obj(3.142, 12);
   // . . .
}
```

Which of the following statement is true?

(*a*) A class cannot have *const* data member.
(*b*) The *const* data member must be initialized in the class itself.
(*c*) The *const* data member cannot be initialized in the constructor.
(*d*) None of above.

10. Given a class named *Book* that has *author* and *title* as its data members, which of the following is valid copy constructor?

(*a*) Book (Book b) { }
(*b*) Book (char *author, char *title) { }
(*c*) Book (Book *b) { }
(*d*) Book (Book &b) { }

REVIEW EXERCISES

1. What is a constructor? Is it mandatory that every class must have constructor?
2. What are the characteristics of a constructor?
3. What is a destructor? Is it mandatory that every class must have destructor?
4. What are the characteristics of a destructor?
5. When is it mandatory for a class to have a destructor?
6. What is a copy constructor?
7. A class has a default constructor and a parameterized constructor with all its arguments as default argument. When an object of the class is created invoking default constructor explicitly, what situation can arise?
8. Is any thing wrong with the following code? If yes, make the necessary fix.

```
class Example
{
    private:
        static int count;
        int k;
    public:
        Example( int b )
        {
            count++;
            k = b;
        }
        void show()
        {
            cout <<"\nCount = " <<count<<"\nk = "<<k<<"\n";
        }
};
```

```
void main()
{
   Example obj(12);
   obj.show();
}
```

9. Is any thing wrong with the following code? If yes, make the necessary fix.

```
class SampleClass
{
   private:
      int a;
      int b;
   public:
      SampleClass( int i, int j )
      {
         a = i;
         b = j;
      }
      void show() {
         cout << "\na = " << a << "\nb = " << b << "\n";
      }
};
void main()
{
   SampleClass obj1(3,12);
   obj1.show();
   SampleClass obj2;
   obj2.show();
}
```

10. What will be the order of execution of constructors in the following program?

```
class Date
{
   // members defined here
};
class Time
{
   // members defined here
};
class Train
{
   private:
      Date depDate; // departure date
      Time depTime; // departure time
   // other members defined here
};
```

```
void main()
{
    Time t1;
    Train tr1;
    Date d1;
    // remaining code goes here
}
```

11. What will be the output when the following program is executed?

```
class Check
{
   public:
      Check()
      {
          calculate();
          cout << "Constructor";
      }
      void calculate()
      {
          show();
          cout << "Calculating ";
      }
      void show()
      {
          cout << "\nI am displaying ";
      }
};
void main()
{
   Check chk;
}
```

12. How many times copy constructor will be invoked in the following code?

```
class Sample
{
    private:
       int i;                                  // data members
    public:
       Sample()
       {                                       // zero argument constructor
          i = 5;
       }
       Sample(Sample &c)                       // copy constructor
       {
          i = c.i;
       }
       ~Sample() {                             // destructor
       }
       friend Sample func(Sample y);           // friend function
}; // end of class definition
```

```
Sample func(Sample y)
{
    Sample x(y);
    Sample z = x;
    return z;
}
void main()
{
    Sample a;
    Sample b = func(a);
}
```

PROGRAMMING EXERCISES

1. Design a class from which only one object can be created. If more than one object is created, then the program should terminate.
2. Design a class named *Time* with *hours*, *minutes* and *seconds* (all of type *int*) as its data members declared in private section of the class. Define the following constructors for the class:
   (*i*) Zero argument constructor that initialize the *hours*, *minutes* and *seconds* data members to 2, 10 and 35 respectively.
   (*ii*) Parameterized constructor that takes time in *seconds* as its only argument and initialize the *hours*, *minutes* and *seconds* data members with appropriate values.
   (*iii*) Parameterized constructor which takes three arguments, all of which are declared with default values as 2, 10 and 35 respectively, and initializes the *hours*, *minutes* and *seconds* data members with corresponding arguments.
   (*iv*) Copy constructor.
3. Design a class named *Distance* with *feets* and *inches* (both of type *float*) as its data members declared in private section of the class. Define the following constructors for the class:
   (*i*) Zero argument constructor that initialize the *feets* and *inches* data members to 2 and 35 respectively.
   (*ii*) Parameterized constructor that takes distance in *inches* as its only argument and initialize the *feets* and *inches* data members with appropriate values.
   (*iii*) Parameterized constructor which takes two arguments, both are declared with default values as 2 and 35 respectively, and initializes the *feets* and *inches* data members with corresponding arguments.
   (*iv*) Copy constructor.

4. Design a class named *Date* with *day*, *month* and *year* (all of type *int*) as its data members declared in private section of the class. Define the following constructors for the class:
   (*i*) Zero argument constructor that initialize the *day*, *month* and *year* data members to 12, 3 and 1993 respectively.
   (*ii*) Parameterized constructor which takes three arguments, all of which are declared with default values as 12, 10 and 2000 respectively, and initializes the *day*, *month* and *year* data members with corresponding arguments.
   (*iii*) Copy constructor.
5. Create a class to model a point in 3D space, with following specifications:

   Data Members:

   x, *y*, and *z* as coordinates of a 3D point that are of type *int*.

   Constructors:

   To create a 3D point representing the origin

   To create a 3D point representing an arbitrary point

   To create a 3D point from another 3D point

   Member Functions:

   To input the coordinates of a 3D point

   To output the coordinates of a 3D point in the form (*x*,*y*,*z*)

   To compute the distance between two points

   Write a program to use this class.

❑ ❑ ❑

Chapter 7

Operator Overloading and Type Conversion

Learning Objectives

After reading this chapter, students will be able to

- explain the concept of overloading and its usefulness
- explain the syntax for operator function for overloading an operator
- explain the overloading using member functions and friend functions
- explain the various rules for overloading operators
- overload various operators
- explain the concept of type conversion
- explain various kind of possible type conversions
- implement type conversion in source class as well as destination class

7.1 INTRODUCTION

Operator overloading is one of the exciting features of C++ and it aims to make user-defined data types behave much like built-in data types. Like built-in data types, operator overloading facilitates the use of most of the operations permissible on user-defined data types. These operations include input/output, arithmetic operations, comparisons and assignment. This means that C++ has the facility to provide the operators new meanings as per user-defined data type. This mechanism of giving new meanings to an operator is known as *operator overloading*.

It is important to note that the semantics of an operator can be extended but its syntax can't be changed. This precisely means that the rules that govern its use such as number of operands, precedence and associatively cannot be changed.

7.2 DEFINING OPERATOR OVERLOADING

To give an additional meaning to an operator, we must specify what it means in relation to the class to which the operator is applied. This is done with the help of a special function, called *operator function*, which describes the task. The general syntax for overloading an operator is

```
[friend] ReturnType operator op ( argList )
{
    // function body defining the task
}
```

Figure 7.1: Syntax for overloading an operator

where *op* is the operator being overloaded and *argList* is the list of arguments for the operator that may be empty.

Operator function is either non-static member function or friend function. The basic difference between them is that a friend function will have only one argument for unary operators and two for binary operators while a member function has no argument for unary operators and only one for binary operators. This is because that an object that is used to invoke a member function is passed explicitly and therefore is available for the member function.

This is not the case for friend function. Arguments can be passed either by value or by reference.

The process of overloading involves the following steps:

- Create a class that defines a data type that is to be used for overloading an operator.
- Declare the *operator function op(argList)* in the public part of the class. It can be a member function or friend function.
- Define the operator function to implement the required operation.

Overloaded operator functions can be invoked in following ways:

Using Member Functions:

For unary operators

`op operand` **OR** `operand op`

For binary operators

```
operand1 op operand2
```

and will be interpreted as

```
operand1.operator op(operand2)
```

Using Friend Functions:

For unary operators

```
operator op(operand)
```

For binary operators

operator op (operand1, operand2)

When both the member functions and friend functions are used then standard argument matching is applied to resolve the ambiguity.

7.3 RULES FOR OVERLOADING OPERATORS

The following are some restrictions that must be observed while overloading operators:

- Only existing operators can be overloaded. New operators cannot be created.
- The overloaded operator must have at least one operand of user-defined data type.
- We should not change the meaning of the operator for their behaviour for the built in data types. This precisely means that, for example, we cannot make the plus '+' to subtract one value from the other.
- The overloaded operators follow the syntax rules of the original operators. They cannot be overridden.
- The following operators cannot be overloaded.

Table 7.1: Operators that cannot be overloaded

Operator	Description
sizeof	Size of operator
.	Membership operator
.*	Pointer-to-member operator
::	Scope resolution operator
:?	Conditional operator

- Friend function cannot be used to overload the following operators; however, the member functions can be used.

Table 7.2: Operators where a friend function cannot be used

Operator	Description
=	Assignment operator
()	Function call operator
[]	Subscripting operator
–>	Class member access operator

- Unary operators overloaded by means of a member function take no parameter and returns no value, but overloaded by means of friend function take one parameter of its class and return a value.
- Binary operators overloaded by means of a member function take single parameter and return a value, but overloaded by means of friend function take two parameters of its class and return a value.

7.4 OVERLOADING OF UNARY OPERATORS

In this section, we will consider the overloading of unary operators.

7.4.1 Overloading of Increment and Decrement Operators

When increment (++) and decrement (--) operator is used as prefix, its value is first incremented and decremented, respectively, and then used. However, if used as postfix, first its value is used and then incremented and decremented.

Consider the following *Counter* class

```
class Counter
{
  private:
     int counterValue;
  public:
     Counter()                  // zero argument constructor
     {
       counterValue = 5;
     }
     // overloading of increment operator
     void operator ++ () {
       counterValue++;
     }
     // overloading of decrement operator
     void operator -- ()
     {
       counterValue--;
     }
     void showCounter() {       // display counter value
        cout << "\nCurrent counter value = "
               << counterValue << endl;
     }
}; // end of Counter class definition
```

Note that the overloaded increment and decrement operators can be used on user-defined data type in the prefix form. In the postfix form the compiler will give a warning message like

```
Overloaded prefix 'operator ++' used as a postfix operator
```

But still the system will execute the program.

Note that when these operators are overloaded, no difference exists between prefix and postfix operator loaded functions. Therefore, system has no way of determining that whether these operators are overloaded for prefix or postfix operations. Hence, these operators must be overloaded in such a way that work both for prefix and postfix operations.

To make a distinction between prefix and postfix notation of these operators, the following syntax is used

```
operator ++ ()       // prefix notation
operator ++ (int)    // postfix notation
```

In the above syntax, the use of *int* in parentheses is to indicate the compiler that this operator is being overloaded for postfix use.

Therefore, for *Counter* class, these operators must be overloaded as shown below:

```
// overloading of increment operator for prefix notation
void operator ++ ()
{
   ++counterValue;
}
// overloading of increment operator for postfix notation
void operator ++ (int)
{
   counterValue++;
}
// overloading of decrement operator for prefix notation
void operator -- ()
{
   --counterValue;
}
// overloading of decrement operator for postfix notation
void operator -- (int)
{
   counterValue--;
}
```

The following listing demonstrates the use of *Counter* class.

Listing 7.1

```
// Program to demonstrate the overloading of increment and
// decrement operators

#include <iostream.h>
#include <iomanip.h>

class Counter
{
    private:
```

```
        int counterValue;
    public:
        Counter() {  // zero argument constructor
        {
            counterValue = 5;
            cout << "\nCounter's initial value = "
                 << counterValue << endl;
        }
        // overloading of increment operator for prefix notation
        void operator ++ ()
        {
            ++counterValue;
        }
        // overloading of increment operator for postfix notation
        void operator ++ (int)
        {
            counterValue++;
        }
        // overloading of decrement operator for prefix notation
        void operator -- ()
        {
            --counterValue;
        }
        // overloading of decrement operator for postfix notation
        void operator -- (int)
        {
            counterValue--;
        }
        // display counter value
        void showCounter()
        {
            cout << "\nCurrent counter value = "
                 << counterValue << endl;
        }
}; // end of Counter class definition
void main()  // main program
{
    // create counter object
    Counter counter;
     ++counter;              // increment counter
    counter.showCounter();
    counter++;              // increment counter once more
    counter.showCounter();
    --counter;              // decrement counter
    counter.showCounter();
    counter--;              // decrement counter once more
    counter.showCounter();
}   // end of main function
```

Test Run

```
Counter's initial value = 5
Current counter value = 6
Current counter value = 7
Current counter value = 6
Current counter value = 5
```

7.4.2 Overloading of Unary Minus Operator

The following program illustrates the overloading of unary minus operator.

Listing 7.2

```
// Program to demonstrate overloading of unary minus operator
#include <iostream.h>
#include <iomanip.h>
class ComplexNumber {
   private:
      float realPart;
      float imaginaryPart;
   public:
      // parameterized constructor
      ComplexNumber( float real, float imaginary ) {
         realPart = real;
         imaginaryPart = imaginary;
      }
      // overloading of unary minus operator
      void operator -() {
         realPart = -realPart;
         imaginaryPart = -imaginaryPart;
      }
      // member function to output complex number
      void displayComplexNumber() {
         cout << setiosflags ( ios::showpoint )
              << setprecision ( 2 ) << realPart
              << setiosflags ( ios::showpos )
              << imaginaryPart << "j" << endl;
      }
};  // end of ComplexNumber class definition
void main()   // main program
{
   ComplexNumber number ( 1.5, 2.5 );    // create object
   cout << "\nOriginal complex number : ";
   number.displayComplexNumber();
   -number;          // negate complex number
```

```
   cout << "\nComplex number after negate operation : ";
   number.displayComplexNumber();
}
```

Test Run

```
Original complex number : 1.50+2.50j

Complex number after negate operation : -1.50-2.50j
```

Listing 7.3

```
//  Program to demonstrate the overloading of unary
//  minus operator using friend function
#include <iostream.h>
#include <iomanip.h>
class ComplexNumber
{
   private:
      float realPart;
      float imaginaryPart;
   public:
      ComplexNumber() {       // zero argument constructor
         realPart = 0.0;
         imaginaryPart = 0.0;
      }
      // parameterized constructor
      ComplexNumber( float real, float imaginary ) {
         realPart = real;
         imaginaryPart = imaginary;
      }
      // declaration of global function as a friend
      friend ComplexNumber operator - ( ComplexNumber cn );
      // member function to output complex number
      void displayComplexNumber()
      {
         cout << setiosflags ( ios::showpoint )
              << setprecision ( 2 ) << realPart
              << setiosflags ( ios::showpos )
              << imaginaryPart << "j" << endl;
      }
};  // end of ComplexNumber class definition
// definition of global function
ComplexNumber operator - ( ComplexNumber cn ) {
   cn.realPart = - cn.realPart;
   cn.imaginaryPart = - cn.imaginaryPart;
   return cn;
}
```

```
void main()  // main program
{
    ComplexNumber number1( 1.5, 2.5 ), number2; // create object
    cout << "\nOriginal complex number : ";
    number1.displayComplexNumber();
    number2 = -number1;      // negate original complex number
                             // and assign to other complex number
    cout << "\nComplex number after negate operation : ";
    number2.displayComplexNumber();
}
```

7.4.3 Overloading of << and >> Operators

The following program illustrates the overloading of << and >> operators.

Listing 7.4

```
 //  Program to demonstrate the overloading of
 //  extraction (>>) and insertion (<<) operators

#include <iostream.h>
#include <iomanip.h>
class ComplexNumber
{
   private:
      float realPart;
      float imaginaryPart;
   public:
      // default constructor
      ComplexNumber() { }
      // declaration of overloading of << operator
      friend ostream & operator << (ostream &,ComplexNumber &);
      // declaration of overloading of >> operator
      friend istream & operator >> (istream &,ComplexNumber &);
};    // end of ComplexNumber class definition
// definition of overloading of << operator
ostream & operator << ( ostream &dout, ComplexNumber &c ) {
    dout << endl << setiosflags ( ios::showpoint )
         << setprecision ( 2 ) << c.realPart
         << setiosflags ( ios::showpos ) << c.imaginaryPart
         << resetiosflags ( ios::showpos ) << "j" << endl;
    return dout;
}
// definition of overloading of >> operator
istream & operator >> (istream & din, ComplexNumber &c ) {
    cout << "\nEnter real part : ";
    din  >>  c.realPart;
    cout << "Enter imaginary part : ";
    din  >>  c.imaginaryPart;
```

```
    return din;
}
void main()  // main program
{
    ComplexNumber number;    // create object
    // input complex number using overloaded >> operator
    cin >> number;
    // output complex number using overloaded << operator
    cout << "\nComplex number entered by you is\n";
    cout << number;
}
```

Test Run

```
Enter real part : 1.5
Enter imaginary part : 2.5
Complex number entered by you is
1.50+2.50j
```

7.5 OVERLOADING OF BINARY OPERATORS

In this section we will consider the overloading of binary operators.

7.5.1 Overloading of Arithmetic Operators

The following program show the overloading of plus '+' and minus '-' operators. The same steps can be used to overload multiplication '*' and division '/' operators.

Listing 7.5

```
// Program to demonstrate the overloading of plus and minus
// arithmetic operators
#include <iostream.h>
#include <iomanip.h>
class ComplexNumber
{
    private:
      float realPart;
      float imaginaryPart;
    public:
      // default constructor
      ComplexNumber( ) { }
      // overloading of minus - operator
      ComplexNumber operator - (ComplexNumber &c) {
```

```
        ComplexNumber temp;
        temp.realPart = realPart - c.realPart;
        temp.imaginaryPart = imaginaryPart - c.imaginaryPart;
        return temp;
    }
    // overloading of plus + operator
    ComplexNumber operator + (ComplexNumber & c) {
        ComplexNumber temp;
        temp.realPart = realPart + c.realPart;
        temp.imaginaryPart = imaginaryPart + c.imaginaryPart;
        return temp;
    }
    // declaration of overloading of << operator
    friend ostream & operator << (ostream &,ComplexNumber &);
    // declaration of overloading of << operator
    friend istream & operator >> (istream &,ComplexNumber &);
};    // end of ComplexNumber class definition
// definition of overloading of << operator
ostream & operator << ( ostream &dout, ComplexNumber &c ) {
    dout << setiosflags ( ios::showpoint )
         << setprecision ( 2 ) << "( " << c.realPart
         << setiosflags ( ios::showpos ) << c.imaginaryPart
         << resetiosflags ( ios::showpos ) << "j" << " )";
    return dout;
}
// definition of overloading of >> operator
istream & operator >> (istream & din, ComplexNumber &c ) {
    cout << "\nEnter real part : ";
    din  >>  c.realPart;
    cout << "Enter imaginary part : ";
    din  >>  c.imaginaryPart;
    return din;
}
void main()  // main program
{
    // create objects
    ComplexNumber number1, number2, number3, number4;
    // Input two complex numbers
    cout << "\nEnter first complex number\n";
    cin >> number1;
    cout << "\nEnter second complex number\n";
    cin >> number2;
    number3 = number1 + number2;   // add complex numbers
    cout << endl << number1 << " + " << number2 << " = "
         << number3 << endl;
    number4 = number2 - number1;  //subrtaction complex numbers
    cout << endl << number2 << " - " << number1 << " = "
         << number4 << endl;
}
```

Test Run

```
Enter first complex number

Enter real part : 1
Enter imaginary part : 2

Enter second complex number

Enter real part : 2
Enter imaginary part : 3

( 1.00+2.00j ) + ( 2.00+3.00j ) = ( 3.00+5.00j )

( 2.00+3.00j ) - ( 1.00+2.00j ) = ( 1.00+1.00j )
```

7.5.2 Overloading of Relational Operators

The following program shows the overloading of all relational operators on a user-defined *MyString* class.

Listing 7.6

```
// Program to demonstrate overloading of relation operators

#include <iostream.h>
#include <iomanip.h>
#include <string.h>
class MyString
{
   private:
      char *stringName;
      int length;
   public:
      MyString () { // zero argument constructor
         length = 0;
         stringName = new char [ length + 1 ];
      }
      // parameterized constructor that takes string as argument
       MyString ( char *str ) {
          length = strlen ( str );
          stringName = new char [ length + 1 ];
          strcpy ( stringName, str );
      }
      // member function to display the string
      void  displayString()
      {
         cout << endl << StringName << endl;
      }
      // overloading of "==" operator
```

```
      int operator == ( String &st ) {
          if ( strcmp ( StringName, st.StringName ) == 0 )
             return 1;
          else
             return 0;
      }
      // overloading of "!=" operator
      int operator != ( String &st ) {
         if ( strcmp ( StringName, st.StringName ) != 0 )
            return 1;
         else
            return 0;
      }
      // overloading of ">" operator
      int operator > ( String &st ) {
         if ( strcmp ( StringName, st.StringName ) > 0 )
            return 1;
         else
            return 0;
      }
      // overloading of ">=" operator
      int operator >= ( String &st ) {
         if ( strcmp ( StringName, st.StringName ) >= 0 )
            return 1;
         else
            return 0;
      }
      // overloading of "<" operator
      int operator < ( String &st ) {
         if ( strcmp ( StringName, st.StringName ) < 0 )
            return 1;
         else
            return 0;
      }
      // overloading of "<=" operator
      int operator >= ( String &st ) {
         if ( strcmp ( StringName, st.StringName ) <= 0 )
            return 1;
         else
            return 0;
      }
};    // end of class definition
void main()  // main program
{
   MyString string1 ( "good" );
   MyString string2 ( "bad" );
   cout << "First string : ";
   string1.displayString();
   cout << "\nFirst string : ";
```

```
    string2.displayString();
    cout << endl;
    if ( string1 == string2 )
       cout << "Strings are identical.";
    else
       cout << "Strings are not identical.";
    cout << endl;
}
```

Test Run

```
First string : good
Second string : bad
Strings are not identical.
```

7.6 OVERLOADING OF *new* AND *delete* OPERATORS

Following program demonstrates overloading of memory management operators.

Listing 7.7

```
//Program to demonstrate overloading of 'new' & 'delete' operators
#include <iostream.h>
#include <iomanip.h>
#include <alloc.h>
class Myclass
{
   private:
      int i;
      int j;
   public:
      Myclass(int a, int b)
      {
         i = a;
         j = b;
      }
      void show()
      {
         cout << "\nObject's data members:\n\n";
         cout << "i = " << i << endl;
         cout << "j = " << j << endl;
      }
      void * operator new ( size_t size )
      {
         void *voidPointer;
         cout << "\nMemory allocated to object.\n";
         voidPointer = (Myclass *) malloc(size);
```

```
        if ( voidPointer == NULL ) {
            bad_alloc ba;
            throw ba;
        }
        return voidPointer;
    }
    void operator delete ( void * voidPointer ) {
        cout << "\nMemory occupied by object released.\n";
        free(voidPointer);
    }
};  // end of class definition
void main()
{
    // create object
    try {
        Myclass *ptr = new Myclass(7,8);
    }
    catch ( bad_alloc xa ) {
        cout << "\nUnable to allocate memory . . .\n";
        return;
    }
    // access member function through pointer to object
    ptr->show();
    delete(ptr);        // destroy object
}
```

Test Run

```
Memory allocated to object.

Object's data members:

i = 7
j = 8

Memory occupied by object released.
```

7.7 TYPE CONVERSION

From the knowledge of basic data type we know that

- When a constant and variable is assigned to another variable of different data type, the value is automatically converted to the data type of the variable to the left of the assignment operator.

```
int intVar1, intVar2;
float floatVar1 = 1.4142, floatVar2;
// . . .
```

```
intVar1 = 4.5;              // constant 4.5 is converted to 4
intVar2 = floatVar1;        // value of floatVar converted to type int
```

- When constants and variables are used together in an expression, the values are automatically converted depending on the hierarchy of data types.

```
int intVar1 = 4;
float floatVar1 = 1.4142, floatVar2;
// . . .
floatVar2 = 5 * floatVar1 / intVar1;
```

  In the above expression, before multiplication, first integer constant 5 is converted to float constant 5.0. The result of multiplication will be a float value. Next, before division operation, the value of integer variable *intVar1* is converted to float value and then the division operation is performed. The resulting value of the expression will be of type *float* that is finally assigned to float variable *floatVar2*.

With user-defined data types, when operations are performed on objects of same type, every thing works fine. However, when objects of different types are used, compiler has no idea about their conversion from one type to another.

Therefore, compiler cannot perform automatic type conversion for such types and hence need to be told the way type conversion can be performed explicitly.

Following situations might arise in the type conversion between incompatible types:

- Conversion from basic type to class type.
- Conversion from class type to basic type.
- Conversion from one class type to another class type.

Each of these cases is described below.

7.7.1 Conversion from Basic Type to Class Type

The conversion from basic type to class is simple and easiest of all the conversions. Just recall the way constructors were used to construct an object from basic types. When a value of basic type is assigned to an object, the constructor is implicitly invoked, and thus this type of conversion resembles to automatic conversion of basic types.

To fix the idea, consider the following examples.

Consider the parameterized constructor of *MyString* class of listing 7.6

```
MyString ( char *str )
{
   length = strlen ( str );
   stringName = new char [ length + 1 ];
   strcpy ( stringName, str );
}
```

This constructor builds a *MyString* type object from a *char* * type variable *str*.

Now consider, the following code

```
MyString strObj1, strObj2;

char *str1 = "first string";
char *str2 = "second string";

strObj1 = MyString(str1);    // 1
strObj2 = str2;              // 2
```

The statement numbered 1, first converts *str1* from *char* * type to *MyString* type and then assigns the converted value to the object *strObj1*.

The statement numbered 2, also does the same job by invoking the constructor implicitly.

The following is another example of *int* type to class type conversion.

```
class Time
{
  private:
    int hours;
    int minutes;
    int seconds;
  public:
    Time( int timeInSeconds ) {
       hours = timeInSeconds / 3600;
       timeInSeconds %= 3600;
       minutes = timeInSeconds / 60;
       timeInSeconds %= 60;
       seconds = timeInSeconds;
    }
          // . . .
}
```

Now consider, the following statements

```
Time t1 = Time(3738);
Time t2 = 3738;
```

Both of these statements create *Time* objects with data members *hours* initialized to 1, *minutes* initialized to 2, and *seconds* initialized to 18, respectively from an *int* type value 3738 representing time in seconds.

- The constructor used for type conversion from basic type to class type takes a single argument.
- The left hand operand of assignment operator '=' is always a class object. Therefore, this type of conversion can also be performed by overloading assignment operator.

7.7.2 Conversion from Class Type to Basic Type

We have seen how constructor did the job of type conversion from a basic type to class type. But what about the conversion from a class type to basic type? The constructors do not support this type of conversion. However, C++ allow us to define an overloaded *cast operator* function, usually referred to as *conversion function* that can be used to convert a class type to a basic type.

The general form of an overloaded *conversion function* is

```
operator typename()
{
  // statements
}
```

It converts a class type object to *typeName*.

The cast operator function has following characteristics:

- It must be a class member.
- It has no rcturn type.
- It has no arguments.

To fix the idea, consider the following examples.

```
class IntFloatPair
{
   private:
     int intMember;
     float floatMember;
   public:
     // default constructor
     IntFloatPair()
     {
        intMember = 0;
        floatMember = 0.0;
     }
     // parametrized constructor
     IntFloatPair( int x, float y )
     {
        intMember = x;
        floatMember = y;
     }
     // conversion function that returns int member
     operator int()
     {
        return intMember;
     }
     // conversion function that returns float member
     operator float()
     {
        return floatMember;
     }
};
```

The following program illustrates the use of above class.

Listing 7.8

```
// Program to demonstrate definition & use of conversion function

#include <iostream.h>
#include <iomanip.h>
class IntFloatPair
{
     private:
       int intMember;
       float floatMember;
     public:
       IntFloatPair() {    // zero argument constructor
          intMember = 0;
```

```
        floatMember = 0.0;
     }
     // parametrized constructor
     IntFloatPair( int x, float y ) {
        intMember = x;
        floatMember = y;
     }
     // conversion function that returns int member
     operator int() {
        return intMember;
     }
     // conversion function that returns float member
     operator float() {
        return floatMember;
     }
     // member function to display pair
     void showPair() {
        cout << "\nIntFloatPair : (" << intMember << ","
             << setprecision(2) << floatMember << ")\n";
     }
};  // end of class definition
void main()
{
   int intVar;
   float floatVar;
   IntFloatPair pair(100, 12.25);
   intVar = int(pair);       // convert class type to int
   floatVar = float(pair);  // convert class type to float
   pair.showPair();
   cout << "\nInteger part of IntFloatPair : "<< intVar << endl;
   cout << "Float part of IntFloatPair : " << floatVar << endl;
}
```

Test Run

```
IntFloatPair : (100,12.25)
Integer part of IntFloatPair : 100
Float part of IntFloatPair : 12.25
```

7.7.3 Conversion from one Class Type to another Class Type

We have seen type conversions from basic type to class type and from class type to basic type. Now the final turn is for type conversion from one class type to another class type.

Consider the following statement

```
objX = objY; // objects of different types
```

where *objX* is an object of class *X* and *objY* is an object of class *Y*. We want that object *objY* of type *Y* be converted to object of type *X* and then assigned to *objX*. Since the conversion in the above statement will take from class *Y* to class *X*, the class *Y* will act as *source* class and class *X* as *destination* class. Conversion from one class to another can be done using both through constructor approach and conversion function approach. Compiler treats both of these approaches in identical manner. Therefore, question arises — *which approach to use*?

It depends upon where you want conversion facility to be located. The following guidelines will help you:

- If you want to place the conversion facility in the source class, then use conversion function with name of the destination class as *typename*.

```
class X;            // declaration, used for forward reference

class Y             // source class
{
   private:
      // . . .
   public:
      // . . .
   operator X()     // conversion function
   {
      // . . .
   }
   // . . .
};
class X             // destination class
{
   private:
      // . . .
   public:
      // . . .
};
```

- If you want to place the conversion facility in the destination class, then use constructor that takes object of source class as its only argument.

```
class Y;            // declaration, used for forward reference

class X             // destination class
{
```

```
   private:
      // . . .
   public:
      X ( Y obj )          // constructor for conversion
      {
         // . . .
      }
      // . . .
};
class Y                    // source class
{
   private:
      // . . .
   public:
      // . . .
};
```

Let us consider a complete workable example.

Listing 7.9

```
//  program to demonstrate the conversion from one class
//  type to another class type when the conversion facility
//  is defined in the source class

#include <iostream.h>
#include <iomanip.h>
class Time24Hours;          // declaration for forward reference
class Time12Hours
{
   private:
      int hours;
      int minutes;
      char meridian[5];
   public:
      Time12Hours() {       // zero argument constructor
         hours = minutes = 0;
         strcpy ( meridian, "" );
      }
      // parameterized constructor
      Time12Hours ( int hh, int mm, char *s ) {
         hours = hh;
         minutes = mm;
         strcpy ( meridian, s );
      }
      // member function to display 12 hour time
      void showTime() {
         cout << hours << ":" << minutes;
         if ( hours < 12 )
```

```
            cout << " AM";
        else if ( hours == 12 )
            cout << " Noon";
        else
            cout << " PM";
        cout << endl;
    }
    // conversion function
    operator Time24Hours() {
        Time24Hours temp;
        int hh = hours;
        if ( ( stricmp(meridian, "PM" ) == 0 ) ||
             ( stricmp(meridian, "Noon" ) == 0 ) ) {
            hh += 12;
            if ( hh >= 24 )
                hh -= 24;
        }
        hh = hh * 100;
        hh = hh + minutes;
        temp.setHours(hh);
        return temp;
    }
};      // end of Time12Hours class definition
class Time24Hours
{
   private:
    int hours;
   public:
    Time24Hours() {                // zero argument constructor
       hours = 0;
    }
    // parameterized constructor
    Time24Hours ( int hh ) {
       hours = hh;
    }
    void setHours( int hh ) {     // setter method
       hours = hh;
    }
    // member function to display the 24 hour time
    void showTime() {
       if ( hours <= 9 )
          cout << "000";
       else if ( hours <= 59 )
          cout << "00";
       else if ( hours <= 959 )
          cout << "0";
       cout << hours << " hrs." << endl;
    }
};      // end of Time24Hours class definition
```

```
void main()  // main program
{
   Time12Hours time1 ( 12, 15, "PM" );
   cout << "Time in 12 hours system is ";
   time1.showTime();
   Time24Hours time2 = time1;
   cout << "\nIts equivalent time in 24 hour system is ";
   time2.showTime();
}
```

Listing 7.10

```
//  program to demonstrate the conversion from one class
//  type to another class type when the conversion facility
//  is defined in the destination class
#include <iostream.h>
#include <iomanip.h>
class Time12Hours
{
   private:
      int hours;
      int minutes;
      char meridian[5];
   public:
      Time12Hours() {      // zero argument constructor
         hours = minutes = 0;
         strcpy ( meridian, "" );
      }
      // parameterized constructor
      Time12Hours ( int hh, int mm, char *s ) {
         hours = hh;
         minutes = mm;
         strcpy ( meridian, s );
      }
      int getHours() {
         return hours;
      }
      int getMinutes() {
         return minutes;
      }
      char *getMeridian() {
         return meridian;
      }
      // member function to display the string
      void showTime()
      {
         cout << hours << ":" << minutes << " "<<meridian<<endl;
      }
};     // end of Time12Hours class definition
```

```
class Time24Hours
{
   private:
     int hours;
   public:
     Time24Hours() {   // zero argument constructor
        hours = 0;
     }
     // parameterized constructor
     Time24Hours ( int hh ) {
        hours = hh;
     }
     // constructor that perform conversion
     Time24Hours( Time12Hours obj ) {
        int hh;
        hh = obj.getHours();
        if ( (stricmp(obj.getMeridian(),"PM" )==0) ||
             (stricmp(obj.getMeridian(),"Noon" )==0)) {
           hh += 12;
           if ( hh >= 24 )
              hh -= 24;
        }
        hh = hh * 100;
        hh = hh + obj.getMinutes();
        hours = hh;
     }
     // member function to display the 24 hour time
     void showTime() {
        if ( hours <= 9 )
           cout << "000";
        else if ( hours <= 59 )
           cout << "00";
        else if ( hours <= 959 )
           cout << "0";
        cout << hours << " hrs." << endl;
     }
};     // end of Time24Hours class definition
void main()  // main program
{
   Time12Hours time1 ( 12, 15 );
   cout << "Time in 12 hours system is ";
   time1.showTime();
   Time24Hours time2 = time1;
   cout << endl << "Its equivalent time in 24 hour system is ";
   time2.showTime();
}
```

Table 7.3: Summary of Type Conversion

Type Conversion from	Conversion takes place in	
	Source Class	Destination Class
Basic type to Class type	Not applicable	Constructor
Class type to Basic type	Conversion function	Not applicable
Class type to Class type	Conversion function	Constructor

QUICK RECAP

In this chapter, we have learnt that

- Operator overloading makes the user-defined data types behave like built-in data types.
- Operator function is used to overload an operator, which can be a member function or friend function.
- Only existing operators can be overloaded. New operator cannot be created.
- Overloaded operator must have at least one operand of user-defined data type.
- The overloaded operators follow the syntax rules of the original operators. They cannot be overridden.
- *sizeof* operator, membership operator (.), pointer-to-member operator (.*), scope resolution operator (::) and conditional operator (:?) cannot be overloaded.
- Friend function cannot be used to overload assignment operator, function call, subscripting operator and class member access operator.
- Unary operators overloaded by means of a member function take no parameter and return no value, but overloaded by means of friend function take one parameter of its class and return a value.
- Binary operators overloaded by means of a member function take single parameter and return a value, but overloaded by means of friend function take two parameters of its class and return a value.
- In postfix overloading of increment and decrement operators, the additional argument should be of type *int*?
- Type conversion is the process of converting incompatible values from one type to another type. For built-in types it happens automatically (implicitly), but for user-defined types, we have to define them.
- Possible type conversions are from basic type to class type, class type to basic type, and class type to class type.

- Basic type to class type conversion takes place automatically using one argument constructor of the destination class.
- Class type to basic type conversion can be performed by defining conversion function in the source class.
- Class type to class type conversion can be performed by defining conversion function in the source class or through one argument constructor that takes an object of the source class, in the destination class.

MULTIPLE CHOICE QUESTIONS

1. Which of the following operators cannot be overloaded?

   (*a*) *new* (*b*) ?:
   (*c*) * (*d*) >>

2. In postfix overloading of increment and decrement operators using friend function, the second argument should have which of the following type?

   (*a*) void (*b*) float
   (*c*) char (*d*) None of above

3. Which of the following statement is not valid about operator overloading?

   (*a*) Only existing operators can be overloaded. New operators cannot be created.
   (*b*) Overloaded operator must have at least one operand of its class type.
   (*c*) The overloaded operators follow the syntax rules of the original operators.
   (*d*) None of above

4. Which of the following operators cannot be overloaded using a friend function?

   (*a*) = (*b*) ()
   (*c*) [] (*d*) ->
   (*e*) All of above

5. Which of the following operators can only be overloaded using a friend function?

   (*a*) Binary arithmetic operators (*b*) Memory management operators
   (*c*) Stream operators (*d*) Relational operators

6. Which of the following type of conversion resembles automatic conversion of basic types?

   (*a*) Class type to basic type
   (*b*) Basic type to class type
   (*c*) Class type to class type
   (*d*) All of above

7. Which of the following is not a characteristic of a conversion function?

   (*a*) It must be a class member
   (*b*) It has no return type
   (*c*) It takes no arguments
   (*d*) It must have same name as that of class

8. The class type to basic type conversion can . . . . .

   (*a*) only take place in source class.
   (*b*) only take place in destination class.
   (*c*) not take place.
   (*d*) take place in source class as well as destination class.

9. The class type to class type conversion can . . . . .

   (*a*) only take place in source class.
   (*b*) only take place in destination class.
   (*c*) not take place.
   (*d*) take place in source class as well as destination class.

10. The basic type to class type conversion can . . . . .

    (*a*) only take place in source class.
    (*b*) only take place in destination class.
    (*c*) not take place.
    (*d*) take place in source class as well as destination class.

11. If you want to place the conversion facility in the destination class, which of the following will be used?

    (*a*) Overloaded assignment operator
    (*b*) Constructor
    (*c*) Conversion function
    (*d*) None of above

12. If you want to place the conversion facility in the source class, which of the following will be used?

    (*a*) Overloaded assignment operator
    (*b*) Constructor
    (*c*) Conversion function
    (*d*) None of above

13. When the conversion facility is defined in the destination class, what happens when an object of source class is assigned to destination class?

    (*a*) Copy constructor of the destination class is invoked
    (*b*) No argument constructor of the destination class is invoked
    (*c*) One argument constructor of the destination class that takes object of the source class as its argument is invoked

(*d*) One argument constructor of the source that takes object of the destination class as its argument is invoked

14. When the conversion facility is defined in the source class, what happens when an object of source class is assigned to destination class?

    (*a*) Conversion function of the source class is invoked
    (*b*) Conversion function of the destination class is invoked
    (*c*) No argument constructor of the destination class is invoked
    (*d*) No argument constructor of the source class is invoked

15. Which of the following statement about operator overloading is not true?

    (*a*) Operator overloading makes user-defined data types behave like built-in data types
    (*b*) Semantics of an operator can be extended
    (*c*) Syntax of an operator can be changed
    (*d*) An operator can be overloaded using an operator function or a friend function

REVIEW EXERCISES

1. What is operator overloading? Explain the usefulness of operator overloading.
2. What is operator function? Give examples.
3. What are the steps in overloading an operator?
4. What are the rules that govern the operator overloading?
5. List the operators that cannot be overloaded. Also explain why they cannot be overloaded?
6. How is it possible to distinguish between prefix and postfix notation while overloading increment '++' and decrement '—' operators?
7. Can we overload *new* and *delete* operators? If yes, how?
8. What is type conversion?
9. How conversion from basic type to class type can be performed?
10. How conversion from class type to basic type can be performed?
11. How conversion from one class to another class type can be performed?

PROGRAMMING EXERCISES

1. Design a class named *Time* to represent time in hours, minutes and seconds. Overload the appropriate set of operators for performing I/O of time and manipulating objects of Time class. Write a program to use this class.

2. Design a class named *Vector* to model a one-dimensional array with integer elements. Overload the following operators to perform the intended task:

   (*i*) Operator '<<' to output a vector object.
   (*ii*) Operator '>>' to input a vector object in the form [10, 20, 30, . . .].
   (*iii*) Operator '+' to add two vector objects.
   (*iv*) Operator '–' to subtract a given vector object from another vector object.

   Write a program to use this class.

3. Design a class named *Matrix* to model a matrix of size *m*×*n*. Overload the following operators to perform the intended task:

   (*i*) Operator '<<' to output a matrix object.
   (*ii*) Operator '>>' to input a matrix object.
   (*iii*) Operator '+' to add two matrix objects.
   (*iv*) Operator '–' to subtract a given matrix object from another matrix object.
   (*v*) Operator '*' to multiply two matrix objects.

   Write a program to use this class.

4. Design two classes named *Rupees* and *Dollars* to represent currency in Indian system and American system, respectively. Write conversion routines for converting currency from one system to another system using both the features — when conversion facility is built in source and when conversion facility is built in destination class. Write a program to use this class.

5. Design two classes named *Distance1* and *Distance2* to represent length of an object in meters & centimeters and feet & inches, respectively. Write conversion routines for converting length from meters & centimeters to feet & inches and vice a versa. Write a program to use this class.

6. Design two classes named *Polar* and *Cartesian* to represent a point in plane using polar coordinate system and cartesian coordinate system, respectively. Write conversion routines for converting coordinates of a point from one system to another system using both the features — when conversion facility is built in source and when the conversion facility is built in destination class. Write a program to use this class.

7. Design a class named *Polar* that models polar coordinate system in which a point in a plane is described using polar coordinates — *radius* (*r*) and *angle* (θ) as shown in figure 7.1. Overload operators '+' and '–' to perform addition and subtraction of two objects of *Polar* class.

Note that coordinates in polar coordinate system cannot be added or subtracted directly. In order to do that, following steps need to be performed:

(*i*) Polar coordinate are converted to cartesian coordinates

(*ii*) Add or subtract cartesian coordinates

(*iii*) Covert the result obtained in (*ii*) to polar coordinates.

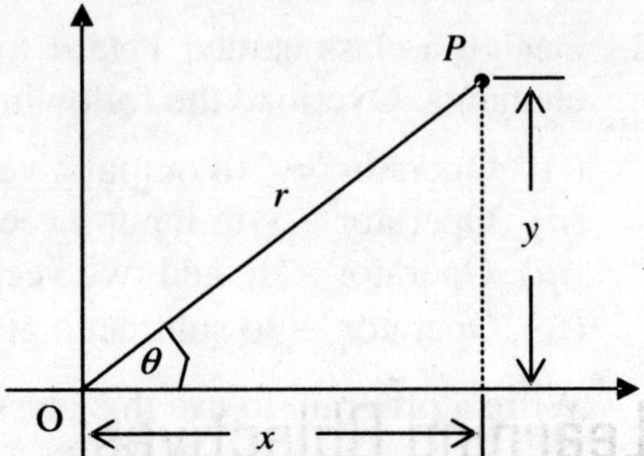

Figure 7.1: Polar coordinate system

The relations between polar coordinates and Cartesian coordinates are

$$x = r\cos\theta \qquad y = r\sin\theta \qquad r = \sqrt{x^2 + y^2} \qquad \theta = \tan^{-1}(x/y)$$

Write a program to use this class.

❑ ❑ ❑

Chapter 8

Inheritance

Learning Objectives

After reading this chapter, students will be able to explain the

- concept of inheritance and its usefulness
- syntax for defining derived classes
- role of access specifiers in class derivation
- various forms of inheritance
- source of ambiguity and its handling in multiple inheritance
- source of ambiguity and its handling in multipath inheritance
- concept of virtual derivation
- concept of object slicing
- overriding of member functions
- difference between overriding and overloading
- order of constructors and destructors

8.1 INTRODUCTION

Reusability and extensibility is among the most important features of object-oriented programming paradigm. It is always nice if we can reuse something that already exists instead of creating it afresh. The reusability offers following advantages:

- It saves time and effort.
- It reduces development cost of new software product.
- Increases reliability because the class is already tested and used many times.

Inheritance allows new class, *called derived class*, to be built from the existing and generalized class, called *base class*, instead of building from the scratch. New classes can be build by first inheriting the general features of some given class and then adding specific features.

The derived class inherits all of the capabilities of the base class and can add refinements and extensions of its own. The derivation of a new class from the existing class is represented in a simplistic view as shown in Figure 8.2.

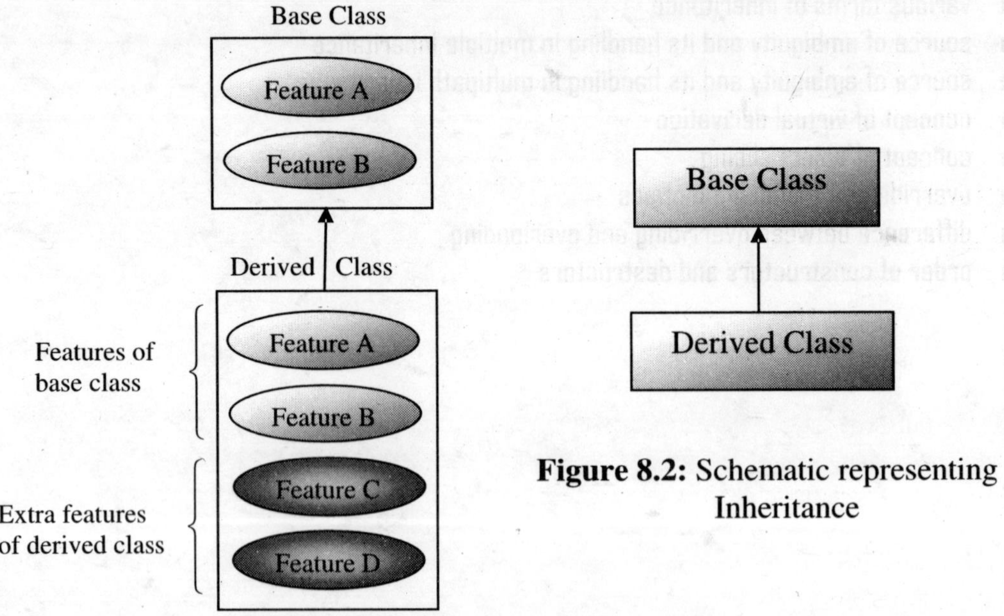

Figure 8.2: Schematic representing Inheritance

Figure 8.1: Inheritance showing relationship between base class & derived class

A number of terms are used to describe classes that are related through inheritance. A base class is often called the *ancestor*, *parent* or *superclass*. The derived class is called *descendent*, *child* or *subclass*. A derived class may itself be a base class from which additional classes can be derived. There is no specific limit on the number of classes that may be derived from one another, which forms a class hierarchy.

In this chapter, we will discuss about various aspects of inheritance.

8.2 CLASS DEFINITION REVISITED

The C++ language supports three access specifiers: *private*, *protected* and *public*. As for as the access limit from within a class or from the object of a class is concerned, the *protected* access-limit behaves same as *private* access-limit. The *protected* access specifier plays an important role in inheritance.

In general, a class can use all these access specifiers as illustrated below:

```
class ClassName
{
   private:
        . . . . .              // members visible within the class only
        . . . . .
        . . . . .

   protected:
        . . . . .              // members visible within the class and
        . . . . .              // its derived classes
        . . . . .

   public:
        . . . . .              // members visible within the class, its
        . . . . .              // derived classes and objects of these
        . . . . .              // classes
}; // end of class template
```

Figure 8.3: Syntax for class template

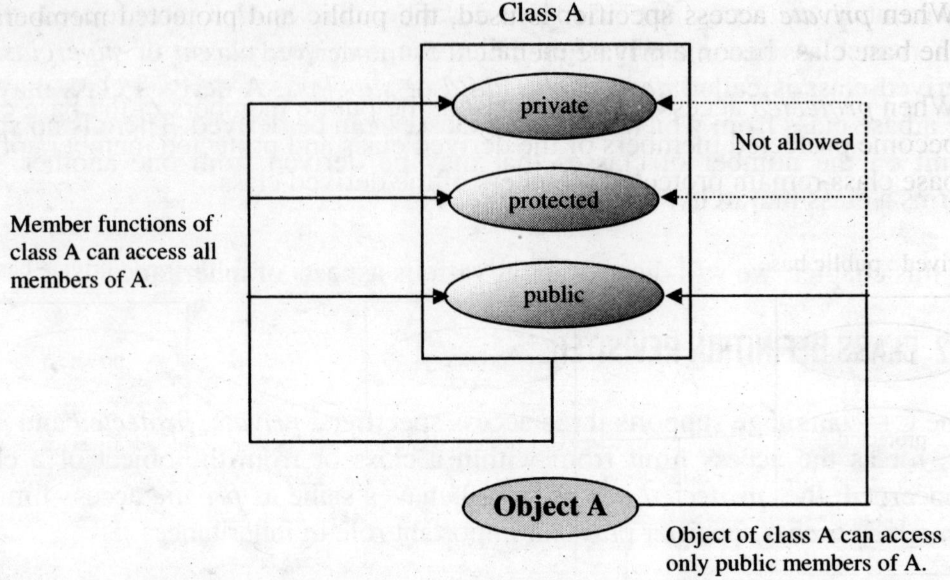

Figure 8.4: Access limits without inheritance

8.3 DEFINING DERIVED CLASSES

The syntax for defining a derived class is

```
class DerivedClassName : [AccessSpecifier] BaseClassName
{
    . . . . .
    . . . . .    // members of the derived class
    . . . . .
};
```

Figure 8.5: Syntax for class derivation

The *AccessSpecifier* is optional and can be *public*, *private* or *protected*. The default access specifier is *private*.

The role of the access specifier is described below:

- When *public* access specifier is used, the public members of the base class remain public members of the derived class. Similarly, the protected members of the base class remain protected members of the derived class.

- When *private* access specifier is used, the public and protected members of the base class become private members of the derived class.
- When *protected* access specifier is used, the public members of the base class become protected members of the derived class and protected members of the base class remain protected members of the derived class.

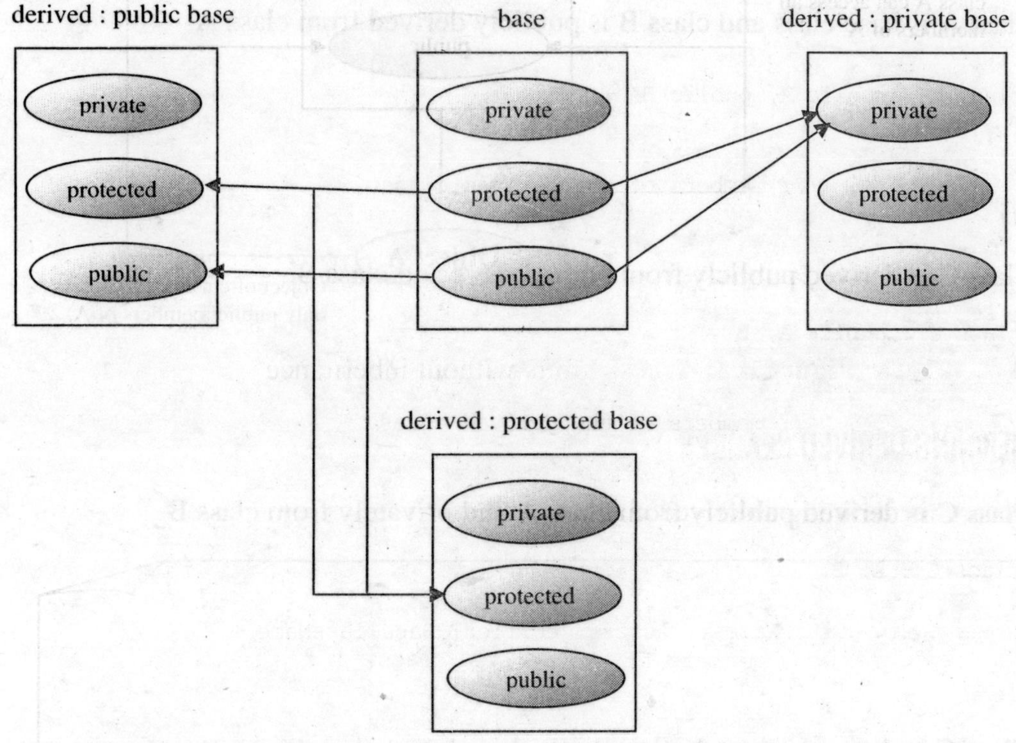

Figure 8.6: Effect of inheritance on visibility of members

The visibility of the inherited members is also summarized in Table 8.1.

Table 8.1: Visibility of Inherited Members

Base Class Visibility	Derived Class Visibility		
	Public derivation	Private derivation	Protected derivation
private	Not affected	Not affected	Not affected
protected	Protected	Private	Protected
public	Public	Private	Protected

Following are some examples to illustrate the syntax of class derivation.

```
class B : public A
{
    . . . . .
    . . . . .    // members of the derived class
};
```

Class A is base class and class B is publicly derived from class A.

```
class C : public A, public B
{
    . . . . .
    . . . . .    // members of the derived class
};
```

Class C is derived publicly from both class A and class B.

```
class C : public A, B
{
    . . . . .
    . . . . .    // members of the derived class
};
```

Class C is derived publicly from class A and privately from class B.

```
class C : A, B
{
    . . . . .
    . . . . .    // members of the derived class
};
```

Class C is derived privately from both class A and class B.

```
class C : A, public B
{
    . . . . .
    . . . . .    // members of the derived class
};
```

Class C is derived privately from class A and publicly from class B.

```
class C : public A, private B
{
    . . . . .
    . . . . .    // members of the derived class
};
```

Class C is derived publicly from class A and privately from class B.

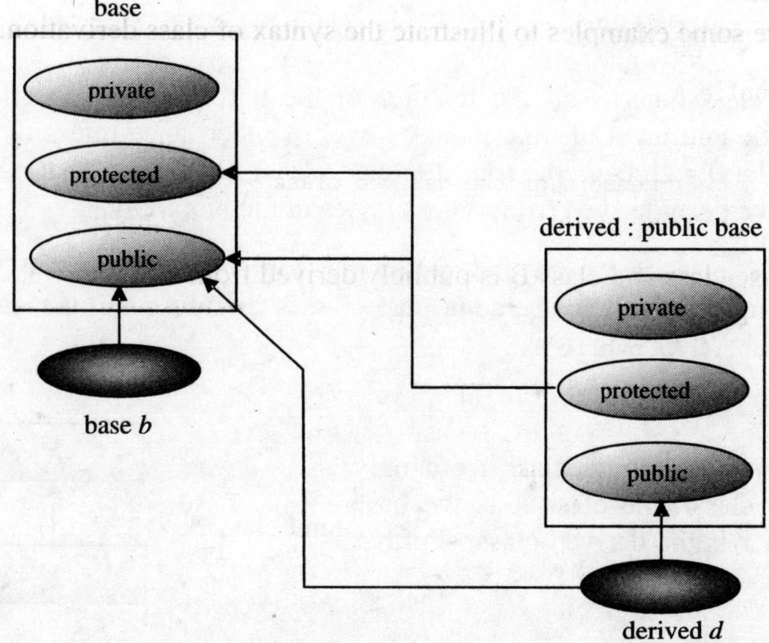

Figure 8.7: Access limits with *public* derivation

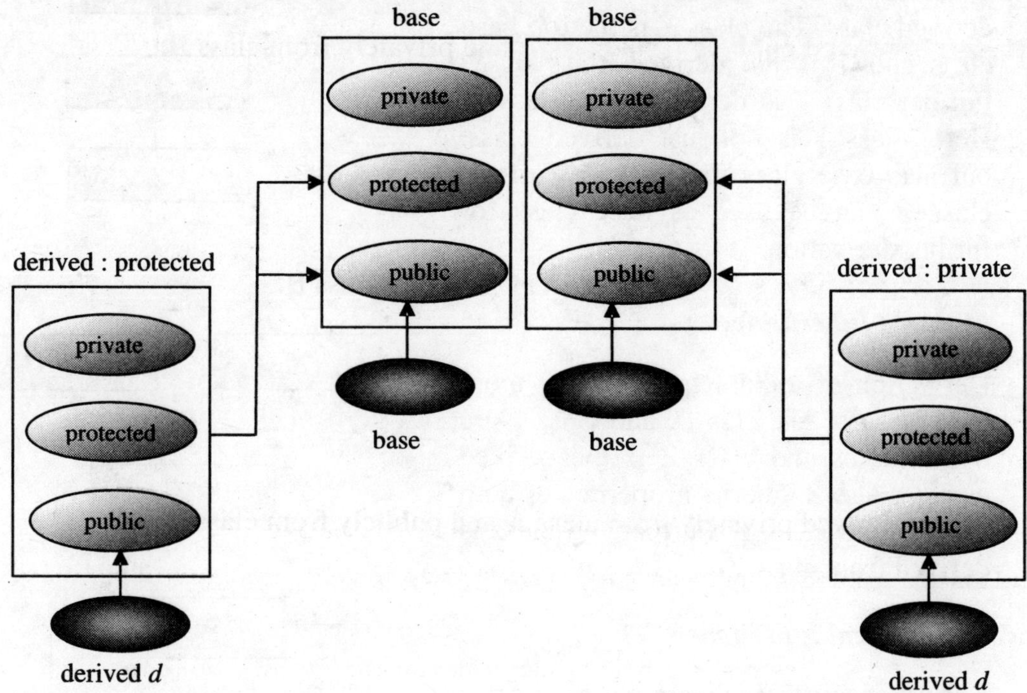

Figure 8.8: Access limits with *protected* derivation

Figure 8.9: Access limits with *private* derivation

8.4 FORMS OF INHERITANCE

The derived class inherits all the features of the base class irrespective of the visibility mode and level of inheritance. Level of inheritance refers to length of its (derived class) path from the root (top base class). Remember that a base class itself may have been derived from other classes in the hierarchy.

Inheritance is classified into the following forms based on the levels of inheritance and interrelation among the classes involved in the inheritance process:

- ***Single Inheritance***

  Derivation of a single class from only one base class. The class *X* is the base class and *Y* is the derived class. Further no class is derived from *Y*.

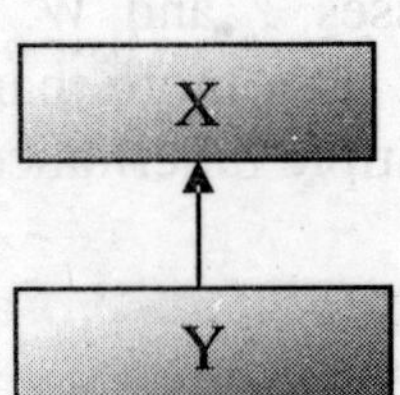

- ***Multilevel Inheritance***

  Derivation of a class from another derived class. The class *X* is the top base class and *Y* is the derived class of *X*. Further class *Z* is derived from class *Y*. Here, class *Y* is not just derived class, but also base class for class *Z*. Further, class *Z* can be used as base class for further derivation.

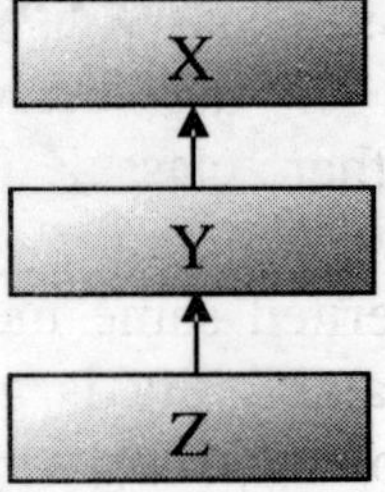

- ***Multiple Inheritance***

  Derivation of a class from two or more base classes. The class *X* and class *Y* are base classes and class *Z* is the derived class. Class *Z* inherits properties of both class *X* and class *Y*. Further, no class is derived from class *Z*.

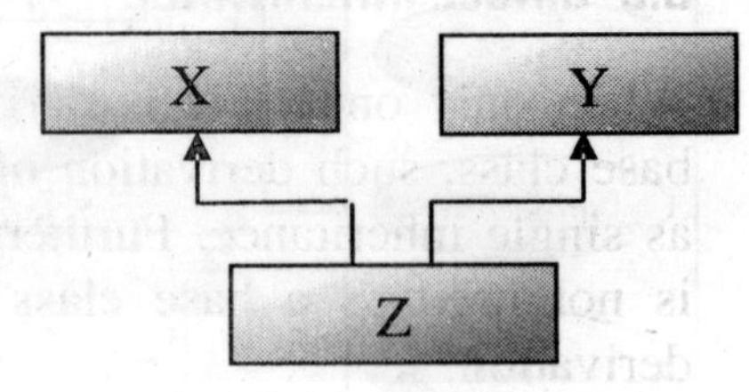

- ***Hierarchical Inheritance***

  Derivation of two or more classes from a single base class. Class *W* is the only base class and classes *X*, *Y* and *Z* are derived

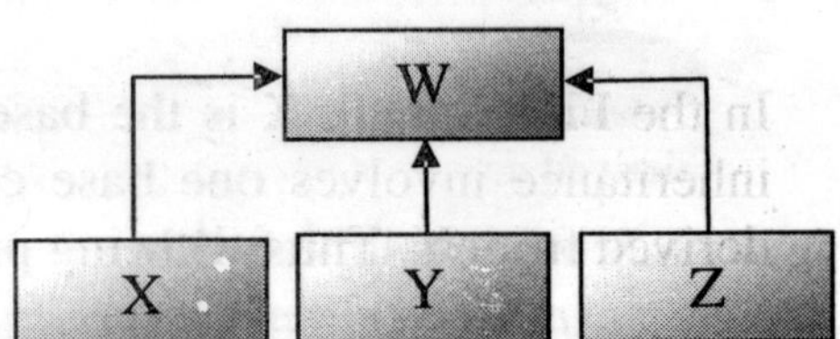

classes. Further, none of the class *X*, *Y* and *Z* is used as base class.

- ***Hybrid Inheritance***

Derivation of a class involving two or more forms of inheritance. In this case, multilevel and multiple inheritances are involved. Class *Y* is derived from class *X*. It is a single type of inheritance. Further, derived class *Y* acts as a base class. The class *Z* is derived from classes *Y* and *W*. This type of inheritance that uses more than one base class is called multiple inheritance.

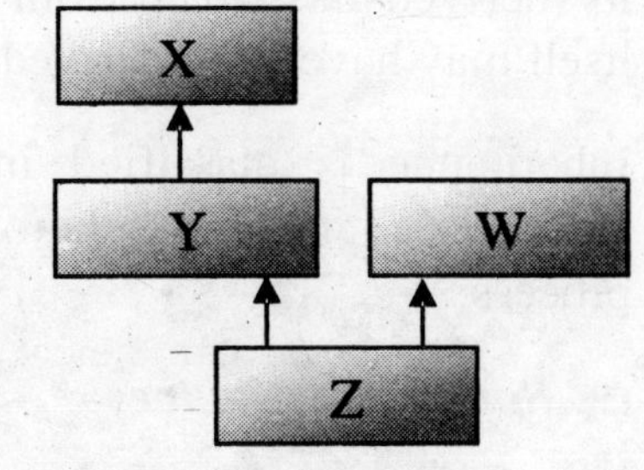

- ***Multipath Inheritance***

Derivation of a class from two or more classes that are derived from the same base class. Class *X* is the base class. Classes *Y* and *W* are derived from base class *X*. Further, class *Z* is derived from classes *Y* and *W*. Since, classes *Y* and *W* have inherited same members of *X*. In this case, an ambiguity is generated which in turn is resolved using virtual keyword. The virtual mechanism is explained later.

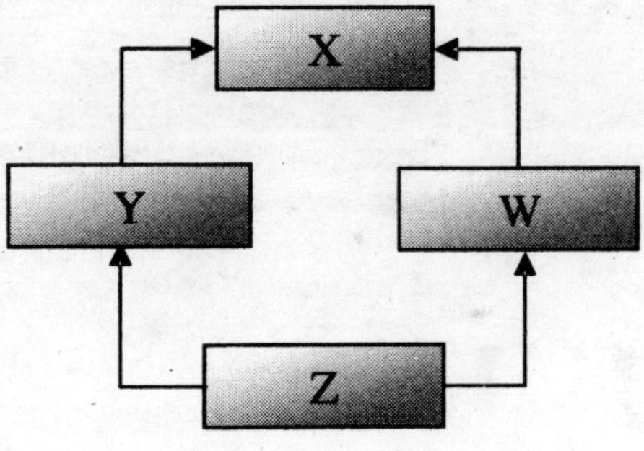

8.5 SINGLE INHERITANCE

When only one class is derived from a single base class, such derivation of a class is known as single inheritance. Further, the derived class is not used as a base class for another class derivation.

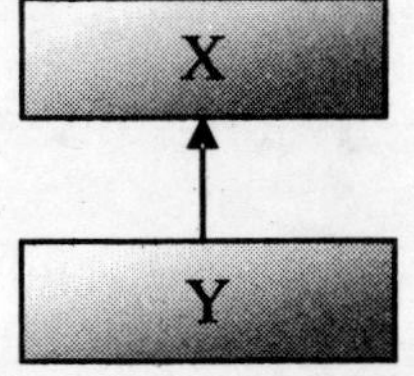

Figure 8.10: Single inheritance

In the Figure 8.10, X is the base class and Y is the derived class. This type of inheritance involves one base class and one derived class. Further no class is derived from Y. The following program demonstrates the single inheritance.

Listing 8.1

```
// Program to demonstrate single inheritance
#include <iostream.h>
#include <iomanip.h>
#include <string.h>
class X                    // base class
{
    protected:
       char name[30];
       int age;
    public:
      //  some member functions can be added
};
class Y : public X {           // derived class
    private:
       int weight;
    public:
       void getData() {
          cout << "Enter Name : ";
          cin >> name;
          cout << "Enter age : ";
          cin >> age;
          cout << "Enter weight : ";
          cin >> weight;
       }
       void showData() {
          cout << "\nName   : " << name;
          cout << "\nAge    : " << age;
          cout << "\nWeight : " << weight << endl;
       }
};
void main()
{
   Y objY;
   objY.getData();
   objY.showData();
}
```

Test Run

```
Enter Name : Mehak
Enter age : 12
Enter weight : 30

Name   : Mehak
Age    : 12
Weight : 30
```

In this program, class X is the base class and is having two data members, *name* and *age*, which are declared in the protected section. These data members are accessible from any class that is derived from class X. Class Y is the derived class which adds one data member *weight* and two member functions *getData()* and *showData()*. In the *main()* function, an object of derived class Y, *objY*, is created on which member functions *getData()* and *setData()* are invoked.

8.6 MULTILEVEL INHERITANCE

When a class is derived from a single base class and further can be used as a base class for deriving another class. This derivation can continue up to any level.

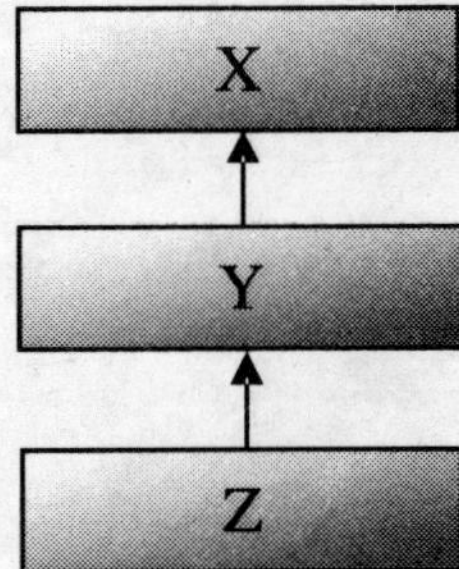

Figure 8.11: Multilevel inheritance

In the Figure 8.11, X is the top base class and Y is the derived class of X. At next level, class Z is derived from class Y. Therefore, class Y is not just a derived class of class X, but also base class for class Z. Further, Z can be used as base class.

The following program demonstrates the multilevel inheritance.

Listing 8.2

```
// Program to demonstrate multilevel inheritance
#include <iostream.h>
#include <iomanip.h>
#include <string.h>
class X                          // base class
{
    protected:
        char name[30];
        int age;
    public:
     //  some member functions can be added
};
```

```
class Y : public X  // derived class
{
   protected:
      int weight;
   public:
      // some member functions can be added here also
};
class Z : public Y  // derived class
{
   private:
      char sex[7];
   public:
      void getData(void) {
         cout << "Enter Name : ";
         cin >> name;
         cout << "Enter age : ";
         cin >> age;
         cout << "Enter sex : ";
         cin >> sex;
         cout << "Enter weight : ";
         cin >> weight;
      }
      void showData(void) {
         cout << "\nName   : " << name;
         cout << "\nAge    : " << age;
         cout << "\nSex    : " << sex
         cout << "\nWeight : " << weight << endl;
      }
};
void main()
{
   Z objZ;
   objZ.getData();
   objZ.showData();
}
```

Test Run

```
Enter Name : Kartik
Enter age : 2
Enter sex : male
Enter weight : 15

Name   : Kartik
Age    : 2
Sex    : male
Weight : 15
```

In this program, class X is the topmost base class and is having two data members, *name* and *age*, which are declared in the protected section. These data members are accessible from any class that is derived from class X. Class Y is derived from class X which adds one data member *weight* also in the protected section. Class Z is derived from class Y and adds one data member *sex* and two member functions *getData()* and *showData()*. In the *main()* function, an object of class Z, *objZ*, is created on which member functions *getData()* and *showData()* are invoked.

8.7 MULTIPLE INHERITANCE

When a class is derived from two or more than two base classes. The derived class inherits the properties of all the base classes. The derived class is not used further in deriving another classes.

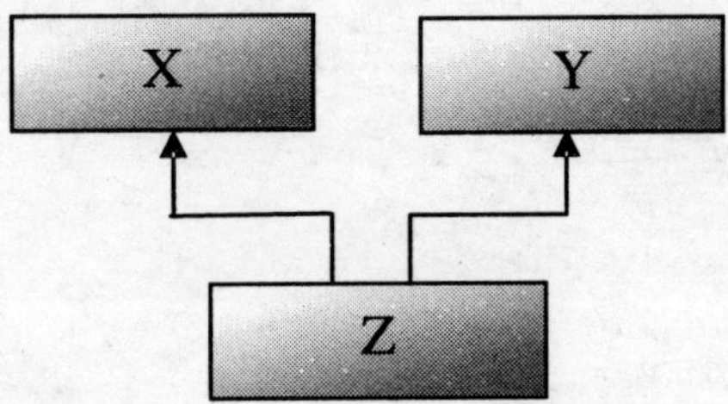

Figure 8.12: Multiple inheritance

In the Figure 8.12, X and Y are base classes and Z is the derived class. Class Z inherits properties of both X and Y. Further, no class is derived from Z.

Since, Z is derived from X and Y, therefore inherit members from both of these classes. However, if the base classes have any member with same name, then accessing that member from the derived class may cause an ambiguity. The mechanism to handle this ambiguity is explained later.

Listing 8.3

```
// Program to demonstrate multiple inheritance

#include <iostream.h>
#include <iomanip.h>
#include <string.h>
class X
{
    protected:
        int x;
    public:
        void showX() {
```

```
        cout << "\nX::x = " << x << endl;
    }
};
class Y
{
  protected:
    int y;
  public:
    void showY()
    {
        cout << "\nY::y = " << y << endl;
    }
};
class Z : public X, public Y
{
  private:
    int z;
  public:
    void setData(int i, int j, int k) {
        x = i;
        y = j;
        z = k;
    }
    void showZ() {
        cout << "\nZ::z = " << z << endl;
    }
};
void main()
{
  Z objZ;                         // object of derived class
  objZ.setData(5, 10, 15);        // from derived class
  objZ.showX();                   // from base class X
  objZ.showY();                   // from base class Y
  objZ.showZ();                   // from derived class Z
}
```

Test Run

```
X::x = 5
Y::y = 10
Z::z = 15
```

In this program, class X and class Y are two base classes each having one data member and one member function. Class Z is derived from both class X and class Y. Class Z add one data member and two member functions. In the *main()* function, an object of class Z, *objZ*, is created on which first member function *setData()* is invoked to initialize the data members and then member functions *showX(), showY()* and *showZ()* are invoked to display data members.

8.7.1 Ambiguity in Multiple Inheritance

As mentioned earlier, when the base classes have members with same name, while the classes derived from these classes have no member with that name, then accessing that common member causes ambiguity. When an object of the derived class access the member of the base class, the compiler will not be able to figure out which of these members should be used.

The following program demonstrates this ambiguity.

Listing 8.4

```
// Program to demonstrate the ambiguity that may arise when
// two or more base classes have same member function, but
// the derived class have no such function.
#include <iostream.h>
#include <iomanip.h>
class X
{
    public:
       void show() {
           cout << "\n Class X\n";
       }
};
class Y {
   public:
      void show() {
          cout << "\n Class Y \n";
      }
};
class Z : public X, public Y { };
void main()
{
    Z objZ;
    objZ.show();     // ambiguity
}
```

When this program is compiled, the compiler will give the error message something like

Member is ambiguous: 'X::show' and 'Y::show'

when object of derived class attempt to access the *show()* method of the base classes.

This ambiguity can be resolved using scope-resolution operator to specify the class in which the function lies. Thus

```
objZ.X::show();
```

refer to the version of *show()* that is in the class X, while

```
objZ.Y::show();
```

refer to the version of *show()* that is in the class Y.

Therefore, the statement *objZ.show()* can be replaced with either of the above statements.

8.8 HIERARCHICAL INHERITANCE

When more than one class is derived from the same base class. Further, the derived classes are not used as base classes.

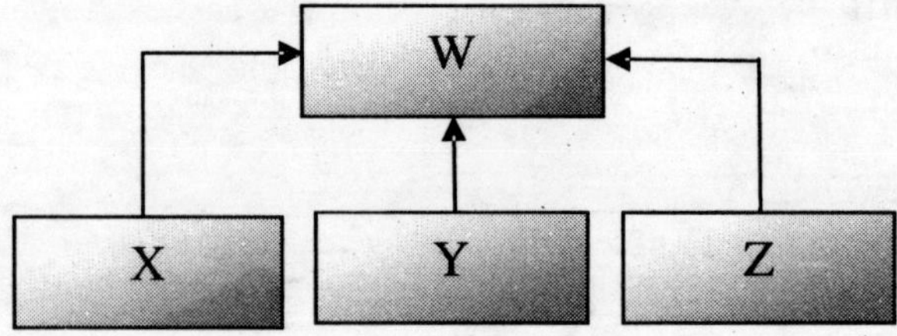

Figure 8.13: Hierarchical inheritance

In the Figure 8.13, W is the base class and X, Y and Z are derived classes. Further, classes X, Y and Z are not used as base classes. The following program demonstrates the hierarchical inheritance.

Listing 8.5

```
// Program to demonstrate hierarchical inheritance
#include <iostream.h>
#include <iomanip.h>
#include <string.h>
class W
{
  public:
    void showW() {
      cout << "\nBase class W\n";
    }
};
```

```
class X : public W
{
   public:
      void showX() {
         cout << "\nDerived class X \n";
   }
};
class Y : public W
{
   public:
      void showY() {
         cout << "\nDerived class Y \n";
   }
};
class Z : public W
{
   public:
      void showZ() {
         cout << "\nDerived class Z \n";
      }
};
void main()
{
   W objW;
   X objX;
   Y objY;
   Z objZ;
   clrscr();
   objW.showW();
   objX.showX();
   objY.showY();
   objZ.showZ();
}
```

Test Run

```
Base class W
Derived class X
Derived class Y
Derived class Z
```

In this program, class W is the base class. Classes X, Y and Z are derived from base class W. In the *main()* function, an object of each class is created on which the respective *show* function is invoked.

8.9 HYBRID INHERITANCE

When a class is derived involving two or more forms of inheritance. In the Figure 8.14, multilevel and multiple inheritances are involved. Class Y is derived from X. It is a single type of inheritance. Further, derived class Y acts as a base class. The class Z is derived from classes Y and W. This type of inheritance that uses more than one base class is called multiple inheritance.

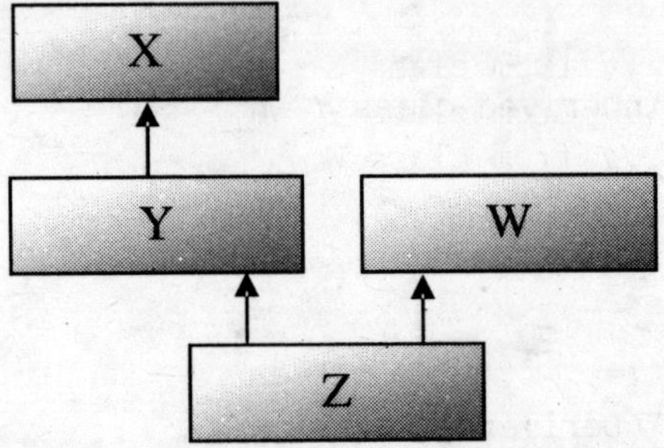

Figure 8.14: Hybrid inheritance

Listing 8.6

```
// Program to demonstrate hybrid inheritance

#include <iostream.h>
#include <iomanip.h>
#include <string.h>
class X
{
   public:
      void showX() {
         cout << "\nClass X\n";
      }
};
class Y : public X
{
   public:
      void showY() {
         cout << "\nClass Y \n";
      }
};
class W {
   public:
      void showW() {
         cout << "\nClass W \n";
      }
};
```

```
class Z : public Y, public W
{
  public:
    void showZ() {
      cout << "\nClass Z \n";
    }
};
void main()
{
    Z objZ;
    objZ.showX();   // from class X
    objZ.showY();   // from class Y
    objZ.showW();   // from class W
    objZ.showZ();
}
```

Test Run

```
Class X

Class Y

Class W

Class Z
```

In this program, class X and W are the base classes. Class Y is derived from single base class X and is further used in inheritance. Thus it is a case of multilevel inheritance. Class Z is derived from class Y as well as class W, and thus is a case of multiple inheritance. Thus, in the derivation of class Z, multilevel as well as multiple inheritance is used, and hence the name hybrid inheritance.

8.10 MULTIPATH INHERITANCE

When a class is derived from two or more classes that in turn are derived from the same base class.

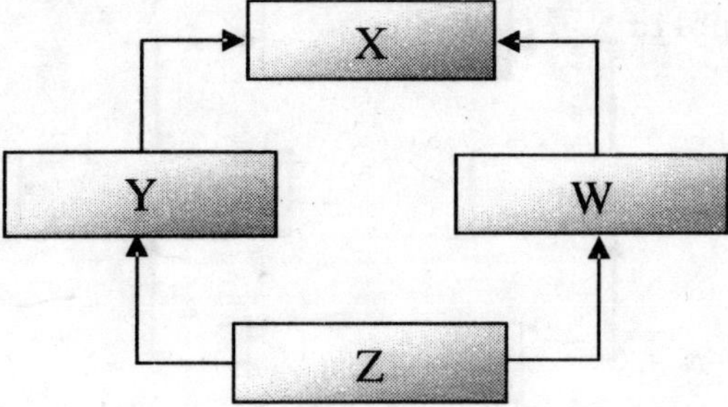

Figure 8.15: Multipath inheritance

In the Figure 8.15, X is the base class. Classes Y and W are derived from base class X. Further, class Z is derived from Y and W. Since Y and W have inherited same members of X, an ambiguity is generated which in turn is resolved using *virtual* keyword. The virtual mechanism is explained later. The following program demonstrates the multipath inheritance.

Listing 8.7

```
// Program to demonstrate multipath inheritance

#include <iostream.h>
#include <iomanip.h>
#include <string.h>
class X
{
   public:
        void showX()
       {
           cout << "\nClass X\n";
       }
};
class Y : public X
{
   public:
      void showY()
      {
         cout << "\nClass Y\n";
      }
};
class W : public X
{
   public:
      void showW()
      {
         cout << "\nClass W\n";
      }
};
class Z : public Y, public W
{
   public:
      void showZ() {
         cout << "\nClass Z\n";
      }
};
void main()
{
     Z objZ;
     // objZ.showX();        // error; ambiguity
```

```
    objZ.showY();           // from class Y
    objZ.showW();           // from class W
    objZ.showZ();
}
```

Test Run

```
Class Y
Class W
Class Z
```

In this program, class X is the base class. Classes Y and W are derived from base class X. Class Z is derived from class Y as well as class W. Thus, in the derivation of class Z, multilevel as well as multiple inheritance is used, and hence the name hybrid inheritance.

8.10.1 Ambiguity in Multipath Inheritance

When a class is derived from two or more base classes and these base classes are derived from the same class, this creates a diamond shaped inheritance tree as shown in Figure 8.16.

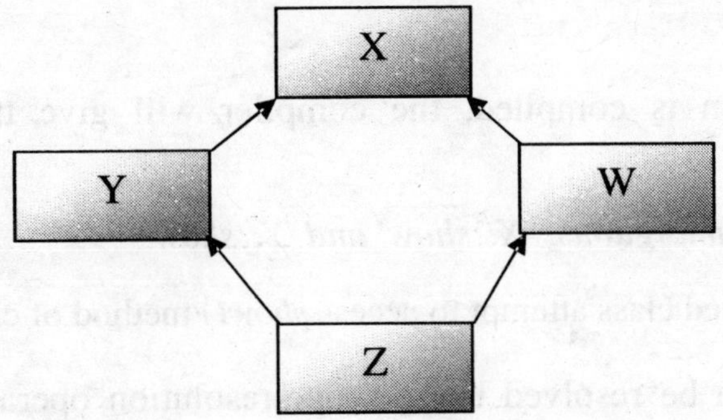

Figure 8.16: Diamond shaped inheritance tree

Class Y and W are both derived from class X, and class Z is derived by multiple inheritance from both Y and W classes. Ambiguity occurs when an object of class Z accesses a member of class X. Since both classes Y and W contain a copy of the members of class X, the compiler will no be able to figure out which copy of the member, inherited from class X, to use.

The following program demonstrates this type of ambiguity.

Listing 8.8

```
// Program to demonstrate the ambiguity that may arise when
// two or more classes are derived from the same class, and
// a new class is derived from these classes.

#include <iostream.h>
#include <iomanip.h>

class X
{
   public:
      void show()
      {
         cout << "\n Class X \n";
      }
};

class Y : public X { };
class W : public X { };
class Z : public Y, public W {  };

void main()
{
   Z objZ;
   objZ.show();       // ambiguity
}
```

When this program is compiled, the compiler will give the error message something like

Member is ambiguous: 'X::show' and 'Y::show'

when object of derived class attempt to access *show()* method of class X.

This ambiguity can be resolved using scope-resolution operator to specify the class whose copy to use. Thus, substituting the statement with either

```
objZ.X::show();          or          objZ.Y::show();
```

will solve the ambiguity.

The other approach, which is more professional, is to handle this ambiguity is using *virtual base class,* the mechanism also called *virtual inheritance.*

8.10.2 Virtual Base Class

When more than one class derives from the same class and these derived classes are further used in the derivation, prefix the keyword *virtual* before the access specifier in the class derivation. With *virtual derivation*, only single shared copy of the base class sub object is inherited regardless of how many times the base class occurs within the derivation hierarchy. The shared base class sub object is called *virtual base class.*

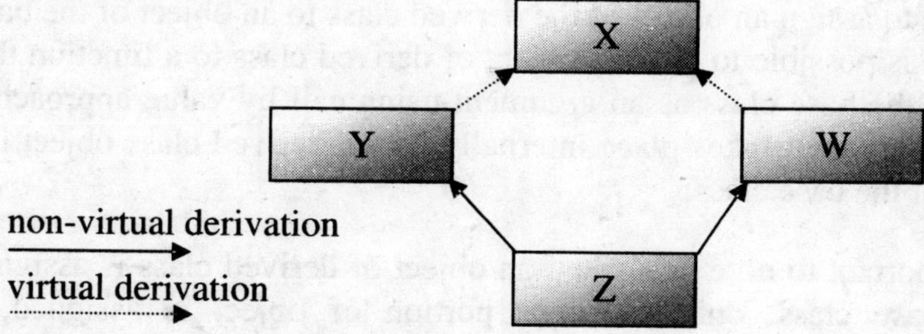

Figure 8.17: Virtual Inheritance

Using virtual inheritance, the duplication of base class sub objects and the ambiguity to which the duplication gives rise are removed.

Listing 8.9

```
// Program to demonstrate how ambiguity that may arise when
// two or more classes are derived from the same class, and
// a new class is derived from these classes is handled
// using virtual derivation

#include <iostream.h>
#include <iomanip.h>

class X
{
  public:
     void show() {
          cout << "\n Class X \n";
     }
};
class Y : virtual public X { }          // virtual derivation
class W : virtual public X { }          // virtual derivation
class Z : public Y, public W { }

void main()
{
     Z objZ;
     objZ.show();    // No ambiguity
}
```

This program works fine.

In *virtual derivation*, the *virtual* and *public* keywords can be used in any order.

8.11 OBJECT SLICING

It is possible to assign an object of the derived class to an object of the base class. Like wise, it is possible to pass an object of derived class to a function that takes an object of the base class as an argument using call by value approach. In this case also, assignment takes place internally as the derived class object is copied into object of the base class.

But it is important to note that when an object of derived class is assigned to an object of base class, only the base portion of object is assigned, portion corresponding the derived class is *chopped off* (*sliced off*). This phenomenon is called *object slicing*.

The following programs demonstrate the phenomenon of object slicing.

Listing 8.10

```
// Program to demonstrate the phenomenon of object slicing
// when an object of the derived class is assigned to
// an object of the base class

#include <iostream.h>
class A
{
   private:
     int a;
   public:
     A(int x)
     {
        a = x;
     }
     void show()
     {
        cout << "\na = " << a << "\n";
     }
};

class B : public A
{
```

```
   private:
     int b;
   public:
     B(int r, int s) : A(r) {
        b = s;
     }
     void show()
     {
        cout << "\nb = " << b << "\n";
     }
};

void main()
{
    A objA(10);
    B objB(12,25);
    objA = objB;
    objA.show();
}
```

Test Run

```
a = 12
```

Listing 8.11

```
// Program to demonstrate the phenomenon of object slicing when an
// object of the derived class is passed as argument to a global
// function that takes object of the base class as an argument

#include <iostream.h>
class A
{
   private:
     int a;
   public:
     A(int x)
     {
        a = x;
     }
     void show()
     {
        cout << "\na = " << a << "\n";
     }
};

class B : public A
{
```

```
    private:
      int b;
    public:
      B(int r, int s) : A(r) {
         b = s;
      }
      void show()
      {
         cout << "\nb = " << b << "\n";
      }
};

void func(A obj)
{
    obj.show();
}

void main()
{
    A objA(10);
    B objB(12,25);
    func(objB);
}
```

Test Run

```
a = 12
```

8.12 OVERRIDING MEMBER FUNCTIONS

The derived class can have a member functions with same *name*, same *return type* and same *list of arguments*, as defined in the base class. In such a case, the member function of the derived class overrides the member function of the base class. The overriding function can make refinements or enhancements suited to the derived class. With overriding functions, the calls in the program work the same way for objects of both base and derived classes.

Listing 8.12

```
// Program to demonstrate the overriding of functions

#include <iostream.h>
#include <iomanip.h>

class X
{
    protected:
```

```
      int a;
      float b;
   public:
      void read() {
         cout << "\nEnter a = ";
         cin >> a;
         cout << "Enter b = ";
         cin >> b;
      }
      void display() {
         cout << "\na = " << a;
         cout << "\nb = " << b << "\n";
      }
};

class Y : public X
{
   protected:
      int c;
   public:
      void read() {
         X::read();
         cout << "Enter c = ";
         cin >> c;
      }
      void display() {
         X::display();
         cout << "c = " << c << "\n";
      }
};

void main()
{
   Y objY;
   objY.read();
   objY.display();
}
```

Test Run

```
Enter a = 5
Enter b = 2.75
Enter c = 10

a = 5
b = 2.75
c = 10
```

In the above program, class *X* contains two data members *a* and *b* of type *int* and *float* declared in the protected section of the class. The class *X* also contains two member functions *read()* and *display()* to input the values for the data members and to display them. The class *Y* is derived from class *X* publicly, and adds its own data member named *c* of type *int*, and overrides *read()* and *display()* methods in the base class *X*.

The overriding methods in the derived class invokes the corresponding overridden methods of the base class *X* to handle the parts of the object that pertains to the class *X* and adds additional instructions to handle the parts of the object that are added in the derived class *Y*.

Listing 8.13

```
// Another program to demonstrate the overriding of functions

#include <iostream.h>
#include <iomanip.h>
#include <stdlib.h>
const int MAX = 10;

class Stack1
{
    protected:
       int elements[MAX];
       int top;
    public:
       Stack1()
       {
          top = -1;
       }
       void push(int num)
       {
          elements[++top] = num;
       }

       int pop()
       {
          return elements[top--];
       }
};
class Stack2 : public Stack1
{
   public:
      void push(int num)
      {
         if ( top == MAX - 1 )
```

```
        {
            cout << "\nERROR: Stack is full.";
            exit(1);
        }
        Stack1::push(num);
    }
    int pop()
    {
        if ( top == - 1 )
        {
            cout << "\nERROR: Stack is empty.";
            exit(1);
        }
        return Stack1::pop();
    }
};
void main()
{
    Stack2 s;
    s.push(1);
    s.push(5);
    s.push(7);
    cout << endl << s.pop();
    cout << endl << s.pop();
    cout << endl << s.pop() << endl;
}
```

Test Run

```
7
5
1
```

In the above program, class *Stack1* is designed to model a stack whose elements are of type *int*. It allows pushing integers onto the stack and popping them off. However, this design has a potential flaw. If you try to push too many elements onto the stack, the program might behave strangely, since data would be placed in memory beyond the end of *elements* array. Similarly, if you try to pop too many elements, the result would be meaningless, since you would be reading data from memory locations outside the *elements* array.

To cure these defects, a new class *Stack2*, derived from *Stack1*, is created. Objects of *Stack2* behave in exactly the same way as those of *Stack1*, except that a warning will be there if an attempt is made to push too many elements on the stack or pop too many elements from the stack.

The *Stack2* class contains two member functions, *push()* and *pop()*. These functions have the same name, the same arguments, and same return type, as the corresponding functions in the *Stack1* class.

When these functions are called from the *main()* functions using statement like

```
s.push(1);
```

how does the compiler know which of the two *push()* functions to use? The rule is simple — When the same function exists in both the base class and the derived class, the function in the derived class will be executed. We say that the derived class function *overrides* the base class function. So in the preceding statement, since *s* is an object of *Stack2* class, the *push()* function in *Stack2* will be executed not the one in *Stack1*.

The *push()* function in *Stack2* checks to see whether the stack is full. If it is full, it displays error message and causes the program to exit; otherwise, it calls the *push()* function in *Stack1*. Similarly, the *pop()* function in *Stack2* checks to see whether the stack is empty. If it is empty, it displays error message and causes the program to exit; otherwise, it calls the *pop()* function in *Stack1*.

From within the *push()* and *pop()* member functions of *Stack2* class, the *push()* and *pop()* functions are called using the scope resolution operator. In the absence of scope resolution operator, the compiler would consider that *push()* and *pop()* functions in the *Stack2* are calling themselves, which would lead to failure. Thus, the scope resolution operator allows specifying exactly to which class the member function belongs.

8.13 OBJECT COMPOSITION AND DELEGATION

By now I hope you understand concepts such as objects, classes, interfaces, and inheritance. The challenge lies in applying them to build flexible and reusable software. The two most common techniques for reusing functionality in object-oriented systems are *class inheritance* and *object composition*.

As explained, inheritance is a mechanism of building new classes by deriving from existing classes, and the relationship is called *is-a* or *kind-of* relationship.

There are many situations where objects are used as data members in a class. The mechanism of using objects in a class as data members is referred to as object composition. Object composition is an alternative to class inheritance. Here, new functionality is obtained by assembling or composing objects to support more powerful functionality. This new approach takes a view that an object can be a collection of many other objects and the relationship is called *has-a* relationship or *containership*.

In object-oriented programming, the *has-a* relationship occurs when an object of one class is contained in another class as a data member. In other words, a class can contain objects of other classes as its members.

```
class B {
   // . . .
};
class D {
   // . . .
   B objB;
   // . . .
};
```

In the case of inheritance, the constructors of base classes are invoked before the constructor of the derived class. However, in the case of composition, the constructor of the derived class *D* is invoked first and then the object of class *B* is created. The concept of creating the member objects first using respective member constructors and then the other ordinary members can also be accomplished in *has-a* relationship by using member initialization list in the constructor of the derived class as shown below.

```
class B
{
   // . . .
};
class D
{
   // . . .
   B objB;
   // . . .
   public:
      D(arg-list1) : objB(arg-list2)
      {
         // ordinary member initialization
      }
};
```

where *arg-list1* is the list of arguments to be supplied during the creation of object of class *D*. From *arg-list1*, the *arg-list2* is used to initialize the members of class *B*, and the remaining is used to initialize the ordinary member of class *D*. In this case, first the constructor of class *B* is executed and then the constructor of class *D* is executed.

Listing 8.14

```
// Program to demonstrate object composition
#include <iostream.h>
class B
{
  private:
     int a;
  public:
     B() {          // zero argument constructor
        a = 0;
     }
     B(int i) {     // single argument constructor
        cout << "\nConstructor B(int i) is invoked\n";
        a = i;
     }
     void showB()
     {
        cout << a;
     }
};
class D
{
   private:
     int d;
     B objB;
   public:
     D(int r, int s) : objB(r) {
        cout << "\n\nConstructor D(int r, int s) is invoked\n";
        d = s;
     }
     void showD() {
        cout << "\nObject member of class D = ";
        objB.showB();
        cout << "\nOrdinary member of class D = ";
        cout << d << "\n";
     }
};
void main()
{
   D objD(10,20);
   objD.showD();
}
```

Test Run

```
Constructor B(int i) is invoked

Constructor D(int r, int s) is invoked

Object member of class D = 10

Ordinary member of class D = 20
```

Delegation is a way of making object composition as powerful as inheritance for reuse. In delegation, two objects are involved in handling a request — a receiving object delegates operation to its delegate. This is analogous to subclasses deferring requests to parent classes. In certain situations, inheritance and composition can serve the same purpose.

It is illustrated by the following code:

```
class Publication
{
   // body of Publication class
};
class Sales
{
   // body of Sales class
};
```

The *book* class can be derived from the *Publication* and *Sales* classes using multiple inheritance as follows:

```
class Books : public Publication, public Sales
{
   // body of Book class
};
```

The above functionality can also be achieved by composing objects of classes *Publication* and *Sales* as data members of *book* class as follows:

```
class Books
{
   // . . .
   Publication pub; // object of Publication class
   Sales sal;       // object of Sales class
   // . . .
};
```

The classes *Publication* and *Sales* have same declarations in both the cases, but are used in different way by the *book* class. Although, containership is an alternative to inheritance and offers the functionality of inheritance, it does not provide flexibility of ownership. Inheritance relationship is simpler to implement and offers a clearer conceptual framework.

Listing 8.15

```
// Program to demonstrate object composition and delegation
#include <iostream.h>
class Publication
{
  private:
    char title[40];
    int price;
  public:
    void getData()
    {
      cout << "Enter title : ";
      cin.getline(title, 40);
      cout << "Enter price : ";
      cin >> price;
    }
    void showData()
    {
      cout << "Title : " << title;
      cout << "\nPrice : " << price;
    }
};
class Sales
{
  private:
    int saleFigures[3];  // sales Figures for last 3 months
  public:
    void getData();
    void showData();
};
void Sales::getData()
{
  for ( int i = 0; i < 3; i++ )
  {
    cout << "Enter sales of Month #" << i+1 << " : ";
    cin >> saleFigures[i];
  }
}
void Sales::showData()
{
```

```
   int totalSales = 0;
   for ( int i = 0; i < 3; i++ )
   {
      cout << "\nSales of Month #" << i+1 << " = "
           << saleFigures[i];
      totalSales += saleFigures[i];
   }
   cout << "\n\nTotal Sales = " << totalSales;
}
class Book
{
   private:
      int pages;
      Publication pub;
      Sales sal;
   public:
      void getData()
      {
         pub.getData();
         cout << "Enter number of pages : ";
         cin >> pages;
         sal.getData();
      }
      void showData()
      {
         pub.showData();
         cout << "\nNumber of pages = " << pages;
         sal.showData();
      }
};
void main()
{
   Book bookObj;
   cout << "\n\nEnter book publication data\n\n";
   bookObj.getData();
   cout << "\n\nBook publication data entered by u\n\n";
   bookObj.showData();
}
```

Test Run

```
Enter book publication data

Enter title : C++ for C Programmers
Enter price : 195
Enter number of pages : 400
Enter sales of Month #1 : 200
Enter sales of Month #2 : 500
```

```
Enter sales of Month #3 : 300

Book publication data entered by u

Title : C++ for C Programmers
Price : 195
Number of pages = 400
Sales of Month #1 = 200
Sales of Month #2 = 500
Sales of Month #3 = 300

Total Sales = 1000
```

The above purpose can also be served using inheritance as shown below.

Listing 8.16

```
// Program to demonstrate how inheritance and composition
// can serve the same purpose

#include <iostream.h>
class Publication
{
   private:
      char title[40];
      int price;
   public:
      void getData()
      {
         cout << "Enter title : ";
         cin.getline(title, 40);
         cout << "Enter price : ";
         cin >> price;
      }
      void showData()
      {
         cout << "Title : " << title;
         cout << "\nPrice : " << price;
      }
};

class Sales
{
   private:
      int saleFigures[3];   // sales Figures for last 3 months
   public:
      void getData();
      void showData();
};
```

```
void Sales::getData()
{
   for ( int i = 0; i < 3; i++ )  {
      cout << "Enter sales of Month #" << i+1 << " : ";
      cin >> saleFigures[i];
   }
}
void Sales::showData()
{
   int totalSales = 0;
   for ( int i = 0; i < 3; i++ )
   {
      cout << "\nSales of Month #" << i+1 << " = "
           << saleFigures[i];
      totalSales += saleFigures[i];
   }
   cout << "\n\nTotal Sales = " << totalSales;
}
class Book : public Publication, public Sales
{
   private:
      int pages;
   public:
      void getData()
      {
         Publication::getData();
         cout << "Enter number of pages : ";
         cin >> pages;
         Sales::getData();
      }
      void showData()
      {
         Publication::showData();
         cout << "\nNumber of pages = " << pages;
         Sales::showData();
      }
};
void main()
{
   Book bookObj;
   cout << "\n\nEnter book publication data\n\n";
   bookObj.getData();
   cout << "\n\nBook publication data entered by u\n\n";
   bookObj.showData();
}
```

The output of this program will be same as that of previous program.

8.14 ORDER OF EXECUTION OF CONSTRUCTORS

Constructors play an important role in initializing an object's data members and allocating required resources such a memory. The derived class need not have a constructor as long as the base class has a no-argument (default) constructor.

However, if the base class has one or more constructors with arguments then it is mandatory for the derived class to have a constructor with arguments and pass the arguments to the base class constructor.

In case of inheritance, usually the objects of derived class are created instead of base class. Hence, it makes sense for the derived class to have a constructor and pass arguments to the constructor of the base class. When an object of the derived class is created, the constructor of the base class is executed first and then the constructor of the derived class.

Basically, when the object of the derived class is created, the constructors in the class hierarchy build their own part of sub object, *i.e.*, part of the object that corresponds to that class. Ultimately when all the constructors finish their execution, a complete object of the derived class is in place and ready for use.

The order of execution of constructors is always as following:

1. *Base class constructor*. If there is more than base class, the constructors are executed in the order the base classes appear in the class derivation list, not in the order in which they are listed in the member initialization list. However, if there is a virtual base class in the class derivation list, its constructor will be executed first irrespective of its position the derivation list.
2. *Member class object constructor*. If there is more than one member class object, the constructors are executed in order the objects are declared in the class, not in the order in which they are listed in the member initialization list.
3. *Derived class constructor*.

As a general rule, the derived class constructor should never assign a value to the base class data member directly, but rather pass the value to the appropriate base class constructor. Otherwise, the implementation of two classes becomes *tightly coupled*, and it can be more difficult to modify or extend the base class implementation correctly. It is our responsibility, as the base class designed, to provide appropriate set of base class constructors.

Following points must be kept in mind about constructors in relation to inheritance:

- If no constructor is defined in a class, the compiler inserts no-argument constructor with empty body, *i.e.*, constructor of type

```
className() { }
```

- If a class contains parameterized constructor(s), the compiler will not insert zero argument constructor, even if it is not defined in the class. In this case, if you want to use no-argument constructor, you have to define yourself.
- In case of multiple inheritance, the constructors are invoked in the order of derivation. However, if a class is virtually derived, its constructor will be invoked first irrespective of its position the derivation.
- If a base class has a parameterized constructor, then the derived class must make an explicit call to the base class constructor and pass the required parameter.

8.15 ORDER OF EXECUTION OF DESTRUCTORS

Unlike constructors, destructors in the class hierarchy are invoked in the reverse order of constructor invocation. The destructor of that class, whose constructor was executed last, while building the object of derived class, will be executed first whenever the object of the derived class goes out of scope.

Basically, when the object of the derived class goes out of scope, the destructors in the class hierarchy destroy their own part of sub object, *i.e.*, part of the object that corresponds to that class. Ultimately when all the destructors finish their execution, complete object of the derived class is destroyed.

If the destructors are missing in any class in the class hierarchy, then nothing is done to sub object that corresponds to that class.

Following program illustrates the order of execution of constructors and destructors in handling the objects of a derived class.

Listing 8.17

```
//Program to demonstrate order of execution of constructors

#include <iostream.h>
class A {
    private:
      int a;
```

```
    public:
      A() {
         a = 1;
         cout << "\nConstructor of Class A\n";
      }
      ~A() {
         cout << "\nDestructor of Class A\n";
      }
};
class B {
    private:
      int b;
    public:
      B() {
         b = 2;
         cout << "\nConstructor of Class B\n";
      }
      ~B() {
         cout << "\nDestructor of Class B\n";
      }
};
class C
{
    private:
       int c;
    public:
       C() {
          c = 3;
          cout << "\nConstructor of Class C\n";
       }
       ~C() {
          cout << "\nDestructor of Class C\n";
       }
};
class D : public A, virtual public B
{
    private:
       int d;
       C objC;
     public:
       D() {
          d = 4;
          cout << "\nConstructor of Class D\n";
       }
       ~D() {
          cout << "\nDestructor of Class D\n";
       }
};
```

```
void main()
{
    D objD;
}
```

Test Run

```
Constructor of Class B
Constructor of Class A
Constructor of Class C
Constructor of Class D
Destructor of Class D
Destructor of Class C
Destructor of Class A
Destructor of Class B
```

However, if the object of the derived class is created dynamically using the *new* operator, then it must be destroyed explicitly using the *delete* operator.

Listing 8.18

```
// Program to demonstrate the order of execution of destructors
// in class hierarchy, when object is created dynamically

#include <iostream.h>
class A
{
    public:
       A() {
          cout << "\nConstructor of class A\n";
       }
       ~A() {
          cout << "\nDestructor of class A\n";
       }
};
class B
{
    public:
       B() {
          cout << "\nConstructor of class B\n";
       }
       ~B() {
          cout << "\nDestructor of class B\n";
       }
};
```

```
class C : public A, public B
{
    public:
       C() {
          cout << "\nConstructor of class C\n";
       }
       ~C() {
          cout << "\nDestructor of class C\n";
       }
};
void main()
{
    C *ptr = new C(); // object created dynamically
    delete ptr;          // delete object created dynamically
}
```

Test Run

```
Constructor of class A
Constructor of class B
Constructor of class C
Destructor of class C
Destructor of class B
Destructor of class A
```

However, if you forget to destroy the object using *delete* operator, the destructors will not be invoked, and the output of the program will be as shown below:

```
Constructor of class A
Constructor of class B
Constructor of class C
```

QUICK RECAP

In this chapter, we have learnt that

- Inheritance is a mechanism that allow new classes to be derived from existing class(es) that facilitates reusability, where existing class(es) is/are known as base class(es) and the newly created class is known as derived class.
- Derived class inherits all the properties of the parent class and adds its own.

- Inheritance represents *is-a* or *kind-of* relationship.
- A class can be derived using *public*, *private* and *protected* derivation.
- In public derivation, public and protected members of the base class remain public and protected members of the derived class, respectively.
- In private derivation, public and protected members of the base class become private members of the derived class.
- In protected derivation, public members of the base class become protected members of the derived class.
- Various forms of inheritance are single, multiple, multilevel, hierarchical, hybrid and multipath.
- Multiple inheritance may cause ambiguity when more than one base class have same member function. This ambiguity is resolved using scope resolution operator.
- Multipath inheritance may also cause ambiguity when a class is derived from more than one base class that in turn are derived from the same base class(es). This ambiguity is resolved using virtual base classes.
- Object slicing is the phenomenon that causes portion of the object corresponding to the derived class is chopped/sliced off when an object of the derived class is assigned to an object of the derived class or when an object of the derived class is passed as an argument to a function that takes object of the base class as its argument.
- Derived class can have a same member function as in the base class. In this class, the member function of the derived class overrides the base class member function. However, the member function of the base class can be called on an object of the derived class using scope resolution operator.
- Another technique for reusing functionality is *object composition*, where an object is contained in another class as a data member.
- Composition represents *has-a* relationship.
- Order of execution of constructors is — constructors of the base class(es) are executed in order the base class(es) appear in the class derivation list, however if there is a virtual base class in the class derivation list, its constructor will be executed first irrespective of its position in the derivation list; constructors of the member class objects in order of their declaration; constructor of the derived class.
- Order of execution of destructors is reverse of constructor execution.

MULTIPLE CHOICE QUESTIONS

1. **Consider the following code**

```
class B {
    // ... members of the class
}
class D : private B {
    // ... members of the class
}
void main()
{
    D objD;
    // ... more code
}
```

Which of the following can object *objD* access?

(*a*) Public members of class B (*b*) Protected members of class B
(*c*) Public members of class D (*d*) Protected members of class D

2. **Consider the following code**

```
class B
{
    // ... members of the class
}
class D : protected B
{
    // ... members of the class
}
void main()
{
    D objD;
    // ... more code
}
```

Which of the following can object *objD* access?

(*a*) Public members of class B (*b*) Public members of class D
(*c*) Protected members of class B (*d*) Protected members of class D

3. **Consider the following code**

```
class B
{
    // ... members of the class
}
class D : public B
{
    // ... members of the class
}
```

```
void main()
{
   D objD;
   // ... more code
}
```

Which of the following can object *objD* access?

(*a*) Public members of class B
(*b*) Protected members of class B
(*c*) Protected members of class D
(*d*) Public members of class D

4. Consider the following code

```
class B {
   // ... members of the class
}
class D : public B {
   // ... members of the class
}
```

Which of the following statement(s) are true about member functions of class D?

(*a*) Can access private members of class D.
(*b*) Can access protected members of class B
(*c*) Can access protected members of class D
(*d*) All of above

5. Which of the following statement is true about protected derivation?

(*a*) Private members of base class become protected members of derived class.
(*b*) Protected members of base class become public members of derived class.
(*c*) Public members of base class become protected members of derived class.
(*d*) Protected derivation does not affect private and protected members of base class.

6. Which of the following statement is true about private derivation?

(*a*) Only protected members of base class become private members of derived class.
(*b*) Private derivation does not affect protected members of base class.
(*c*) Only public members of base class become private members of derived class.
(*d*) Protected as well as public members of base class become private members of the derived class.

7. Which of the following statement is true about public derivation?
   (*a*) All members of base class become public members of derived class.
   (*b*) Only protected of base class become public members of derived class.
   (*c*) Protected members of base class remain protected members of derived class and public members of base class remain public members of derived class.
   (*d*) Public derivation is not a valid derivation.
8. Which of the following statement about the execution of constructors is true?
   (*a*) Constructors of the object class members are executed first.
   (*b*) Constructor of the derived class is executed first.
   (*c*) Constructors of the base class(es) is/are executed first in order of their derivation.
   (*d*) None of above.
9. Which of the following statement about the execution of destructors is true?
   (*a*) Destructors of the object class member are executed first.
   (*b*) Destructor of the derived class is executed first.
   (*c*) Destructors of the base class(es) is/are executed first in order of their derivation.
   (*d*) None of above.
10. Which of the following is not a valid type of relationship in the context of object-oriented programming?
   (*a*) The *is-a* relationship. (*b*) The *has-a* relationship.
   (*c*) The *was-a* relationship. (*d*) None of above.
11. In which form of inheritance, you have to use virtual base class to resolve the ambiguity?
   (*a*) Multiple inheritance (*b*) Multilevel inheritance
   (*c*) Hierarchical inheritance (*d*) None of above.
12. Object slicing takes place when ______________
   (*a*) Object of derived class is assigned to base class type.
   (*b*) Object of base class is assigned to derived class type.
   (*c*) Object of base class is passed as an argument to a function that takes object of derived class type as its argument.
   (*d*) All of above.
13. The use of inheritance facilitates . . . . .
   (*a*) Extensibility (*b*) Reusability
   (*c*) Scalability. (*d*) Interoperability

14. Which of the following statement is not true?
    (*a*) An object of a derived class cannot access private and protected members of the base class.
    (*b*) There is no difference between private and protected derivation.
    (*c*) The size of a derived class object is equal to the sum of sizes of data members in the derived class and base class.
    (*d*) Multiple inheritance is different from multilevel inheritance.

15. Which of the following character is used in class derivation?
    (*a*) :   (*b*) –
    (*c*) ;   (*d*) ::

REVIEW EXERCISES

1. What is inheritance?
2. What is the usefulness of inheritance?
3. What are various forms of inheritance?
4. Does the source code of the base class is required in order to derive a class from it?
5. Can a member function of a base class access any member of the derived class?
6. What is the difference between *private*, *public*, and *protected* derivation?
7. When do we use the protected visibility specifier for a class member?
8. In case of multiple inheritance, what is order of execution of constructors?
9. What is virtual derivation? Where is it used?
10. When objects are created statically, the constructors and destructors are invoked automatically. What is the case when objects are created dynamically?
11. When does an ambiguity occur in multiple inheritance? How can this ambiguity be resolved?
12. When does an ambiguity occur in multipath inheritance? How can this ambiguity be resolved?
13. A class is derived using private derivation. In private derivation, all the members of the base class become private members of the derived class. Is it possible, to make a member function of the base class as public member

function of the derived class? If yes, demonstrate with the help of a suitable example.

14. A class is derived using public derivation. In public derivation, the private, protected and public members of the base class remain as private, protected and public members of the derived class. Is it possible, to make a public member function of the base class as private member function of the derived class? If yes, demonstrate with the help of a suitable example.

15. Consider the following program.

```
class A
{
    private:
        int a, b;
    public:
        A(int x, int y) {
            a = x;   b = y;
        }
};
class B : public A
{
    private:
        int d, e, f;
    public:
        B(int r, int s, int t, int u, int v)  : A(r,s) {
            d = t; e = u; f = v;
        }
};
void func(A a)
{
    cout << endl << sizeof(a) << ",";
}
void main() {
    B bb(1,2,3,4,5);
    func(bb);
    cout << sizeof(bb) << endl;
}
```

16. Is there any error? If yes, what is the error and what is its solution? If not, then what will be its output?

```
class A
{
    protected:
        int a;
    public:
        A() { }
        A(int x) {
            a = x;
```

```
        }
        void show()
        {
            cout << "\na = " << a << "\n";
        }
};
class B : public A
{
    private:
        int b;
    public:
        B(int r, int s) : A(r) {
            b = s;
        }
        void show()
        {
            cout << "\na = " << a << "\nb = " << b << "\n";
        }
};
void main()
{
    A objA;
    B objB(10,20);
    objA = objB;   //assign derived class object to base class
    objA.show();
}
```

PROGRAMMING EXERCISES

1. Assume that a bank maintains two types of accounts – *savings* and *current*. The savings account provides compound interest, cash deposit and cash withdrawal facilities but no cheque book facility. The current account provides no interest, no cash deposit and no cash withdrawal facilities but provides cheque book facility. However, the current account holder needs to main certain minimum balance otherwise a service charge is imposed. Create a class *Account* with data members *account holder's name*, *account number*, and *opening balance*. From *Account* class, derive two classes named *Saving* and *Current* to model saving account and current account respectively.

   Include the required member functions to accomplish the following tasks:

   - Deposit an amount in an account
   - Display the account details
   - Compute interest and update balance
   - Withdraw an amount from an account

Write a program that creates objects of *Saving* and *Current* classes, and performs above mentioned operation on these objects.

2. Assume that a publishing company markets prints books and digital books (electronic form – CD'). Create a class named *Publication* with data members named *title*, *price*, and *author's name*. From *Publication* class, derive two classes named *Book* and *Ebook*. The *Book* class adds a page count data member named *pcount* while *Ebook* adds data member playing time name *ptime*. Each of these classes must have member function *getData()* to read class specific data from keyboard and *displayData()* to output the class specific data to the computer screen. Write a program to test these classes.
3. If a class *D* is derived from two base classes *B1* and *B2*, then write these classes, each containing a no-argument constructor. Ensure that while building an object of type *D*, firstly constructor of *B2* gets called, followed by that of *B1*. Also provide a destructor in each class. In what order would these destructors get called?
4. A small organization wish to maintain a data base of its employees. The following figure models the relationship between classes representing employees of the organization.

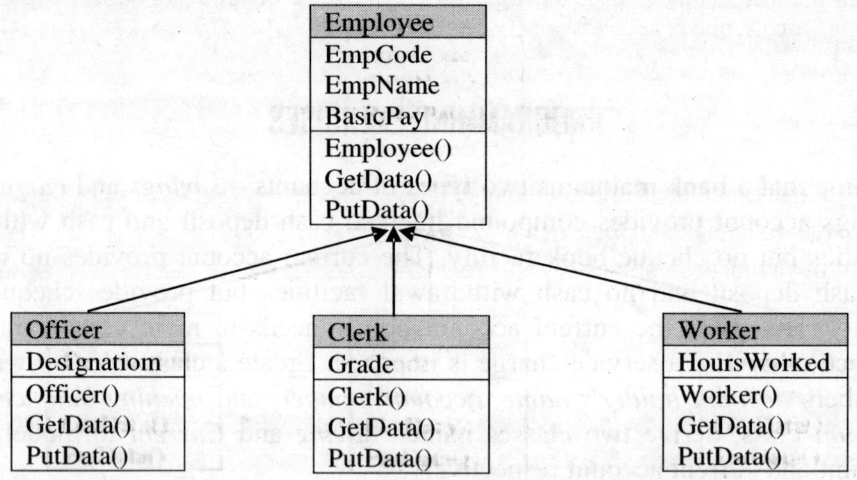

Create the specified class and using these classes write a program to test them.

❑ ❑ ❑

Chapter 9

Virtual Functions and Polymorphism

Learning Objectives

After reading this chapter, students will be able to explain the

- concept of polymorphism and its usefulness
- types of polymorphism
- concept of binding
- difference between early binding and late binding
- concept of virtual functions
- use of virtual functions in implementing runtime polymorphism
- pure virtual functions and their use
- concept of virtual destructors

9.1 INTRODUCTION

Polymorphism is another important feature of object-oriented programming. Polymorphism is a combination of two words *poly* and *morphism*. The word *poly* means *many* and the word *morphism* means *forms*. Thus, *polymorphism* means *many forms*. More formally, polymorphism can be defined as a technique that allows defining various forms of a single function that can be shared by various objects to perform the operations.

We have already seen how concept of polymorphism is implemented using overloaded operators and functions. The overloaded functions are selected for call by matching the arguments, both in number and type, also called as *signature* of a function. Note that the compiler knows the information about the number and type of arguments at the time of compilation, therefore, the compiler is able to select the appropriate function for a particular call at the compile time itself. This is called *early binding* or *static binding*. It is *early* in the sense that a function definition is bound to its call at the compile time and *static* in the sense that this binding cannot be changed at execution time.

There have been situations, where it is more appropriate that member function could be selected while the program is executing. At execution time, when it is known what objects are under consideration, the appropriate version of member is invoked. This is known as *run time polymorphism*. Since, the function is linked with a particular object after the compilation, *i.e.*, during program execution, the process is called *late binding* or *dynamic binding*. It is *late* in the sense that a function definition is bound to its call at the execution time and *dynamic* in the sense that this binding can be changed at execution time.

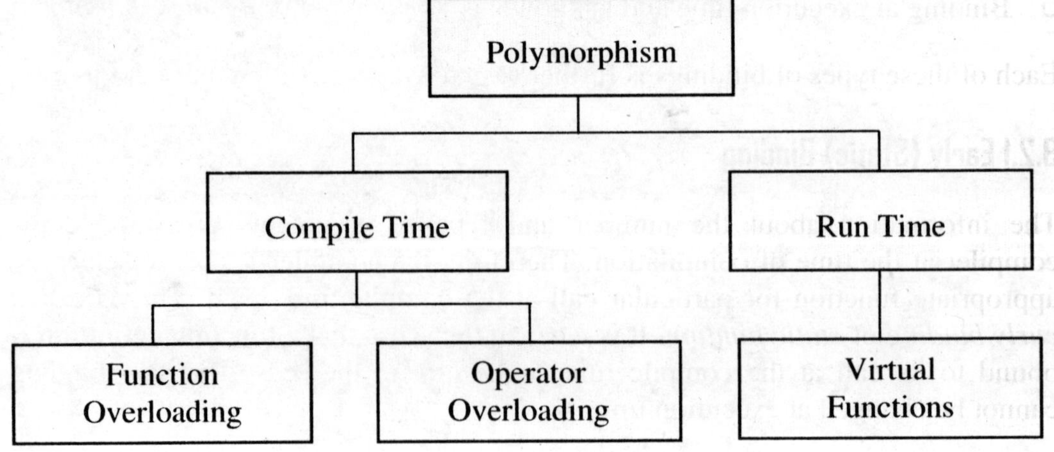

Figure 9.1: Polymorphism in C++

9.2 CONCEPT OF BINDING

Before we talk about the concept of binding, let us review the possible way of organizing the programs. When we write a program, either of the following approach to organize the programs can be used:

- Declare the prototype of each function to be used in the subsequent parts of the program and then define these functions at later course. In this way, a function call can appear before its definition. The compiler gets the information about the functions from the prototype and does the necessary type checking about its return type, number and type of arguments.
- Define the functions before the first place of its call. In this way, when the compiler encounters function call, it has complete information about the function from its definition and can perform the necessary type checking about its return type, number and type of arguments.

The preferred approach is to declare the function prototypes in the beginning of the program. This approach will also let the reader know the number and type of functions used in the program just by reading the first few lines of the program.

Now let us move to concept of binding.

Binding is the process of resolving the function call, *i.e.*, linking the function call to its definition. The binding can take place at either of the following stages:

- Binding at compilation time and is known as *early binding* or *static binding*.
- Binding at execution time and is known as *late binding* or *dynamic binding*.

Each of these types of bindings is further explained in the following sections.

9.2.1 Early (Static) Binding

The information about the number and type of arguments is available the compiler at the time of compilation. Therefore, the compiler is able to select the appropriate function for particular call at the compile time itself. This is called *early binding* or *static binding*. It is *early* in the sense that a function definition is bound to its call at the compile time and *static* in the sense that this binding cannot be changed at execution time.

Consider the following listings:

Listing 9.1

```
// Program to illustrate concept of early binding without classes
#include <iostream.h>
#include <iomanip.h>
void swap(int &, int &);     // prototype for integer variables
void swap(float &, float &); // prototype for float variables
void main()
{
   int intVar1 = 10, intVar2 = 20;
   cout << "Before swapping" << endl;
   cout << "---------------" << endl;
   cout << "First integer variable  = " << intVar1 << endl;
   cout << "Second integer variable = " << intVar2 << endl;
   // invoke integer version of swap function
   swap ( intVar1, intVar2 );
   cout << endl << "After swapping" << endl;
   cout << "---------------" << endl;
   cout << "First integer variable  = " << intVar1 << endl;
   cout << "Second integer variable = " << intVar2 << endl;
   float floatVar1 = 10.25, floatVar2 = 20.75;
   cout << endl << "Before swapping" << endl;
   cout << "---------------" << endl;
   cout << "First float variable  = " << floatVar1 << endl;
   cout << "Second float variable = " << floatVar2 << endl;
   // invoke float version of swap function
   swap ( floatVar1, floatVar2 );
   cout << endl << "After swapping" << endl;
   cout << "---------------" << endl;
   cout << "First float variable  = " << floatVar1 << endl;
   cout << "Second float variable = " << floatVar2 << endl;
} // end of main() functions
// integer version of the swap function
void swap ( int &a, int &b) {
    int temp;
    temp = a;
    a = b;
    b = temp;
 }
 // float version of the swap function
 void swap ( float &a, float &b) {
    float temp;
    temp = a;
    a = b;
    b = temp;
 }
```

Test Run

```
Before swapping
---------------
First integer variable  = 10
Second integer variable = 20

After swapping
--------------
First integer variable  = 20
Second integer variable = 10

Before swapping
---------------
First float variable  = 10.25
Second float variable = 20.75

After swapping
--------------
First float variable  = 20.75
Second float variable = 10.25
```

In the above program, the function prototypes of overloaded function *swap()* are given. From these prototypes, the compiler gets the information that this function is overloaded where one takes integer arguments and other takes float arguments. When the *swap()* function is called, the compiler performs the type checking with its respective prototypes, and if the match is OK, it goes ahead otherwise signals a syntax error at this point. The definition of the integer version of *swap()* function and float version is also given. When the call for *swap()* function for swapping integer variables is found, at this point the compiler binds (links) the function call statement for integer arguments with this definition. Similarly, when the call for *swap()* function for swapping float variables is found, the compiler binds (links) the function call statement for float arguments with its corresponding definition. Thus, all function calls are resolved at the compilation time.

Listing 9.2

```
// Program to illustrate concept of early binding with classes
#include <iostream.h>
#include <iomanip.h>

class BaseClass                  //  base class
{
    protected:
```

```
        int d;
    public:
        BaseClass() { }
        BaseClass(int arg) {
            d = arg;
        }
        void display() {
            cout << endl << "Display method of base class";
            cout << endl << "d = " << d << endl;
        }
};
class DerivedClass : public BaseClass     //derived class
{
    private:
        int k;
    public:
        DerivedClass() { }
        DerivedClass(int arg) {
            k = arg;
        }
        void display() {
            cout << "\nDisplay method of derived class";
            cout << endl << "d = " << d << endl;
            cout << endl << "k = " << k << endl;
        }
};
void main()          // main function
{
    // create instance of base class
    BaseClass varB(10);
    // call display function on instance of base class
    varB.display();
    // create instance of base class
    DerivedClass varD(20);
    // call display function on instance of derived class
    varD.display();
}
```

Test Run

```
Display method of base class
d = 10

Display method of derived class
d = 10
k = 20
```

In the above program, the base class and the derived class have the same member function *display()* as shown. When the member function *display()* is called on an instance of base class, *i.e.*, object *varB*, compiler binds (links) this call with the definition of the *display()* function in the base class. When the member function *display()* is called on an instance of derived class, *i.e.*, object *varD*, compiler binds (links) this call with the definition of the *display()* function in the derived class.

Thus, all calls to functions are resolved at the compilation time.

9.2.2 Late (Dynamic) Binding

There have been situations, where it is more appropriate that member function could be selected while the program is running. At run time, when it is known what objects are under consideration, the appropriate version of member is invoked. This is known as *run time polymorphism*. Since, the function is linked with a particular class after the compilation, *i.e.*, during program execution, the process is called *late binding* or *dynamic binding*. It is *late* in the sense that a function definition is bound to its call at the execution time and *dynamic* in the sense that this binding can be changed at execution time.

Run time polymorphism is achieved using following steps:

- Preceding the member function with keyword *virtual* in the base class.
- Accessing the member function through a pointer of a base class.

Consider the following listings.

Listing 9.3

```
// Program to illustrate the concept of late binding when
// member functions are accessed using a pointer
// variable of base class

#include<iostream.h>
#include<iomanip.h>

class BaseClass          // base class
{
    private:
       int d;
    public:
       BaseClass() { }
       BaseClass(int arg) {
          d = arg;
       }
```

```
        virtual void display() {                  // 1
            cout << endl << "Display method of base class";
            cout << endl << "d = " << d << endl;
        }
};
class DerivedClass : public BaseClass    // derived class
{
    private:
        int k;
    public:
        DerivedClass() { }
        DerivedClass(int arg) {
             k = arg;
        }
        void display() {
            cout << "\nDisplay method of derived class";
            cout << endl << "d = " << d << endl;
            cout << endl << "k = " << k << endl;
        }
};
void main()     // main function
{
    // declare pointer to base class
    BaseClass *basePtr;                           // 2
    // create instance of base class
    BaseClass varB(10);
    // assign address of base class to pointer
    basePtr = &varB;                              // 3
    // call display function using pointer
    basePtr->display();                           // 4
    // create instance of base class
    DerivedClass varD(20);
    // assign address of derived class to pointer
    basePtr = &varD;                              // 5
    // call display function
    basePtr->display();                           // 6
}
```

Test Run

```
Display method of base class
d = 10

Display method of derived class
d = 10
k = 20
```

You can see, in the above program at line labeled 1, the only difference from program of *Listing 9.2* is that we have prefixed keyword *virtual* with *display()*

member function of base class. The *virtual* keyword tells the compiler that binding for this member function, whether the function is called on object of base class or an object of derived class, be delayed till the program execution. In statement labeled 2, a pointer to the base class is declared, that can be used to call the appropriate version of *display()* member function in the class hierarchy. In statement labeled 3, the address of an object *varB*, which is an object of base class, is assigned to pointer variable *basePtr*. In statement labeled 4, the *display()* member function of base class is invoked as the address assigned to the pointer variable is of an object of base class. In statement labeled 5, the address of an object *varD*, which is an object of derived class, is assigned to pointer variable *basePtr*. In statement labeled 6, the *display()* of derived class is invoked as the address assigned to the pointer variable is of an object of base class.

Thus, all calls to *display()* member functions are resolved at the execution (run) time, whereas for other functions, still all calls are resolved at compilation time.

However, if you remove the keyword *virtual* from the header of the *display()* member function, the program will give the following output.

Test Run

```
Display method of base class
d = 10

Display method of base class
d = 10
```

9.3 VIRTUAL FUNCTIONS

A member function whose function declaration is preceded by *virtual* keyword is known as a virtual function. These functions are defined in a base class in the public section and they provide a mechanism by which the derived classes can override it. These functions are bound dynamically.

The syntax for defining a virtual function is

```
class SampleClass
{
   private:
      . . . . .   // data members of the class
   public:
      . . . .     // function members of the class
      virtual ReturnType FunctionName( agruments )
      {
```

```
        . . . . . // body of the virtual function
    }
};
```

At run time, it allows to decide which overridden form of the function is to used based on the type of object pointed by the base pointer rather than the type of derived pointer.

9.4 PURE VIRTUAL FUNCTIONS

Virtual function, normally, serves as a framework for the future design of the class hierarchy as they can be overridden in the derived classes. In many cases, these virtual functions are declared without any body, *i.e.*, they don't have any definition. Such virtual functions are called *pure virtual functions*. These functions are also called *do-nothing* functions.

The syntax for defining a pure virtual function is

```
class SampleClass
{
  private:
    . . . .     // data members of the class
  public:
    . . . .     // function members of the class
    virtual ReturnType FunctionName ( agruments ) = 0;
};
```

Any derived class of a base class containing pure virtual functions must either define these functions or re-declare them as pure virtual functions.

It is not possible to define the body of a pure virtual function in class template, however, it can be defined outside the class template.

9.5 ABSTRACT CLASSES

In is important to note that any class containing pure virtual functions cannot be used to define objects and hence such classes are called *abstract classes*. In contrast, the classes without virtual functions are called *concrete classes*.

9.6 VIRTUAL DESTRUCTORS AND POLYMORPHISM

A problem can occur when using polymorphism to process dynamically allocated objects of a class of hierarchy. If an object with a non-virtual destructor is destroyed explicitly by applying a *delete* operator to a base class pointer to the object, the base class destructor, matching the pointer type, is called on the object. This occurs regardless of the type of fact that each class's destructor has a different name. This fact is illustrated in the following program.

Listing 9.4

```
// Program to illustrate that execution of destructors in
// class hierarchy when destructors are non-virtual
#include <iostream.h>
class A
{
    public:
        A() {
            cout << "\nConstructor of class A invoked\n";
        }
        ~A() {
            cout << "\nDestructor of class A invoked\n";
        }
};
class B : public A {
    public:
        B() {
            cout << "\nConstructor of class B invoked\n";
        }
        ~B() {
            cout << "\nDestructor of class B invoked\n";
        }
};
class C : public B {
    public:
        C() {
            cout << "\nConstructor of class C invoked\n";
        }
        ~C() {
            cout << "\nDestructor of class C invoked\n";
        }
};
void main()
{
    A *ptrObjA = new C();
    delete ptrObjA;
}
```

Test Run

```
Constructor of class A invoked

Constructor of class B invoked

Constructor of class C invoked

Destructor of class A invoked
```

Note that in the above program, pointer to the base class is used to point the object of the derived class *C*. When object of derived class *C* is created dynamically, the constructors in the class hierarchy are invoked in the right order. However, when the same object is deleted explicitly using the *delete* operator, only destructor of the base class is invoked.

The simple solution to this problem is that you declare the base-class destructor as *virtual*. This makes all derived class destructors virtual even they do not have the same name as the base class destructor. Now, if an object in the hierarchy is destroyed explicitly by applying a *delete* operator to a base class pointer to the derived class object, the destructor for the appropriate class is invoked. Remember that when a derived class object is destroyed, the base class part of the derived class object is also destroyed — the base class destructor automatically executed after the derived class destructor.

This fact is illustrated in the next program.

Listing 9.5

```
// Program to illustrate that the execution of destructors in
// the class hierarchy when destructors are declared virtual

#include <iostream.h>

class A
{
   public:
      A() {
         cout << "\nConstructor of class A invoked\n";
      }
      virtual ~A() {
          cout << "\nDestructor of class A invoked\n";
      }
};

class B : public A
{
   public:
      B() {
```

```
        cout << "\nConstructor of class B invoked\n";
      }
      ~B() {
        cout << "\nDestructor of class B invoked\n";
      }
};
class C : public B
{
   public:
      C() {
        cout << "\nConstructor of class C invoked\n";
      }
      ~C() {
        cout << "\nDestructor of class C invoked\n";
      }
};
void main()
{
   A *ptrObjA = new C();
   delete ptrObjA;
}
```

Test Run

```
Constructor of class A invoked
Constructor of class B invoked
Constructor of class C invoked
Destructor of class C invoked
Destructor of class B invoked
Destructor of class A invoked
```

- If a class has *virtual* functions, provide a *virtual* destructor, even if one is not required for the class. Classes derived from this class may contain destructors that must be called properly.
- When a destructor in a base class is declared as *virtual*, the destructors of all the derived classes, down the line, in the class hierarchy automatically become *virtual*.
- Constructors cannot be *virtual*. Declaring a constructor as a virtual is a syntax error. The reason why constructors cannot be virtual is that virtual mechanism works on objects, and an object exists only after the successful execution of constructor.

9.7 POLYMORPHISM, VIRTUAL FUNCTIONS AND DYNAMIC BINDING UNDER THE HOOD

Let us look at how polymorphism, virtual functions and dynamic binding is being handled internally. This will give you a basic understanding of how these capabilities really work. More importantly, it will help you to appreciate the overhead of polymorphism — in additional memory consumption and processor time. This will help you determine when to use polymorphism and when to avoid it.

For every class that contains virtual functions, the compiler creates a VTABLE for each class and for class that are derived from it. The VTABLE contains the addresses in the order in which virtual functions are defined within the class. The address of VTABLE is stored in the pointer variable VPTR that is added in the beginning of an object. Consider the following example

```
class Shape
{
  public:
     virtual void draw1() {
       cout << "\ndraw1 of base class\n";
     }
    virtual void draw2() {
       cout << "\ndraw2 of base class\n";
    }
};
class Circle : Shape
{
    public:
        void draw1() {
          cout << "\ndraw1 of derived class\n";
        }
        void draw2() {
          cout << "\ndraw2 of derived class\n";
        }
};
void main()
{
    Shape *p, q;
    Circle c;
    p = &q;
    p->draw2();
    p = &c;
    p->draw2();
}
```

Whenever we create an object of a class, the VTABLE gets created. In this program, we have created an object of *Shape* class as well as of *Circle* class

Hence, there will be two VTABLEs in memory as shown below.

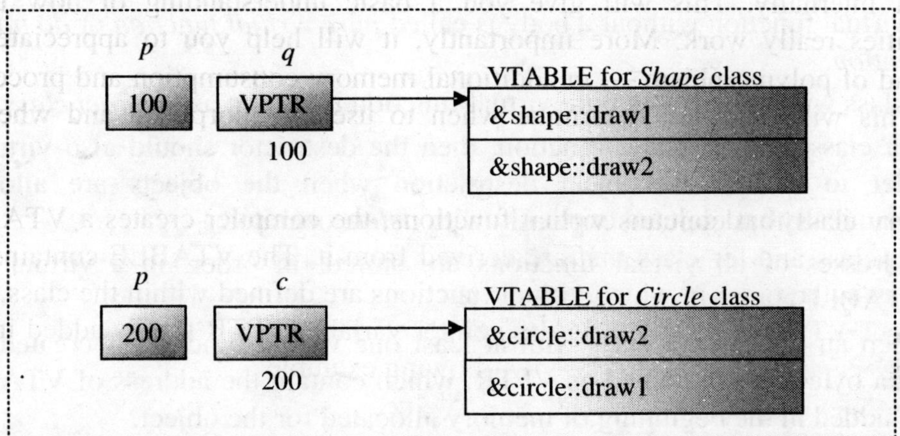

When the compiler encounters a call

```
p->draw2();
```

it generates the code to extract the first two bytes of the object whose address is stored in the pointer *p*. Before, a call to *draw2()*, we have assigned the address of object *q* to pointer *p*. Hence first two bytes of *q* will be extracted. This gives the address of VTABLE. The compiler also adds a number to this address. This number is actually an offset in the VTABLE. Since we have called *draw2()*, 2 would be added to the address of the VTABLE.

QUICK RECAP

In this chapter, we have learnt that

- Polymorphism is a technique that allows defining various forms of a single function that can be shared by various objects to perform the identical operations.
- Polymorphism can be implemented at compile time as well as run time.
- At compile time, polymorphism is implemented using function overloading and operator overloading.
- At run time, polymorphism is implemented using virtual functions.
- Binding is the process of tying the function call to function definition.
- When binding happens at compile time, it is known as *early binding*.

- When binding happens at run time, it is known as *late binding*.
- To implement run time polymorphism, you need to make a function virtual and access the virtual function through pointer to the base class.
- A function in a class prefixed by keyword *virtual* becomes virtual function.
- A virtual function without a body is called *pure virtual function* or *do nothing function*.
- A class with at least one pure virtual function is known as *abstract class*.
- In a class with a virtual function, then the destructor should also virtual in order to ensure the object destruction when the objects are allocated dynamically and deleted explicitly with *delete* operator.
- Addresses of all virtual functions are stored, in order, in a virtual table (VTABLE).
- When an object of a class with at least one virtual function is created, two extra bytes – field named as VPTR, which contain the address of VTABLE, are added in the beginning of memory allocated for the object.
- When a virtual function is called on an object, it retrieves the address of VTABLE from VPTR and adds the offset value to retrieve the address of the function from VTABLE and then function is invoked using that address.

MULTPLE CHOICE QUESTIONS

1. Which of the following statement is not true about polymorphism?
   (*a*) Polymorphism can be implemented at run time only.
   (*b*) To implement run time polymorphism, you need a pointer to the base class and virtual functions in the base class.
   (*c*) When a function is declared as virtual in base class, it is automatically becomes virtual in the derived classes.
   (*d*) Polymorphism provides uniform interface to access a method in a class hierarchy.
2. A pointer to the base class can hold address of
   (*a*) base class object as well as derived class object
   (*b*) only base class object
   (*c*) only derived class object
   (*d*) None of above
3. When a class contains a pure virtual function, it is known as
   (*a*) concrete class (*b*) container class
   (*c*) base class (*d*) abstract class

4. **Consider the statement appearing in a class definition**

```
virtual void display() = 0;
```

Which of the following statement is true about *display()* function?

(*a*) It is virtual function (*b*) It is pure virtual function
(*c*) It is a friend function (*d*) None of above

5. **The do-nothing function is nothing but**

(*a*) a virtual function (*b*) a friend function
(*c*) a pure virtual function (*d*) a global function

6. **When a class contains no pure virtual function, it is known as**

(*a*) concrete class (*b*) container class
(*c*) base class (*d*) abstract class

7. **Which of the following keyword is used to achieve runtime polymorphism?**

(*a*) mutable (*b*) const
(*c*) explicit (*d*) virtual

8. **A pointer to the derived class can hold address of**

(*a*) only base class object
(*b*) only derived class object
(*c*) base class object as well as derived class object
(*d*) None of above

9. **Suppose *objB* is an object of the base class and *objD* is an object of the derived class. The statement**

```
objB = objD;
```

(*a*) Copies all data members and member function of *objD* to *objB*
(*b*) Copies only all data members of *objD* to *objB*
(*c*) Copies only those data members of *objD* to *objB* which are inherited from base class
(*b*) Copies only member functions of *objD* to *objB*

10. **The address of all virtual functions defined is a class are stored in**

(*a*) *this* pointer (*b*) virtual table (VTABLE)
(*c*) pointer variable VPTR (*d*) pointer to the base class

REVIEW EXERCISES

1. What does binding mean? Distinguish between static binding and dynamic binding.
2. What is polymorphism? In what ways polymorphism can be achieved?
3. Is there any alternative to polymorphism? How it compares with polymorphism?
4. What are virtual functions? What are the circumstances in which virtual functions would be appropriate?
5. Distinguish between virtual functions and pure virtual functions.
6. How does polymorphism promote extensibility?
7. Can we make a constructor virtual? If not, why.
8. Can we make a destructor virtual? What purpose a virtual destructor will serve?
9. What is an abstract class?
10. Is it possible to declare an object of the class that contains virtual function?
11. Is it possible to declare an object of the class that contains pure virtual function?

PROGRAMMING EXERCISES

1. Write a program to demonstrate the way to access member functions of the base class and derived class using a pointer to the base class.
2. Write a program to demonstrate the use of pure virtual functions.
3. Write a program to demonstrate the use of abstract class.
4. Create a class named *shape* and define a pure virtual function named *draw()*. Create classes named *rectangle*, *square*, *circle* and *triangle* that inherit from shape class and provides the class specific implementation of *draw()* in each of these derived classes. Create objects of these derived classes and store their addresses in an array of type pointer to *shape* class. Write a polymorphic program that walks through the array and invokes *draw()* method. This walk continues till user strikes any key.

❑ ❑ ❑

Chapter 10

Exception Handling

Learning Objectives

After reading this chapter, students will be able to explain

- the concept of exceptions
- how exception handling is different from traditional error handling
- the basic mechanism of exception handling
- the use of *try* and *catch* keywords in implementing exception handling
- the concept of throwing an exception
- the mechanism of restricting a function to throw only selected exceptions
- the use exception handling to write efficient programs

10.1 INTRODUCTION

Exception handling is another powerful feature of C++ that enables the programmer to write clearer, robust, and fault-tolerant programs.

Recall that it is very rare that the program works correctly first time. It may have *errors* (*bugs*) in it. These bugs can be classified as either *syntax errors* or *logical errors*. The cause of syntax errors is incorrect use of language constructs, whereas the cause of logical errors is the poor understanding of the solution procedure. The syntax errors are caught by the compiler where as the logical errors can be tracked and fixed (corrected) by carefully debugging the program.

There is another kind of problem that can cause your program to fail. This problem is known as *exception*. Exceptions are basically runtime anomalies or unusual conditions that the program may encounter during execution. Examples include division by zero, attempting to access an array element outside array index bound, running out of memory, etc. When program encounters such a situation, the program may terminate abnormally in the absence of error handling mechanism.

In this chapter, we will learn about exceptions and the way they can be handed.

10.2 TRADITIONAL ERROR HANDLING

The most common and traditional way of error handling is to deal with errors at the place where they can occur. The advantage of this approach is that a programmer reading the code can see the error processing in the immediate vicinity of the code and determines if the proper error checking mechanism has been implemented. But the problem with this approach is that in some sense the code becomes polluted with the error processing. It becomes more difficult for a programmer concerned with the application itself to read the code and determine if the code is functioning correctly. This makes it more difficult to understand and to maintain the program.

10.3 BASICS OF EXCEPTION HANDLING

The C++'s exception handling features enable the programmer to remove the error handling code from the main code of the program. This improves program readability and modifiability. With C++ style of exception handling, it is possible to catch all kind of exceptions, to catch all exceptions of a certain type or to catch all exception of related types. This makes program more robust by reducing the likelihood that a program will not catch errors. Exception handling is provided to enable programs to catch and handle errors rather than letting them occur and suffering the consequences. If the programmer does not provide a means of handling a fatal error, the program terminates.

Exception handling is designed for dealing with synchronous errors such as an attempt to divide by zero (that occurs as the program executes the divide instruction). With exception handling, before the program executes the divide instruction, it checks the denominator and throws (issues) an exception if the denominator is zero.

Exception handling is not designed to deal with asynchronous errors such as disk I/O completions, network message arrivals, mouse clicks, and the like; these are best handled through other means, such as interrupt processing.

Exception handling is used in situations in which the system can recover from the error causing the exception. The recovery procedure is called an *exception handler*. Exception handling is typically used when the error will be dealt with by a different part of the program (i.e., a different scope) from that which detected the error. The program that carries on interactive dialog with a user should not use exceptions to process input errors.

Exception handling is especially appropriate for situations in which the program will not be able to recover, but needs to provide orderly cleanup and then terminates gracefully.

Exception handling helps improve a program's fault tolerance. It becomes more pleasant to write error-processing code, so programmers are more likely to provide it. It also becomes possible to catch exceptions in a variety of ways such as by type or even by specifying that exceptions of any type can be caught.

The mechanism of exception handling involves the following steps:

1. Find the problem (*Hit the exception*).
2. Inform that an error has occurred (*Throw the exception*).
3. Receive the error information (*Catch the exception*).
4. Take corrective actions (*Handle the exception*).

The style of exception handling varies in nature and amount depending on the language and the application. Commercial software products tend to contain for more error-handling code that casual software product.

10.4 EXCEPTION HANDLING MECHANISM

The C++ exception handling mechanism is built upon three keywords: *try*, *throw* and *catch*. The keyword *try* is used to preface the block of statements that may generate exception(s). This block of statements is known as *try block*. When an exception is detected, it is thrown using keyword *throw* in the try block. A *catch block* that is defined by prefacing a block of statement with *catch* keyword, catches the exception thrown by the throw statement in the try block, and handles it appropriately.

The *catch block* that catches an exception must immediately follow the *try block* that throws the exception.

This entire sequence is shown in Figure 10.1.

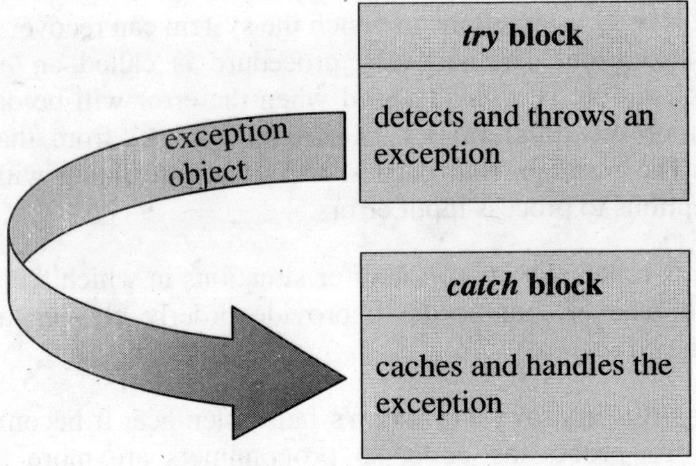

Figure 10.1: Try block throwing exception

Following program skeleton shows program structure with exceptional handling features.

```
void main()
{
    . . . . .
    try
    {
        . . . . .   // statements which can cause,
        . . . . .   // detect and throw an exception
        throw exception;
        . . . . .
```

```
    }
    catch (DataType argument)
    {
        . . . . .   // statements that handles
        . . . . .   // the exception
    }
    . . . . .
}
```

As soon as the *try block* throws an exception, the program control leaves the try block and enters the catch block. Note that exceptions are objects used to transmit information about a problem. If the type of the object thrown matches the data type of the *argument* in the catch statement, then catch block is executed for handling the exception. If they do not match, the program is aborted with the help of *abort()* function which is invoked by default. When no exception is detected, the control goes to the statement immediately after the catch block, *i.e.*, catch block is skipped.

Listing 10.1

```
//  Program to demonstrate the division by zero exception
#include <iostream.h>
#include <string.h>
class DivideByZeroException
{
   private:
      char *msg;
   public:
      DivideByZeroException()
      {
         strcpy(msg, "Attempt to Divide by Zero." );
      }
      char *getMessage()
      {
         return msg;
      }
};
void main()
{
   int intDividend, intDivisor, intQuotient;
   cout << "Enter dividend : ";
   cin >> intDividend;
   cout << "Enter divisor  : ";
   cin >> intDivisor;
   try  {
      if ( intDivisor == 0 )
            throw DivideByZeroException();
      intQuotient = intDividend / intDivisor;
```

```
        cout << "Quotient = : " << intQuotient << "\n";
    }
    catch( DivideByZeroException e ) {
        cout << "\nException occurred: " << e.getMessage();
        cout << "\n";
    }
}
```

Test Runs

First Run

```
Enter dividend  : 25
Enter divisor   : 10
Quotient = : 2
```

Second Run

```
Enter dividend  : 25
Enter divisor   : 0

Exception occurred: Attempt to Divide by Zero.
```

Listing 10.2

```
// Program to demonstrate array index out of bound exception
#include <iostream.h>
#include <string.h>
class ArrayIndexOutOfBoundException
{
   private:
      char *msg;
   public:
      ArrayIndexOutOfBoundException()
      {
          strcpy(msg,"Array index out of bound exception.");
      }
      char *getMessage()
      {
          return msg;
      }
};
void main()
{
   int intArray[10] = { 0, 1, 2, 3, 4, 5, 6, 7, 8, 9 };
   try {
       for ( int i = 0; ; i++ )
       {
          if ( ( i < 0 ) || ( i > 9 ) )
                throw ArrayIndexOutOfBoundException();
```

```
        cout << "\nElement[" << i << "] = ";
        cout << intArray[i];
      }
      cout << "\n";
   }
   catch( ArrayIndexOutOfBoundException e )
   {
      cout << "Exception occurred: " << e.getMessage();
      cout << "\n";
   }
}
```

Test Run

```
Element[0] = 0
Element[1] = 1
Element[2] = 2
Element[3] = 3
Element[4] = 4
Element[5] = 5
Element[6] = 6
Element[7] = 8
Element[8] = 9
Element[9] = 10
Exception occurred: Array index out of bound exception.
```

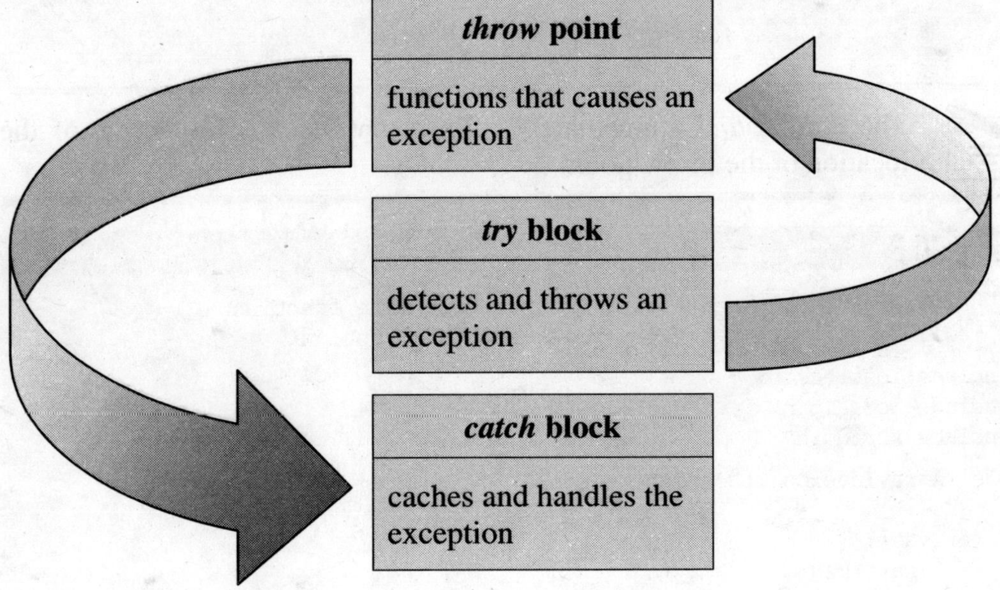

Figure 10.2: Function invoked in try block throws exception

There are many situations when the functions called from within try block throw exceptions. The point at which exception is thrown is called *throw* point. Once an exception is thrown to catch block, control cannot return to the throw point. This kind of relationship is shown in Figure 10.2.

```
DataType functionName( formal argument list )
{
    . . . . .          // statements which can cause,
    . . . . .          // detect and throw an exception
    throw exception;
    . . . . .
}
void main()
{
    . . . . .
    try {
        . . . . .
        . . . . .
        functionName(actual argument list);
        . . . . .
    }
    catch (DataType argument)
    {
        . . . . .    // statements that handles
        . . . . .    // the exception
    }
    . . . . .
}
```

The *catch block* immediately follows *try block*, irrespective of the location of the throw point.

Listing 10.3

```
//  Program to demonstrate the mechanism when the function
//  called from within the try block throws exception

#include<iostream.h>
#include<iomanip.h>
#include<string.h>

class ArrayIndexOutOfBoundException
{
    private:
       char *msg;
    public:
       ArrayIndexOutOfBoundException() {
```

```
        strcpy(msg,"Array index out of bound exception.");
    }
    char *getMessage() {
        return msg;
    }
};
void printArray(int *array, int size)
{
    for ( int i = 0; ; i++ ) {
        if ( (i < 0) || (i > (size-1)) )
            throw ArrayIndexOutOfBoundException();
        cout << "\nElement[" << i << "] = ";
        cout << array[i];
    }
    cout << endl;
}
void main ()
{
    int intArray[10] = { 0, 1, 2, 3, 4, 5, 6, 7, 8, 9 };
    try {
       printArray(intArray, 10);
    }
    catch( ArrayIndexOutOfBoundException e ) {
        cout << "\nException occurred: " << e.getMessage();
        cout << endl;
    }
}
```

10.5 THROWING MECHANISM

The *throw* keyword is used to indicate that an exception has occurred. This is called *throwing an exception.* A throw specifies one operand that can be of any data type (built-in or user-defined). If the operand is an object, we call it an exception object. The value of any type can be thrown.

An exception can be thrown in any of the following forms:

```
throw(exception);
throw exception;
throw;      //used for re-throwing an exception
```

When an exception is thrown it will be caught by the nearest catch block whose argument type match with the type of the exception.

Throw point can be in a deeply nested scope within a try block or in a deeply nested function call. In any case, control is transferred to the catch statement.

10.6 CATCHING MECHANISM

As stated earlier, code for handling exceptions is included in catch block. A catch block looks like a function definition and is of the form

```
catch (DataType argument)
{
     . . . . .
     // statements for handling exception
}
```

The catch statement catches an exception whose data type matches with the data type of the argument of catch statement. When it is caught, the code in the catch block is executed.

The catch argument is like a local variable and can be used in the exception handling code. After executing the handler, the control goes to the statement immediately following the catch block.

If there is no match, an exception is not caught and abnormal program termination will occur. It is important to note that the catch block is simply skipped if the catch statement does not catch an exception.

10.6.1 Multiple Catch Statements

It is possible that a program segment can throw more than one exception. In such cases, we can associate more than one-catch blocks with a try block:

```
catch (DataType1 arg1) {
     . . . . .
     // statements for handling exception
}
catch (DataType2 arg2) {
     . . . . .
     // statements for handling exception
}
  :
catch (DataTypeN argN) {
     . . . . .
     // statements for handling exception
}
```

When an exception is thrown, the exception handlers are searched in order for an appropriate match. The first handler that yields a match is executed. After executing the handler, the control goes to the first statement after the last catch block for that try block, *i.e.*, all other handlers are bypassed. When no match is found, the program is terminated.

10.6.2 Catch all Exceptions

There may situations where it may not be possible to anticipate the possible type of exceptions. In such situations it will not be possible to write separate catch handlers to catch them. What we can do is that we can write a catch handler that can catch all exception instead of catching an exception of particular type.

This is achieved by defining the *catch* statement using three ellipses as follows:

```
catch (...)
{
    . . . .
    // statements for handling all exception
}
```

It may be good idea to use the *catch(. . .)* as a default statement along other catch handlers that it can catch all those exceptions which are not handled explicitly.

The *catch(. . .)* handler must be placed last in the list of handlers. Placing it before other catch handlers would prevent those blocks from catching exceptions.

10.7 RETHROWING AN EXCEPTION

A handler may decide to rethrow the exception caught without or partially processing it. In such situations, we can simply invoke throw without any argument as shown below:

```
throw;
```

This causes the current exception to be thrown to the next enclosing try/catch sequence and is caught by a catch statement listed after that enclosing try block.

10.8 SPECIFYING EXCEPTIONS

It is possible to restrict a function to throw only certain specified exceptions. This is achieved by adding a throw list clause to the function prototype/definition.

The general form of using an exception specification is:

```
DataType functionName(arg-list) throw (exceptions-list)
{
    . . . . .                   // function body
    . . . . .
}
```

Throwing any other type of exception will cause abnormal program termination. If we wish to prevent a function from throwing any exception, we may do so by making the exception-list empty as shown below:

```
DataType functionName(arg-list) throw ()
{
    . . . . .                   // function body
    . . . . .
}
```

QUICK RECAP

In this chapter, we have learnt that

- Errors can be of compile time (syntax), logical and run-time type.
- Traditional error handling hinders understandability of the logic of the code.
- Exception handling is designed to handle run-time errors.
- Exception handling helps in separating the code implementing the logic of the problem and code responsible for error handling.
- Exception handling is built on *try*, *throw* and *catch* keywords.
- Try block encloses the code that can throw an exception.
- Exception is thrown using throw keyword.
- Catch keyword is used to define block responsible for dealing with the exception thrown.
- Catch block with ellipses, as its argument can be defined to handle all exceptions.
- Exception can be rethrown from a catch block.
- A function can be restricted to throw only certain type of exception.
- In absence of an exception handler, default handler is invoked that calls *terminate()* function which in turn invokes *abort()* function which ultimately terminates the program and displays the message "Abnormal program termination".

MULTIPLE CHOICE QUESTIONS

1. Exception handling is targeted at . . .
   (*a*) Compile time errors (*b*) Logical errors
   (*c*) Run-time errors (*d*) All of above
2. The main advantage of exception handling is that . . .
   (*a*) It clearly separates the main code and error handling code.
   (*b*) It can be implemented very easily.
   (*c*) It can handle compile time as well as logical errors in addition to runtime errors.
   (*d*) All of above.
3. In the absence of an appropriate catch block, which of the following function is executed that ultimately terminates the program, in case an exception is thrown?
   (*a*) exit() (*b*) set_terminate()
   (*c*) terminate() (*d*) abort()
4. An exception can be thrown . . .
   (*a*) Outside the try block. (*b*) Only inside the try block.
   (*c*) Inside the catch block. (*d*) All of above.
5. Which of the following declaration is more restrictive?
   (*a*) void fname (int, float)
   (*b*) void fname (int, float) throw()
   (*c*) void fname (int, float) throw(int)
   (*d*) void fname (int,float) throw(int, float)
6. Which of the following is not a keyword used in exception handling?
   (*a*) throw (*b*) try
   (*c*) catchAll (*d*) catch
7. Which of the following function prototype prevents a function from throwing any exception?
   (*a*) void fname (int, float)
   (*b*) void fname (int, float) throw()
   (*c*) void fname (int, float) throw(void)
   (*d*) void fname (int, float) throw(…)
8. Which of the following statement is used to throw an exception from a handler?
   (*a*) throw; (*b*) throw exceptObj;
   (*c*) rethrow; (*d*) throw new exceptClass;

9. Which of the following statement is true about exception handling?
   (*a*) An exception can be rethrown from a try block.
   (*b*) Only catch block can rethrow an exception.
   (*c*) An exception cannot be rethrown.
   (*d*) None of above.

REVIEW EXERCISES

1. What are various types of errors? What is the source of these errors? Which of these errors are most difficult to debug?
2. What is/are the drawback(s) of traditional error handling?
3. What is an exception? Give some reasons that cause exceptions.
4. What is an exception handler?
5. What is the default exception handler?
6. What are the steps involved in exception handling?
7. What are the keywords on which exception handling is built in C++? Explain each of these keywords, with suitable examples.
8. Is it possible to have try block in one functional unit and catch block another functional unit of a program? Justify your viewpoint.
9. Is it possible to have a block that throws an exception and a block that catches that exception in different functional units? Justify your viewpoint.
10. Is it possible to have only one catch block to handle all possible exception? If yes, how?
11. Suppose we have built a class hierarchy, and using exception handling in our program with multiple catch blocks. If the type of the argument of first catch is of base class type, then what will happen when exceptions of all possible types are thrown?
12. Is it possible to have a block that throws an exception and a block that catches that exception in different functional units? Justify your viewpoint.
13. What does re-throwing an exception mean? What purpose it can serve?
14. Is it possible to restrict a function to throw only some specified exception? If yes how?
15. Is it possible to stop a function from throwing any exception? If yes, how?
16. Is it possible to throw an exception outside the scope of try block?
17. Suppose an exception is thrown, but there is no catch block to handle that exception then what will happen?

PROGRAMMING EXERCISES

1. Write a program to multiply two matrices? Program should throw an exception if the order of these matrices is not compatible.
2. Write a program to demonstrate a situation when the function called from within a try block throws an exception.
3. Write a program to demonstrate a deep nesting of try blocks.
4. Write a program to demonstrate the use of multiple catch blocks.
5. Write a program to demonstrate the way user can specify default exception handler.
6. Write a program to demonstrate the rethrowing of an exception.
7. Write a program to demonstrate the way a function can be restricted to throwing only certain type of exceptions.
8. Design your own exception class to handle memory allocation failures. Write a program to demonstrate the use of above class
9. Write a program that accepts a string, which may contain spaces, from the user and throws an exception if it encounters a space during its scan.
10. Write a program to accomplish the following tasks:
    - (*i*) Input an array of integer number.
    - (*ii*) Sum the elements of the array, if during the summing of elements, the running sum becomes zero it should throw an exception.
    - (*iii*) If exception is not thrown, it should display the final sum of elements.

❑ ❑ ❑

Chapter 11

Templates and Generic Programming

Learning Objectives

After reading this chapter, students will be able to explain

- the concept of templates and their usefulness
- the syntax for defining function templates
- the syntax for defining class templates
- how nontype parameters can be used with templates
- how templates relates to inheritance
- how templates relates to friends
- how templates relates to static members
- the use templates to write efficient generic programs

11.1 INTRODUCTION

Templates are one of the C++'s most powerful features for software reuse. Templates enable us to specify, with a single code segment, an entire range of related (overloaded) functions — called *template functions*; or an entire range of related classes — called *template classes.*

We can write a single *function template* to sort an array and then C++ compiler will generate separate functions that will sort an array of *int*, sort an array of float, sort an array of double, etc.

Likewise, we can write a single *class template* for a stack class and then C++ compiler will generate separate classes such as stack of *int* class, stack of float class, stack of string class, etc.

In this chapter, we will learn about the way function templates and class templates defined and used.

11.2 FUNCTION TEMPLATES

Note that overloaded functions are normally used to perform similar kind of operations on different types of data. However, if the operations are same, they can be performed in more compact and convenient way using function templates.

The programmer writes a single function template definition. Based on the argument types in the function call, the compiler generates separate object code to handle each call appropriately.

The syntax of function template is

```
template < class T1, class T2, ...>
DataType FunctionName(arguments of type T1, T2, ... )
{
    //local variables of type T1, T2, or any other type
    //function body, operating on variable of type T1, T2
    //any other variables
}
```

Figure 11.1: Syntax for function template

All function templates begin with the keyword `template` followed by a list of formal arguments to the function template enclosed in angle brackets where each formal argument must be preceded by the keyword `class`.

The following examples illustrate this concept:

1. `template <class T>`
2. `template <class T1, class T2>`
3. `template <class T, int intArg>`
4. `template <class T1, class T2, float floatArg>`

The formal arguments of a template definition are used in the same way as built-in types or user-defined types. They can be used to specify formal argument(s) for the function, to declare variables within the function, to specify the return type of the function. The function definition follows and is defined like any other function.

A function template for swapping two variables

```
template <class T>
void swapTwoVariables( T &a, T &b )
{
    T temp;
    temp = a;
    a = b;
    b = temp;
}
```

Let us examine *swapTwoVariables* function template.

The *swapTwoVariables* function template declares a single formal type parameter *T* (*T* can be any valid identifier) for the type of the variables to be swapped by the function. Here T is referred to as a *type parameter*.

When the compiler detects a *swapTwoVariables* function call in the source code, the type of the actual arguments is substituted for T throughout the template definition and creates a complete function for swapping two variables of specified data type. Then, the newly created function is compiled.

For example, if the function call statement appears as

```
swapTwoVariables( first, second );
```

where actual argument *first* and *second* are of type *float*.

Then the C++ compiler first creates the following function definition

```
void swapTwoVariables( float &a, float &b )
{
    float temp;
    temp = a;
    a = b;
    b = temp;
}
```

by replacing *T* by *float* throughout the template definition, and then compiles it to create an object code.

The use of the *swamTwoVariables* function template is described in the following example program for all built-in data types.

Listing 11.1

```
//  Program to demonstrate the use of template function
#include<iostream.h>
#include<iomanip.h>
template <class T>
void swapTwoVariables ( T &a, T &b) {
    T temp;
    temp = a;
    a = b;
    b = temp;
}
void main()
{
    char charVar1 = '*', charVar2 = '+';
    cout << "Before swapping\n";
    cout << "First character variable  = "<<charVar1<<endl;
    cout << "Second character variable = "<<charVar2<<endl;
    swapTwoVariables ( charVar1, charVar2 );
    cout << "\n\nAfter swapping\n";
    cout << "First character variable  = "<<charVar1<<endl;
    cout << "Second character variable = "<<charVar2<<endl;
    int intVar1 = 10, intVar2 = 20;
    cout << "Before swapping \n";
    cout << "---------------\n\n";
    cout << "First integer variable  = "<<intVar1<<endl;
```

```
    cout << "Second integer variable = "<<intVar2<<endl;
    swapTwoVariables ( intVar1, intVar2 );
    cout << "\n\nAfter swapping\n";
    cout << "--------------\n\n";
    cout << "First integer variable  = " << intVar1<<endl;
    cout << "Second integer variable = " << intVar2<<endl;
    float floatVar1 = 10.25, floatVar2 = 20.75;
    cout << "Before swapping\n";
    cout << "---------------\n\n";
    cout << "First float variable  = " << floatVar1 << endl;
    cout << "Second float variable = " << floatVar2 << endl;
    swapTwoVariables ( floatVar1, floatVar2 );
    cout << "\n\nAfter swapping\n";
    cout << "--------------\n\n";
    cout << "First float variable  = " << floatVar1 << endl;
    cout << "Second float variable = " << floatVar2 << endl;
}
```

Test Run

```
Before swapping
---------------
First character variable  = *
Second character variable = +
After swapping
---------------
First character variable  = +
Second character variable = *
Before swapping
---------------
First integer variable  = 10
Second integer variable = 20
After swapping
---------------
First integer variable  = 20
Second integer variable = 10
Before swapping
---------------
First float variable  = 10.25
Second float variable = 20.75
After swapping
---------------
First float variable  = 20.75
Second float variable = 10.25
```

Following are some more examples of template function for handling arrays.

A function template for sorting an array with Bubble sort method.

```
template <class T>
void sortArray( T *array, int size )
{
   T temp;
   for ( int i = 0;  i < size - 1;  i++ )
   {
       for ( int j = 0; j <= size - i -1; j++ )
       {
           if ( array[j] > array[j+1] ) {
               temp = array[j];
               array[j] = a[j+1];
               array[j+1] = temp;
           }
       }
   }
}
```

A function template for reading an array

```
template <class T>
void readArray( T *array, int size )
{
   cout << "\n\nEnter Elements of array" << endl;
   for ( int i = 0;  i < size - 1;  i++ )
   {
       cout << "Element[" << i << "] : ";
       cin >> array[i];
   }
}
```

A function template for printing an array

```
template <class T>
void printArray( T *array, int size )
{
   cout << "\n\nElements of array are\n\n";
   for ( int i = 0;  i < size - 1;  i++ )
       cout << array[i] << " ";
}
```

These template functions are used in the following program that sorts an array of numbers of type float in the ascending order.

Listing 11.2

```
//  Program to sort an array of any type in ascending order
#include<iostream.h>
#include<iomanip.h>
#define  MAX  100
template <class T>
void sortArray( T *array, int size )
{
    T temp;
    for ( int i = 0;  i < size - 1;  i++ ) {
       for ( int j = 0; j <= size - i -1; j++ ) {
          if ( array[j] > array[j+1] ) {
             temp = array[j];
             array[j] = a[j+1];
             array[j+1] = temp;
          }
       }
    }
}
template <class T>
void readArray( T *array, int size )
{
    cout << "\n\nEnter Elements of array" << endl;
    for ( int i = 0;  i < size - 1;  i++ ) {
       cout << "Element[" << i << "] : ";
       cin >> array[i];
    }
}
template <class T>
void printArray( T *array, int size )
{
    cout << "\n\nElements of array are\n\n";
    for ( int i = 0;  i < size - 1;  i++ )
         cout << array[i] << " ";
}
void main()
{
   float a[MAX];
   int n;
   cout << "\nEnter size of array : ";
   cin >> n;
   readArray( a, n );  //call function to read array
   cout << "Before Sorting\n";
   printArray( a, n );  //call function to print array
   sortArray( a, n );  //call function to sort array
   cout << "\n\n\nAfter Sorting\n";
   printArray( a, n );  //call function to print array
}
```

Test Run

```
Enter size of array: 7
Enter elements of the array
Element[0] : 75
Element[1] : 80
Element[2] : 65
Element[3] : 59
Element[4] : 72
Element[5] : 35
Element[6] : 55
Before Sorting
Elements of array are
75 80 65 59 72 35 55
After Sorting
Elements of array are
35  55  59  65  70  72  80
```

11.3 OVERLOADING TEMPLATE FUNCTIONS

A template function can be overloaded either by another template function or normal function. In such case the compiler uses overloading resolution to call the proper function.

The compiler performs a matching process to determine what function to call when a function call is encountered in the source code. This is done in the following order:

1. At first step, the compiler tries to find a match where the function name and argument types match perfectly with those of the function call, i.e. call the normal function that has an exact match.
2. If first step fails, then in the second step, the compiler checks if any function template is available that can be used to generate a template function with a precise match of function name and argument types. If such a function template is found, the compiler generates and uses the appropriate template function.
3. And, if the second step also fails, then the compiler flags an error message.

Compiler also flags an error if it finds multiple matches for a given function call.

Listing 11.3

```
// Program to demonstrate overloading of function templates

#include<iostream.h>
#include<iomanip.h>

template <class T>
void displayArgument( T argument )
{
   cout << "Template Function called" << endl;
   cout << "Value of arg = " << argument << endl;
}
void displayArgument( float argument )
{
   cout << "Normal function called" << endl;
   cout << "Value of arg = " << argument << endl;
}
void main()
{
   displayArgument(20.25);
   displayArgument(200);
   displayArgument('H');
}
```

Test Run

```
Normal function called.
Value of argument = 20.25

Template function called.
Value of argument = 200

Template function called.
Value of argument = H
```

11.4 CLASS TEMPLATES

We know that stack is a data structure that works on the principle of Last-In-First-Out (LIFO) principle. The items in the stack are inserted (pushed) and removed (poped) in a manner that is independent of the type of the items. But when it comes to actually implementing a stack, the data type of the items must be specified. Therefore, if we want to have a stack class that could handle all the data types, then we would have to define a stack class generically and then instantiating classes that are type-specific. The class templates in C++ provide this capability.

The syntax of class template is

```
template < class T1, class T2, ... >
class className
{
     //class member specification with type T1, T2
     //wherever appropriate
}
```

All class templates begin with the keyword template followed by a list of formal parameters to the class template enclosed in angle brackets where each formal parameter must be preceded by the keyword *class* or type name.

The following examples illustrate this concept:

Listing 11.4

```
//   Program to demonstrate the class template
#include<iostream.h>
#include<iomanip.h>
enum boolean { false, true };
template <class T>
class Stack
{
    private:
       T *stackPointer;
       int size;
       int top;
    public:
       Stack (int n = 10)
       {
          size = n;
          top = -1;
          stackPointer = new T[size];
       }
       ~Stack ()
       {
          delete [] stackPointer;
       }
       boolean isEmpty()
       {
          return ( (top == -1) ? true : false );
       }
```

```
      boolean isFull()
      {
         return ( (top == size-1) ? true : false );
      }
      boolean push ( T element )
      {
         if ( !isFull() ) {
              stackPointer[++top] = element;
              return true;
         } else
              return false;
      }
      boolean pop (T & popValue)
      {
           if ( !isEmpty() ) {
                popValue = stackPointer[top--];
               return true;
           } else
               return false;
      }
};
void main()  // main function
{
   Stack <float> floatStack(6);
   float floatVariable = 1.1;
   cout << "Pushing Elements onto floatStack\n\n";
   while ( floatStack.push ( floatVariable ) )
       floatVariable += 0.1;
    cout << "Stack is full. Cannot push element";
    cout << floatVariable;
    cout << "\n\nPoping Elements from floatStack\n\n";
    while ( floatStack.pop ( floatVariable ) )
       cout << floatVariable << "  ";
    cout << "\n\nStack is empty. Cannot pop.\n";
    Stack <int> intStack(10);
    int intVariable = 0;
    cout << "\n\n\nPushing Elements onto intStack\n\n";
    while ( intStack.push ( intVariable ) )
       intVariable++;
    cout << "Stack is full. Cannot push element";
    cout << intVariable;
    cout << "\n\nPoping Elements from intStack\n\n";
    while ( intStack.pop ( intVariable ) )
       cout << intVariable << "  ";
    cout << "\n\nStack is empty. Cannot pop.\n";
}
```

Test Run

```
Pushing Elements onto floatStack

Stack is full. Cannot push element 1.7

Poping Elements from floatStack

1.6 1.5 1.4 1.3 1.2 1.1

Stack is empty. Cannot pop.

Pushing Elements onto intStack

Stack is full. Cannot push element 10

Poping Elements from intStack

9 8 7 6 5 4 3 2 1 0

Stack is empty. Cannot pop.
```

In above program, all the member functions are defined in the class body. However, if we want to define the member function outside the class body, then we have to prefix each member function with the template header. This is illustrated below.

Listing 11.5

```
//  Program to demonstrate the class template when template
//  member function are defined outside the class template
#include<iostream.h>
#include<iomanip.h>
enum boolean { false, true };
template <class T>
class Stack
{
   private:
      T *stackPointer;
      int size;
      int top;
   public:
      Stack (int n = 10) {
         size = n;
         top = -1;
         stackPointer = new T[size];
      }
      ~Stack () {
         delete [] stackPointer;
      }
      boolean isEmpty() {
        return ( (top == -1) ? true : false );
```

```
    }
    boolean isFull() {
        return ( (top == size-1) ? true : false );
    }
    boolean push ( T element );
    boolean pop (T & popValue);
};
template <class T>
boolean Stack <T> :: push ( T element ) {
   if ( !isFull() ) {
      stackPointer[++top] = element;
      return true;
   } else
      return false;
}
template <class T>
boolean Stack <T> :: pop ( T & popValue) {
   if ( !isEmpty() ) {
       popValue = stackPointer[top--];
       return true;
   } else
       return false;
}
void main()  // main function
{
   Stack <float> floatStack(6);
   float floatVariable = 1.1;
   cout << "Pushing Elements onto floatStack\n\n";
   while ( floatStack.push ( floatVariable ) )
       floatVariable += 0.1;
   cout << "Stack is full. Cannot push element ";
   cout << floatVariable;
   cout << "\n\nPoping Elements from floatStack\n\n";
   while ( floatStack.pop ( floatVariable ) )
       cout << floatVariable << " ";
   cout << "\n\nStack is empty. Cannot pop.\n";
   Stack <int> intStack(10);
   int intVariable = 0;
   cout << "\n\n\nPushing Elements onto intStack\n\n";
   while ( intStack.push ( intVariable ) )
      intVariable++;
   cout << "Stack is full. Cannot push element ";
   cout << intVariable;
   cout << "\n\nPoping Elements from intStack\n\n";
   while ( intStack.pop ( intVariable ) )
      cout << intVariable << " ";
   cout << "\n\nStack is empty. Cannot pop.\n";
}
```

11.5 CLASS TEMPLATES AND NONTYPE PARAMETERS

In the *Stack* class of the previous section used only type parameters in the template header. However, it is possible to use *nontype parameters*; a nontype parameter can have a default argument and the nontype parameter is treated as *const*. For example, the template header for *Stack* class can be modified to take a nontype parameter as follows:

```
template < class T, int elements >
```

Then, a declaration such as

```
Stack <double, 10> doubleStack;
```

would instantiate (at compile time) a 10-element *Stack* template class named *doubleStack* of double values.

The class header might then contain a private data member with an array declaration such as

```
T stackHolder [ elements ];
```

The next program illustrates this.

Listing 11.6

```
//Program to demonstrate use nontype parameters in template header
#include<iostream.h>
#include<iomanip.h>
enum boolean { false, true };
template <class T, int elements>
class Stack
{
    private:
       T stackHolder[elements];
       int size;
       int top;
    public:
       Stack () {
          size = elements;
          top = -1;
       }
       ~Stack () { }
       boolean isEmpty()
       {
          return ( (top == -1) ? true : false );
```

```
        }
        boolean isFull()
        {
           return ( (top == size-1) ? true : false );
        }
        boolean push ( T element )
        {
           if ( !isFull() ) {
                stackHolder[++top] = element;
                return true;
           } else
                return false;
        }
        boolean pop (T & popValue)
        {
           if ( !isEmpty() )
           {
                popValue = stackHolder[top--];
                return true;
           } else
                return false;
        }
};
void main()           // main function
{
    Stack <double, 10> doubleStack;
    double doubleVariable = 1.1;
    cout << "Pushing Elements onto doubleStack\n\n";
    while ( doubleStack.push ( doubleVariable ) )
       doubleVariable += 0.2;
    cout << "Stack is full. Cannot push element";
    cout << doubleVariable;
    cout << "\n\nPoping Elements from doubleStack\n\n";
    while ( doubleStack.pop ( doubleVariable ) )
       cout << doubleVariable << "  ";
    cout << "\n\nStack is empty. Cannot pop.\n";
}
```

Test Run

```
Pushing Elements onto doubleStack

Stack is full. Cannot push element 3.1

Poping Elements from doubleStack

2.9 2.7 2.5 2.3 2.1 1.9 1.7 1.5 1.3 1.1

Stack is empty. Cannot pop.
```

11.6 TEMPLATES AND INHERITANCE

Templates and inheritance relate to each other in following ways:

1. A class template can be derived from a template class.
2. A class template can be derived from a non-template class.
3. A template class can be derived from a class template.
4. A non-template class can be derived from a class template.

11.7 TEMPLATES AND FRIENDS

We have seen that a function and an entire class can be declared as *friend* of a non-template class. With class templates, the obvious kind of friendship arrangement can also be declared. Friendship can be established between a class template and a global function, a member function of another class (possibly a template class), or even an entire class (possibly a template class). The notation required establishing these friendship relationships can be cumbersome.

Consider the following cases:

1. Inside a class template for class *X* that has been declared with

   ```
   template < class T > class X
   ```

   a friendship declaration of the form

   ```
   friend void functionName1();
   ```

   makes function *functionName1* a friend of every template class instantiated from the preceding class template.

2. Inside a class template for class *X* that has been declared with

   ```
   template < class T > class X
   ```

   a friendship declaration of the form

   ```
   friend void functionName2( X <T> &);
   ```

   for a particular type *T* such as *float* makes function *functionName2* friend of *X* <*float*> only.

Inside a class template, you can declare that a member function of another class is a *friend* of any template class generated from the class template. Simply name the member function of the other class using the class name and the scope resolution operator.

Consider the following cases:

1. Inside a class template for class *X* that has been declared with

```
template < class T > class X
```

a friendship declaration of the form

```
friend void A::f4();
```

makes member function *f4* of class *A* a friend of every template class instantiated from the preceding class template.

2. Inside a class template for class *X* that has been declared with

```
template < class T > class X
```

a friendship declaration of the form

```
friend void C<T>::f5(X<T> &);
```

for a particular type *T* such as *float* makes function

```
C<float>::f5(X<float> &);
```

a friend function of only template class *X<float>*.

3. Inside a class template for class *X* that has been declared with

```
template < class T > class X
```

a second class *Z* can be declared with

```
friend class Z<T>;
```

then when a template class is instantiated with a particular type for *T* such as float, all members of class *Z<float>* become friends of template class *X<float>*.

11.8 TEMPLATES AND STATIC MEMBERS

Recall that for a non-template class, one copy of a static data member is shared among all objects of the class and the static data member must be initialized at file scope.

Each template class instantiated from a class template has its own copy of each static data member of the class template; all objects of that template class share that one static data member. And as with static data members of non-template classes, static data members of template classes must be initialized at file scope. Each template class gets its own copy of the class template's static member functions.

QUICK RECAP

In this chapter, we have learnt that

- Templates are one of the C++'s most powerful features for software reuse.
- Using templates, we can create generic functions and generic classes capable of handling variety of data types.
- The definition of every function template and class template starts with *template* keyword, and followed by list of generic arguments enclosed in angle brackets, where each argument is preceded by *class* keyword.
- A template function can be overloaded either by another template function or a normal function.
- Compiler performs a matching process to determine what function to call when a function call is encountered. First it tries to find the exact match (normal function), and if it fails to find such a match then it tries to find a function template from which it can generate template function, and if it fails here as well, it will flag an error message.
- We can also use non-type parameters that can be of basic types or derived types. A non-type parameter is treated as constant.

MULTIPLE CHOICE QUESTIONS

1. Templates are useful when the template parameter is of type . . .

   (*a*) Basic type (*b*) Derived type
   (*c*) Basic type as well as derived type (*d*) Basic type but not derived type

2. The template facilitates software reuse . . .

   (*a*) at compile time
   (*b*) at execution time
   (*c*) at compile time as well as execution time
   (*d*) None of above

3. Template class is also known as . . . . . . class.

   (*a*) virtual (*b*) container
   (*c*) generic (*d*) abstract

4. Which of the following is a correct template definition?
   (*a*) template < class T > (*b*) template < T >
   (*c*) class < template T > (*d*) template class < T >
5. Function templates can accept . . .
   (*a*) only one parameter (*b*) only parameter of basic type
   (*c*) only parameter of derived type (*d*) any number of parameters
6. Function templates can be defined . . .
   (*a*) in the main function (*b*) in a class
   (*c*) globally (*d*) All of above
7. If template functions and normal functions are overloaded, then the compiler will tie the function call to . . .
   (*a*) normal function (*b*) template function
   (*c*) which is smaller in size (*d*) which requires less execution time
8. Which of the following is not a correct template definition?
   (*a*) template < class T > (*b*) template < class T, class T >
   (*c*) template < class T, int x > (*d*) template < class T1, class T2 >
9. Consider the following code

```
#include <iostream.h>
void display ( int x )                  // normal function
{
   cout << "\nx = " << x << "\n";
}
template < class T >
void display ( T y ) {                  // template function
   cout << "\ny = " << y << "\n";
}
void main() {
  display(5);
}
```

   What will happen when the above code is compiled?
   (*a*) Function call will be tied to the template function.
   (*b*) Function call will be tied to the normal function.
   (*c*) An error regarding ambiguity will be generated.
   (*d*) None of above
10. In the following statement, parameter *T* is referred as . . .

```
template < class T >
```

   (*a*) argument (*b*) type parameter
   (*c*) non-type parameter (*d*) formal parameter

REVIEW EXERCISES

1. What is generic programming? How is it implemented in C++?
2. What are templates?
3. How do templates compare with macros?
4. Distinguish between overloaded functions and function templates.
5. Distinguish between function template and template function.
6. What are the steps to create a class template and function template?
7. How overloading of template function with other template functions or normal function is handled?
8. What are type parameters?
9. Is it possible to use non-type parameters in function templates?
10. How do templates and inheritance relate to each other?
11. How friendship works with templates?

PROGRAMMING EXERCISES

1. Create a function template to display the absolute value of an argument of basic type. Using this function template, write a program to display the absolute value of a variable of type *int*, *float*, *double*.
2. Create a function template that returns the largest element in an array of basic type. Using this function template, write a program to find and display the largest element of an array.
3. Create a class template to represent a generic vector. Include member functions to perform the following tasks:
   (*i*) To create an empty vector
   (*ii*) To input the elements of the vector
   (*iii*) To modify the value of a given element
   (*iv*) To output the vector in the form (10,20,30,…)
4. Create a class template to represent a generic matrix. Include member functions to perform the following tasks:
   (*i*) To create a default matrix of size 4×4 with all elements initialized to zero
   (*ii*) To input the elements of the matrix
   (*iii*) To multiply two compatible matrices
   (*iv*) To output the matrix in matrix form
   (*v*) To output the matrix in matrix form, *i.e.*, elements of each row on separate line

❑ ❑ ❑

Chapter 12

File Handling

Learning Objectives

After reading this chapter, students will be able to

- explain the concept of data file and its usefulness
- explain the file streams supported by C++'s I/O subsystem
- explain the hierarchy of file stream classes
- explain the steps in processing a file
- explain possible ways of opening a file in appropriate mode
- explain reading/writing of files
- explain the concept of file pointers
- explain how to access records randomly
- explain the possible ways of updating a file
- write efficient programs for file handling

12.1 INTRODUCTION

The programs described so far, accepts the input data from the keyboard at the time of execution. The main limitation of this approach is that it is very difficult to handle large volume of data. As an example, suppose there are about 100 data items to enter. Some of the problems that may arise are enumerated below:

- It takes lot of time to enter the entire data.
- If the user makes a mistake while entering the data, he has to start from the beginning.
- If the same data is to be processed again at some later stage, again we have to enter it again. That is, for every program run, we have to enter the same data again and again.

Therefore, if the data is entered in computer's memory, checked for its correctness, and finally stored in a disk file, a program can read it directly from the disk and that too at very high speed.

In addition, the output of one program may become input for another program. In such a situation, it is more efficient to store the output of a program in a disk file, which can subsequently be read by other program(s).

In this chapter, we discuss in detail about data files and their management using file stream classes.

12.2 DATA FILE DEFINED

A data file is a collection of related records. For example, file containing records of all students in class; a file containing records of all employees of an organization; a file containing records of all items in a stock, etc.

A record is a collection of related data-items, where a data item refers to a single unit of values. Examples of data items are *roll number*, *name*, *date of birth*, *sex*, and *class*, etc. The collection of *roll number*, *name*, *date of birth*, *sex*, and *class* data items of a particular student such as *1234*, *Surbhi*, *12/03/1993*, *F*, *9* constitutes a record.

File organization refers to the way records are physically arranged on a storage device.

12.3 FILE STREAMS

The C++ I/O subsystem is designed to work with a wide variety of devices that includes keyboard, monitor, disks, tape drives, etc. The working principle (characteristics) of each of these devices is quite different. The C++ I/O subsystem is designed in such a way that it provides a uniform interface that is independent of the actual device being used. Thus, the programmer can write a C++ program that can receive input from, and send output to any device without bothering about the characteristics of device being used. This interface is called a *stream*.

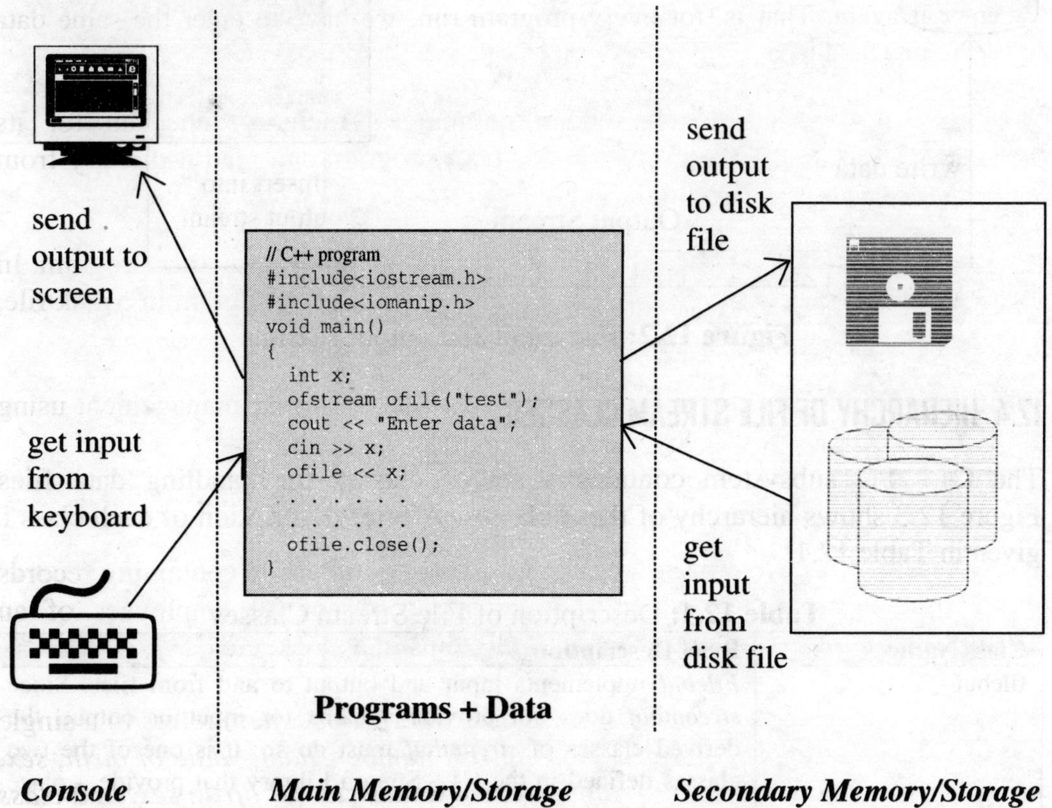

Figure 12.1: Console-program-file interaction

A stream basically is a sequence of bytes. It can either act as a *source* from which the program can take (extract) input data or as a *destination* to which the program can send (insert) output data. The source stream that supplies data to the program is called *input stream* and the destination stream that receives data from the program is called *output stream*.

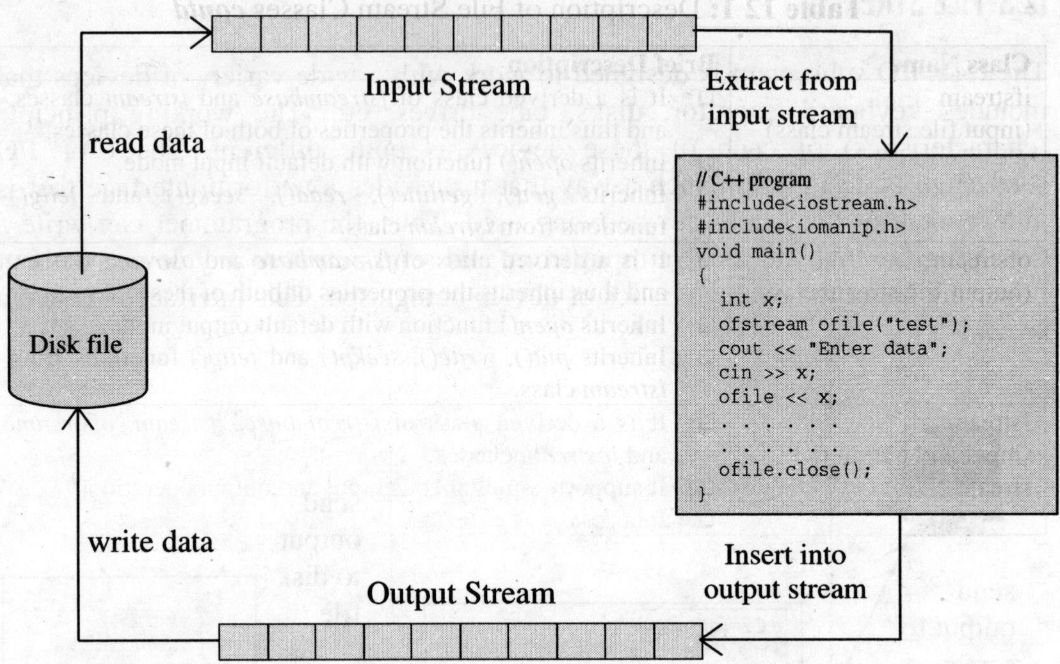

Figure 12.2: File input and output streams

12.4 HIERARCHY OF FILE STREAM CLASSES

The C++ I/O subsystem contains a set of classes for handling data files. Figure 12.3 shows hierarchy of these classes. A brief description of each class is given in Table 12.1.

Table 12.1: Description of File Stream Classes

Class Name	Brief Description
filebuf	*Filebuf* implements input and output to and from files. Since *streambuf* does not provide streams for input or output, the derived classes of *streambuf* must do so. It is one of the two classes defined in the C++ Stream Library that provide a place for input to be gathered from and a place for output to go. The I/O functions of class *istream* and *ostream* make calls to the functions of *filebuf* to do the actual insertion or extraction on the streams. This occurs if the *bp* (pointer to *streambuf*) data member of class *ios* has been assigned a pointer to class *filebuf*.
fstreambase (Base class for file streams)	❑ It is a base class for all file stream classes. Thus, supports operations common to file streams. ❑ Contains *open()* and *close()* function in addition to other member functions.

Table 12 1: Description of File Stream Classes ***contd***

Class Name	Brief Description
ifstream (input file stream class)	❑ It is a derived class of *fstreambase* and *istream* classes, and thus inherits the properties of both of these classes. ❑ Inherits *open()* function with default input mode. ❑ Inherits *get()*, *getline()*, *read()*, *seekg()* and *tellg()* functions from *istream* class.
ofstream (output file stream class)	❑ It is a derived class of *fstreambase* and *ostream* classes, and thus inherits the properties of both of these classes. ❑ Inherits *open()* function with default output mode. ❑ Inherits *put()*, *write()*, *seekp()* and *tellp()* functions from *istream* class.
fstream (input and output file stream class)	❑ It is a derived class of *fstreambase*, *ifstream*, *ofstream*, and *iostream* classes. ❑ It supports simultaneous input and output operations. ❑ Inherits *open()* function with default input mode.

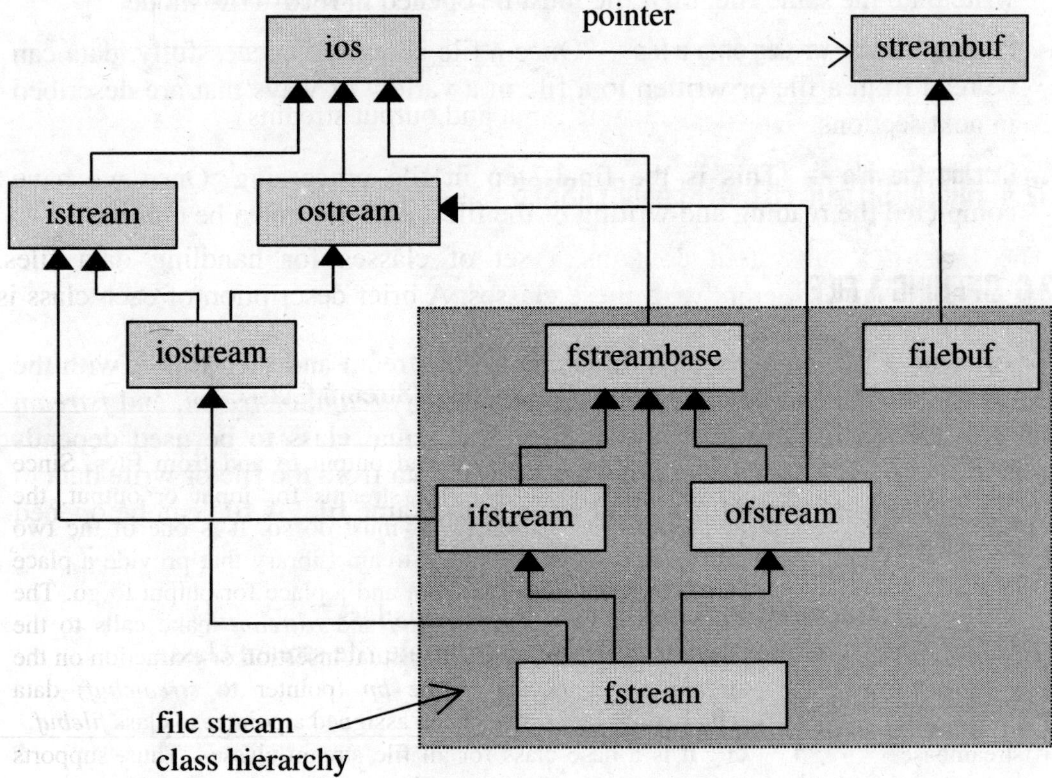

Figure 12.3: Hierarchy of file stream classes

12.5 STEPS IN PROCESSING A FILE

The processing of a file involves following steps:

1. **Naming a file** — First step in file processing is to select an appropriate name. It is recommended that name of the file should indicate the type of its contents and its purpose. The rules for naming a file may be different for different operating systems. The following are examples of some valid file names:

```
input.dat, output.dat, inventory, result,
data.txt, master.dat, tax.in, savings
```

2. **Opening a file** — The second step in file processing is to open the file in appropriate mode. If you want to read from a file in your program, the file must be opened in the read/input mode. Similarly, if you want to write the output of your program to a file, the file must be opened in the write/output mode. However, there may be cases when you want to read from and also write onto the same file, then file must be opened in read-write mode.
3. **Reading from or writing onto a file** — Once a file is opened successfully, data can be read from a file or written to a file in a variety of ways that are described in next sections.
4. **Closing the file** — This is the final step in file processing. Once we have completed the reading and writing of the files, each file must be closed.

12.6 OPENING A FILE

For opening a file, first we have to create a file stream and then link it with the file. A file stream can be created using the class *ifstream*, *ofstream*, and *fstream* that are defined in *fstream.h* header file. The actual class to be used depends upon the purpose, *i.e.*, whether we want to read data from the file or write data to the file or we want to read from and write to the same file. A file can be opened in two ways:

- Using constructor of the appropriate file stream class.
- Using *open()* member function of the appropriate file stream class.

12.6.1 Opening a File Using Constructor

We know that a constructor is used to initialize an object while it is being created. Here, filename is used as an argument for the constructor, which is then used to initialize the file stream object.

The prototype of generalized constructor of *ifstream* class is

```
ifstream( const char *path, int mode = ios::in,
          int prot = filebuf::openprot );
```

where *path* is filename with path information, however, if path information is omitted, file is considered to be in the working directory; *mode* is file opening mode, default argument with default value 'in' for input mode; *prot* is access specifier, default argument with default value 'openprot' for read and write access permissions.

The prototype of generalized constructor of *ofstream* class is

```
ofstream( const char *path, int mode = ios::out,
          int prot = filebuf::openprot );
```

where *path* is filename with path information, however, if path information is omitted, file is considered to be in the working directory; *mode* is file opening mode, default argument with default value 'out' for output mode; *prot* is access specifier, default argument with default value 'openprot' for read and write access permissions.

The prototype of generalized constructor of *fstream* class is

```
fstream( const char *path, int mode = ios::in | ios::out,
         int prot = filebuf::openprot );
```

where *path* is filename with path information, however, if path information is omitted, file is considered to be in the working directory; *mode* is file opening mode, default argument with default value 'in' and 'out' for input-output mode; *prot* is access specifier, default argument with default value 'openprot' for read and write access permissions.

Table 12.2: File mode parameters

Parameter	Purpose
`binary`	Open file in binary mode. By default, file is opened in text mode.
`in`	Open file for read only.
`out`	Open file for write only.
`trunc`	Delete the contents of the file if it exists.
`app`	Append to the end of file.
`ate`	Move the file pointer to the end-of-file on opening.
`nocreate`	Open fails if the file does not exist.
`noreplace`	Open file if file already exists.

Table 12.3: Access permission parameters

Parameter	Access Permission
S_IREAD	Read permission.
S_ IWRITE	Write permission.
S_IEXEC	Execute permission.

***These parameters, in both the tables, can be combined using bit-wise OR operator ('|').**

Following examples illustrate the mechanism to open a file using a constructor.

1. The statement

```
ifstream inFile( "score.dat" );
```

opens a file named *score.dat* in text mode for input only with read and write permissions.

2. The statement

```
ofstream outFile ( "result.dat" );
```

opens a file named *result.dat* in text mode for output only with read and write permissions.

3. The statement

```
fstream ioFile( "inventory.dat" );
```

opens a file named *inventory.dat* in text mode for input and output with read and write permissions.

4. The statement

```
ofstream outFile( "rating.dat", ios::binary | ios::out );
```

opens a file named *rating.dat* in binary mode for output with read and write permissions.

12.6.2 Opening a File Using *open()* Member Function

The prototype of *open()* function is

```
void open ( const char *path, int mode, int prot = filebuf::openprot );
```

where *path* is filename with path information, however, if path information is omitted, file is considered to be in the working directory; *mode* is file opening mode; *prot* is access specifier, default argument with default value 'openprot' for read and write access permissions.

The *open()* function is invoked on a file stream object as

```
file-stream-object.open("filename", mode );
```

Following examples illustrate mechanism to open a file using *open()* function.

1. The statement

   ```
   ifstream inFile;
   inFile.open( "score.dat", ios::in );
   ```

   opens a file named *score.dat* in text mode for input only with read and write permissions.

2. The statements

   ```
   ofstream outFile;
   outFile.open( "result.dat", ios::out );
   ```

   opens a file named *result.dat* in text mode for output only with read and write permissions.

3. The statement

   ```
   fstream ioFile;
   ioFile.open( "inventory.dat", ios::in | ios::out );
   ```

   opens a file named *inventory.dat* in text mode for input and output with read and write permissions.

4. The statement

   ```
   ofstream outFile;
   outFile.open( "rating.dat", ios::binary | ios::out );
   ```

   opens a file named *rating.dat* in binary mode for output with read and write permissions.

12.6.3 Possible Trouble with Opening a File

When we make an attempt to open a file, the open operation may fail. There may be many reasons for the failure of open operations.

Some of the possible reasons are enumerated below:

- Trying to open a file for reading that does not exist.
- Trying to open a file for writing, but sufficient space is not available on the disk.
- Trying to open a file that has been corrupted, *i.e.*, media error.
- Trying to open a file with invalid filename.
- Trying to open a file for writing that has been created with read-only permission.

Thus, it is important for the program that uses a data file to check whether a file has been opened successfully before trying to read from or write onto the file.

Every file stream class inherits a data member named *state* from *ios* class. The state data member represents the state of the corresponding stream after performing the open, read, or write operation. Testing this state appropriately does the error handling. The information of stream status recorded in state variable is as shown in Figure 12.4.

There are number of member functions that can be used to detect errors occurred during file operation. One of them is *fail()* function that can be used to see whether the file is opened successfully or not.

The *fail()* function returns non-zero (*true*) value if open, read, or write operations has failed; otherwise returns zero (*false*) value to indicate success of operation.

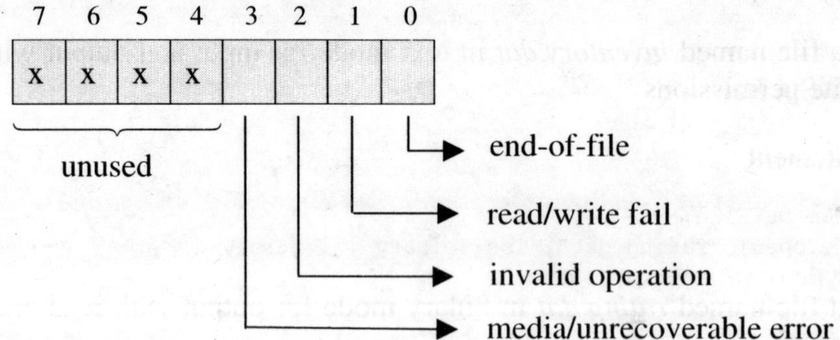

Figure 12.4: Interpretation of individual bits of *state* variable

The next examples illustrate the mechanism used to check whether the file is opened successfully.

1. **Opening a non-existent file in read-only mode:**

```
ifstream inFile;
inFile.open ( "test.dat");
if ( inFile.fail() ) {
    cout << "\nEither file does not exist or "
         << "unable to open it because of media error\n"
    return;
}
```

2. **Opening a file for writing that has been previously created with read-only permission:**

```
ofstream outFile;
outFile.open ( "test.dat");
if ( outFile.fail() ) {
    cout << "\nEither file does not exist or "
         << "is created with read only permission\n"
    return;
}
```

3. **Opening a file with invalid file name:**

```
ofstream outFile;
outFile.open ( "|^*+");
if ( outFile.fail() ) {
    cout << "\nInvalid file name\n"
         << endl;
    return;
}
```

12.7 CLOSING A FILE

When a program has finished with reading/writing of a file, it must be closed. This task is carried out by using *close()* member function of *fstreambase* class.

The prototype of *close()* function is

```
void close();
```

When invoked on a file stream object, it closes the associated file.

The following statement

```
sampleFile.close();
```

closes file associated with file stream object *sampleFile* irrespective of whether the file is opened for reading, writing, appending etc.

12.8 ERROR HADNLING DURING FILE OPERATIONS

So far we have been opening and using the files for reading and writing on the assumption that everything is fine with the files. This may not always be true. The following situations may arise while handling files:

1. Attempting to open a non-existence file in read-mode.
2. Attempting to open a file in write mode that was created with read-only access permission.
3. Attempting to open a file with invalid filename.
4. Attempting invalid operations, such as reading past the end-of-file, writing onto a file that is opened in read-only mode, etc.
5. Sufficient disk space is not available when writing to a file.
6. Attempting to open a file in write or append mode when disk is write protected.
7. Attempting a read or write operation on an area on disk that is damaged will result in media errors.
8. Attempting to manipulate an unopened file.

Such conditions must be detected while manipulating files and appropriate action should be taken to achieve consistent access to files.

Every file stream inherits a *state* data member from *ios* class associated with it.

Table 12 7: Error handling functions

Function	Purpose
`.eof()`	Return non-zero (true) value if end-of-file (EOF) encountered while reading a file, otherwise returns zero (false) value.
`fail()`	Return non-zero (true) value if open, read, or write operations has failed; otherwise returns zero (false) value to indicate success of operation.
`bad()`	Return non-zero (true) value if invalid operation is attempted or any media (unrecoverable) error occurs; otherwise returns zero (false) value.
`good()`	Return non-zero (true) value every thing is fine; otherwise returns zero (false) value.
`rdstate()`	Returns the value of the state data member of ios class.
`clear()`	Clear the current error state so that further operations can be attempted.

12.9 READING/WRITING OF FILES

In this section, we will discuss about possible ways of reading and writing of files. In C++ I/O file subsystem, files can be of type text and binary. In text format, numbers are stored as sequence of characters, whereas in binary files numbers are stored in the similar fashion as they are stored in main memory. We will discuss reading/writing of both types of files.

12.9.1 Reading/Writing of Text Files

12.9.1.1 Reading and Writing of Character Data

Character data is read and written using character input/output member function of *ifstream* and *ofstream* classes.

12.9.1.1.1 Writing Character Data

The following interactive program illustrates the approach to write/create a file using character output function *put()* of *ofstream* class. The program reads data from the keyboard and writes into a file.

Listing 12.1

```
// Interactive program to demonstrate the writing of a file
// using character output function of ofstream class

#include <iostream.h>
#include <fstream.h>

void main()
{
   char ch;
   char fileName[12];
   cout << "\nEnter name of file to write/create : ";
   cin >> fileName;
   ofstream outFile ( fileName );
   if ( outFile.fail() ) {
      cout << "\nUnable to open file " << fileName <<endl;
      return;
   }
   cout << "\nEnter some text and terminate by "
      << "^Z followed by <Enter> key\n"
   while ( !cin.eof() ) {
     cin.get(ch);
     outFile.put(ch);
   }
   outFile.close();
}
```

Test Run

```
Enter name of file to write/create : file1.dat
Enter some text and terminate by ^Z followed by <Enter> key
It is better to keep your word soft and sweet, you never know
when you have to eat them.^Z↵
```

12.9.1.1.2 Reading Character Data

The following program illustrates the approach to read a file (written/created using character output) using character input function *get()* of *ifstream* class. The program reads data from the file and displays on the monitor (screen).

Listing 12.2

```
//  Program to demonstrate the reading of a file using
//  character input function of ifstream class

#include <iostream.h>
#include <fstream.h>

void main()
{
    char ch;
    char fileName[12];
    cout << "\nEnter name of file to read : ";
    cin >> fileName;
    ifstream inFile ( fileName );
    if ( inFile.fail() ) {
        cout << "\nUnable to open file " << filename <<endl;
        return;
    }
    cout << "Contents of file : " << filename << "\n\n";
    while ( !inFile.eof() ) {
       inFile.get(ch);
       cout << ch;
    }
    inFile.close();
}
```

Test Run

```
Enter name of file to read : file1.dat
Contents of file: file1.dat
It is better to keep your word soft and sweet, you never know
when you have to eat them.
```

12.9.1.2 Reading and Writing of String Data

String data is read and written using string input/output member function of *ifstream* and *ofstream* classes.

12.9.1.2.1 Writing String Data

The following interactive program illustrates the approach to write/create a file using string output function *write()* of *ofstream* class. The program reads data from the keyboard and writes into a file.

Listing 12.3

```
// Interactive program to demonstrate the writing of a
// file using string output function of ofstream class

#include <iostream.h>
#include <fstream.h>
#include <string.h>

void main()
{
    char fileName[12], strName[81];
    int strLength;

    cout << "\nEnter name of file to write/create : ";
    cin >> fileName;
    ofstream outFile ( fileName );

    if ( outFile.fail() )
    {
        cout << "\nUnable to open file " << filename <<endl;
        return;
    }

    cout << "Enter some strings & terminate by null string."
        << endl;

    while ( 1 )
    {
       cin.getline(strName, 80);
       strLength = strlen(strName);

       if ( strLength == 0 )
          break;
       outFile.write(strName, strLength);
    }

    outFile.close();
}
```

Test Run

```
Enter name of file to write/create : file2.dat

Enter some strings & terminate by null string.

The winner never quits and quitter never wins.↵

Actions are best interpreters of one's thoughts.↵

Eyes are the index of your heart.↵

Hard work always pays dividends.↵

↵
```

12.9.1.2.2 Reading String Data

The following program illustrates the approach to read a file (written/created using string output) using string input function *getline()* of *ifstream* class. The program reads data from the file and displays on the monitor (screen).

Listing 12.4

```
//  Program to demonstrate the reading of a file using
//  string input function of ofstream class

#include <iostream.h>
#include <fstream.h>
void main()
{
    char fileName[12], strName[81];
    cout << "\nEnter name of file to read : ";
    cin >> fileName;
    ifstream inFile ( fileName );
    if ( inFile.fail() )
    {
        cout << "\nUnable to open file " << filename <<endl;
        return;
    }
    cout << "\nContents of file : " << filename << endl;
    while ( !inFile.eof() )
    {
       inFile.getline(strName, 80);
       cout.write(strName, strlen(strName));
       cout << endl;
    }
    inFile.close();
}
```

Test Run

```
Enter name of file to read : file2.dat

Contents of file : file2.dat

The winner never quits and quitter never wins.
Actions are best interpreters of one's thoughts.
Eyes are the index of your heart.
Hard work always pays dividends.
```

12.9.1.3 Reading and Writing of Formatted Data

So far we have considered reading and writing of characters and strings. *What about numbers*? Let us suppose that we want to store information about an student comprising his/her *roll number* (an integer), *first name* (a string), *marks in four subjects* (integer numbers). We want to create a data file for a given list of students.

It is important to note that in formatted I/O, numbers are stored as a series of characters. Thus, number 6.352 which may be of type *float* or *double*, will be stored as character '6', '.', '3', '5', and '2' rather that being stored as 4-byte type *float* or 8-byte type *double*. This type of storage of numbers is inefficient particularly with numbers having large number of digits, but may be appropriate in many situations and is easy to implement. Characters and strings are stored in this fashion only.

12.9.1.3.1 Writing Formatted Data

The following interactive program illustrates the approach to write/create a file using formatted output. The program reads data from the keyboard and writes into a file.

Listing 12.5

```
//  Interactive program to demonstrate the writing of a
//  file using formatted output

#include <iostream.h>
#include <fstream.h>

void main()
{
   char fileName[12];
   int rollNo;
   char firstName[20];
   float engMarks;
```

```
    float mathMarks;
    float phyMarks;
    float chemMarks;
    char more;
    cout << "\nEnter name of file to write/create : ";
    cin >> fileName;
    ofstream outFile ( fileName );
    if ( outFile.fail() ) {
        cout << "\nUnable to open file " << filename <<endl;
        return;
    }
    while ( 1 ) {
       cout << endl << "Enter roll number          : ";
       cin >> rollNo;
       cout << "Enter first name           : ";
       cin >> firstName;
       cout << "Enter marks in English     : ";
       cin >> engMarks;
       cout << "Enter marks in Mathematics : ";
       cin >> mathMarks;
       cout << "Enter marks in Physics     : ";
       cin >> phyMarks;
       cout << "Enter marks in Chemistry   : ";
       cin >> chemMarks;
       outFile << rollNo << " " << firstName
               << " " << engMarks << " ";
       outFile << mathMarks << " " << phyMarks
               << " " << chemMarks << endl;
       cout << "\nAny more record to enter (y/n) : ";
       cin >> more;
       if ( more == 'y' || more == 'Y' )
          continue;
       else
          break;
    }
    outFile.close();
}
```

Test Run

```
Enter name of file to write/create : file3.dat

Enter roll number          : 1000
Enter first name           : happy
Enter marks in English     : 50
Enter marks in Mathematics : 65
Enter marks in Physics     : 55
Enter marks in Chemistry   : 70
```

```
Any more record to enter (y/n) : y

Enter roll number           : 1001
Enter first name            : dolly
Enter marks in English      : 70
Enter marks in Mathematics : 65
Enter marks in Physics      : 88
Enter marks in Chemistry    : 72

Any more record to enter (y/n) : n
```

The contents of the file will be stored as

```
1000 happy 50 65 55 70
1001 dolly 70 65 88 72
```

12.9.1.3.2 Reading Formatted Data

The following program illustrates the approach to read a file (written/created using formatted output) using formatted input. The program reads data from the file and displays on the monitor (screen).

Listing 12.6

```
//  Program to demonstrate the reading of file using
//  formatted input

#include <iostream.h>
#include <fstream.h>
void main()
{
   char fileName[12];
   int rollNo;
   char firstName[20];
   float engMarks;
   float mathMarks;
   float phyMarks;
   float chemMarks;
   cout << "\nEnter name of file to read : ";
   cin >> fileName;
   ifstream inFile ( fileName );
   if ( inFile.fail() ) {
       cout << "\nUnable to open file " << filename << endl;
       return;
   }
   while ( !inFile.eof() )
   {
      inFile >> rollNo >> firstName >> engMarks
             >> mathMarks >> phyMarks >> chemMarks;
```

```
        cout << endl
             << "Roll number           : " <<rollNo<<endl;
        cout << "First name            : " <<firstName<<endl;
        cout << "Marks in English      : " <<engMarks<<endl;
        cout << "Marks in Mathematics  : " <<mathMarks<< endl;
        cout << "Marks in Physics      : " <<phyMarks<<endl;
        cout << "Marks in Chemistry    : " <<chemMarks<< endl;
    }
    inFile.close();
}
```

Test Run

```
Enter name of file to read : file3.dat

Contents of file : file3.dat

Roll number          : 1000
First name           : happy
Marks in English     : 50
Marks in Mathematics : 65
Marks in Physics     : 55
Marks in Chemistry   : 70

Roll number          : 1001
First name           : dolly
Marks in English     : 70
Marks in Mathematics : 65
Marks in Physics     : 88
Marks in Chemistry   : 72
```

12.9.1.4 Reading and Writing of Objects

In C++ language, objects can be read and written in text format using overloaded >> and << operators, respectively. The approach used is illustrated in this section.

12.9.1.4.1 Writing of Objects

The following interactive program illustrates the approach of writing objects to a file using overloaded << operator. The program reads data from the keyboard and writes into a file.

Listing 12.7

```
// Interactive program to demonstrate the writing
// of objects to a text file using overloaded << operator
```

```
#include <iostream.h>
#include <iomanip.h>
#include <fstream.h>
class studentType
{
   private:
      int rollNo;
      char firstName[20];
      float engMarks;
      float mathMarks;
      float phyMarks;
      float chemMarks;
   public:
      studentType() { }   // default constructor
      void readData() {
         cout << "\nEnter roll number          : ";
         cin >> rollNo;
         cout << "Enter first name           : ";
         cin >> firstName;
         cout << "Enter marks in English     : ";
         cin >> engMarks;
         cout << "Enter marks in Mathematics : ";
         cin >> mathMarks;
         cout << "Enter marks in Physics     : ";
         cin >> phyMarks;
         cout << "Enter marks in Chemistry   : ";
         cin >> chemMarks;
      }
      void printData() {
         cout <<"Roll number               : "<<rollNo<<endl;
         cout <<"First name                : "<<firstName<<endl;
         cout <<setprecision(2);
         cout <<"Marks in English          : "<<engMarks<<endl;
         cout <<"Marks in Mathematics      : "<<mathMarks<<endl;
         cout <<"Marks in Physics          : "<<phyMarks<<endl;
         cout <<"Marks in Chemistry        : "<<chemMarks<<endl;
      }
      // declaration of overloading of << operator
      friend ofstream & operator << (ofstream &,studentType&);
      // declaration of overloading of >> operator
      friend ifstream & operator >> (ifstream &,studentType&);
};
// definition of overloading of << operator
ofstream & operator << ( ofstream &dout, studentType &st )
{
    dout << st.rollNo << " "
         << st.firstName << " "
         << setprecision(2)
         << st.engMarks << " "
```

```
            << st.mathMarks << " "
            << st.phyMarks << " "
            << st.chemMarks
            << endl;
    return dout;
}
// definition of overloading of >> operator
ifstream & operator >> ( ifstream & din, studentType &st )
{
    din >> st.rollNo >> st.firstName >> st.engMarks
        >> st.mathMarks >> st.phyMarks >> st.chemMarks;
    return din;
}
void main()
{
    studentType student;
    char more = 'y';
    ofstream outFile ( "student.txt", ios::out );
    if ( outFile.fail() ) {
       cout << "\nUnable to open file student.txt\n";
       return;
    }
    while(1) {
       student.readData();
       outFile << student; // write object to file
       if ( outFile.bad() ) {
           cout << "\nError while writing to student.txt\n";
           return;
       }
       cout << "\n\nAny more records (y/n) ? : ";
       cin >> more;
       if ( (more == 'n') || (more == 'N') )
       {
          outFile.close();
          break;
       }
    }
}
```

From the user point of view, its working will be identical to program of listing 12.5.

12.9.1.4.2 Reading of Objects

The following program illustrates the approach of reading objects from a file using overloaded >> operator. The program reads data from file and displays on the monitor (screen).

Listing 12.8

```
// Program to demonstrate the reading of objects
// from a text file using overloaded >> operator

#include <iostream.h>
#include <iomanip.h>
#include <fstream.h>
class studentType
{
    private:
      int rollNo;
      char firstName[20];
      float engMarks;
      float mathMarks;
      float phyMarks;
      float chemMarks;
    public:
      studentType() { }   // default constructor
      void readData() {
         cout << "\nEnter roll number          : ";
         cin >> rollNo;
         cout << "Enter first name           : ";
         cin >> firstName;
         cout << "Enter marks in English     : ";
         cin >> engMarks;
         cout << "Enter marks in Mathematics : ";
         cin >> mathMarks;
         cout << "Enter marks in Physics     : ";
         cin >> phyMarks;
         cout << "Enter marks in Chemistry   : ";
         cin >> chemMarks;
      }
      void printData() {
         cout <<"Roll number          : "<<rollNo<<endl;
         cout <<"First name           : "<<firstName<<endl;
         cout <<setprecision(2);
         cout <<"Marks in English     : "<<engMarks<<endl;
         cout <<"Marks in Mathematics : "<<mathMarks<<endl;
         cout <<"Marks in Physics     : "<<phyMarks<<endl;
         cout <<"Marks in Chemistry   : "<<chemMarks<<endl;
      }
      // declaration of overloading of << operator
      friend ofstream & operator << ( ofstream &, studentType & );
      // declaration of overloading of >> operator
      friend ifstream & operator >> ( ifstream &, studentType & );
};
// definition of overloading of << operator
ofstream & operator << ( ofstream &dout, studentType &st )
```

```
{
    dout << st.rollNo << " "
         << st.firstName << " "
         << setprecision(2)
         << st.engMarks << " "
         << st.mathMarks << " "
         << st.phyMarks << " "
         << st.chemMarks
         << endl;
    return dout;
}
// definition of overloading of >> operator
ifstream & operator >> ( ifstream & din, studentType &st )
{
    din >> st.rollNo >> st.firstName >> st.engMarks
        >> st.mathMarks >> st.phyMarks >> st.chemMarks;
    return din;
}
void main()
{
    studentType student;
    int studentNo = 0;
    ifstream inFile ( "student.txt", ios::in );
    if ( inFile.fail() ) {
       cout << "\nUnable to open file student.txt\n";
       return;
    }
    while( !inFile.eof() ) {
       inFile >> student;         // read object from file
       if ( inFile.bad() ) {
           cout << "\nError while writing to student.txt\n";
           return;
       }
       studentNo++;
       cout << "Student NO : " << studentNo << endl << endl;
       student.printData();
       cout << "\n\nPress any key for next record ...";
       cin.get();
    }
    inFile.close();
}
```

From the user point of view, its working will be identical to program of listing 12.6.

12.9.2 Reading/Writing of Binary Files

When we want to write few numbers to a disk file, it is possible with formatted I/O, though not efficient. But when we want to store a large amount of numerical data, the more efficient way of doing the same is using binary I/O, *also known as block I/O*, in which numbers are stored as they are stored in the computer's main memory, rather than as strings of characters. Likewise, objects can be stored in a file more efficiently using binary I/O.

12.9.2.1 Reading and Writing of Arrays

An entire array can be read and written in a single read and write operation. The following programs illustrates the approach to by first writing an entire array to a file and then reading back using *write()* function of *ofstream* class and *read()* function of *ifstream* class, respectively.

Listing 12.9

```
// Program to demonstrate writing of a file using binary I/O
// It write entire array in single write operation,
// and then reads back in single read operation.
#include <iostream.h>
#include <fstream.h>
const int MAX = 10;
void main()
{
    int intArray[MAX] = { 0, 1, 2, 3, 4, 5, 6, 7, 8, 9 };
    ofstream outFile( "file4.dat", ios::binary | ios::out );
    if ( outFile.fail() ) {
        cout << "\nUnable to open file for writing" << endl;
        return;
    }
    outFile.write( (char*) intArray, MAX*sizeof(int) );
    if ( outFile.fail() ) {
        cout << "\nUnable to write onto file " << endl;
        return;
    }
    outFile.close();
    ifstream inFile ( "file4.dat", ios::binary | ios::in );
    if ( inFile.fail() ) {
        cout << "\nUnable to open file for reading" << endl;
        return;
    }
    inFile.read( (char*) intArray, MAX*sizeof(int) );
    if ( inFile.fail() ) {
        cout << "\nUnable to read from file\n ";
        return;
```

```
    }
    inFile.close();
    cout << "\nContents written and read "
         << "back are using binary I/O" << endl << endl;
    for ( int i = 0; i < 10; i++ )
        cout << intArray[i] << "  ";
    cout << endl;
}
```

Test Run

```
Contents written and read back are using binary I/O

0 1 2 3 4 5 6 7 8 9
```

In above program, we are writing one-dimensional array (linear array) at a time, however, if we have two-dimensional array named *mat* of type *int*, say of size *m*×*n*, then this array can be written in following ways:

- Writing one row at a time as shown below:

```
for ( i = 0; i < m; i++ )
    outFile.write((char*) &mat[i], n*sizeof(int));
```

- Writing entire two-dimensional array as shown below:

```
outFile.write((char*) mat, m*n*sizeof(int));
```

12.9.2.2 Reading and Writing of Structures

A structure can be read and written in a single read and write operation. The following programs illustrates the approach to by first writing a structure to a file and then reading back using *write()* function of *ofstream* class and *read()* function of *ifstream* class, respectively.

Listing 12.10

```
//  Program to demonstrate the writing of a file using
//  binary I/O. It writes entire structure in single write
// operation, and then reads back in single read operation.

#include <iostream.h>
```

```
#include <fstream.h>
struct studentType
{
   int rollNo;
   char firstName[20];
   int engMarks;
   int mathMarks;
   int phyMarks;
   int chemMarks;
};
void main()
{
   studentType student = { 1000, "Mehak", 56, 73, 84, 65 };
   ofstream outFile( "file4.dat", ios::binary | ios::out );
   if ( outFile.fail() )
   {
       cout << "\nUnable to open file for writing" << endl;
       return;
   }
   outFile.write( (char*) &student, sizeof(student) );
   if ( outFile.fail() )
   {
       cout << "\nUnable to write onto file " << endl;
       return;
   }
   outFile.close();
   ifstream inFile ( "file4.dat", ios::binary | ios::in );
   if ( inFile.fail() )
   {
       cout << "\nUnable to open file for reading" << endl;
       return;
   }
   inFile.read( (char*) &student, sizeof(student) );
   if ( inFile.fail() )
   {
       cout << "\nUnable to read from file " << endl;
       return;
   }
   inFile.close();
   cout << "\nContents written and read "
        << "back are using binary I/O" << endl << endl;
   cout << "Roll number         : " << student.rollNo << endl;
   cout << "First name          : " << student.firstName << endl;
   cout << "Marks in English    : " << student.engMarks << endl;
   cout << "Marks in Mathematics : " << student.mathMarks << endl;
   cout << "Marks in Physics    : " << student.phyMarks << endl;
   cout << "Marks in Chemistry  : " << student.chemMarks << endl;
   cout << endl;
}
```

Test Run

```
Contents written and read back are using binary I/O

Roll number          : 1000
First name           : Mehak
Marks in English     : 56
Marks in Mathematics : 73
Marks in Physics     : 84
Marks in Chemistry   : 65
```

In above program, we are writing one structure at a time; however, If we have array of structures, say *n*, then these structures can be written in following ways:

- Writing one structure at a time as shown below:

```
for ( int i = 0; i < n; i++ )
  outFile.write((char*)&student[i],sizeof(student[i]));
```

- Writing entire array of structures as shown below:

```
outFile.write((char*)&student, n*sizeof(student[0]));
```

12.9.2.3 Writing of Objects

An object can be written to a file using *write()* function as

```
outFile.write ( (char *) &object, sizeof(object) );
```

The first argument is address of the object, and the second argument is the size of the argument in bytes. The address of the object must be cast of type *char* * (pointer to *char* type).

The following interactive program illustrates the approach to writing an object to a file. The program reads data from the keyboard and writes into a file.

Listing 12.11

```
// Interactive program to demonstrate the writing
// of objects to a file

#include <iostream.h>
#include <fstream.h>
class studentType
{
    private:
```

```
        int rollNo;
        char firstName[20];
        float engMarks;
        float mathMarks;
        float phyMarks;
        float chemMarks;
    public:
        studentType() { }   // default constructor
        void readData() {
            cout << "\nEnter roll number          : ";
            cin >> rollNo;
            cout << "Enter first name           : ";
            cin >> firstName;
            cout << "Enter marks in English     : ";
            cin >> engMarks;
            cout << "Enter marks in Mathematics : ";
            cin >> mathMarks;
            cout << "Enter marks in Physics     : ";
            cin >> phyMarks;
            cout << "Enter marks in Chemistry   : ";
            cin >> chemMarks;
        }
        void printData() {
            cout << "Roll number           : " << rollNo << endl;
            cout << "First name            : " << firstName << endl;
            cout << "Marks in English      : " << engMarks << endl;
            cout << "Marks in Mathematics  : " << mathMarks << endl;
            cout << "Marks in Physics      : " << phyMarks << endl;
            cout << "Marks in Chemistry    : " << chemMarks << endl;
        }
};
void main()
{
    studentType student;
    char more = 'y';
    ofstream oFile( "student.dat", ios::binary | ios::out );
    if ( oFile.fail() ) {
        cout << "\nUnable to open file student.dat" << endl;
        return;
    }
    while(1)
    {
        student.readData();
        oFile.write( (char *) &student, sizeof(student) );
        if ( oFile.bad() ) {
            cout << "\nError while writing to student.dat"<<endl;
            return;
        }
        cout << "\n\nAny more records (y/n) ? : ";
```

```
        cin >> more;
        if ( (more == 'n') || (more == 'N') ) {
            oFile.close();
            break;
        }
    }
}
```

From user point of view, its working will be identical to program of listing 12.7.

12.9.2.4 Reading of Objects

An object can be read from a file using *write()* function as

```
inFile.read ( (char *) &object, sizeof(object) );
```

The first argument is address of the object, and second argument is the size of argument in bytes. The address of the object must be cast of type *char* * (pointer to *char* type).

The following program illustrates the approach to reading an object from a file. The program reads objects from a file and displays on the monitor (screen).

Listing 12.12

```
//  Program to demonstrate the reading of objects written
//  previously with program of listing 12.11

#include <iostream.h>
#include <fstream.h>

class studentType
{
    private:
       int rollNo;
       char firstName[20];
       float engMarks;
       float mathMarks;
       float phyMarks;
       float chemMarks;
   public:
       void readData()
       {
          cout << "\nEnter roll number          : ";
          cin >> rollNo;
          cout << "Enter first name           : ";
          cin >> firstName;
          cout << "Enter marks in English     : ";
```

```
        cin >> engMarks;
        cout << "Enter marks in Mathematics : ";
        cin >> mathMarks;
        cout << "Enter marks in Physics     : ";
        cin >> phyMarks;
        cout << "Enter marks in Chemistry   : ";
        cin >> chemMarks;
      }
      void printData()
      {
        cout << "Roll number              : " << rollNo << endl;
        cout << "First name               : " << firstName << endl;
        cout << "Marks in English         : " << engMarks << endl;
        cout << "Marks in Mathematics : " << mathMarks << endl;
        cout << "Marks in Physics         : " << phyMarks << endl;
        cout << "Marks in Chemistry   : " << chemMarks << endl;
      }
};
void main()
{
    studentType student;
    int studentNo = 0;
    ifstream iFile ("student.dat", ios::binary | ios::in);
    if ( iFile.fail() )
    {
      cout << "\nUnable to open file student.dat" << endl;
      return;
    }
    while ( !iFile.eof() )
    {
      iFile.read( (char *) &student, sizeof(student) );
      if ( iFile.bad() )
      {
        cout << "\nError while reading file student.dat"
             << endl;
        return;
      }

      studentNo++;
      cout << "Student NO : " << studentNo << "\n\n";
      student.printData();
      cout << "\n\nPress any key for next record ...";
      cin.get();
    }
    iFile.close();
}
```

From user point of view, its working will be identical to program of listing 12.8.

12.10 ACCESSING RECORDS RANDOMLY

In all the previous programs, the reading and writing has been sequential. While writing to a file, data items (which may be a character, a string, an array or a structure or an object) are placed one after the other in a sequence. Similarly, while reading from a file, the data items are read from the beginning of the file in sequence until we came to the end of the file is reached.

It is also possible to access a particular data item that may be in the middle of the file. This way of accessing a file is called *direct accessing* or *random accessing*. The only restriction for direct/random addressing is that all the data items must be of same size, *i.e.*, record length must be fixed.

12.10.1 File Pointer

A *file pointer* is a pointer to a particular byte in a file. Every time, when we write to a file, the file pointer moves to the end of the data item written so that writing can continue from that point. When a file is closed, and subsequently opened for reading, the file pointer is set to the beginning of the file. So we can read the file from beginning. After reading a data item, the file pointer moves to the beginning of the next data item, this can be subsequently read. However, if the file is opened in append mode, then the file pointer will be positioned at the end of the exiting file, so that new data items can be written from there onwards.

12.10.2 File Pointers and their Manipulations

The C++ language file management system associates *file pointers* with files. These pointers are called *get pointer* (input pointer) and *put pointer* (output pointer). It associates get pointer with a file that is opened for reading, put pointer with a file that is opened for writing, and both of these pointers with a file that is opened for reading and writing.

These pointers serve the following purpose:

1. *Get pointer* specifies a location in input file from where the current read operation is initiated.
2. *Put pointer* specifies a location in output file from where the current write operation is initiated.

On successful completion of a read or write operation, the appropriate pointer is advanced automatically.

When a file is opened, then by default, the file pointers are initially positioned as per following:

1. When a file is opened in read-only mode, the get pointer is automatically positioned at the beginning of the file so that the file can be read from the beginning.
2. When a file is opened in write-only mode, the following possibilities can happen:

   (*a*) If the file already exists, its contents will be deleted.
   (*b*) If the file does not exist, it is created.

   In both the cases, the put pointer is set at the beginning of the file so that the file can be written from the beginning.
3. When a file is opened in append mode, the following possibilities can happen:

   (*a*) If the file already exists, its existing contents will remain unaffected, and the put pointer is positioned at the end-of-file so that the data can be written (appended) at the end of the existing contents.

   (*b*) If the file does not exist, it is created, and the put pointer is set at the beginning of the file so that the file can be written from the beginning.

However, there may be situations where these file pointers are to be set at desired position in a file so the read or write operation can take place. The file stream classes contain member functions that allow moving these file pointers within a file. In addition, there may be situations, when we want to know the current position of the file pointer in a file. The file stream classes also contain member functions that return the current position of the file pointer in a file. The member functions are listed in Table 12.4.

Table 12.4: File pointer control functions

Function	Class in which defined	Action Performed
`seekg()`	`ifstream` class	Moves get file pointer to specified position.
`seekp()`	`ofstream` class	Moves put file pointer to specified position.
`tellg()`	`ifstream` class	Returns the position of the get pointer.
`tellp()`	`ofstream` class	Returns the position of the put pointer.

The *seek()* functions have the following prototypes:

```
ifstream & seekg( long offset, seek_dir origin = ios::beg );
ofstream & seekp( long offset, seek_dir origin = ios::beg );
```

where *offset* specifies number of bytes by which file pointer is to be moved; *origin* specifies the reference point from where the offset is to measured, default argument with default value beginning of the file as reference point.

These functions return a reference to the respective streams.

Using an enumeration named *seek_dir* defined in the *ios* class, specifies the reference point.

```
enum seek_dir { beg, cur, end };
```

Table 12.5: Description of file seek origins

Origin value	Offset is measured from
`beg`	Reference point is the beginning of the file.
`cur`	Reference point is the current position of the file pointer in the file.
`end`	Reference point is the end of the file.

The *tell()* functions have the following prototypes:

```
long tellg();
long tellp();
```

These functions return the current position as number of bytes from the beginning of the respective files.

For example, the statement

```
inFile.seekg(20);

          or

inFile.seekg(20, ios::beg);
```

moves the file pointer to the byte number 20. Here, by default the reference point is beginning of the file. Remember that the bytes in a file are numbered beginning from 0. Therefore, the get pointer will be positioned at the 21st byte in the file.

Consider the following the statements

```
ifstream inFile;
inFile.open("test.dat", ios::app);
int length = inFile.tellg();
```

or

```
ifstream inFile("test.dat", ios::app);
int length = inFile.tellg();
```

On execution of these statements, the get pointer will be moved to the end-of-file, and the value of variable length will represent the bytes in *test.dat* file, *i.e.*, current size of *test.dat* file.

Some more examples of file pointer positioning are listed in Table 12.6. Here, *outFile* is an *ofstream* object that is linked to *result.dat* file.

Table 12.6: Some examples illustrating the use of *seekp()/seekg()* functions

Seek Call	Action performed
`outFile.seekp(0,ios::beg);`	Moves the put pointer to the beginning of the file. If file pointer is currently at beginning of file, it results in no action.
`outFile.seekp(n,ios::beg);`	Moves the put pointer forward by *n* bytes, i.e., move put pointer filed to (*n*+1)th bytes in the file.
`outFile.seekp(-n,ios::cur);`	Moves the put pointer backward by *n* bytes from the current position.
`outFile.seekp(0,ios::end);`	Moves the put pointer to the end of the file. If file pointer is currently at end of file, it results in no action.
`outFile.seekp(n,ios::cur);`	Moves the put pointer forward by *n* bytes from the current position.
`outFile.seekp(1,ios::cur);`	Moves the put pointer to the next byte.
`outFile.seekp(-1,ios::cur);`	Moves the put pointer to the previous byte.
`outFile.seekp(m,ios::end);`	Moves the put pointer backward by *m* bytes from the end of the file.

Listing 12.13

```
//  Filename : fsize.cpp
//  Program to demonstrate the use of seek & tell functions.
//  It displays the size of the file in bytes.
```

```
#include <iostream.h>
#include <fstream.h>
#include <iomanip.h>
void main( int argc, char *argv[] )
{
   if ( argc != 2 ) {
      cout << "Usage: fsize <file>" << endl;
      return;
   }
   ifstream inFile;
   inFile.open ( argv[1], ios::in );
   if ( inFile.fail() ) {
      cout << "\nError in file: " << argv[1] << endl;
      return;
   }
   inFile.seekg(0, ios::end);
   if ( inFile.bad() ) {
      cout << "\nError in file: " << argv[1] << endl;
      return;
   }
   long size = inFile.tellg();
   cout << "Size of file : " << size << " bytes." << endl;
   inFile.close();
}
```

Test Run

```
> fsize fsize.cpp
Size of file : 1145 bytes.
```

12.11 FILE UPDATION

The most usual way of updating a sequential file is to read data items from one file, update the required data items and write onto a new file. This is illustrated below by an example. We have with us a file containing students' awards in five subjects namely *English*, *Maths*, *Physics*, and *Chemistry*. It is decided that those students who had secured less than 50 marks in English be given 5 grace marks. The following program illustrates the various steps required.

Listing 12.14

```
//  Program to demonstrate updation of a file
//  while creating a new file

#include <iostream.h>
```

```
#include <fstream.h>
class studentType
{
   private:
      int rollNo;
      char firstName[20];
      float engMarks;
      float mathMarks;
      float phyMarks;
      float chemMarks;
   public:
      studentType() { }   // default constructor
      void readData() {
         cout << "Enter roll number          : ";
         cin >> rollNo;
         cout << "Enter first name           : ";
         cin >> firstName;
         cout << "Enter marks in English     : ";
         cin >> engMarks;
         cout << "Enter marks in Mathematics : ";
         cin >> mathMarks;
         cout << "Enter marks in Physics     : ";
         cin >> phyMarks;
         cout << "Enter marks in Chemistry   : ";
         cin >> chemMarks;
      }
      void printData() {
         cout << "Roll number          : " << rollNo << endl;
         cout << "First name           : " << firstName << endl;
         cout << "Marks in English     : " << engMarks << endl;
         cout << "Marks in Mathematics : " << mathMarks << endl;
         cout << "Marks in Physics     : " << phyMarks << endl;
         cout << "Marks in Chemistry   : " << chemMarks << endl;
      }
      void updateData() {
         if ( engMarks < 50 )
            engMarks += 5;
      }
};
void main()
{
   studentType student;
   ifstream inFile ("oldfile.dat", ios::binary | ios::in);
   if ( inFile.fail() ) {
      cout << "\nUnable to open file oldfile.dat" << endl;
      return;
   }
   ofstream outFile("newfile.dat", ios::binary | ios::out);
   if ( outFile.fail() ) {
```

```
        cout << "\nUnable to open file newfile.dat" << endl;
        return;
    }
    while ( !inFile.eof() ) {
        inFile.read((char *) &student, sizeof(student));
        if ( inFile.bad() ) {
            cout << "\nError while reading file oldfile.dat\n";
            return;
        }
        student.updateData();
        outFile.write ( (char *) &student, sizeof(student) );
        if ( inFile.bad() ) {
            cout << "\nError while writing to file newfile.dat\n";
            return;
        }
    }
    inFile.close();
    outFile.close();
}
```

Since C++ permits reading and writing of files at the same time, so instead of creating a new updated file, the data items can be updated in the original file itself. The following program illustrates the various steps required.

Listing 12.15

```
//  Program to demonstrate updation of a file
//  without creating a new file
#include <iostream.h>
#include <fstream.h>
class studentType
{
    private:
      int rollNo;
      char firstName[20];
      float engMarks;
      float mathMarks;
      float phyMarks;
      float chemMarks;
    public:
      studentType() { }   // default constructor
      void readData() {
         cout << "\nEnter roll number            : ";
         cin >> rollNo;
         cout << "Enter first name            : ";
         cin >> firstName;
         cout << "Enter marks in English      : ";
         cin >> engMarks;
         cout << "Enter marks in Mathematics : ";
```

```
      cin >> mathMarks;
      cout << "Enter marks in Physics     : ";
      cin >> phyMarks;
      cout << "Enter marks in Chemistry   : ";
      cin >> chemMarks;
   }
   void printData() {
      cout << "Roll number           : " << rollNo << endl;
      cout << "First name            : " << firstName << endl;
      cout << "Marks in English      : " << engMarks << endl;
      cout << "Marks in Mathematics  : " << mathMarks << endl;
      cout << "Marks in Physics      : " << phyMarks << endl;
      cout << "Marks in Chemistry    : " << chemMarks << endl;
   }
   int updateData() {
      if ( engMarks < 50 ) {
         engMarks += 5;
         return 1;      // return 1 if record updated
      }
      else
         return 0;      // return 0 if record is not updated
   }
};
void main()
{
   studentType student;
   fstream ioFile("student.dat",ios::binary|ios::in|ios::out);
   if ( ioFile.fail() ) {
      cout << "\nUnable to open file student.dat\n";
      return;
   }
   while ( !ioFile.eof() ) {
      ioFile.read( (char *) &student, sizeof(student));
      if ( ioFile.bad() ) {
         cout << "\nError while reading file\n";
         return;
      }
      if ( student.updateData() == 1 ) {
         ioFile.seekp(-long(sizeof(student)),ios::cur);
         ioFile.write((char *)&student,sizeof(student));
         if ( ioFile.bad() ) {
            cout << "\nError while writing file\n";
            return;
         }
      }
   }
   ioFile.close();
}
```

We have used the *seekp()* with second argument as a long negative number, which requests the operating system that file pointer is to moved in the backward direction. We know that after reading the current data item, the file pointer is moved to the beginning of the next data item. Since we want to update the current data item, we have to bring back the file pointer to the beginning of the data item to be updated. Thus after modifying the data item in memory, the *write()* function overwrites the existing data item with the modified one.

In C++, files can also be updated in a random manner. The only thing required is that we must know the record number of the data item(s) to be updated. If we know the record number of the data item, we can access it directly, and after modifying the data item, we can write it back.

Deletion of a data item(s) in the file itself is not possible. To delete a data item, we have to create a new file that contains all the data items of the original file except the data item to be deleted.

QUICK RECAP

In this chapter, we have learnt that

- If the volume of the input data is very large, it can be best handled using data files.
- If the data generated by some instrument is in machine-readable form (binary form), then you have to use data file to pass on this data to your program.
- If volume of output is large and can't be viewed on screen properly, it is better to write output to data file that you can refer later on without re-executing your program.
- If the output generated by one program is to be used as input for another program, again the use of data files will be advantageous.
- A data file can be a text file or a binary file.
- C++ provides file stream classes to handle various I/O operations on files.
- A file can be opened using the constructor of the appropriate stream class.
- A file can be also opened using the *open()* member function of the appropriate stream class.
- There can be a problem while opening a file or while doing I/O operations, therefore, your program should be capable of catching these problems and proving safe exit from the program.
- It is not possible to delete a record from he disk directly.

MULTIPLE CHOICE QUESTIONS

1. Which of the following is not an attribute of a data file?

(a) Name (b) Structure
(c) Access method (d) Storage device

2. Which of the following statement is true about master file?

(a) It is used to hold the data which is relatively permanent.
(b) A record in master file keeps track of some thing such as employee of an organization.
(c) A record in master file represents an event or change in something whose status is tracked to transaction file.
(d) None of above

3. In what kind of files the information is stored in exactly the same way as it is stored in computer's main memory?

(a) Master file (b) Text file (c) Binary file (d) Input file

4. Which is the topmost base class in the hierarchy of file stream classes?

(a) fstream (b) ofsteam (c) fstreambase (d) ifstream

5. Which of the following is not a stream object which automatically is created when a program begins execution?

(a) cin (b) cerr (c) cout (d) cprn

6. Which of the following is not an error handling function?

(a) fail() (b) bad() (c) good() (d) ok()

7. Member function *close()* of *fstreambase* class is, usually, used to

(a) delete a file (b) disconnect file from program
(c) read data from a file (d) write data to a file

8. A file stream object is created using . . . . function of *fstreambase* class.

(a) fclose() (b) open() (c) fopen() (d) OPEN()

9. Member function of input stream class used to read a character from a file is

(a) getc() (b) get() (c) getchar() (d) fgetc()

10. Member function of output stream used to write a character to a file is

(a) putchar() (b) put() (c) fputc() (d) char()

11. Function that allows a file to read randomly is

(a) seek() (b) seekg() (c) fseek() (d) fseekg()

12. Consider the statement

```
inFile.seekg(20, ios::end);
```

What can you say about identifier *inFile*?

(*a*) It is the name of the object of output file stream class
(*b*) It is the name of the object of input file stream class
(*c*) It is the name of pre-defined input file stream object
(*d*) None of above

13. Member function *ftellg()* of input stream class returns

(*a*) the beginning position of the file (*b*) the end position of the file
(*c*) the current position of the file (*d*) the middle position of the file

14. The task performed by the statement "`inFile.seekg(0,ios::end)`" is

(*a*) positioning of the file pointer at the beginning of the file
(*b*) positioning of the file pointer at the end of the file
(*c*) positioning of the file pointer at the middle of the file
(*d*) positioning of the file pointer at the second last record

15. Which of the following statements about data files in C++ is true?

(*a*) File can only be accessed sequentially
(*b*) The C++ file system supports handling of only text files
(*c*) The C++ file system provides a way to access to contents of a data file using member functions of file stream classes only
(*d*) None of above

REVIEW EXERCISES

1. What is a data file? Explain the usefulness of data files.
2. How can the data files be classified?
3. Compare and contrast between a master file and a transaction file.
4. What are the steps involved in using a data file in a C++ program?
5. What you mean by a *file pointer*?
6. What the text and binary modes have to do with files?
7. How data is stored when a file is opened in text mode?
8. How data is stored when a file is opened in binary mode?
9. Given a choice between text mode and binary mode, which mode you would prefer? What are the factors on basis of that you will decide about the mode to be used?

10. Suppose a program wants to examine every byte of a file, which mode will be more appropriate?
11. What do you mean by term *offset* in reference to a data file?
12. What is the task performed by the *seekg()* function?
13. What is the task performed by the *tellg()* function?
14. Which value is returned by the *fopen()* if some error occurs in opening a file?
15. What are the possible reasons for failure while opening a data file?

PROGRAMMING EXERCISES

1. Write a program that read some text from the keyboard and write it into a file named TEXT. The program then reads this file and displays its contents on the computer screen.
2. Write a program to copy the contents of one file to another file byte-by-byte. The names of the files are taken as command line argument.
3. Given a text file containing some text. Write a program that prompts the user to input name of a text file, reads this file and outputs the number of vowels and number of words in the text.
4. You are given a binary file named *student.dat* that contains information about some students. The information about each student consists of — his/her roll number (an integer), name (25 characters), father's (25 characters), and address (30 characters). Write a program that permits to modify a student's record, whose roll number is given.
5. You are given a binary file named *student.dat* that contains information about some students. The information about each student consists of his/her roll number (an integer), name (25 characters), father's (25 characters), and address (30 characters). Write a program that permits the user to delete a student's record, whose roll number is given.
6. Given a text file containing some text. Write a program that prompts the user to input name of a text file, reads this file and replaces each occurrence of character 'x' with uppercase 'X'.
7. A beginner to the C++ language has typed the entire program in uppercase letter. As you know that the normal convention in C++ language is to type the source code using lowercase letters only except for macros and defined constants. Write a program that converts the source code into lowercase letter. Comments should be left unchanged.

8. We have to maintain a database of members of a club. The information recorded about a member includes his/her membership number (int), name (20 characters), address (40 characters), and telephone number (long integer). Write a menu driven program that permits the user to add members, modify member's information except membership number, delete member from database, and generate a list of members.

9. Write a program to compare two files. Program should accept the file names as command line arguments. The program should report where the respective bytes differ.

❑ ❑ ❑

Chapter 13

Introduction to Standard Template Library

Learning Objectives

After reading this chapter, students will be able to

- explain STL and its programming model
- understand and explain various containers
- describe various algorithms that operate on containers
- explain the type of iterators and their working
- use STL in solving real-life problems

13.1 INTRODUCTION

Besides maintainability and understandability, another great promise of object orientation is reuse, reuse, and reuse. We have already studied templates using that we can write generic functions or generic classes that support all data types. The C++ language includes a Standard Template Library (STL) of many reusable components. **Alexander Stepanov** and **Meng Lee** at Hewlett-Packard developed the STL library. It is based on their research in the field of generic programming, with significant contribution from **David Musser**. STL contains several functions and operators that help the programmer develop complex programs rapidly. The programmers only need to include appropriate header file in their program file.

The STL is now widely used and has been accepted as part of the C++ standard. All famous compiler vendors provide support for STL in their C++ compilers.

STL is quite large and a complete book can be written on it. In this chapter we will attempt to present STL in a manner so that reader can start using it effectively.

13.2 PROGRAMMING MODEL OF STL

It is very easy to use STL once you understand how it is constructed and what elements it employs. Therefore, in this section we will have an overview of STL.

At the heart of the programming model of STL are three foundational items: *containers*, *algorithms*, and *iterators*. These items work in tandem to provide off-the-shelf solutions to a variety of programming problems.

Each of these items is described below.

13.2.1 Containers

Containers are the objects that hold other objects. STL has number of container classes that allow programmers to perform common tasks. These container classes support generic programming and can be used for handling data of different data types. Each container class defines a set of functions that may be applied to the container. For example, a *list* container includes functions that *insert*, *delete*, and *merge* elements; a *stack* container includes functions to *push* and *pop* values.

Containers are further classified as *sequence containers* and *associative containers*. In sequence containers, the elements are stored in a sequence and only can be retrieved in that sequence where as in associative containers the elements can be retrieved according to keys. In addition, STL provides three containers that are derived from sequence containers, and are known as *derived containers* or *container adapters*.

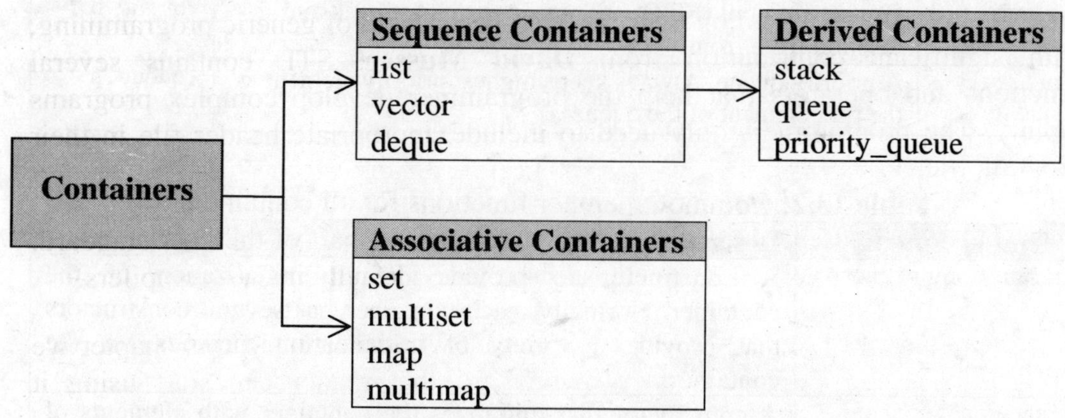

Figure 13.1: Classification of Containers

Table 13.1: Containers, their description, and required header files

Container	Description	Required header file
Sequence Containers		
`list`	A doubly linear list. Allows rapid insertions and deletion anywhere.	<list.h>
`vector`	A dynamic array. Allows rapid insertions and deletion at back. Allows direct access to any element.	<vector.h>
`deque`	A double-ended queue. Allows rapid insertions and deletion at front and back.	<deque.h>
Associative Containers		
`set`	A set in which each element is unique. Allows rapid lookup.	<set.h>
`multiset`	A set in which each element is not necessarily unique. Allows rapid lookup.	<set.h>
`map`	Stores key/value pairs in which each key is associated with only one value (no duplicates), *i.e.*, one-to-one mapping. Allows rapid key-based lookup.	<map.h>
`multimap`	Stores key/value pairs in which one key may be associated with two or more values (duplicates allowed), *i.e.*, one-to-many mapping. Allows rapid key-based lookup.	<map.h>

Table 13.1: Containers, their description, and required header files (*Contd.*)

Container	Description	Required header file
Derived Containers		
`stack`	Last-in-first-out (LIFO). Allows insertions and deletion only at one end, called *top*.	`<stack.h>`
`queue`	First-in-first-out (FIFO). Allows insertions at back and deletion from front.	`<queue.h>`
`priority queue`	A priority queue. Always keeps highest priority element as the first element of the queue.	`<queue.h>`

Table 13.2: Common member functions for all containers

Member Function	Description
`default constructor`	A constructor to provide default initialization of the container. Normally, each container has several constructors that provide a variety of initialization methods for the container.
`copy constructor`	A constructor that initializes the container with elements of another container of same type.
`Destructor`	A destructor for cleanup after a container is no longer needed.
`Empty`	Returns *true* if there are no elements in the container, otherwise, return *false*.
`max_size`	Returns the maximum number of elements for a container.
`Size`	Returns the number of elements currently in the container.
`operator =`	Assigns one container to another.
`operator <`	Returns *true* if the first container is less than the second container, otherwise, return *false*.
`operator <=`	Returns *true* if the first container is less than or equal to the second container, otherwise, return *false*.
`operator >`	Returns *true* if the first container is greater than the second container, otherwise, return *false*.
`operator >=`	Returns *true* if the first container is greater than or equal to the second container, otherwise, return *false*.
`operator ==`	Returns *true* if the first container is equal to the second container, otherwise, return *false*.
`operator !=`	Returns *true* if the first container is not equal to the second container, otherwise, return *false*.
`swap`	Swaps the elements of two containers.

Table 13 3: Common member functions for *first class* containers

Member Function	Description
`begin`	Returns an iterator that refers to the first element of the container.
`end`	Returns an iterator that refers to the next position after the last element of the container.
`rbegin`	Returns an iterator that refers to the last element of the container.
`rend`	Returns an iterator that refers to the position before the first of the container.
`erase`	Erases one or more elements from the container
`clear`	Erases all elements from the container

13.2.2 Algorithms

Algorithms act on containers. They provide the means by which you will manipulate the contents of the containers. Their capabilities include *initializing*, *sorting*, *searching*, and *transforming* the contents of containers. Many algorithms operate on a range of elements within a container. It is important to note that these algorithms are neither member functions nor friends of containers. These are standalone template functions. To use these algorithms, we must include header file *algorithm.h* in the program. These algorithms, depending on the nature of operations they perform, can be categorized as follows:

- *Non-mutating algorithms* – algorithms that do not modify the container.
- *Mutating algorithms* – algorithms that modify the container.

Table 13.4: Some Mutating algorithms

Algorithm	Description
`copy()`	Duplicates sequence from beginning
`copy_backward()`	Duplicates sequence from end
`fill()`	Fills up a sequence with a given element
`fill_n()`	Fills up first *n* elements of a sequence with a given element
`generate()`	Substitutes all elements of a sequence with the result of an operation
`generate_n()`	Substitutes first *n* elements of a sequence with result of an operation
`iter_swap()`	Swaps elements pointer to by the iterator
`remove()`	Erases elements with given value
`replace()`	Substitutes elements with a given value
`reverse()`	Reverses the order of elements
`swap()`	Swaps two elements
`transform()`	Applies an operation on all elements
`unique()`	Removes similar contiguous elements

Table 13.5: Some Non-mutating algorithms

Algorithm	Description
`binary_search()`	Performs a binary search on an indexed sequence
`count()`	Counts occurrences of a value in a sequence
`count_if()`	Counts occurrences of a value in a sequence that satisfies the condition
`equal()`	Returns true if two sequences are identical
`find()`	Searches the first occurrence of a value in a sequence
`find_end()`	Searches the last occurrence of a value in a sequence
`for_each()`	Perform an operation on each element of a sequence
`max()`	Returns largest element of a sequence
`merge()`	Combines two sorted sequences
`min()`	Returns smallest element of a sequence
`mismatch()`	Searches elements for which two sequences differs
`partial_sort()`	Sorts a portion of a sequence
`search()`	Searches a subsequence in another sequence
`sort()`	Sorts the elements of a sequence

Table 13.6: Some generic numerical algorithms

Algorithm	Description
`accumulate()`	Accumulates the results of operation on a sequence
`adjacent_difference()`	Computes the differences between adjacent pairs of elements of a sequence and stores the results in the same sequence or another sequence.
`inner_product()`	Computes inner product of two sequences.
`partial_sum()`	Computes partial sums and stores the results in the same sequence or another sequence.

Numerical algorithms are defined in header file *numeric.h*.

13.2.3 Iterators

Iterators are objects that allow to cycle through the contents of a container in much the same way that you would use a pointer to cycle through a linked list. Iterators are of five types — *random access*, *bidirectional*, *forward*, *input*, and *output*.

Table 13.7: Types of Iterators

Iterator	Access Allowed
`Random Access`	Stores and retrieve values. Elements can be accessed randomly.
`Bidirectional`	Stores and retrieve values. Elements can be accessed in forward and backward order.
`Forward`	Stores and retrieve values. Elements can be accessed only in forward direction.
`Input`	Retrieve, but not store, values. Forward moving only.
`Output`	Store, but not retrieve, values. Forward moving only.

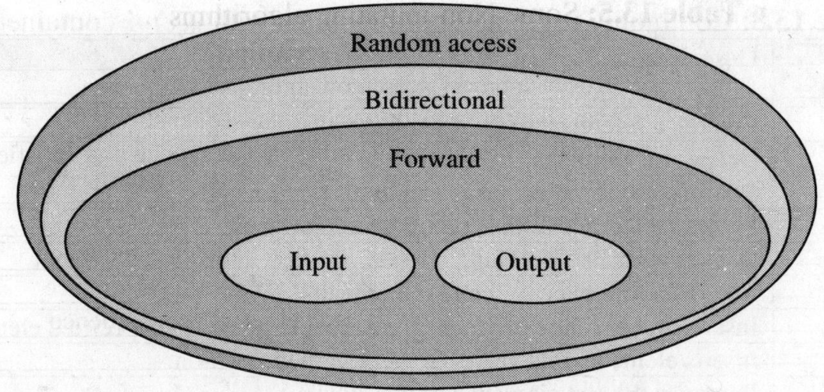

Figure 13.2: Functionality Venn diagram of Iterators

In general, an iterator that has greater access capabilities can be used in place of one that has lesser capabilities. For example, a forward iterator can be used in place of an input iterator.

Iterators are handled just like pointers. You can increment and decrement them. You can apply '*' operator to them. Iterators are declared using the *iterator* type defined by various containers.

The STL also supports *reverse iterators*. Reverse iterators are either bidirectional or random access iterators but move through a sequence in the reverse direction. Thus, if a reverse iterator points to the end of a sequence, incrementing that iterator will cause it to point one element before the end.

13.3 DESCRIPTION OF SELECTIVE CONTAINERS

In this section, we will describe commonly used containers namely *vector*, *list*, and *map*.

13.3.1 Vector Container

The most general-purpose sequence container among all containers is the *vector* container. It supports a dynamic array, dynamic in the sense that it can grow as needed. We know that the size of an array is usually fixed at compile time. This approach is most efficient to implement arrays but is also most restrictive because the size of the array cannot be adjusted at run time to accommodate changing program conditions. A *vector* solves this problem by allocating memory as needed. Further, though *vector* is dynamic, still we can use standard array subscript notation to access its elements. Header file *vector.h* must be included in order to use vector container.

Table 13.8: Commonly used member functions with *vector* container

Member Function	Description
`back()`	Returns a reference to the last element.
`clear()`	Deletes all elements.
`empty()`	Returns true if the vector is empty else returns false.
`end()`	Returns reference to the end of the vector.
`erase()`	Deletes specified element.
`front()`	Returns a reference to the first element.
`insert()`	Inserts one or range of values immediately before the specified element.
`insert()`	Inserts elements in a vector at the specified position.
`pop_back()`	Removes the last element.
`push_back()`	Adds an element with the value specified by *val* to the end of the vector.

13.3.1.1 Creating a Vector

The vector can be declared in following ways:

```
// creates zero-length vector with elements of type int.
vector<int> intVector1;

//creates five element vector with elements of type char.
vector<char> charVector(5);

//creates five element vector with elements of type char and
// initializes all its elements with character 'x'.

vector<char> charVector(5, 'x');

// creates a vector with elements of type int with size equal
// to size of vector intVector2 and initializes all its
// elements with the elements of vector intVector2.

vector<int> intVector2(intVector2);
```

13.3.1.2 Inserting Elements in a Vector

The elements in a vector can be inserted in following ways:

- Elements can be inserted, one at a time, at the end of the vector. This is done using either the subscript notation or *push_back()* function. For example, if *charVector* is a vector with character elements, then element at end can be inserted in following ways:

```
charVector[charVector.size()] = 'x';
```

OR

```
charVector.push_back('x');
```

- Elements can be inserted at the middle of the vector. This is done using *insert()* function. The *insert()* function also requires an iterator to the vector as argument, in addition to the element to be inserted. For example, if *charVector* is a vector with character elements, then element at position 5 can be inserted in the following way:

```
vector <char> iter = charVector.begin();
iter += 5;
charVector.insert(iter, 'x');
```

Since, the *begin()* member function returns an iterator that points to the first element, *i.e.*, with index 0, therefore iterator *iter* is incrementing by 5, so that element can be inserted at the 5th position in the vector.

13.3.1.3 Accessing Elements in a Vector

The elements in a vector can be accessed in following ways:

- The first element can be accessed either using the subscript notation or the *front()* function. For example, if *charVector* is a vector with character elements, then its first element can be accessed in following ways:

```
charVector[0];   // first element is always at index 0

  OR

charVector.front();
```

- The last element can be accessed either using the subscript notation or the *back()* function. For example, if *charVector* is a vector with character elements, then its last element can be accessed in following ways:

```
charVector[charVector.size()-1];

  OR

charVector.back();
```

- Elements other than the first and last element can be accessed either using subscript notation or an iterator. Note that the iterator needs to be updated so that it refers to the desired position in the vector. For example, if *charVector* is a vector with character elements, then its 5th element can be accessed in following ways:

```
charVector[4];   // note that elements are indexed from 0

  OR

vector <char> iter = charVector.begin();
iter += 4;
charVector[iter];
```

- In orderAccessing all elements other than the first and last element can be accessed either using subscript notation or an iterator. Note that the iterator needs to be updated so that it refers to the desired position in the vector. For example, if *charVector* is a vector with character elements, then its 5th element can be accessed in following ways:

```
charVector[4];   // note that elements are indexed from 0
```

Listing 13.1

```
//  Program to demonstrate the vector creation, insertion,
//  size, retrieve, and expanding operations
#include <iostream.h>
#include <vector.h>
#include <cctype.h>
void main()
{
   // create a char vector with size 10
   vector<char> charVector(10);
   int i;
   // output initial size
   cout << "Initial size = " << charVector.size()
         << endl;
    // store some elements in vector
    for ( i = 0; i < 10; i++ )
       charVector[i] = i + 'a';
    // output current contents of the vector
    cout << "Current contents : ";
    for ( i = 0; i < 10; i++ )
        cout << charVector[i] << " ";
    cout << endl << endl;
    cout << "Expanding vector" << endl;
    for ( i = 10; i < 20; i++ )
        charVector.push_back(i + 'a');
    // output current size
    cout << "\nCurrent size = "<<charVector.size()<< endl;
    // output current contents of the vector
    cout << "Current contents : ";
    for ( i = 0; i < charVector.size(); i++ )
        cout << charVector[i] << " ";
    cout << endl << endl;
}
```

Test Run

```
Initial size = 10
Current contents : a b c d e f g h i
```

```
Expanding vector
Current size = 20
Current contents : a b c d e f g h i j k l m n o p q r s t
```

Table 13.9: Commonly used member functions with *list* container

Member Function	Description
back()	Returns a reference to the last element.
begin()	Returns a reference to the first element.
clear()	Deletes all elements.
empty()	Returns true if the list is empty else return false.
end()	Returns reference to the end of the list.
erase()	Deletes specified elements.
insert()	Inserts element at the specified location.
merge()	Merges two ordered lists.
pop_back()	Deletes the last element.
pop_front()	Deletes the first element.
push_back()	Adds element to the end of the list.
push_front()	Adds element to the front of the list.
reverse()	Reverses the list.
sort()	Sorts the list.

13.3.2 List Container

The list container is another useful sequence container that provides an efficient implementation for insertion and deletion operations at any location in the container. List is implemented as a doubly linked list, *i.e.*, every node in the list contains pointer to the previous node and the next node in the list. This enables list to support bi-directional iterators that allow the container to be traversed in both the directions – forward and backward. Any algorithm that requires input, output, forward or bi-directional iterators can operate on a list. Header file *vector.h* must be included in order to use vector container. Following program demonstrates the creations and manipulation of list container.

Listing 13.2

```
// Program to demonstrate the use of list container
#include <iostream.h>
#include <iomanip.h>
#include <list.h>
// prototype for function to display contents of list container
template <class T>
void printList(list<T> &listRef);
void main()
{
    list<int> intList;        // create an empty list
```

```
    // output initial size
    cout << "Initial size of list = "<<intList.size()<<endl;
    intList.push_back(5);   // store some elements in list
    intList.push_back(10);
    intList.push_back(12);
    intList.push_back(3);
    intList.push_back(11);
    // output current contents of the list
    cout << "Contents of list after adding some elements:\n";
    printList(intList);
    intList.push_front(9);  // add element in the beginning
    cout <<"Contents of list after adding element at front:\n";
    printList(intList);
    // remove element from the end of the list
    intList.pop_back();    // output current contents
    cout <<"Contents of list after removing element from back:\n";
    printList(intList);    // sort list
    intList.sort();        // output sortedlist
    cout << "Elements of list after sorting :\n";
    printList(intList);    // reverse list
    intList.reverse();             // output reversed list
    cout << "Elements of the reversed list:\n";
    printList(intList);    // remove all element of list
    intList.clear();
    cout << "List after deleting all its elements:\n";
    printList(intList);
} // end of main function
// function to display the contents of the list container
template <class T>
void printList(list<T> &listRef)
{
    if ( listRef.empty() )
        cout << "\nList is empty. . .\n";
    else {
        list <T> :: iterator ptr;
        for (ptr=listRef.begin();ptr!=listRef.end();ptr++)
            cout << *ptr << "   ";
        cout << endl;
    }
}
```

Test Run

```
Initial size of list = 0
Contents of list after adding some elements:
5  10  12  3  11
Contents of list after adding element at the front:
9  5  10  12  3  11
```

```
Contents of list after removing element from back:
9  5  10  12  3
Elements of list after sorting:
3  5  9  10  12
Elements of the reversed list:
12  10  9  5  3
List after deleting all its elements:
List is empty...
```

13.3.3 Map Container

The map is an associative container and is used for storage and retrieval of unique keys and associated values. Duplicate keys are not allowed in a map, therefore only a single value can be associated with each key. This is called one-to-one mapping. A map is also known as an associative array. Providing the key in map's subscript operator [] locates the value associated with the key in the map. Insertions and deletions can be made anywhere in the map. Header file *map.h* must be included in order to use map container.

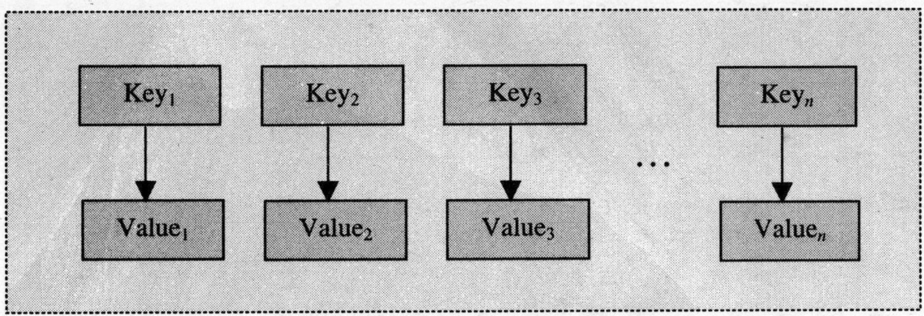

Figure 13.3: A *map* container

Table 13.10: Commonly used member functions with *map* container

Member Function	Description
`begin()`	Returns a reference to the first element.
`clear()`	Deletes all elements.
`empty()`	Returns true if the map is empty else return false.
`end()`	Returns reference to end of the map.
`erase()`	Deletes specified elements.
`find()`	Gives the location of the specified element.
`insert()`	Inserts element at the specified location.

Following program demonstrates creation and manipulation of map container.

Listing 13.3

```
//  Program to demonstrate the use of map container
#include <iostream.h>
#include <iomanip.h>
#include <map.h>
#include <string.h>
typedef map<string, int> namePhoneMap;
// prototype of function to display the contents of a map
void printMap(namePhoneMap &mapRef);
void main()
{
    string name;
    int number;
    namePhoneMap myMap;
    // store some elements in map
    myMap["dhillon"] = 1000;
    myMap["gill"] = 2000;
    myMap["kahlon"] = 3000;
    myMap.insert(pair<string,int>("Salaria",4000));
    myMap.insert(pair<string,string>("Katal",5000 ));
    // output current contents of the map
    cout << "\nCurrent contents of map:\n";
    printMap(myMap);
    cout << "Size of map: " << myMap.size();
    cout << "\nEnter name to search: ";
    cin >> name;
    cout << "\nPhone number of " << name << " = "
         << myMap[name];
}
void printMap(namePhoneMap &mapRef)
{
    if ( mapRef.empty() )
       cout << "\nMap is empty. . .\n";
    else {
       namePhoneMap :: iterator ptr;
       for (ptr=mapRef.begin(); ptr!=mapRef.end();ptr++)
           cout <<ptr->first<< "   " << ptr->second << "\n";
       cout << endl;
    }
}
```

Test Run

```
Current contents of map:
Dhillon  1000
```

```
Gill  2000
Kahlon  3000
Salaria  4000
Katal  5000
Enter name to search: Kahlon
Phone number of Kahlon = 3000
```

13.4 FUNCTION OBJECTS

A function object is basically a function that has been wrapped in a class so that it looks like an object. This class has only one member function, the overloaded operator '()' and contains no data member. The class is created as template class so that it can be used with variety of data types.

Table 22 11: Relational function objects

Function Object	Type	Description
equal_to<T>	relational	$x == y$
greater<T>	relational	$x > y$
greater_equal<T>	relational	$x >= y$
less<T>	relational	$x < y$
less_equal<T>	relational	$x <= y$
not_equal_to<T>	relational	$x != y$

Table 22.12: Arithmetic function objects

Function Object	Type	Description
divides<T>	arithmetic	x / y
Minus<T>	arithmetic	$x - y$
Modulus<T>	arithmetic	$x \% y$
Negate<T>	arithmetic	$-x$
Plus<T>	arithmetic	$x + y$
Multiplies<T>	arithmetic	$x * y$

Table 13.13: Logical function objects

Function Object	Type	Description
logical_and<T>	logical	$x \&\& y$
logical_or<T>	logical	$x \| y$
Logical_not<T>	logical	$!x$

These function objects are often used as arguments to certain containers and algorithms. For example, in the following statement

```
sort( a, a + 10, greater<int>() );
```

the function object *greater<int>* is used as an argument in *sort()* algorithm to sort the first eleven elements contained in array named *a* in descending order.

The STL provides many predefined function objects for performing arithmetic and logical operations. To use these predefined function objects, include header file *functional.h* in your program file.

Listing 13.4

```
//  Program to demonstrate the use function object
#include <iostream>
#include <iomanip>
#include <vector>
#include <numeric>
#include <algorithm>
#include <functional>
// function adds square of second argument to first argument
int sumOfSquares( int total, int value )
{
   return ( total + value * value );
}
// function adds square of second argument to first argument and
// binary function class template which defines an overloaded
// operator () that adds square of its second argument
// and running total in its first argument and returns sum
template <class T>
class sumOfSquaresClass : public binary_function<T,T,T>
{
   public:
     const T operator () ( const T &total, const T &value ) {
         return ( total + value * value );
     }
};
void main()
{
   const int SIZE = 10;
   int a[] = { 0, 1, 2, 3, 4, 5, 6, 7, 8, 9 };
   vector <int> myVector ( a, a + SIZE );
   vector<int> :: iterator ptr;
   int result = 0;
   cout << "\nContents of myVector:\n";
   for (ptr=myVector.begin();ptr!=myVector.end();ptr++)
      cout << *ptr << " ";
   result = accumulate ( myVector.begin(), myVector.end(),
                         0, sumOfSquares );
   cout << "\n\nSum of squares of elements of myVector using"
        << "\nbinary function sumOfSquares = " << result;
   result = accumulate ( myVector.begin(), myVector.end(),
                         0, sumOfSquaresClass<int>() );
   cout << "\n\nSum of squares of elements of myVector using"
        << "\nbinary function object of type "
        << "sumOfSquaresClass = " << result;
}
```

Test Run

```
Contents of myVector:
0 1 2 3 4 5 6 7 8 9

Sum of squares of elements of myVector using
binary function sumOfSquares = 285

Sum of squares of elements of myVector using
binary function object of type sumOfSquaresClass = 285
```

The above program demonstrates the use of numeric algorithm *accumulate* that calculates the sum of squares of the elements of a vector. The fourth argument to *accumulate* is a binary function object or a function pointer to a binary function that takes two arguments and returns a result. Function *accumulate* is used twice – once with a function pointer to a binary function and once with a function object.

QUICK RECAP

In this chapter, we have learnt that

- Standard Template Library (STL) is a collection of generic classes and functions.
- Programming model of STL is built on three components named as *containers*, *iterators* and *algorithms*.
- Containers are basically objects that hold other objects. These containers are classified as *sequence containers*, *associative containers* and *derived containers*.
- In sequence containers the elements are stored in a sequence can only be accessed in that sequence.
- In associative containers the elements are stored according to keys, and any element can be accessed using the key.
- Derived containers are containers that are derived from sequence containers.
- Algorithms are standalone functions that operate on containers. Algorithms that don't modify the contents of a container are known as *non-mutating algorithms* whereas those who modify the container are known as *mutating algorithms*.
- Iterators are objects that allow to cycle through the contents of a container. Iterators are just like pointers. Iterators are of five type's — *random access*, *bidirectional*, *forward*, *input*, and *output*.
- Random access iterator allows storing and retrieving elements of a container randomly.
- Forward iterator allows storing and retrieving elements of a container in forward direction only.
- Input iterator allows only retrieving the elements in forward direction.
- Output iterator allows only storing elements in forward direction.

- A function object is basically a function that has been wrapped in a class so that it looks like an object. A function object is created by a class that contains only one overloaded operator '()' function.
- Certain algorithms use function objects for some operations.

REVIEW EXERCISES

1. What is STL? How is it different from standard library?
2. Describe the programming model of STL?
3. What are containers? Describe various types of containers.
4. What are iterators? Describe various types of iterators.
5. What are algorithms? Describe various types of algorithms.
6. What is the difference between sequence and associative containers?
7. How do iterators compare with pointers?
8. Describe in brief various containers defined in STL? Also give some examples to suggest where these containers can be used.
9. What are functions objects?

PROGRAMMING EXERCISES

1. Write a program to demonstrate the use of *for_each()*.
2. Write a program to demonstrate the use of *fill()* on a vector container.
3. Write a program to display the elements of a list container.
4. Write a program to merge two lists and display the contents of the merged list.
5. Write a program to create a map whose elements are pairs of husband's name and wife's name. Husband's name is to be used as key.
6. Write a program to demonstrate the creations and use of a function object.

❑ ❑ ❑

Appendix A

Preprocessor Directives

Learning Objectives

After reading this chapter, students will be able to

- comprehend the actual compilation process, and the preprocessing of the source code prior to compilation
- comprehend the usage of preprocessing directives
- use them for efficient program handling and making then generalized programs

A.1 INTRODUCTION

The C++ source code may include instructions for the compiler. These instructions are known as *preprocessor commands or directives*. Each directive begins with character '#' (hash character). Although, these directives are not part of the C++ language, they expand the scope of the C++ programming environment.

The C++ compiler is made up of two functional parts – *a preprocessor* and *a translator*. The preprocessor processes all the directives and as a result produces an intermediate code known as *translation unit*, which is then translated by the translator to machine code and places it in object file.

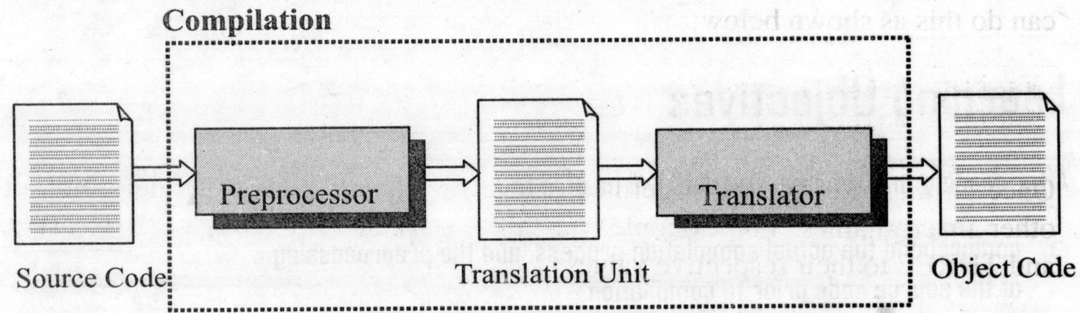

Figure A.1: Compilation process

In this chapter, the various preprocessor directives and built-in macros are described.

A.2 THE #*include* DIRECTIVE

The *#include* directive instructs the compiler to include another source file with the one that has *#include* directive in it. The source file to be included must be enclosed between double quotes or angle brackets. For example, the two directives

```
#include <filename.h>
#nclude "filename.h"
```

The first form directs the preprocessor to include the header file from the standard directory while the second form directs the preprocessor to look for the specified header file in the user directory.

A.3 THE *#define* DIRECTIVE

The *#define* directive is used to define an identifier and a character string that is substituted for the identifier each time it is encountered in the source file. The identifier is called a *macro name*, and the replacement process is called *macro-substitution*. The general form of the directive is

```
#define identifier string
```

Please note that the semicolon is not used after the *#define* directive. There can be any number of spaces between the identifier and the string, but once the string begins, only a new line terminates it.

For example, if we want to use *true* for a value 1 and *false* for a value 0, then we can do this as shown below:

```
#define true  1
#define false 0
```

Once an *identifier* has been defined, it can be used as part of the definition of other macro-names. For example, the following segment defines ONE, TWO, and THREE to their respective values:

```
#define ONE       1
#define TWO       ONE+ONE
#define THREE     TWO+ONE
```

It is important to understand that macro-substitution simply replaces an identifier with its associated string. However, no text substitutions occur within a string.

For example

```
#define XYZ  "This is test string"
    :
printf( "XYZ" );
```

does not print *This is a test string* rather prints *XYZ.*

If a string is longer than one line, it can be continued on the next line by placing a backslash character \ at the end of the line, as shown in the following example:

```
#define LONG_STRING "This is a long string, \
        and is used to illustrate this feature"
```

It is a common practice to use capital letters for the defined identifiers. With this convention, anyone reading the program can understand at a glance that a macro-substitution will take place. It is always better to put all *#define* directives at the beginning of the program file or perhaps in a separate include file, rather than sprinkling them throughout the program.

The maximum use of macro-substitution is to define names for *magic numbers* that occur in a program. For example, you may have a program that defines an array and have several routines that access that array. Instead of *hard coding* the array's size with a constant, it is better to define a size and use that name whenever the size of the array is needed. If the size of the array changes, you only have to change it at one place in the file and recompile. For example,

```
#define MAX_SIZE 100
float a[MAX_SIZE];
```

The *#define* directive has another powerful feature — a macro-name can have arguments. Each time macro-name is encountered, the arguments associated with it are replaced by the actual arguments found in the program. This is illustrated in the following program.

```
#include<stdio.h>
#define MIN(x, y)   ( x < y ) ? x : y
void main()
{   int a = 5, b = 20;
    cout << endl
         << "Minimum of " << a << " and "
         << b << " is " << MIN(a,b) << endl;
}
```

When this program is compiled, the expression defined by *MIN*(*x*, *y*) is substituted except that *a* and *b* are used as the operands. The following statements

```
cout << "\nMinimum of " << a << " and "
     << b << " is " << MIN(a,b) << endl;
```

will look like

```
cout << "\nMinimum of " << a << " and "
     << b << " is " << ( a < b ) ? a : b << endl;
```

If you are not very careful in defining macros that take arguments, there can be some surprising results.

For example

```
#include <stdio.h>
#define  EVEN(x)    x % 2 ? 0 : 1
void main()
{
    int a = 5;
    if ( EVEN(a + 1) )
       cout << endl << a << " is even" << endl;
    else
       cout << endl << a << " is odd" << endl;
}
```

does not work correctly because of the way the macro-substitution is made. When this program is compiled, the *EVEN*(*a*+1) is expanded to

```
a + 1 % 2 ?  0 : 1
```

Because the % (modulus) operator has higher precedence over the + (plus) operator, the modulus operation is performed on 1 first and then the result is added to *a*, which of course does not equal 0. To fix the trouble, there must be parentheses around *a* in the macro definition of EVEN as shown in this corrected version of the program:

```
#include <iostream.h>
#define EVEN(x)    (x) % 2 ? 0 : 1
void main()
{
   int a = 5;
   if ( EVEN(a + 1) )
      cout << endl << a << " is even" << endl;
   else
      cout << endl << a << " is odd" << endl;
}
```

Now the expression *a*+1 is evaluated before the modulus operation. In general, it is good idea to surround macro parameters with parentheses to avoid troubles like the one just described.

The use of macro-substitution in place of real functions one major benefit: it increases the speed of the code because no overhead for a function call is incurred. However, this increased speed is paid for with an increase in the size of the program because of duplicated code.

A.4 THE #*error* DIRECTIVE

The *#error* directive forces the Turbo C++ compiler to stop compiling when it is encountered. It is used primarily for debugging.

The general form of the directive is

```
#error error-message
```

The error-message is not between double quotes. When the compiler encounters this directive, it displays the following information and terminates compilation

```
fatal: filename linenum Error directive: error-message
```

A.5 CONDITIONAL COMPILATION DIRECTIVES

The conditional compilation directives, as their name implies, permit you to compile selective portion of the program. This process of selective compilation is known as *conditional compilation* and is widely used by commercial software houses that provide and maintain many customized versions of one program.

A.5.1 The #*if* Directive

If the *constant expression* following *#if* is true, the code between it and *#endif* is compiled; otherwise the code is ignored by the compiler. The *#endif* is used to mark the end of a *#if* block. The general form of *#if* directive is

```
#if constant-expression
   statement(s)
#endif
```

Consider the following program:

```
#include <iostream.h>
#define MAX 100
void main()
{
    #if MAX > 99
      cout << "compiled for large array";
    #endif
}
```

This program display the message on the screen because, as defined in the program, MAX is greater than 99. This example illustrates an important point --

the expression that follows the *#if* is evaluated at compile time. Therefore, it must contain only identifiers that have been previously defined and constants; the use of variables is not permitted.

A.5.2 The *#elseif* Directive

The *#else* directive works the same way as the *else* statement that forms a part of the C++ language. It provides an alternative to the *#if* directive. The previous example can be expanded as shown here:

```
#include <iostream.h>
#define MAX 100
void main()
{
    #if MAX > 99
       cout << "Compiled for array greater than 99";
    #else
       cout << "Compiled for small array";
   #endif
}
```

In this case, MAX is defined to be less than 99, so the part of the code between *#if* directive and *#else* directive is not compiled, but the part of the code between *#else* directive and *#endif* directive is compiled.

A.5.3 The *#elif* Directive

The *#elif* directive means *else if* and is used to establish an *if–else if* ladder for compilation options. The *#elif* is followed by a *constant expression.* If the expression is true, that block of code is compiled and no other *#elif* expressions are tested. Otherwise, the next in the series is checked. The general form is

```
#if expression-1
   statement sequence-1
#elif expression-2
   statement sequence-2
#elif expression-3
   statement sequence-3
         :
#elif expression-N
   statement sequence-N
#endif
```

As an example, consider the following segment

```
#define US 0
#define UK 1
#define INDIA 2
#if COUNTRY == US
   char curreny[] = "Dollar";
#elif COUNTRY == UK
   char curreny[] = "Pound";
#elif COUNTRY == INDIA
   char curreny[] = "Rupee";
#endif
```

This segment uses the value of COUNTRY to define the currency sign.

A.5.4 The *#ifdef and #ifndef* Directive

The directive *#ifdef* means *if defined*, and its general form is

```
#ifdef macro-name
   statement sequence
#endif
```

If the macro-name has been previously defined in a *#define* statement, the statement sequence between the *#ifdef* and *#endif* is compiled.

The directive *#ifndef* means *if not defined*, and its general form is

```
#ifndef macro-name
   statement sequence
#endif
```

If the macro-name is currently not defined by a *#define* statement, the statement sequence between the *#ifndef* and *#endif* is compiled.

Both the *#ifdef* and *#ifndef* directives can use *#else* directive but not the *#elif* directive.

A.5.5 The *#undef* Directive

The *#undef* directive is used to remove a previous definition of the macro-name that follows it. Its general form is

```
#undef macro-name
```

As an example, consider the following segment

```
#define  LEN 100
#define WIDTH 100
char a[LEN][WIDTH];
#undef LEN
#undef WIDTH
```

Both LEN and WIDTH are defined until the *#undef* statements are encountered. The principal use of *#undef* is to allow macro-names to be localized only to those sections of code that needed them.

A.6 THE *#line* DIRECTIVE

The *#line* directive is used to change the contents of __LINE__ and __FILE__, which are predefined macro-names in Turbo C++. The __LINE__ macro contains the line number of the line currently being compiled and __FILE__ contains the name of the file being compiled. The general form of the *#line* directive is

```
#line number "filename"
```

where *number* is any positive integer, and the *filename* is any valid file identifier, which is optional. The line number is the number of the current source line and the file name is the name of the source file. The *#line* directive is used primarily for debugging purposes and special applications.

As an example, consider the following program

```
#include <iostream.h>
#line 100
void main (void)
{
   cout << endl << "Current Line#" << __LINE__;
}
```

This program specifies that line count will begin from 100. The output statement displays the number 102 because it is the third line in the program after #line 100.

A.7 THE *#pragma* DIRECTIVE

The *#pragma* directive is defined by ANSI standard to be an implementation-defined directive that allows various instructions, defined by the compiler's creator to be given to the compiler.

The general form of *#pragma* directive is

```
#pragma  directiveName
```

where *directiveName* is the name of the *#pragma* you want to use. The Turbo C++ defines following *#pragma* directives

- argsused
- exit
- hrdfile
- hdrstop
- inline
- option
- saveregs
- startup
- warn

The key directives names are described are described below:

A.7.1 The *inline* Directive Name

It takes the form

```
#pragma inline
```

It tells the Turbo C++ compiler that *in-line assembly* code is contained in the program. For the greatest efficiency, the Turbo C++ compiler needs to know this in advance.

A.7.2 The *saveregs* Directive Name

It takes the form

```
#pragma saveregs
```

It prevents a function declared as *huge* from altering the value of any registers. This directive must immediately precede the function and affects only that function to which it precedes.

A.7.3 The *warn* Directive Name

It takes the form

```
                 + xxx
#pragma warn   { -xxx
                 .xxx
```

where

+xxx — Turns on warning *xxx*.
-xxx — Turns off warning *xxx*.
.xxx — Toggles on/off state for warning *xxx*.

A.7.4 The *startup* Directive Name

It takes the form

```
#pragma startup functionName [priority]
```

It allows the program to specify function(s) that should be called before the *main()* function is called. The specified function(s) must be declared or defined so that they take no arguments and have return type as void, *i.e.*, they should be declared as

```
void functionName(void);
```

The optional *priority* parameter is an integer in the range 64 to 255, with 100 as default value. The lower the value of the parameter, the higher is the priority. The numbers in the range 0 to 63 are used by libraries and therefore should not be used. The functions with high priority are called first.

A.7.4 The *exit* Directive Name

It takes the form

```
#pragma exit functionName [priority]
```

It allows the program to specify function(s) that should be called just before the program terminates through *_exit()* function. The specified function(s) must be declared or defined so that they take no arguments and have return type as void, *i.e.*, they should be declared as

```
void functionName(void);
```

The optional *priority* parameter is an integer in the range 64 to 255, with 100 as default value.

The lower the value of the parameter, the higher is the priority. The numbers in the range 0 to 63 are used by libraries and therefore should not be used. The functions with high priority are called last.

Listing A.1

```
// Program to demonstrate the use of startup and exit
// directive names with #pragma directive
#include <iostream.h>
void first(void);
void second(void);
```

```
oid secondLast(void);
void last(void);
#pragma startup  first    65
#pragma startup  second   66
#pragma exit  last        99
#pragma exit  secondLast 100
void main()
{
    cout << "\nMain function invoked\n";
}
void first() {
    cout << "\nFirst function invoked\n";
}
void second() {
    cout << "\nSecond function invoked\n";
}
void last() {
    cout << "\nLast function invoked\n";
}
void secondLast() {
    cout << "\nSecond last function invoked\n";
}
```

Test Run

```
First function invoked.

Second function invoked.

Main function invoked.

Second last function invoked.

Last function invoked.
```

A.8 PREDEFINED MACRO-NAMES

The Turbo C++ standard has following predefined macro-names:

__LINE__	__FILE__	__DATE__
__TIME__	__STDC__	__CDECL__
__COMPACT__	__HUGE__	__LARGE__
__MEDIUM__	__SMALL__	__TINY__
__MSDOS__	__PASCAL__	__TURBOC__

- The __LINE__ and __FILE__ macros are already described, let describe the remaining ones.

- The __DATE__ macro contains a string that has the form *month/day/year*, which is the date the source file is compiled.

- The length of time since beginning of the compilation of the source code into object code to the point at which the __TIME__ macro is encountered is contained in the string in __TIME__. The form of the string is *hour:minute:second.*

- The __STDC__ macro contains the decimal constant 1. This means that the implementation is a standard-conforming implementation. If it contains any other number, the implementation must vary from the standard.

- The __CDECL__ macro is defined if the standard C++ calling conventions are used, *i.e.*, if the Pascal calling conventions are not in use. If this is not the case, the macro is undefined.

- Only one of these macros is defined, based on the memory model used during the compilation: __TINY__, __SMALL__, __COMPACT__, __MEDIUM__, __LARGE__, and __HUGE__.

- The __MSDOS__ macro is defined with the value 1 in all situations for the MS-DOS version of Turbo C++.

- The __PASCAL__ macro is defined only if the Pascal calling conventions are used to compile a program; otherwise it is undefined.

- The __TCPLUSPLUS__ macro contains the version number of Turbo C++. It is represented as a hexadecimal constant. The two rightmost digits represent the minor revision numbers and the leftmost digit represents the major revision, *e.g.*, the number 300 represents Version 3.00.

Consider the following program

Listing A.2

```
//   Program to output the macros (Filename : APPA.CPP
#include <iostream.h>
#include <iomanip.h>
void main()
{
    cout << "File name       : " << __FILE__ << endl;
    cout << "Current Line Number   : " <<  __LINE__ << endl;
    cout << "Date Compiled : " <<  __DATE__ << endl;
    cout << "Time Compiled : " <<  __TIME__ << endl;
    cout <<  endl << endl
         << "Program being compiled using the ";
    #ifdef __TINY__
```

```
    cout << "Tiny";
  #endif
  #ifdef __SMALL__
    cout << "Small";
  #endif
  #ifdef __COMPACT__
    cout << "Compact";
  #endif
  #ifdef __MEDIUM__
    cout << "Medium";
  #endif
  #ifdef __LARGE__
    cout << "Large";
  #endif
  #ifdef __HUGE__
    cout << "Huge";
  #endif
  cout << " Model" << endl << endl;
  cout << "Using version " << hex << __TCPLUSPLUS__
       << " of Turbo C++." << endl;
}
```

Test Run

```
File name               : APPA.CPP
Current Line Number     : 13
Date Compiled           : Oct 06 2003
Time Compiled           : 18:22:32

Program being compiled using the Small Model

Using version 300 of Turbo C++.
```

❑ ❑ ❑

Appendix B

FAQs on OOP Concepts

Question #1

What is procedural (structured) programming?

Answer

In *procedural programming*, also known by other names as *structured programming*, *functional programming* or *traditional programming*, the problem in hand is viewed as a sequence of things to be done such as reading, calculating and printing. Separate functions are written to accomplish these tasks. Thus, the primary focus is on functions.

In other words, we can say that a given problem is divided into small sized sub problems; each sub problem represents a specific task that can be handled efficiently and effectively. Then to solve each sub problem, a function is written. The technique of hierarchical decomposition has been used to specify the tasks to be completed to find the solution of a problem.

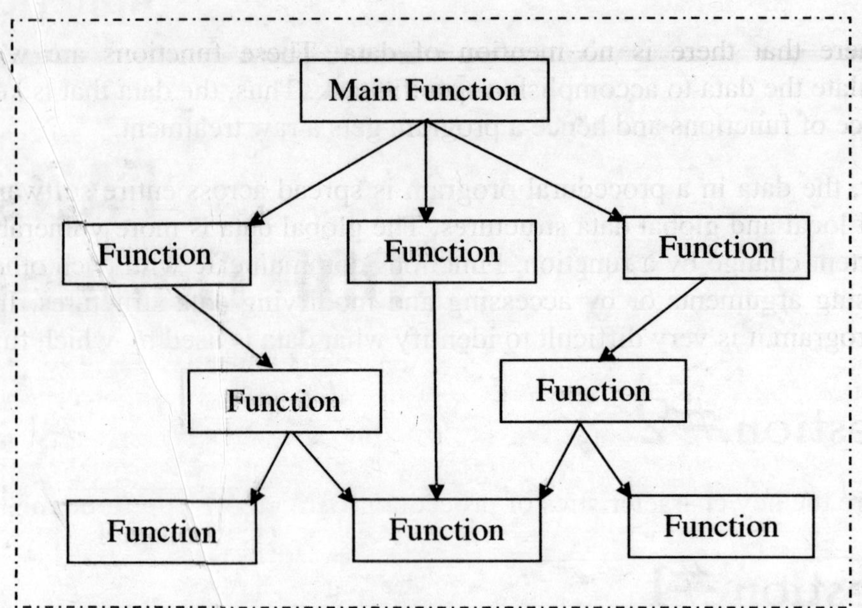

Figure A.1: Typical structure of a procedural program

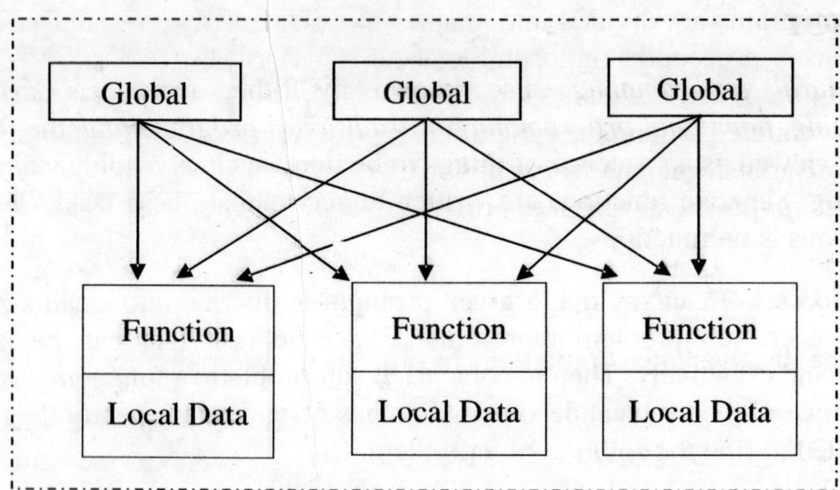

Figure A.2: Relationship of data and functions in a procedural program

Note here that there is no mention of data. These functions are written to manipulate the data to accomplish a specific task. Thus, the data that is key to the existence of functions and hence a program gets a raw treatment.

Further, the data in a procedural program is spread across entire software in the form of local and global data structures. The global data is more vulnerable to an inadvertent change by a function. Functions communicate with each other either by passing arguments or by accessing and modifying data structures. In a very large program it is very difficult to identify what data is used by which function.

Question #2

What are the key characteristics of procedural (structured) programming?

Answer

Key characteristics of procedural (structured) programming are

- Emphasis is on doing things (algorithms).
- Large programs are divided into smaller independent subprograms known as functions or procedures (algorithmic decomposition).
- Majority the functions share global data.
- Data is scattered around the program in the form of local and shared data.
- Functions transform data from one form to another.
- Employs *top-down* approach to program design.

Question #3

What are the disadvantages/limitations of procedural programming?

Answer

- The procedural programming approach does not model the real world problems very well.

- The program logic is dependent on the organization of the data and the vice a versa. You cannot change one without change to another.
- The parts of the program are heavily dependent on each other, *i.e.*, tightly coupled to each other. Therefore, it is very difficult to make a change in one part of the program without affecting the other part.

These problems magnify further as the size and the complexity of the problem under consideration increases, and almost become unmanageable for very large and complex systems.

Question #4

What is object-oriented programming?

Answer

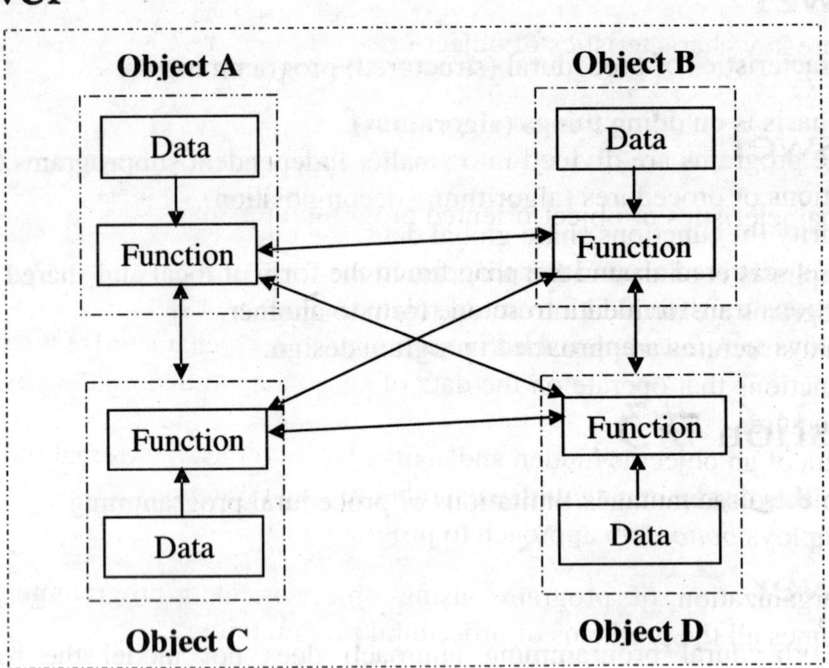

Figure A.3: Typical Structure of an object-oriented program

The major motivation for the invention of new programming approach, object-oriented programming, was to remove the flaws of procedural programming approach. Object- oriented programming treats the data as a most critical element in the program design and does not allow it be scattered around the program. It ties the data and the functions that operate on it and protects it from the other functions.

Object-oriented programming allows decomposition of a problem into a number of entities called *objects* and then builds data and functions around these objects.

The data of an object can only be accessed by functions associated with it. However, function of one object can access the function of another object. The communications among functions of different objects is called *messaging*.

Question #5

What are key characteristics of object-oriented programming?

Answer

Key characteristics of object-oriented programming are:

- Emphasis is on data rather than functions.
- Programs are divided into set of related objects.
- Data structures are designed in such way so as to characterize the objects.
- Functions that operate on the data of an object are tied together with the data structure.
- Data of an object is hidden and cannot be accessed by external functions.
- Objects communicate with each other through functions.
- Employs *bottom-up* approach to program design.

The organization of programs using object-oriented programming approach overcomes all the problems of procedural programming.

Question #6

What is an object model?

Answer

Object model is a description of an object-oriented architecture, including the details of the object structure, interfaces between objects and other object-oriented features and functions.

It encompasses the principles of *abstraction*, *encapsulation*, *data hiding*, *inheritance*, *overloading*, and *polymorphism*.

Nothing is new about these principles. The important feature of the object model is that these elements are brought together in a synergistic way.

Question #7

How formally can we define object-oriented programming?

Answer

The object-oriented programming can formally be defined as *a method of implementation in which programs are organized as cooperative collection of objects, each of which represent an instance of some class, and whose classes are all members of a hierarchy of classes united via inheritance relationship*.

The object-oriented programming use objects as basic building blocks, where each object is an instance of some class, and classes are related to each other through inheritance.

Question #8

List various concepts and terms that are used extensively in object-oriented programming.

Answer

Extensively used concepts and terms in object-oriented programming include:

- Object
- Class
- Abstraction
- Encapsulation
- Data Hiding
- Inheritance
- Overloading
- Polymorphism
- Dynamic binding
- Message passing

Question #9

Differentiate between a class and an object?

Answer

The concepts of class and object are tightly interwoven, for example, we cannot talk about an object without regard for its class.

However, there are important differences between these two terms. An object is a concrete entity that exists in time and space. A class represents only an abstraction, the *essence* of an object, as it were. Thus, we may speak of the class mammal, which represents characteristics common to all mammals. To identify a particular mammal in this class, we must speak of *this mammal* or *that mammal*.

In the context of object-oriented programming, we define class as a set of objects that share a common structure and a common behaviour. A single object is simply an instance of a class.

Question #10

What is an object?

Answer

An *object* is an entity that has *state*, *behavior* and *identity*. The structure and behavior of similar objects are defined in their common class. The term *instance* and *object* are interchangeable.

Question #11

Give some examples of classes and objects from the real-world and programming world?

Answer

Examples from real-world:

Class	Objects
Bird	Sparrow, Parrot, Peacock, etc.
Car	Santro, Swift, Punto, etc.
Mammal	Cow, Buffalo, Goat, etc.
Human Being	Meahk, Pradeep, Shalini, etc.

Examples from programming-world:

Class	Objects
Complex Number	2.5+7.5*i*, 3.0 -5.5*i*, etc.
Shape	Cricle, Line, Rectangle, etc.
GUI Element	Menu, Toolbar, Button, etc.
Linked List	L1, L2, L3, etc.

Question #12

What are the characteristics of an object?

Answer

Each object has following characteristics:

- *State* – The *state* of an object encompasses all of the (usually static) property of the object plus the current (usually dynamic) values of each of these properties.
- *Behavior* – The *behavior* of an object tells how it acts and reacts to the outside world in terms of its state changes and message passing.

  With this, the state of the object can now be defined as - *the state of an object represents the cumulative results of its behaviour.*
- *Identity* – The *identity* of an object is that property which distinguishes it from all other objects.

Question #13

List the possible operations that are performed on an object.

Answer

The kind of operations that are performed on objects comprises:

- *Modifier* – An operation that alters the state of an object.
- *Selector* – An operation that access the state of the object but does not alter it.
- *Iterator* – An operation that permits all parts of an object to be accessed in some well-defined order.
- *Constructor* – An operation that creates an object and/or initializes its state.
- *Destructor* – An operation that frees the state of an object and/or destroys the object itself.

Question #14

What are the possible relationships that exist between objects?

Answer

Objects contribute to the behaviour of a system by collaborating with one another. The relationship between any two objects encompasses the assumptions that each make about the other, including what operations can be performed and what behaviour results.

Objects communicate with each other through links, where a link defined as a physical or a conceptual connection between objects.

As a participant in a link, an object may play one of the following roles:

- *Client/Actor* – that operate on other objects, but is never operated upon by other objects.
- *Server* – that never operates upon other objects, it is only operated upon by other objects.
- *Agent* – that can operate on other objects and be operated upon by other objects; an agent is usually created to do some work on behalf of an actor or another agent.

Question #15

What does interface of a class represent?

Answer

The interface of a class represents outside view of a class and encompasses the abstraction while hiding its structure and the secrets of its behaviour.

This interface primarily consists of the declarations of all the operations applicable to instances of this class, but it may include the declarations of other classes, constants, variables, and exceptions that are needed to complete the abstraction.

Interface of a class is divided into following parts:

- *Public* – A part that is accessible to all clients.
- *Protected* – A part that is accessible to the class and its subclasses.
- *Private* – A part that is accessible to the class only.

Different object-oriented programming languages provide different mixtures of *public*, *protected*, and *private* parts, which developers can choose among to establish specific access rights for each part of the class's interface, and thereby exercise control over what clients can see and what they cannot see.

Question #16

What does implementation of a class represent?

Answer

Implementation of a class represents inside view of a class that encompasses the secrets of its behaviour. It primarily consists of implementation of all the operations defined in the interface of the class.

Question #17

What is the advantage of separating interface from implementation of a class?

Answer

By separating implementation of a class from its interface, we have the flexibility of changing its implementation.

Popular technologies, such as Component Object Model (COM) and Enterprise Java beans (EJB), are based on this facet of object-oriented programming.

Question #18

What is abstraction?

Answer

Dictionary meaning of word *abstraction* refers to the act of emphasizing and representing essential features and ignoring the irrelevant features. In the context of object-oriented programming, word *abstraction* refers to the separation between the specification of data and its implementation.
It results in better quality programs and more efficient programming techniques. These, in turn, reduce the number of man-hours required to develop a software system, and hence reduce the total cost of the final software product.

Since classes use the concept of data abstraction, they are also known as *abstract data types* (ADTs).

Question #19

What is encapsulation?

Answer

Encapsulation is the concealing of the implementation details of a data object from the outside world. The data and functions are wrapped into a single unit, called *class*. Encapsulation is the most striking feature of a class.

Question #20

Give a real life example to demonstrate the use of abstraction and encapsulation.

Answer

The notion of abstraction and encapsulation are commonly used in human-machine interaction and are widely prevalent in the technology-oriented world in which we are living.

Consider, for example, the Video Cassette Player (VCP), which is an integral part of every household today. We make two observations about how VCPs are packaged and used.

- All our interactions with a VCP are made through buttons on the control panel such as PLAY, FF (forward), REW (rewind), REC (record), STOP, EJECT, etc.
- The VCP is packaged in such a way that we cannot interact directly with the internal circuitry. So, the *internal representation* of the VCP is *hidden* from the user. This is the principle of *encapsulation*.
- The instruction manual that accompanies the VCP tells us what the VCP is supposed to do if we press a particular button. It does not tell us how it is implemented inside the VCP. For example, it does not explain the sequence of electronic and mechanical events that result when the REW button is pressed. So, the instruction manual makes a clear distinction between what the VCP does and how it does. This distinction is the principle of *abstraction*.

Question #21

What is data hiding?

Answer

Data hiding deals with visibility of the members. The level of visibility determines which parts of the code can access the member.

All most all the object-oriented programming languages provide three levels of visibility – *private*, *protected*, and *public*.

Private members are accessible to members of the class only.

Protected members are accessible to members of the class and members of the derived class.

Public members are accessible from everywhere.

Question #22

What is inheritance?

Answer

Inheritance is the process of creating new class(es), called *derived class(es)*, from existing class(es), called *base class(es)*. The derived class inherits all the features and capabilities of the base class(es) and can either refine some of its features or add new features of its own.

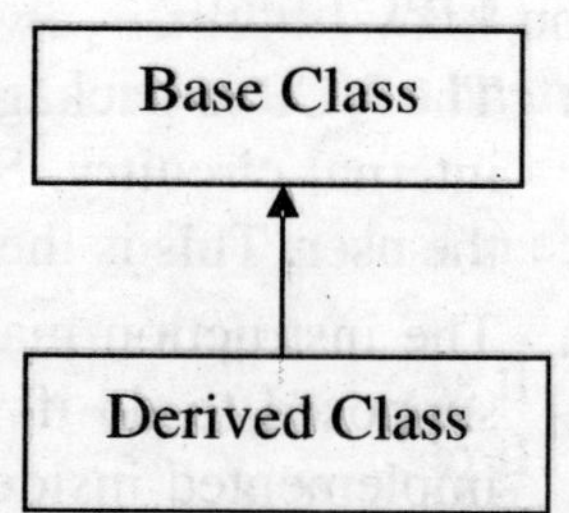

A number of terms are used to describe classes that are related through inheritance. A base class is often called the *ancestor*, *parent* or *superclass*. The derived class is called *descendent*, *child* or *subclass*.

Question #23

Whether private member are inherited or not?

Answer

Private members are inherited, but they cannot be accessed directly by the derived class. Only member functions of the class can access the private members. However, if the derived class member function wants to access the private member of the base class, it can do so indirectly by calling the member function of the base class.

Question #24

Explain the usefulness of inheritance?

Answer

The concept of inheritance provides reusability, *i.e.*, we can add new features to an existing class without modifying it. The new class will have combined features of base class and its own.

You know that it is always nice if we can reuse something that already exists instead of creating it afresh.

The reusability offers following advantages:

- It saves time and effort.
- It reduces development cost of new software product.
- Increases reliability because the class is already tested and used many times.

Question #25

Explain the possible types (forms) of inheritance?

Answer

The derived class inherits some or all of the features of the base class depending on the visibility mode and level of inheritance. Level of inheritance refers to length of its (derived class) path from the root (top base class). Remember that a base class itself may have been derived from other classes in the hierarchy.

Inheritance is classified into the following forms based on the levels of inheritance and interrelation among the classes involved in the inheritance process.

❑ *Single Inheritance*

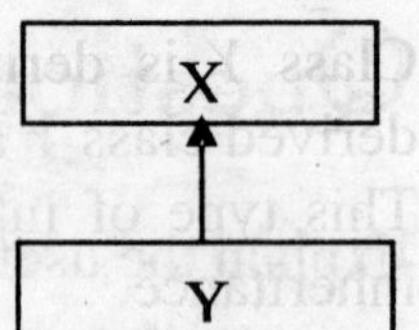

Derivation of a single class from only one base class. The class *X* is the base class and *Y* is the derived class. Further no class is derived from *Y*.

❑ *Multilevel Inheritance*

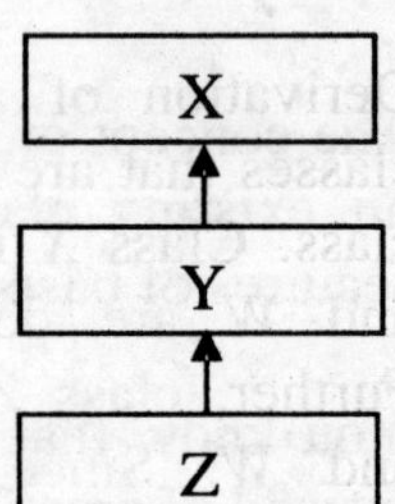

Derivation of a class from another derived class. The class *X* is the top base class and *Y* is the derived class of *X*. Further class *Z* is derived from class *Y*. Here, class *Y* is not just derived class, but also base class for class *Z*. Further, class *Z* can be used as base class for further derivation.

❑ *Multiple Inheritance*

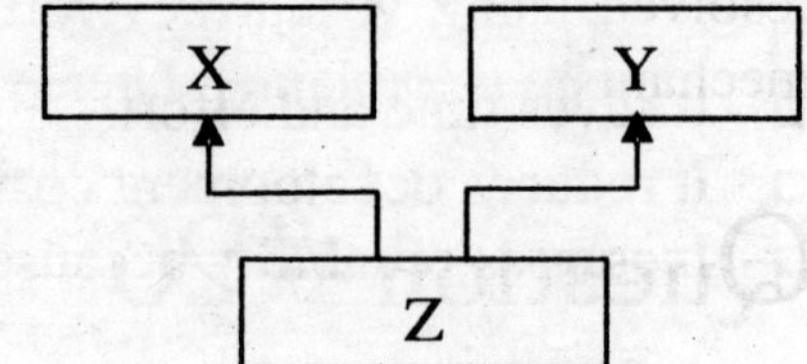

Derivation of a class from two or more base classes. The class *X* and class *Y* are base classes and class *Z* is the derived class. Class *Z* inherits properties of both class *X* and class *Y*. Further, no class is derived from class *Z*.

❑ *Hierarchical Inheritance*

Derivation of two or more classes from a single base class. Class *W* is the only base class and classes *X*, *Y* and *Z* are derived classes. Further, none of the class *X*, *Y* and *Z* is used as base class.

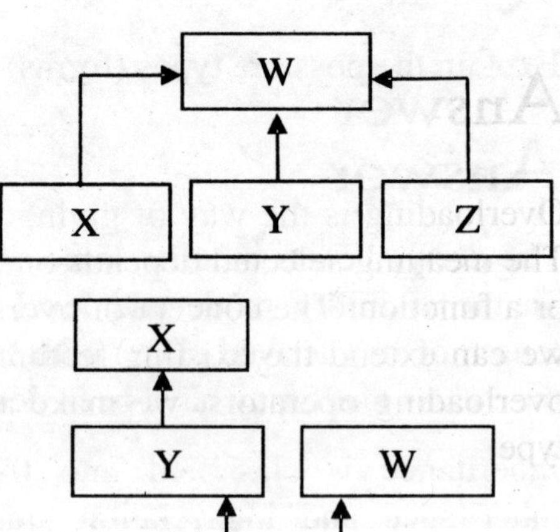

❑ *Hybrid Inheritance*

Derivation of a class involving two or more forms of inheritance. In this case, multilevel and multiple inheritances are involved.

Class *Y* is derived from class *X*. It is a single type of inheritance. Further, derived class *Y* acts as a base class. The class *Z* is derived from classes *Y* and *W*. This type of inheritance that uses more than one base class is called multiple inheritance.

❑ *Multipath Inheritance*

Derivation of a class from two or more classes that are derived from the same base class. Class *X* is the base class. Classes *Y* and *W* are derived from base class *X*. Further, class *Z* is derived from classes *Y* and *W*. Since, classes *Y* and *W* have inherited same members of *X*. In this case, an ambiguity is generated which in turn is resolved using virtual keyword. The virtual mechanism is explained later.

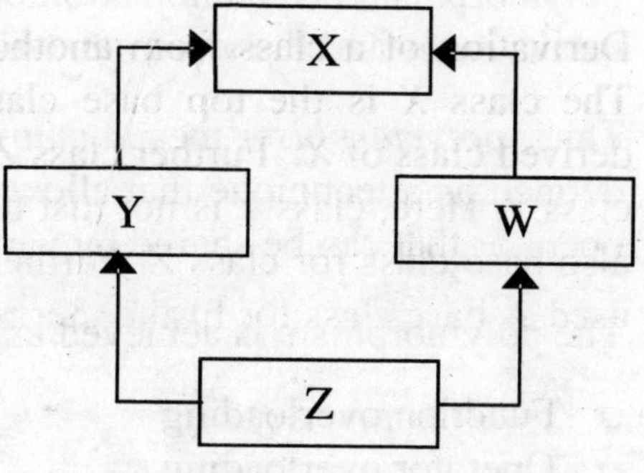

Question #26

What is overloading?

Answer

Overloading is the way of giving several meanings to an operator or a function. The meaning selected depends on the types of the arguments used by an operator or a function. The concept of overloading provides extensibility. This means that we can extend the existing features to meet new requirements. For example, by overloading operators, we make a new data type to behave like a built-in data type.

Question #27

What is polymorphism?

Answer

Polymorphism is a combination of two words *poly* and *morphism*. The word *poly* means *many* and the word *morphism* means *forms*.

Thus, *polymorphism* means *many forms*. More formally, polymorphism can be defined as a technique that allows defining various forms of a single function or operator that can be shared by various objects to perform the operation.

The polymorphism is achieved using the following:

- Function overloading
- Operator overloading
- Dynamic binding (virtual functions)

Question #28

What is dynamic binding?

Answer

Binding is the linking of a function call to the function definition that will be executed on the call during program execution. Normally the function call is tied to the function definition during the linking process. This process is known as *early binding*.

However, the OOP permits dynamic binding, also called *late binding*, where the tie-up of function call to the address code is delayed until the run-time.

Question #29

What is messaging?

Answer

An object-oriented program consists of set of objects that communicate with each other in order to solve a particular problem. Objects communicate with one another by sending and receiving information much the same way as people pass messages to one another. A message for an object is a request for execution of a function, and therefore will invoke a function in the receiving object that generates the desired results. Message passing involves specifying the name of the object, the name of the function and the information to be sent.

Every object has a life cycle – they are created and destroyed. Communication with an object is feasible as long as it is alive.

Question #30

What is the difference between an object-based language and object-oriented language?

Answer

Languages that support only objects and classes are called object-based languages. Such languages do not support features like inheritance and polymorphism. These languages only allow you to create objects and call methods using these objects. Visual Basic (VB) language is an example of object-based language.

On the other hand, object-oriented languages support full range of object-oriented concepts including inheritance and polymorphism. Java, C++, C#, Visual C++ (VC++) languages is example of object-oriented languages.

Question #31

What is UML?

Answer

UML (Unified Modeling Language) is a modeling language used in designing object models for software applications. It helps to specify, visualize and document models of software systems.

Question #32

What are different UML diagrams?

Answer

UML defines a total of 12 diagrams which are grouped as

- *Structures diagrams* – These diagrams include class diagram, object diagram, component diagram and deployment diagram.
- *Behavior diagrams* – These diagrams include use case diagram (used during requirement gathering), sequence diagram, activity diagram and collaboration diagram.
- *Model management diagrams* – These diagrams include packages, subsystems and models.

Question #33

What is a class diagram?

Answer

A class diagram in UML is a type of static structure diagram that describes the structure of a system by showing the system's classes, their attributes, operations (or methods), and the relationships among the classes.

The class diagram is the main building block of object oriented modeling. It is used both for general conceptual modeling of the systematics of the application, and for detailed modeling translating the models into programming code.

Class diagrams can also be used for data modeling. The classes in a class diagram represent both the main objects and/or interactions in the application and the objects to be programmed.

In class diagram, a class is represented with boxes which contain three parts:

BankAccount
String owner float balance
deposit (float amount) withdrawal (float amount)

- Upper part holds the name of the class.
- Middle part contains the attributes of the class.
- Bottom part gives the methods or operations the class can take or undertake.

Question #35

What are design principles?

Answer

Software design principles represent a set of guidelines that helps us to avoid having a bad design. According to Robert Martin there are three important characteristics of a bad design that should be avoided:

- *Rigidity* - It is hard to change because every change affects too many other parts of the system.
- *Fragility* - When you make a change, unexpected parts of the system break.
- *Immobility* - It is hard to reuse in another application because it cannot be disentangled from the current application.

Question #36

What are design patterns?

Answer

These are standard solutions for certain common problems that occur while designing a software system. For example, whenever we want restrict an application to create only one instance of a class, we can make use of the Singleton design pattern.

Various design patterns are divided into following three main categories:

- Creational
- Behavioral
- Structural

Question #37

Explain Singleton design pattern.

Answer

The Singleton design pattern is one of the simplest design patterns. It involves only one class which is responsible to instantiate itself, to make sure it creates not more than one instance. It provides a global point of access to that instance. The same instance can be used from everywhere, being impossible to invoke directly the constructor each time.

❑ ❑ ❑

Appendix C

Answers of MCQs

Chapter 1: Introduction to Object-Oriented Programming

1.	(*a*)	2.	(*c*)	3.	(*d*)	4.	(*a*)	5.	(*b*)
6.	(*c*)	7.	(*d*)	8.	(*b*)	9.	(*d*)	10.	(*d*)
11.	(*d*)	12.	(*c*)	13.	(*b*)	14.	(*a*)	15.	(*d*)
16.	(*d*)								

Chapter 3: Standard Input/Output

1.	(*b*)	2.	(*a*)	3.	(*d*)	4.	(*d*)	5.	(*a*)
6.	(*d*)	7.	(*c*)	8.	(*a*)	9.	(*a*)	10.	(*c*)
11.	(*b*)	12.	(*a*)	13.	(*c*)	14.	(*b*)	15.	(*c*)

Chapter 4: Classes and Objects

1.	(*a*)	2.	(*b*)	3.	(*c*)	4.	(*c*)	5.	(*b*)
6.	(*a*)	7.	(*c*)	8.	(*a*)	9.	(*a*)	10.	(*d*)
11.	(*d*)	12.	(*c*)	13.	(*b*)	14.	(*b*)	15.	(*d*)

Chapter 5: Pointers and Dynamic Memory Management

1.	(*b*)	2.	(*d*)	3.	(*a*)	4.	(*d*)	5.	(*b*)
6.	(*b*)	7.	(*a*)	8.	(*a*)	9.	(*d*)	10.	(*c*)
11.	(*c*)	12.	(*b*)	13.	(*c*)	14.	(*c*)	15.	(*a*)
16.	(*b*)	17.	(*c*)	18.	(*d*)	19.	(*c*)	20.	(*b*)

Chapter 6: Constructors and Destructors

1.	*(b)*	2.	*(c)*	3.	*(b)*	4.	*(d)*	5.	*(c)*
6.	*(d)*	7.	*(b)*	8.	*(c)*	9.	*(c)*	10.	*(d)*

Chapter 7: Operator Overloading and Type Conversion

1.	*(b)*	2.	*(d)*	3.	*(d)*	4.	*(e)*	5.	*(c)*
6.	*(b)*	7.	*(d)*	8.	*(a)*	9.	*(d)*	10.	*(b)*
11.	*(b)*	12.	*(c)*	13.	*(c)*	14.	*(a)*	15.	*(c)*

Chapter 8: Inheritance

1.	*(c)*	2.	*(b)*	3.	*(d)*	4.	*(d)*	5.	*(c)*
6.	*(d)*	7.	*(c)*	8.	*(c)*	9.	*(b)*	10.	*(c)*
11.	*(d)*	12.	*(a)*	13.	*(b)*	14.	*(b)*	15.	*(a)*

Chapter 9: Virtual Functions and Polymorphism

1.	*(a)*	2.	*(a)*	3.	*(d)*	4.	*(b)*	5.	*(c)*
6.	*(a)*	7.	*(d)*	8.	*(b)*	9.	*(c)*	10.	*(b)*

Chapter 10: Exception Handling

1.	*(c)*	2.	*(a)*	3.	*(d)*	4.	*(a)*	5.	*(b)*
6.	*(c)*	7.	*(b)*	8.	*(a)*	9.	*(b)*		

Chapter 11: Templates and Generic Programming

1.	*(c)*	2.	*(a)*	3.	*(c)*	4.	*(a)*	5.	*(d)*
6.	*(c)*	7.	*(a)*	8.	*(b)*	9.	*(b)*	10.	*(b)*

Chapter 12: File Handling

1.	*(d)*	2.	*(a)*	3.	*(c)*	4.	*(c)*	5.	*(d)*
6.	*(d)*	7.	*(b)*	8.	*(b)*	9.	*(b)*	10.	*(b)*
11.	*(b)*	12.	*(b)*	13.	*(c)*	14.	*(b)*	15.	*(d)*

❑ ❑ ❑

Appendix D

Comparison Between C++ and Java

Although the Java language is modeled on C++, it has several fundamental differences. It is important to keep in mind the fact that Java was designed to allow portable applications to be safely downloaded over a network. In its current form, it is not designed to replace C or C++ as systems programming language, and this will not happen in the near future.

There are a number of C++ features that Java does not support. Perhaps the single biggest difference between Java and C++ is that Java does not support pointers. In C++, pointer is one of C++ most important language features. It is also one of the most dangerous if used improperly. Pointers don't exist in Java for two reasons. First, pointers are inherently insecure. For example, using a C++ pointer, it is possible to gain access to memory addresses outside a program's code and data. Second, the designers of Java probably think that they were too troublesome. Since pointers don't exist in Java, neither does the arrow '–>' operator.

Following are some features that Java does not support, as does C++:

- Java does not support global variables. Everything has to be part of an object.
- Java built-in data types are defined as fixed length, irrespective of the underlying platform.
- Java does not support enumerated data type.
- Java does not include structures and unions.

- Java does not support pointers.
- Java does not support typedefs.
- Java does not support operator overloading.
- Java does not include a preprocessor or support the preprocessor directives.
- Java does not perform automatic type conversions.
- Java does not allow default arguments.
- Java does not allow variable number of arguments.
- Java does not support templates.
- Java does not support multiple inheritance.
- There are no friends in Java
- There are no destructors in Java as such. The finalize function in Java corresponds to a destructor in C++.

Following are some new features added by Java that are not in C++:

- Java support multithreading that allows two or more pieces of the same program to execute concurrently.
- Java contains a built-in string data type named *String*.
- In Java, most of the exceptions must be caught, whereas in C++ there is no requirement that a thrown exception be caught.
- Java built-in data types are defined as fixed length, irrespective of the underlying platform.
- Java supports the concept of packages.
- Java supports the concept of interfaces.
- Java uses garbage collection that frees the developer from the hackles of having to manage memory.
- Java supports security issues to ensure that the bytecode that can come from unknown sources is safe and can be executed by the interpreter.

❑ ❑ ❑

Glossary

Abstract Class - A class that has at least one pure virtual function, *i.e.*, a class which is incomplete. An abstract class is written with the expectation that its concrete subclasses will add to its structure and behavior, typically by implementing its abstract operations.

Abstract Operation - An operation that is declared but not implemented by an abstract class. In C++, an abstract operation is declared as a pure virtual member function.

Abstraction - The essential characteristics of an object that distinguishes it from all other kinds of objects and thus provides crisply-defined conceptual boundaries relative to the perspective of the viewer; the process of focusing upon the essential characteristics of an object. Abstraction is one of the fundamental elements of the object model.

Access Control - The mechanism for control of access to the structure or behavior of a class. Public items are accessible by all; protected items are accessible only by the subclasses, implementation, and friends of the class containing the item; private items are accessible only by the implementation and friends of the class containing the item; implementation items are accessible only by the implementation of the class containing the item.

Action - An operation that, for all practical purposes, takes zero time. An action may denote the invocation of a method, the triggering of another event, or the starting or stopping of an activity.

Active Object - An object that encompasses its own thread of control.

Activity - An operation that takes some time to complete.

Actor - An object that can operate upon other objects but is never operated upon by other objects. In some contexts, the terms active object and actor are interchangeable.

Agent - An object that can both operate upon other objects and be operated upon by other objects. An agent is usually created to do some work on behalf of an actor or another agent.

Aggregate Object - An object composed of one or more other objects, each of which is consider a part of the aggregate object.

Algorithmic Decomposition - The process of breaking a system into parts, each of which represents some small step in a larger process. The application of structured design methods leads to an algorithmic decomposition, whose focus is upon the flow of control within a system.

Architecture - The logical and physical structure of a system, forged by all the strategic and tactical design decisions applied during development.

Assertion - The Boolean expression of some condition whose truth must be preserved.

Association - A relationship denoting a semantic connection between two classes.

Attribute - A part of an aggregate object.

Base Class - The most generalized class in a class structure. Most applications have many such root classes. Some languages define a primitive base class, which serves as the ultimate superclass of all classes.

Behavior - How an object acts and reacts, in terms of its state changes and message passing; the outwardly visible and testable activity of an object.

Blocking Object - A passive object whose semantics are guaranteed in the presence of multiple threads of control. Invoking an operation of a blocking object blocks the client for the duration of the operation.

Cardinality - The number of instances that a class may have; the number of instances that participate in a class relationship.

CASE Tool - Computer Assisted Software Engineering Tool is any program which provides a programmer with additional means of designing and/or analyzing the structure of their program. Traditionally, these are programs which provide an interactive graphical representation of a programs object structure.

Class - A set of objects that share a common structure and a common behavior. The terms class and type are usually (but not always) interchangeable; a class is a slightly different concept that a type, in that it emphasizes the classifications of structure and behavior.

Class Diagram - Part of the notation of object-oriented design, used to show the existence of classes and their relationships in the logical design of a system. A class diagram may represent all or part of the class structure of a system.

Class Operation - An operation, such as a constructor or destructor, directed at a class rather than an object.

Class Structure - A graph whose vertices represent classes and whose arcs represent relationships among these classes. The class structure of a system is represented by a set of class diagrams.

Class Variable - Part of the state of a class. Collectively, the class variables of a class constitute its structure. A Class variable is shared by all instances of the same class. In C++, a class variable is declared as a static member.

Client - An object that uses the services of another object, either by operation upon it or by referencing its state.

Collaboration - The process whereby several objects cooperate to provide some high-level behavior.

Concrete Class - A class whose implementation is complete and thus may have instances.

Concurrency - The property that distinguishes an active object from one that is not active.

Concurrent Object - An active object whose semantics are guaranteed in the presence of multiple threads of control.

Constraint - The expression of some semantic condition that must be preserved.

Constructor - An operation that creates an object and/or initializes its state.

Container Class - A class whose instances are collections of other objects. Container classes may denote homogeneous collections (all of the objects in the collections are of the same class) or heterogeneous collections (each of the objects in the collections may be of a different class, although all must generally share a common superclass). Container classes are most often defined as parameterized classes, with some parameter designating the class of the contained objects.

CRC Cards - Class/Responsibilities/Collaborators; a simple tool for brainstorming about the key abstractions and mechanisms in a system.

Data Dictionary - A comprehensive repository enumerating all the classes in a system.

Delegation - The actor of one object forwarding an operation to another object, to be performed on behalf of the first object.

Destructor - An operation that frees the state of an object and/or destroys the object itself.

Dynamic Binding - Binding denotes the association of a name (such as a variable declaration) with a class; dynamic binding is a binding in which the name/class association is not made until the object designated by the name is created at execution time.

Encapsulation - The process of compartmentalizing the elements of an abstraction that constitute its structure and behavior; encapsulation serves to separate the contractual interface of an abstraction and its implementation.

Event - Some occurrence that may cause the state of a system to change.

Exception - An indication that some invariant has not or cannot be satisfied. In C++, we throw an exception to abandon processing and alert some other object of the problem, which in turn may catch the exception and handle the problem.

Field - A repository for part of the state of an object; collectively, the fields of an object constitute its structure. The terms field, instance variable, member object, and slot are interchangeable.

Framework - A collection of classes that provide a set of services for a particular domain; a framework thus exports a number of individual classes and mechanisms that clients can use or adapt.

Friend - A class or operation whose implementation may reference the private parts of another class, who alone can extend the offer of friendship.

Function - An input/output mapping resulting from some object's behavior.

Generic Class - A class that serves as a template for other classes, in which the template may be parameterized by other classes, objects, and/or operations. A generic class must be instantiated (its parameters filled in) before objects can be created. Generic classes are typically used as container classes. The terms generic class and parameterized class are interchangeable.

Generic Function - An operation upon an object. A generic function of a class may be redefined in subclasses; thus, for a given object, it is implemented through a set of methods declared in various classes related via their inheritance hierarchy. The terms generic function and virtual function are usually interchangeable.

Hierarchy - A ranking or ordering of abstractions. The two most common hierarchies in a complex system include its class structure (including "kind of" hierarchies) and its object structure (including "part of" and collaboration hierarchies); hierarchies may also be found in the module and process architectures of a complex system.

Identity - The nature of an object that distinguishes it form all other objects

Implementation - The inside view of a class, object, or module, including the secrets of its behavior.

Information Hiding - The process of hiding all the secrets of an object that do not contribute to its essential characteristics; typically, the structure of an object is hidden, as well as the implementation of its methods.

Inheritance - A relationship among classes, wherein one class shares the structure or behavior defined in one (single inheritance) or more (multiple inheritance) other classes. Inheritance defines an "is-a" hierarchy among classes in which a subclass inherits from one or more generalized superclasses; a subclass typically specializes its superclasses by augmenting or redefining existing structure and behavior.

Instance - Something you can do things to. An instance has state, behavior, and identity. The structure and behavior of similar instances are defined in their common class. The terms instance and object are interchangeable.

Instance Variable - A repository for part of the state of an object. Collectively, the instance variables of an object constitute its structures. The terms field, instance variable, member object, and slot are interchangeable.

Instantiation - The process of filling in the template of a generic or parameterized class to produce a class from which one can create instances.

Interaction Diagram - Part of the notation of object-oriented design, used to show the execution of a scenario in the context of an object diagram.

Interface - The outside view of a class, object, or module, which emphasizes its abstraction while hiding its structure and the secrets of its behavior.

Iterator - An operation that permits the parts of an object to be visited.

Key - An attribute whose value uniquely identifies a single target object.

Key Abstraction - A class or object that forms part of the vocabulary of the problem domain.

Layer - The collection of class categories or subsystems at the same level of abstraction.

Level of Abstraction - The relative ranking of abstractions in a class structure, object structure, module architecture, or process architecture. In terms of its "part of" hierarchy, a given abstraction is at a higher level of abstraction than other if it builds upon the others; in terms of their "kind of" hierarchy, high-level abstractions are generalized, and low-level abstractions are specialized.

Link - Between two objects, one instance of an association.

Mechanism - A structure whereby objects collaborate to provide some behavior that satisfies a requirement of the problem.

Member Function - An operation upon an object, defined as part of the declaration of a class; all member functions are operations, but not all operations are member functions. The terms member function and method are usually interchangeable. In some languages, a member function stands alone and may be redefined in a subclass; in other languages, a member function may not be redefined, but serves as part of the implementation of a generic function or virtual function, both of which may be redefined in a subclass.

Member Object - A repository for part of the state of an object; collectively, the member objects of an object constitute its structure. The terms field, instance variable, member object, a slot are interchangeable.

Message - An operation that one object performs upon another. The terms message, method, and operation are usually interchangeable.

Method - An operation upon an object, defined as part of the declaration of a class; all methods are operations, but not all operations are methods, The terms message, method and operation are usually interchangeable. In some languages, a method stands alone and may be redefined in a subclass; in other languages, an method may mot be redefined, but serves as part of the implementation of a generic function or a virtual function, both of which may be redefined in a subclass.

Modularity - The property of a system that has been decomposed into a set of cohesive and loosely coupled modules.

Module - A unit of code that serves as a building block for the physical structure of a system; a program unit that contains declarations, expressed in the vocabulary of a particular programming language, that form the physical realization of some or all of the classes and objects in the logical design of the system. A module typically has two parts: its interface and its implementation.

Module Architecture - A graph whose vertices represent modules and whose arcs represent relationships among these modules. The module architecture of a system is represented by a set of module diagrams.

Name Mangling – It is a concept that compilers use to resolve names for overloaded function. The compiler generates unique name for each function by prefixing and/or suffixing additional information. There is no specific standard for it rather it is implementation dependent.

Object - Something you can do things to. An object has state, behavior, and identity; the structure and behavior of similar objects are defined in their common class. The terms instance and object are interchangeable.

Object Diagram - Part of the notation of object-oriented design, used to show the existence of objects and their relationships in the logical design of a system. An object diagram may represent all or part of the object structure of system, and primarily illustrates the semantics of mechanisms in the logical design. A single object diagram represents a snapshot in time of an otherwise transitory event of configurations of objects.

Object Model - The collection of principles that form the foundation of object-oriented design; a software engineering paradigm emphasizing the principles of abstraction, encapsulation, modularity, hierarchy, typing, concurrency, and persistence.

Object-Based Programming - A method of programming in which programs are organized as cooperative collections of objects, each of which represents an instance of some type, and whose types are all members of a hierarchy of types united via other than inheritance relationships. In such programs, types are generally viewed as static, whereas objects typically have a much more dynamic nature, somewhat constrained by the existence of static binding and monomorphism.

Object-Oriented Analysis - A method of analysis in which requirements are examined form the perspective of the class and objects found in the vocabulary of the problem domain.

Object-Oriented Decomposition - The process of breaking a system into parts, each of which represents some class or object from the problem domain. The application of object-oriented design methods leads to an object-oriented decomposition, in which we view the world as a collection of objects that cooperate with one another to achieve some desired functionality.

Object-Oriented Design - A method of design encompassing the process of object-oriented decomposition and a notation for depicting both logical and physical as well as static and dynamic models of the system under design; specifically, this notation includes class diagrams, object diagrams, module diagrams, and process diagrams.

Object-Oriented Programming - A method of implementation in which programs are organized as cooperative collections of objects, each of which represents an instance of some class, and whose classes are all members of a hierarchy of classes united via inheritance relationships. In such programs, classes are generally viewed as static, whereas objects typically have a much more dynamic nature, which is encouraged by the existence of dynamic binding and polymorphism.

Overloading – In C++, overloading applies to functions as well as operators. When applied to functions, it means that single function name may have many definitions; however, each definition must differ in arguments (in number, order or types). Note that the return type of the function doesn't play any role in function overloading.

When applied to operators, it means giving new meaning to existing operators so as to use them on user-defined data types (classes).

Persistence - The property of an object by which its existence transcends time (i.e., the object continues to exist after its creator ceases to exists) and/or space (i.e., the object's locations moves from the address space in which it was created).

Polymorphism - A concept in type theory, according to which a name (such as a variable declaration) may denote objects of many different classes that are related by some common superclass; thus, any object denoted by this name is able to respond to some common set of operations in different ways.

Private - A declaration that forms part of the interface of a class, object, or module; what is declared as private is not visible to any other classes, objects, or modules.

Process - The activation of a single thread of control.

Process Architecture - A graph whose vertices represent processors and devices and whose arcs represent connections among these processors and devices. The process architecture of a system is represented by a set of process diagrams.

Process Diagram - Part of the notation of object-oriented design, used to show the allocation of processes to processors in the physical design of a system. A process diagram may represent all or part of the process architecture of a system.

Processor - A piece of hardware that has computation resources.

Protected - A declaration that forms part of the interface of a class, object, or module, but that is not visible to any other classes, objects, or modules except those that represent subclasses.

Public - A declaration that forms part of the interface of a class, object, or module, and that is visible to all other classes, objects, and modules that have visibility to it.

Reactive System - An event-driven system; the behavior of a reactive system is not a simple input/out mapping.

Real-Time System - A system whose essential processes must meet certain critical time deadlines. A hard-real-time system must be deterministic; missing a deadline may lead to catastrophic results.

Responsibility - Some behavior for which an object is held accountable; a responsibility denotes the obligation of an object to provide a certain behavior.

Role - The purpose or capacity wherein one class or object participates in a relationship with another; the role of an object denotes the selection of a set of behaviors that are well-defined at a single point in time; a role is the face an object presents to the world at a given moment.

Run Time Type Identification (RTTI) - It refers to a C++ system that keeps information about an object's data type in memory at runtime. Run-time type identification can apply to simple data types, such as integers and characters, or to generic objects. This is a C++ implementation of a more generic concept called *reflection*.

Scenario - An outline of events that elicits some system behavior.

Selector - An operation that accesses the state of an object but does not alter that state.

Server - An object that never operates upon other objects, but is only operated upon by other objects; an object that provides certain services.

Service - The behavior provided by a given part of a system.

Signature - The complete profile of an operation's formal arguments and return type.

Slot - A repository for part of the state of an object; collectively, the slots of an object constitute its structure. The terms field, instance variable, member object, and slot are interchangeable.

Space Complexity - The relative or absolute time in which some operation completes.

State - The cumulative results of the behavior of an object; one of the possible conditions in which an object may exist, characterized by definite quantities that are distinct from other quantities; at any given point in time, the state of an object encompasses all of the (usually static) properties of the object plus the current (usually dynamic) values of each of these properties.

Static Binding - Binding denotes the association of a name (such as a variable declaration) with a class; static binding is a binding in which the name/class association is made when the name is declared (at compile time) but before the creation of the object that the name designates.

Strongly Typed - A characteristic of a programming language, according to which all expressions are guaranteed to be type-consistent.

Subclass - A class that inherits from one of more classes, which are called its immediate superclasses.

Subsystem - A collection of modules, some of which are visible to other subsystems and others of which are hidden.

Superclass - The class from which another class inherits (which is called its immediate subclass).

Synchronization - The concurrency semantics of an operation. An operation may be simple (only one thread of control is involved), synchronous (two processes rendezvous), balking (one process may rendezvous with another only if the second process is already waiting), timeout (one process may rendezvous with another, but will wait or the second process only for a specified amount of time), or asynchronous (the two processes operate independently).

Time Complexity - The relative or absolute space consumed by an object.

Type - The definition of the domain of allowable values that an object may possess and the set of operations that may be performed upon the object. The terms class and type are usually (but not always) interchangeable; a type is a slightly different concept than a class, in that it emphasizes the importance of conformance to a common protocol.

Typing - The enforcement of the class of an object, which prevents objects of different types from being interchanged or, at the most, allow them to be interchanged only in very restricted ways.

Virtual Function - An operation upon an object. A virtual function may be redefined by subclasses; thus, for a given object, it is implemented through a set of methods declared in various classes that are related via their inheritance hierarchy. The terms generic function and virtual function are usually interchangeable.

Visibility - The ability of one abstraction to see another and thus reference resources in its outside view. Abstractions are visible to one another only where their scopes overlap. Export control may further restrict access to visible abstractions.

Index

❑ ❑ ❑